The Penguin
GOOD AUSTRALIAN WINE GUIDE
1996–97

Mark Shield
& Huon Hooke

Penguin Books

Penguin Books Australia Ltd
487 Maroondah Highway, PO Box 257
Ringwood, Victoria 3134, Australia
Penguin Books Ltd
Harmondsworth, Middlesex, England
Viking Penguin, A Division of Penguin Books USA Inc
375 Hudson Street, New York, New York 10014, USA
Penguin Books Canada Limited
10 Alcorn Avenue, Toronto, Ontario, Canada M4V 3B2
Penguin Books (NZ) Ltd
182–190 Wairau Road, Auckland 10, New Zealand

First published by Penguin Books Australia 1996

10 9 8 7 6 5 4 3 2 1

Copyright © Penguin Books Australia Ltd., 1996
Copyright © 🅜 1996

All rights reserved. Without limiting the rights under
copyright reserved above, no part of this publication may be
reproduced, stored in or introduced into a retrieval system,
or transmitted, in any form or by any means (electronic,
mechanical, photocopying, recording or otherwise), without the
prior written permission of both the copyright owner and the
above publisher of this book.

Typeset in 10/11 Berner by Midland Typesetters, Maryborough, Victoria
Printed in Australia by Australian Print Group, Maryborough, Victoria

ISBN 014 026009 9
ISSB 1038-6467

Penguin Books

THE PENGUIN GOOD AUSTRALIAN WINE GUIDE

Unlike fine wine, **Mark Shield** gets no better with age. After paying his dues in the wine industry in the field of sales, marketing, wholesale, retail and production, he elbowed his way into wine writing via contributions to Melbourne's *Age* newspaper. He quickly established a reputation of being iconoclastic and the polite description of his style is 'wine larrikin'. For fifteen years he has been a self-supporting wine writer with five weekly wine columns, nine monthly columns as well as his own Wine Guide which is in the fifth year of publication. He has been the author or co-author of sixteen books. Mark is a regular broadcaster on the ABC and has a two-volume video, *Discovering Australian Wine With Mark Shield*. He is working on the 'Great Australian Novel' and an autobiography *Scotch for Breakfast*. When not writing or working for charities, he can be found at Mahogany Ridge (the front bar of the All Nations Hotel) or in the Richmond Rat Shack studying the development of aircraft circa 1939 to 1949. Why? Because man doesn't live by drink alone – almost!

Huon Hooke is in danger of becoming a monomaniac. He writes three weekly wine columns (in the *Sydney Morning Herald*, *Good Weekend* and *Northern Herald*) and a monthly column in *Gourmet Traveller*; contributes to the monthly Microsoft Wine Guide magazine Internet site and two wine guides apart from this one (*The Slow Food Guide to the Wines of the World* in Italy, and *The Oz Clarke Pocket Wine Guide* in the UK). He judges in about eight shows a year in Australia and overseas, runs wine courses in Sydney where he lives, and chairs the judging panel of the annual Tucker & Co. Australia's Wine List of the Year Awards. He does occasionally get time to relax and enjoy a glass of the stuff. In 1994 he published his first major book, *Max Schubert, Winemaker*. He duxed the wine marketing course at Roseworthy College in 1981 and has worked in several wineries.

Contents

Acknowledgements	vi
Introduction	1
The Rating System	6
Best Wines	10
Restaurant Wine List of the Year Awards	14
Finding Your Way Around A Bottle Shop	19
Red Wines	21
White Wines	189
Sparkling Wines	345
Fortified Wines	373
The Overflow	403
Food/Wine Combinations – Reds	409
Food/Wine Combinations – Whites	418
Index of Common Names	428
Wine Terms	430
Tasting Terms	435
Directory of Wineries	438

Acknowledgements

Dougall Robertson, Aria Wine Co.
Russell Bradham, Australian Prestige Wines
Jim Humphrys, BRL Hardy
Sarah Gough, Brown Brothers
Dennis Pender and Nick Guy, De Bortoli
Lesley Ann Grimoldby, Intercontact
Michael Price, Negociants
Sally Evans, McWilliams
Alan Nelson, Curtis Marsh, Marshal Waters
Hugh Cuthbertson, Mildara Blass
Judy Farrow, Richmond Hill Cellars
Pete Sawrey and Greg Pullen, S. Smith & Son
Concourse Café, Sydney Opera House
Lyn Gamwell, Vintage Estates
Andrew Watts, Yarra Valley Wine Shippers

Introduction

Feast or famine, that is ever the lot of the Australian wine industry. Last year we reported on a large shortfall of grapes from the key regions, this year the report is an extra million cases above the best estimates.

Also in the equation is the usual imbalance in terms of varieties. Like the old joke about alligators, we are up to our nether regions in chardonnay. You can expect to find a rash of unwooded chardonnay on the market later this year. It depends on your view of the style, we'd rather a touch of oak, but that's not a matter for argument. Chardonnay could also find itself incarcerated in wine casks.

On the subject of casks, they have been deleted from this edition of the *Guide*. For the first time we witnessed the inclusion of imported wine blended into wine casks. At the same time our cask wine was being exported to meet long-term export contracts. The quality of wine casks seemed to hit a low ebb. While the base level was still above the base level of most vin ordinaire, there were not enough better than average examples to sustain a segment in the book. The message is simple, when supplies get tight the first thing to suffer is the economy end of the market. Hopefully next year the segment will return featuring a shoot-out for the best chardonnay cask.

Also of interest are the corporate shifts that seem to resemble the tectonic plate theory about continental drift. Not being financial journalists, we don't pretend to understand the money side. However, as keen industry watchers, the fundamental plates seem to be evolving into three or four major producers.

It is akin to the Senator Button car plan which deemed there was only room for three major producers. The same seems to be happening to the wine industry. The major players are getting bigger as they gobble up some of the medium-sized and the lame that have strategic vineyards but little label presence. Mildara

Blass got Fostered, (Carlton and United); other big players cast hungry eyes at the likes of the Rothbury group, Coldstream and other choice morsels. It's all part of the corporate tango which will increase in tempo.

The modern Australian wine industry is at a crossroad. Our revivalist winemakers are wearing out. The revival started in the late 1960s and to be part of it players had to have an established base. The costs involved made it a professional's or plumber's sport. Most of the revivalists were in their late thirties or early forties then. Thirty-five years later they are near retirement and in many cases the offspring don't want to inherit the farm, or have radically divergent views from the revivalists. Times are changing and as a consequence many of the vineyards are coming onto the market. These are sweetmeats for the large companies that are looking for strategic acquisitions. Most frequently the vineyard is the main attraction; there is not much value in a small winery except as a crushing facility.

Yet as the old are fading the new are coming like a tidal wave. One of the biggest features of the last year has been the proliferation of new and revised labels. If we are ever reincarnated, we want to come back as label designers. That way we would be able to drop the jewel-encrusted Porsche keyring on the bar next to the Kryptonite sunglasses.

Large companies like Southcorp are spending volumes of money to revamp labels. The results are obviously subjective and, love or hate them, they are different. They are also confusing. Witness the new presentation of the fortified wines in the Seppelt Show series. Right down to the Italian olive bottles, they are different and maybe they will attract a new audience. That's what the marketers hope anyway.

Then there are the new wineries who have spent no money on the label designer but opted for the local printer and a sketch from the daughter who has just started art school. Labelling is a small but vital issue. Their wines need to be noticed on the retail shelves and the major question is where will their products fit in the marketplace?

Very few of the new wineries/vineyards have any marketing savvy or realise the implications of selling their products. There is little understanding about price points and the competition. The 'market owes me a living' syndrome means that in some cases there will be tears before disaster. The very small are classed as cottage industries and will probably be able to dispose of their products through cellar door. The middle-size will experience a crash course in marketing.

Apart from the confusion they cause to both consumers and wine writers, the new are very welcome because, as the volume end of the market centralises, their diversity adds colour and interest.

On the up-side, the export of Australian wine increased in value but decreased in volume because of the lean nature of the 1995 vintage. The demand is still there and as strong as ever.

The Australian wine industry also came of age in terms of pricing wine. Penfolds' Grange made profiteers rich when it sold for well above recommended retail price The going price in Melbourne was $215, and it was similar in Sydney. Disapprove as we do, it does bring Australian wine into the big league. If the First Growths can command such prices, why not Australian wine? Who knows what the inventor of Grange, the late Max Schubert, would have thought?

Other prices have been creeping up. It is getting hard to find a reasonable bottle of table wine and get change out of $10 – the price points have shifted. Expect to spend over $12 for a good bottle of wine now.

Another coming-of-age was marked by Wine Australia, staged at Darling Harbour in June. It was a global focus on the local industry. Australian wine also made its presence known on the Internet with varying degrees of success.

The future looks bright and while there is always danger in predictions, it should continue to be prosperous. It will probably be tested by the multitude of new plantings coming on stream, but that should be good for consumers both here and overseas.

Where wine styles are concerned, shiraz continues to make a triumphal march towards centre stage. Grenache is not that far behind but shows some signs of exploitation as makers leap on the bandwagon with little attention being paid to the quality. While they get plenty of attention, most pinot noirs seem unconvincing.

In whites, pinot gris is making a small blip but the volume is negligible. Chardonnay still rules and the unwooded examples are swelling in numbers – expect more and more because they are cheap to make and there is a quick return. Riesling still languishes as far as price and sales are concerned. It and semillon remain the bargain buys.

INTRODUCTION

Organic wines seem to have lost momentum, the players in the game are few and relatively disorganised. The socks-and-sandals image outweighs the potential health benefits that have not been sold to the public. To date most of the wines bearing organic certification on the label have ranged in quality from worthy to very good. Perhaps it will take a couple of brilliant wines to dispel the 'we know what's good for you' health shop with spotty fruit image.

Bubbles continue to become more sophisticated and although méthode champenoise and traditional varieties are being used, the temptation to clone Champagne is abating and the desire to make a local product is growing.

Fortified sales are continuing to dwindle which is good news for the buffs because the material in the bottles is getting older and more complex. The standard has never been higher but the audience is dwindling. The risk is producers will become discouraged and many will abandon the style altogether. An interesting sideline in the fortified department has been the emergence of ratafia styles both from Mountadam and Seppelt. These fortified varietals are an entertaining drink and relatively cheap to produce. They are a bit of fun in an industry that is becoming more serious by the minute.

Coming-of-age is a bit like puberty, a potentially painful process. Since this *Guide* started in 1990 there has been an accelerating maturity. The industry has developed a global identity and many of the winemakers know as much about the bottle shops of London as they do about Sydney, Melbourne and Perth. Moleskins from the Barossa can be seen boot-scooting along Park Lane. Indeed, this book is also on sale in the UK, it's been CD ROMed, floppied and Internetted. Unlike one of the authors (guess who), it too is coming of age.

In this edition we have included a very necessary 'overflow' column. This is an at-a-glance reference to the wines that simply wouldn't fit in the main body of the text. There are many fine wines in this list and they have been rated for quality and value. The list extends the range of the book and also illustrates the increasing problem we face – there is so much **GOOD** Australian wine!

WINE AND HEALTH

There has been much written about the benefits of drinking wine. It is well documented that sticking to the safe level (don't look at one of the authors) of four standard drinks for men per day and two standard drinks for non-pregnant women, will have a beneficial effect. You are likely to live longer than folks who don't drink.

There is also the so-called 'French paradox'. It is usual to see the likes of railway workers in Lyon tucking into a steaming bowl of tripe with a cream sauce for breakfast before they go to work. But beside each steaming bowl you will see a litre of very ordinary red wine. So much for the safe level, but their cholesterol levels are surprisingly low. Heart problems are not a major aspect of the French lifestyle. Research shows the tannin in red wine is a factor in combating cholesterol. There are also beneficial tannins in wood-aged whites. So drink up.

One problem with wine that is ever present, is the allergic reaction to the sulphite preservative used in wine. The Romans discovered that sulphite (sulphur dioxide) is a preservative that was beneficial for wine. The levels in Roman times must have rendered the wines close to household bleach. These days the level of sulphite is much lower, thanks to technology and, in general, the Australian industry is striving to use less sulphite. As a rule of thumb, bag-in-box wines tend to have the highest levels thanks to the limited shelf-life of the product.

Sparkling wines can cause a problem because of the free sulphur dioxide in the bubbles. The best advice for those with a sensitivity is to drink mature wine. As the wine ages, the free SO_2 level falls as it binds with other components in the wine and adds to the complexity.

Because wine has alcohol, and too much wine will make you 'bezottled' (as they say in the Barossa Valley), wine tends to be cast in the baddie parts. Many other foods contain sulphite, but no one blames the sausages, it was the bottle of red that is supposed to have done the damage. Never mind, cautious experimentation will help those who suffer.

Whichever way you look at the subject, in moderation wine should be the health drink of this nation. Cheers!

The Rating System

The rating system used in this guide is designed to give you an immediate assessment of a wine's attributes, as they will affect your purchasing decision. The symbols provide at-a-glance information, and the written descriptions go into greater depth. Other wine guides are full of numbers, but this one places importance on the written word.

The authors assess quality and value, provide an estimate of cellaring potential and optimum drinking age, and give notes on source, grape variety, organic cultivation where applicable, decanting, and alcohol content. We list previous outstanding vintages where we think they're relevant.

We assess quality using a cut-down show judging system, marking out of a possible ten. Wine show judges score out of 20 points – three for nose, seven for colour, ten for palate – but any wine scoring less than ten is obviously faulty, so our five-glass range (with half-glass increments) indicates only the top ten points. When equated to the show system, two and a half to three glasses is roughly equivalent to a bronze medal, and five glasses, our highest award, equals a high gold medal or trophy-standard wine.

Value is arrived at primarily by balancing absolute quality against price. But we do take some account of those intangible attributes that make a wine more desirable, such as rarity, great reputation, glamour, outstanding cellarability, etc. We take such things into account because they are part of the value equation for most consumers.

If a wine scores more for quality than for value, it does not mean the wine is overpriced. As explained below, any wine scoring three stars for value is fairly priced. Hence, a wine scoring five glasses and five stars is extraordinary value for money. Very few wines manage this feat. And of course good and bad value for money can be found at $50 just as it can at $5.

If there are more stars than glasses, you are looking at unusually good value. We urge readers not to become star-struck: a three-glass three-star wine is still a good drink.

Where we had any doubt about the soundness of a wine, a second bottle was always sampled.

QUALITY

♟♟♟♟♟ The acme of style, a fabulous, faultless wine that Australia should be proud of.

♟♟♟♟⸮ A marvellous wine that is so close to the top it almost doesn't matter.

♟♟♟♟ An exciting wine that has plenty of style and dash. You should be proud to serve this.

♟♟♟⸮ Solid quality with a modicum of style, very good drinking.

♟♟♟ Decent, drinkable wine that is a cut above everyday quaffing. You can happily serve this to family and friends.

♟♟⸮ Sound, respectable wines, but the earth won't move.

♟♟ Just okay, but in quality terms, starting to look a little wobbly.

(Lower scores have not been included.)

VALUE

★★★★★ You should feel guilty for paying so little, this is great value for money.

★★★★½ Don't tell too many people because the wine will start selling and the maker will put the price up.

★★★★ If you complain about paying this much for a wine, you've got a death adder in your pocket.

★★★½ Still excellent value but the maker is also making money.

★★★   Fair is fair, this is a win-win exchange for buyer and maker.

★★½   They are starting to see you coming but it's not a total rip-off.

★★   This wine will appeal to label drinkers and those who want to impress the bank manager.

★½   You know what they say about fools and their money ...

★   Makes the used-car industry look saintly.

GRAPES

Grape varieties are listed in dominant order; percentages are cited when available.

CELLAR

Any wine can of course be drunk immediately, but for maximum pleasure we recommend an optimum drinking time, assuming correct cellaring conditions. We have been deliberately conservative, believing it is better to drink a wine when it is a little too young than to risk waiting until it is too old.

An upright bottle ❛ indicates that the wine is ready for drinking now: it may also be possible to cellar it (for the period shown). Where the bottle is lying on its side ⇐ the wine is not ready for drinking now and should be cellared for the period shown.

❛   Drink now, there will be no improvement achieved by cellaring.

❛ 3   Drink now or during the next three years.

⇐ 3–7   Cellar for three years at least before drinking; can be cellared for up to seven years.

⇐ 10+   Cellar for ten years or more – will be at its best in ten years from this book's publication date.

ALCOHOL BY VOLUME

Australian labelling laws require that alcohol content be shown on all wine labels. It is expressed as a percentage of alcohol by volume, eg. 12.0% A/V means that 12 per cent of the wine is pure alcohol.

RECOMMENDED RETAIL PRICE

Prices were arrived at either by calculating from the trade wholesale using a standard full bottle shop mark-up, or by using a maker-nominated recommended retail price. In essence, however, there is no such thing as RRP because retailers use different margins and there are different state taxes. The prices in this book are indicative of those in Sydney and Melbourne, but they will still vary from shop to shop and city to city. They should only be used as a guide. Cellar-door prices have been quoted when the wines are not available in the retail trade.

ⓥ ORGANIC

The wine has passed the tests required to label it as 'organically grown and made'.

▌ DECANT

The wine will be improved by decanting.

Ⓢ SPECIAL

The wine is likely to be 'on special', so it will be possible to pay less than the recommended retail. Shop around.

Best Wines

It is always difficult deciding which wines receive the ultimate accolade. This year produced more than the usual surfeit of riches. It resolves into a contest among equals, and several wines could easily fill the bill.

It also becomes a balancing act to ensure the winning wines are available to readers. In this respect some of the contenders from the smaller producers are at a disadvantage. Between the time of review and release of the book, the supplies will be exhausted. That raises the question, why include them at all? Without them, it would be a pretty predictable book and there is always the possibility readers will have some of the bottles in the cellar or will be followers of the vineyard/maker.

It boils down to a question of availability with price not really a consideration. Having stated that, it is significant that the Best Wine is also the Bargain Red. It is enough to revive faith in the Tooth Fairy, Santa and the Easter Bunny! You don't have to spend a fortune to drink a great wine. Australia is still the lucky wine country.

So without further preamble, in true Oscar presentation style – the winner is . . .

PENGUIN WINE OF THE YEAR

Barwang Cabernet Sauvignon 1994

Brilliant wine that shows off a relatively unknown area (Young, NSW). It's all about style and a balance of elegance and power. (See page 28)

PENGUIN WINE OF THE YEAR

BEST RED WINE

Penley Estate Cabernet Sauvignon 1993
Loads of style and flavour concentration. This company seems set to make its mark as one of the great labels from the district. (See page 124)

BEST WHITE WINE

Rothbury Barrel Fermented Chardonnay 1994
The goods as far as fruit and winemaking is concerned. The wine is extremely complex, rich and rewarding. (See page 304)

BEST SPARKLING WINE

Grant Burge Pinot Noir Chardonnay Méthode Traditionelle (non-vintage)
Theoretically out of left field, it is great to discover a wine that has not yet been recognised for its quality and value. (See page 353)

BEST FORTIFIED WINE

Chateau Reynella Vintage Port 1993
The last tango for a dinosaur style – hope not. This wine should be a discovery for younger readers and a heavy nostalgia trip for the veterans. Long may it live. (See page 383)

PICKS OF THE BUNCH

BEST CABERNET SAUVIGNON
Taltarni Cabernet Sauvignon 1993
The age of reason has dawned and gone are the bombastic styles of yore. This wine has great poise, structure and elegance. (See page 155)

BEST WINES

BEST PINOT NOIR

Port Phillip Estate Reserve Pinot Noir 1995

This is a graceful style that has depths of fruit and complexity. It is indicative of the evolution of the variety in Australia. (See page 131)

BEST SHIRAZ

Bowen Estate Shiraz 1994

Great wine that shows complexity, elegance – yet power. This company has often been a contender in the finals and it's great to seem them win. It is Coonawarra at its best! (See page 34)

BEST RED BLEND/OTHER VARIETY

Yalumba The Signature Cabernet Shiraz 1992

Smokin'! Get this while it's hot, this is one of the best signature blends ever. It has great structure and balance plus the benefit of bottle-age. (See page 184)

BEST CHARDONNAY

Murrindindi Chardonnay 1995

Discovery time. This small producer has always been in the hunt for an award. Now is the time with a very stylish wine that should live long and well. (See page 279)

BEST RIESLING

Mitchell Watervale Riesling 1995

Wonderful regional style with all the goodies we've come to expect. It's a balancing act between finesse and flavour. (See page 271)

BEST SAUVIGNON BLANC

Mitchelton Chinaman's Bridge Sauvignon Blanc 1995

Never mind the label, this is a very well-made style that has authentic varietal character with none of the pitfalls. It doesn't break the bank either. (See page 271)

BEST SEMILLON

Chateau Xanadu Semillon 1995

'Weave a circle round him thrice...' The secret is out, semillon from this district is a winner and this is a sensational example. (See page 218)

BEST WHITE BLEND/OTHER VARIETY

Brown Brothers Gewurztraminer 1995

Lots of varietal authenticity with none of the flaws that can bedevil the final product. It is very well made and a credit to the marque. (See page 207)

BARGAINS

BEST BARGAIN RED

Barwang Cabernet Sauvignon 1994

(See Penguin Wine of The Year)

BEST BARGAIN WHITE

Leasingham Bin 7 Riesling 1995

Very drinkable style with loads of flavour and refreshing qualities. (See page 260)

BEST BARGAIN SPARKLING

Deakin Estate Brut 1995

Very drinkable style that can stand alone or be mixed with juice. A party animal. (See page 350)

BEST BARGAIN FORTIFIED

All Saints Classic Release Tokay

Only in Australia! This shows evidence of aged material yet retains freshness and power. (See page 374)

Australia's Restaurant Wine List of the Year Awards, 1996

The quality of Australian wine and food is improving all the time, but what about the quality of our restaurant wine lists? And are they offering the dining public good value?

In order to encourage higher standards, wholesale wine and spirit merchants Tucker Seabrook & Co., with co-author of this guide Huon Hooke, organised the inaugural Australia's Wine List of the Year Awards in 1994. It was a great success and was staged again in 1995 and 1996. It is the only national wine list award in Australia and this year six judges from Victoria, South Australia, Western Australia and New South Wales, including Huon as chief judge, perused over 300 wine lists from all states. They allocated awards for the best wine list from each state, and best list in each of five restaurant categories. As well, they gave over 200 establishments a recommended wine list rating – scoring out of a possible three wine glasses.

The judging parameters included the quality and range of choice of the wines, pricing, balance, depth of older vintages, number of wines by the glass, suitability to the type of restaurant and cuisine, and – very important – appearance, layout design and general 'user friendliness'. You can be sure of a decent bottle at a fair price if you go to any of these restaurants.

NATIONAL WINNER

Walter's Wine Bar   VIC.   ▼▼▼

WINE LIST OF THE YEAR AWARDS

HALL OF FAME

(**1995 WINNER**) Dear Friends Garden Restaurant, WA. 🍷🍷🍷

(**1994 WINNER**) Cicada, NSW. 🍷🍷🍷

STATE & TERRITORY WINNERS

- **NSW** Hazi's Wine Bar 🍷🍷🍷
- **SA** Chloe's 🍷🍷🍷
- **VIC** Walter's Wine Bar 🍷🍷🍷
- **WA** 44 King Street 🍷🍷
- **ACT** Fringe Benefits 🍷🍷
- **QLD** The Grape Food & Wine Bar 🍷🍷🍷
- **TAS** Fee & Me 🍷🍷🍷
- **NT** Hanaman Thai 🍷

CATEGORY WINNERS

BEST CAFE/BRASSERIE/TRATTORIA Walter's Wine Bar, VIC. 🍷🍷🍷
BEST RESTAURANT The Restaurant Manfredi, NSW 🍷🍷🍷
BEST SMALL RESTAURANT (max. 50 seats) The Grape Food & Wine Bar, QLD 🍷🍷🍷
BEST PUB RESTAURANT Melbourne Wine Room, VIC. 🍷🍷🍷
BEST CLUB RESTAURANT University House, VIC. 🍷🍷🍷

VERY HIGHLY RECOMMENDED 🍷🍷🍷

Walter's Wine Bar, VIC., The Restaurant Manfredi, NSW, Cicada Restaurant, NSW, Dear Friends Garden Restaurant, WA, Forty One Restaurant, NSW, Hazi's Wine Bar, NSW, The Grape Wine & Food Bar, QLD, The Isthmus of Kra Restaurant, VIC., University House,

VIC., Jacques Reymond Restaurant, VIC., Melbourne Wine Room, VIC., France-Soir Restaurant, VIC., Marchetti's Latin Restaurant, VIC., Merrony's, NSW, Chloe's Restaurant, SA, Rose & Crown Hotel, VIC., Caffe Grossi, VIC., Le Restaurant, VIC., Ozone Hotel, VIC., Ottima Cucina, NSW, Blake's Restaurant, SA, Watermark Restaurant, NSW, The Brooklyn Hotel Restaurant, NSW, Mask of China Restaurant, VIC., Darling Mills, NSW, Ristorante Buon Ricordo, NSW, Adams of North Riding Restaurant, VIC., Dogs Bar, VIC., Fee & Me Restaurant, TAS., Hotel Australia, VIC., Jarmers Restaurant, SA, Wine Bar II, VIC., Alexander's, TAS., Claudine's French Restaurant, NSW, Universal Wine Bar, SA, Armstrongs Brasserie, NSW, Il Bacaro, VIC., Jardines Restaurant, NSW, Morans Restaurant, NSW, Cracklins on Swan, VIC., Eagle on the Hill, SA, La Grillade, NSW, Ristorante Roberto, VIC., The Bathers Pavilion, NSW, Caffe La Strada, VIC., Darleys Restaurant, NSW, The Kent Hotel, VIC.

HIGHLY RECOMMENDED 🍷🍷

Red Ochre Grill, QLD, L'Incontro Italian Restaurant, NSW, Marco Polo East West Cuisine, QLD, 44 King Street, WA, Bilson's, NSW, Cafe Luge, VIC., Chinois Restaurant, VIC., Cottage Point Inn, NSW, Gowings Grace Darling Hotel, VIC., Stokehouse, VIC., Chesser Cellars, SA, Pier Restaurant, NSW, Stella, VIC., Stephanie's Restaurant, VIC., Madam Fang Restaurant, VIC., Café Latte, VIC., Lynch's Restaurant, VIC., Sirens Restaurant, VIC., Criterion, NSW, Fringe Benefits, ACT, Max's Restaurant, VIC., Charcoal Grill on the Hill, VIC., Adelphi Hotel, VIC., Friday's Riverside, QLD, La Madrague, VIC., Morgans Seafood Restaurant, QLD, Prosser's on the Beach, TAS., The Old George & Dragon, NSW, Courtney's Brasserie, NSW, Blake's, VIC., L'Avventura, NSW, Blackmans Swamp Restaurant, NSW, Caffe 48, SA, Lathams Restaurant, NSW, Pieroni, VIC., The Grange Restaurant, SA, Roberto Wine Bar & Ristorante, WA, Berowra Waters Inn, NSW, San Francisco Grill, NSW, Caffé e Cucina, VIC., Near East Restaurant, VIC., Ristorante Sapore, VIC., Tables of Toowong, QLD, Beach Hotel, NSW

RECOMMENDED 🍷

Villa D'Este Restaurant, WA, The Fishy Affair, WA, Witch's Cauldron Restaurant, WA, Melvilles, VIC., Dunwoodys, QLD,

Locarno's, WA, Universal Bar & Grill, WA, Italy 1, VIC., Bretts Wharf Seafood Restaurant, QLD, Fiasco's Restaurant, QLD, Milsons Restaurant, NSW, Harveys Restaurant, VIC., Kable's, NSW, XU Bistro & Bar, NSW, Miro Restaurant & Bar, ACT, Siggi's at the Heritage, QLD, Wrest Point Hotel Casino, TAS., Indigo Bar Bistro, QLD, City Rowers Tavern, QLD, Hardings Restaurant, VIC., I Marcus Restaurant, VIC., Mezzaluna, NSW, Restaurant CBD, NSW, The Melbourne Club, VIC., Toledo, WA, Tresini's, VIC., Gekko, NSW, One Fitzroy Street, VIC., Baguette Restaurant, QLD, Sails Beach Cafe & Bar, QLD, St Mounts Guesthouse, NSW, Grand National Restaurant, NSW, Edwards Waterfront, VIC., A Restaurant Five Ways Paddington, NSW, Scusa Mi Ristorante & Bar, VIC., The Botanic Dining Room, SA, The Stag Restaurant, VIC., Big Mouth, VIC., Bortolotto Restaurant, VIC., Botanic Gardens Restaurant, SA, Kooyong Lawn Tennis Club, VIC., Ristorante Bazzani, VIC., Packards Restaurant, SA, Il Solito Posto, VIC., Lebrina, TAS., Ambrosini's Restaurant, SA, The Red Emperor Chinese Restaurant, VIC., The Stag, SA, Flavour of India, NSW, Flouch's, VIC., San Lorenzo Restaurant, WA, O'Connells Centenary Hotel, VIC., Kingsleys Australian Steakhouse, NSW, Vue Grand Hotel, VIC., Red Ochre Grill, SA, The Anchorage Port Stephens, NSW, The Downtown Motel, NSW, Bobby's Bar & Bistro, VIC., Marylands Country House, VIC., Bistro 1, VIC., Court Wine Bar, WA, Pacific Rim Thai, VIC., Bistro Moncur, NSW, Fiorelli, VIC., Fraser's Restaurant, WA, Monty's Restaurant, QLD, The Empire Grill, VIC., The Mixing Pot Restaurant, NSW, Encore, NSW, The Charles Dickens Tavern, VIC., Jolley's Boathouse Restaurant, SA, Cafe Di Stasio, VIC., Cafe Hobson, VIC., Daniel Shea's Restaurant, WA, Jonah's, NSW, Tally Ho Lodge, SA, The Oxford Hotel, SA, Coco's Riverside Bar & Restaurant, WA, East Empress Restaurant & Bar, VIC., Lennons Restaurant, NSW, Clancy's Restaurant, VIC., Daniel's Restaurant, VIC., Haggers Restaurant, VIC., Robin Hood Bistro, NSW, Society Restaurant, VIC., Drumminor Restaurant, SA, Il Centro Restaurant & Bar, QLD, Catwalk Cafe Bar, VIC., Eros, SA, Juniperberry, ACT, Saltwater, QLD, Michael's Riverside Restaurant, QLD, Windows on the Bay, VIC., Veludo, VIC., Byrne's Mill Restaurant, NSW, Chunagon Japanese Restaurant, WA, Fishermans Pier, VIC., Lake House, VIC., Sorrento Golf Club, VIC., Tang Dynasty Restaurant, ACT, The Argo, VIC., Crown & Sceptre Hotel, SA, Zig Zag Food & Wine Bar, QLD, Prickly Pear, ACT, Clover Cottage, VIC., The Essex Restaurant, WA, The Manse

Restaurant, SA, Barry's Country Guest House, NSW, Chez Pok, NSW, Tory's Seafood Restaurant, NSW, Treehouse Restaurant, QLD, Zarrini, NSW, Punch Lane Wine Bar Restaurant, VIC., Alex's Italian Restaurant, VIC., Bergerac Restaurant, VIC., Macrossans Restaurant, QLD, Lattice Bistro, QLD, Sails Restaurant Williamstown, VIC., The Hanaman Thai Restaurant, NT, Victoria's Restaurant, QLD, Kenloch, VIC., Bayswater Brasserie, NSW, The Three Crowns Restaurant & Bar, VIC., Raphael's Restaurant, NSW, The Candy Bar, VIC., Bluewater Bistro, NSW, Miracle Mile Restaurant, NSW, La Brasserie, VIC., Mentone Hotel, VIC., Shores of Middle Harbour, NSW, Archie's on the Park, NSW, Carmine's, VIC., Diners De Gala, VIC., Doyles on the Beach, NSW, Cafe Provincial, VIC., Corn Exchange Brasserie, NSW.

Finding Your Way Around A Bottle Shop

Given the ever increasing number of labels on the market it is getting more and more difficult to navigate your way around a bottle shop. Add to that the ever-increasing price of wine and there is an added pressure to get things right. After all you've got to drink it! The natural instinct is to ask for advice and therein lies the first problem. Is the advice you are about to get worth acting on? But even before that, is the bottle shop worth your patronage?

A good bottle shop should care for wine and know about wine. Sometimes circumstances decree you need an emergency bottle and the first port of call is the only choice. The Knackers Arms window burns brightly and all the bottles have been standing gathering dust for years as has the bloke behind the counter who has at last discovered that beer comes with a crown seal and wine has corks.

There is nothing for it but to pay your money and take your chance. This is not the place to shop for fine wine and it's only good for an emergency when the bring-your-own restaurant is staging a go slow and you have raised a thirst.

Fine wine shops are a different matter, they should store wine in the right conditions. They should be air-conditioned to deal with the summer heat. The bottles should be horizontal (although cork experts tell us this isn't mandatory, old habits die hard) and the staff should know what they are talking about.

According to statistics, the majority of bottles of wine are consumed within 12 hours of purchase. But there is the cellar consideration for those who like to mature wine. There is little point if the wine has been subjected to maltreatment by clumsy handling in the bottle shop. Whatever the motive, be it an investment in terms of increasing value or complexity, it can be thwarted by bad handling along the distribution chain. The bottle shop should have a controlled environment that won't harm the wine.

Before you buy a case, purchase one bottle, take it home and give it a thorough test. Drink the bottle with food, leave a little in the bottom for tasting the next day. If it tastes as good or better, you know you are on a sound cellar item. The fact you have enjoyed the whole bottle is significant. Quite often the first glass of a given wine can be a joy, the second a duty and the third a trial. This won't change with cellaring, so be sure you enjoy it to the last drop if you do go back and pick up a case.

Single bottle purchases are no less important. Maybe you want to pitch woo, impress the bank manager or match your fail-safe recipe with a great bottle of wine. It is advice time and thankfully in a good bottle shop that is available. If the staff are well-trained, shopping should be a pleasure. The sales assistant should be asking questions like, 'What do you want to serve it with?' Wine and food matching is a key point. Then comes the delicate matter of price. Beware those who want to sell you a bargain or a special. Quite often specials are wholesaler or head office generated. Margin takes precedence over quality and there is pressure on the staff to move the stuff. Even if your budget is strictly limited, it pays to focus on the use of the wine. If you want it for quaffing, that's different, buy the cheapest. But if you want it to match a dish – whatever – take your time and ask questions about what it tastes like. That's assuming the person selling the stuff has actually had a taste! Tasting is a key element in the make-up of a good wine store. They usually have tastings towards the end of the week and on weekends. Some have wine clubs and newsletters. Admittedly the latter is often a selling tool but some of the best examples also have an educational function. Some are actually well written.

One of the most recent developments are loyalty programs, call them 'frequent drinker points' that can lead to savings. They look impressive right down to the plastic card, but they are only as good as the range in the store and the expertise of the staff.

The best piece of advice is to find a good wine merchant and cultivate the friendship. Quite often there are goodies under the counter that don't make the display shelves. Being on the right side of your tame merchant can pay dividends in terms of goodies.

However, if you are caught short and the Knackers Arms beckons, well – tough luck – that is the penalty you pay for not being organised in the first place!

Red Wines

All Saints Estate Selection Shiraz

A sort of reserve selection from the All Saints vineyard. Rutherglen reds can be surprisingly elegant in the cooler years. Maker Neil Jericho.
CURRENT RELEASE 1994 Oak takes centre stage, with an amazingly strong, cedary perfume which would invite criticism if the wine weren't so seductive and delicious to drink. It's a streamlined, stylish, elegant red that's unabashedly oak-driven. The finish has drying but smooth tannin. Goes well with roast suckling pig.

QUALITY ♉♉♉♉♉
VALUE ★★★★
GRAPES shiraz
REGION Rutherglen, Vic.
CELLAR 🍷 7+
ALC./VOL. 14.0%
RRP $25.00

All Saints Maturation Reserve Cabernet Sauvignon

This is a traditional regional style which looks increasingly dinosaur-like in the age of elegant, fruity reds.
CURRENT RELEASE 1990 The developed bouquet shows stewed-prune and leathery, earthy mellow-aged characters. The palate is pretty rough and heavy, with definite astringency on the finish. No pretence to elegance but it's a good honest mouthful for devotees of trad Rutherglen reds. He-men will enjoy it with stuffed pig's trotters.

QUALITY ♉♉♉
VALUE ★★★
GRAPES cabernet sauvignon
REGION Rutherglen, Vic.
CELLAR 🍷 7
ALC./VOL. 13.0%
RRP $18.50 (cellar door)

Allandale Matthew Shiraz

QUALITY ▼▼▼
VALUE ★★★
GRAPES shiraz
REGION Hunter Valley, NSW
CELLAR 🍾 2
ALC./VOL. 12.0%
RRP $16.00

Under Bill Sneddon, Allandale has been a quiet but steady winery whose products are not often seen in the shops, but presumably sell mostly ex-winery.
CURRENT RELEASE 1994 The colour is surprisingly light red-purple; the nose is typical Hunter, with earthy leathery and gamey complexities. It's mediumweight at most, with a certain leanness. Pair it with lighter meats, such as pork.

Andrew Garrett Cabernet Merlot

QUALITY ▼▼▼⁒
VALUE ★★★
GRAPES cabernet sauvignon, merlot
REGION McLaren Vale, Padthaway, SA
CELLAR 🍾 4
ALC./VOL. 13.0%
RRP $12.60 $

This brand was only begun in 1988 but already the changes in ownership and winemaker have become the stuff of legends.
CURRENT RELEASE 1994 Quite a different style to the shiraz of the same maker and year. This has a medium purple-red hue, a green leafy/grassy cabernet nose and a soft, straightforward palate with sweet entry, mild tannins and an acid finish. Try it with veal chops.

Andrew Garrett Shiraz

QUALITY ▼▼▼▼⁒
VALUE ★★★★½
GRAPES shiraz
REGION McLaren Vale & Padthaway, SA
CELLAR 🍾 8+
ALC./VOL. 13.5%
RRP $12.60 $

Big wines with huge colour, fruit and tannin extraction have been the hallmark of this brand, thanks to former winemaker Warren Randall. Present maker is Phil Reschke.
CURRENT RELEASE 1994 Wow! This is impressive stuff. A big wine with impenetrable colour and pungent spicy nose. It has a pepper-grinder intensity. Sensational richness and concentration in the mouth, very ripe and lush, masses of fruit. Unsubtle but generous. Drink with designer hamburger.

Angove's Sarnia Farm Cabernet Sauvignon

Sarnia Farm is Angove's new regional varietal brand. It is named after one of the founder Dr William Angove's first vineyards in the Adelaide foothills.
CURRENT RELEASE 1994 Strong peppermint aromas jump out of the glass: this is an aromatic wine with perfumed oak/fruit character and good solid structure and flavour. It's full-bodied, with authority and depth. The finish lingers with a pleasing grip. Good drinking now, with steak and kidney pie.

QUALITY ????
VALUE ★★★★
GRAPES cabernet sauvignon
REGION Padthaway, SA
CELLAR ▮ 5+
ALC./VOL. 13.5%
RRP $18.50

Annie's Lane Cabernet Merlot

This is a new label from the Mildara Blass-owned Clare Valley winery, Quelltaler. It's a chance for new winemaker David O'Leary to do his own thing.
CURRENT RELEASE 1994 Toasty/charry American oak dominates this wine thoroughly, suggesting it needs a few months in the bottle to come into harmony. The flavours are strongly coconutty at time of tasting, with medium-bodied structure that should mellow into a pleasant drinking red after a year or so. Try it with char-grilled spicy sausages.

QUALITY ???
VALUE ★★★
GRAPES cabernet sauvignon, merlot
REGION Clare Valley, SA
CELLAR ← 1–3
ALC./VOL. 12.5%
RRP $12.60 ⓢ

Ashton Hills Pinot Noir

Stephen George is winemaker of this tiny Adelaide Hills winery. The vineyard is owned by his 'outlaws', Peter and Sophie van Rood.
CURRENT RELEASE 1995 A fine and fragrant pinot that showcases the best attributes of the grape. Good depth of colour, cherry/vanilla oak-influenced bouquet and a fleshy, fruit-sweet, high-extract palate that lingers nicely on the finish. The varietal characters are subdued, but it's a lovely flavoursome drink which has more weight than usually encountered in cool-area pinot. Try a warm duck salad.

QUALITY ?????
VALUE ★★★★
GRAPES pinot noir
REGION Adelaide Hills, SA
CELLAR ▮ 3+
ALC./VOL. 12.9%
RRP $27.00

Red Wines

Baileys Touriga

QUALITY ★★★★
VALUE ★★★
GRAPES touriga
REGION north-east Vic.
CELLAR 🍾 2
ALC./VOL. 12.0%
RRP $14.50

New line from an old company. This variety is usually confined to the making of fortified wine but it seems quite smart as a table wine.
CURRENT RELEASE 1994 Deep colour and a strong pepper-berry nose. The palate is cheeky with lively berry flavours dusted with pepper and there is clean acid on the finish. The wine has not been oaked so you get authentic varietal flavours. It is beaut with a pumped leg of mutton.

Baldivis Estate Blue Rock

QUALITY ★★★
VALUE ★★½
GRAPES pinot noir, cabernet sauvignon
REGION Baldivis, WA
CELLAR 🍾
ALC./VOL. 12.4%
RRP $14.75

Rock around the clock, or at least WA. This is a new treatment for pinot noir with a dash. It is a drink-now style. Maker Jane Gilham.
CURRENT RELEASE 1995 The nose is very leafy and there are also undergrowth aromas. The palate is medium-bodied with soft cherry flavours which are adorned by some clean acid on a gently tannic finish. It could be served chilled. Try it with pasta and a meat sauce.

Balgownie Estate Cabernet Sauvignon

QUALITY ★★★★½
VALUE ★★★★½
GRAPES cabernet sauvignon
REGION Bendigo, Vic.
CELLAR 🍾 8
ALC./VOL. 14.0%
RRP $20.00 Ⓢ 🍾

This was a pioneering venture established in 1969 that did much to prove the viability of the small vineyard. It was later sold by its founder, Stuart Anderson to Mildara Blass. Maker Lindsay Ross. Previous outstanding vintages: '76, '80, '86, '90, '92
CURRENT RELEASE 1993 Right in the groove, these days this is a delightfully old-fashioned style. The nose has strong berry, chocolate and gum-leaf aromas. The palate continues the blackberry and chocolate theme. Then comes the tannin which is a bit like old-time religion – it beats a drum in the mouth. It will cellar well but you can drink it now with a dinkum shepherd's pie.

Balgownie Estate Shiraz

Times change, the founder used to play the oboe and drive a Bugatti. These days it's company cars and corporate flag waving.
Previous outstanding vintages: '76, '80, '86, '90, '91
CURRENT RELEASE 1994 A relatively tame little number that possibly reflects a cooler year. The nose is Rhone-like with a liberal dose of pepper. The medium-bodied palate has plum and spice flavours and the finish is distinguished by some subtle oak. It drinks well now, try it with a T-bone steak and all the trimmings.

QUALITY ▼▼▼▼
VALUE ★★★½
GRAPES shiraz
REGION Bendigo, Vic.
CELLAR 5
ALC./VOL. 13.0%
RRP $17.00

Balgownie Shiraz Cabernet

This wine is a confusion: it is not an estate wine but a blend from all over the south-eastern regions. Why it bears the Balgownie label is one of those marketing foibles.
CURRENT RELEASE 1994 The colour is a deep crimson and the nose has strong berry aromas with a hint of leaf and tobacco aromas. The palate is medium-bodied and there are sweet berry flavours which are followed by cedar and cigar box oak. The fine-grained tannins add positive grip. It goes well with a rare eye fillet.

QUALITY ▼▼▼▼
VALUE ★★★★
GRAPES shiraz, cabernet sauvignon
REGION not stated
CELLAR 4
ALC./VOL. 12.5%
RRP $14.50

Balnaves Cabernet Sauvignon

QUALITY ♛♛♛♛̷
VALUE ★★★
GRAPES cabernet sauvignon
REGION Coonawarra, SA
CELLAR 🍷 3
ALC./VOL. 12.8%
RRP $17.00 (cellar door)

In a district noted for its Mount Gambier stone edifices, the Balnaves family have opted for post-modern corrugated iron. Their architect-designed buildings are eye-catching.

CURRENT RELEASE 1993 The colour is somewhat developed and the bouquet shows some of the briary, leafy green overtones that lead HH to suspect these wines are best drunk young. The wine has some attractive tobacco, gamey characters and seems to be ageing quickly. Drink with aged cheeses.

QUALITY ♛♛♛♛
VALUE ★★★½
GRAPES cabernet sauvignon
REGION Coonawarra, SA
CELLAR 🍷 7
ALC./VOL. 13.0%
RRP $17.00 (cellar door)

CURRENT RELEASE 1994 Nice depth of purple-red colour. The aromas are of green-leaf, herb and mint, with blackcurrant and cedar oak well in the background. Good concentration, ripe sweet flavours with flesh and grip. A good match for herb-stuffed, rolled roast beef.

Balnaves Shiraz

QUALITY ♛♛♛♛
VALUE ★★★★
GRAPES shiraz
REGION Coonawarra, SA
CELLAR 🍷 5
ALC./VOL. 12.9%
RRP $16.00 (cellar door)

Doug Balnaves was hoping to have his new winery up in time for the '96 vintage. It will be worth a detour when it's finished.

CURRENT RELEASE 1993 A classy wine, pushing out captivating aromas of chocolate, spices, cherry and vanilla. A rich, ripe wine with a smooth chunky palate and robust, generous flavour. Try it with devilled kidneys.

Bannockburn Serré Pinot Noir

This is Gary Farr's tilt at great Burgundy, deliberately priced on par with Premier Crus. The yield was 35 hectolitres/hectare, lower than Grand Crus. It's made from the best grapes off a 1984-planted, close-spaced vineyard.
CURRENT RELEASE 1991 A step up from the 1990, this is fabulous stuff and takes the pinophile straight to the Cote d'Or. Wonderful concentration of spicy, sappy rich aromas; marvellously fleshy perfumed palate with profound complexity. Mature, yet encouragingly youthful. Hard to condone the price, but we'd be happy to drink it if someone else paid. What else but truffled squab.

QUALITY 🍷🍷🍷🍷🍷
VALUE ★★★
GRAPES pinot noir
REGION Geelong, Vic.
CELLAR 🍾 4
ALC./VOL. 13.5%
RRP $84.00

Bannockburn Shiraz

Gary Farr vinifies his shiraz in a similar way to his pinot, i.e. using Burgundy methods such as whole bunches and pigeage. The style since the change is softer and much more seductive.
CURRENT RELEASE 1994 A slightly lighter vintage with up-front fruit aromas of pepper and licorice, and a silky fruit-sweet palate texture. The tannins are mild and supple, and the wine is relatively accessible, already drinking well. Try it with sauteed kidneys.

QUALITY 🍷🍷🍷🍷
VALUE ★★★½
GRAPES shiraz
REGION Geelong, Vic.
CELLAR 🍾 5+
ALC./VOL. 13.0%
RRP $23.50

Banrock Station Shiraz Cabernet

This vineyard is situated in the Riverland, and doesn't Kingston-on-Murray sound grand, bit like Stratford-on-Avon. This is a new label that represents value for money.
CURRENT RELEASE *non-vintage* A soft drink-now style with a fruity nose. The palate has a lolly quality that suggests partial carbonic maceration. There are soft strawberry and raspberry flavours which are matched by gentle tannins. It drinks well now and could be served chilled. Take it to a barbecue.

QUALITY 🍷🍷🍷
VALUE ★★★
GRAPES shiraz, cabernet sauvignon
REGION Riverland, SA
CELLAR 🍾 1
ALC./VOL. 12.5%
RRP $8.90

Barratt Pinot Noir

QUALITY ♙♙♙♗
VALUE ★★★
GRAPES pinot noir
REGION Adelaide Hills, SA
CELLAR 🍾 4
ALC./VOL. 13.5%
RRP $24.00

This variety is an infuriating beastie, it breaks all the rules. Quite often the lighter the colour the more powerful the wine.

CURRENT RELEASE 1995 A very pale style that surprises in the mouth. The nose is extremely minty with underlying meat and strawberry aromas. The palate has intense cherry flavours and there is a chewy element to the texture. The finish shows typical, cool-climate acid and modest tannin grip. It goes well with rare char-grilled tuna.

Barwang Cabernet Sauvignon

QUALITY ♙♙♙♙♙
VALUE ★★★★★
GRAPES cabernet sauvignon
REGION Young, NSW
CELLAR 🍾 10 +
ALC./VOL. 13.5%
RRP $14.50 Ⓢ

Penguin Wine of the Year and Best Bargain Red

This McWilliams vineyard is located near Young which claims to be the 'cherry capital' of Australia. It boasts high altitude and terra rossa soil as its main attributes. Maker Jim Brayne. Previous outstanding vintages: '93

CURRENT RELEASE 1994 Fabulous wine that flags the potential of this district. There are cherry, blackberry and chocolate aromas plus a touch of briar of the nose. The palate is a mix of dark cherry, blackberry and leafy characters, the oak on the finish has a strong cedar quality and there is plenty of fine-grained tannin. It will cellar like a champ and the value is enough to make you feel guilty for a micro-second or more. Grab it while you can! Try it with baked squab.

Barwang Shiraz

This exciting McWilliams vineyard on terra rossa soil has limits to growth. The region is prone to frost and the vineyard had to be planted in the frost-free areas.
CURRENT RELEASE 1994 Bold wine with lots of flavour. It's all about plums. They dominate the nose and palate. There is also plenty of pepper and a macerated character to the fruit. The finish offers soft black tea-like tannins. The wine is a tad disjointed but cellaring should bring harmony. It goes well with doner kebab.

QUALITY ♛♛♛♛
VALUE ★★★★
GRAPES shiraz
REGION Young, NSW
CELLAR ➝ 3–7
ALC./VOL. 13.0%
RRP $14.50

Basedow Oscar's Heritage

Basedow is part of the Grant Burge stable and it is developing new lines to augment the range. Oscar's (after Oscar Basedow) is a fighting brand. Maker Grant Burge.
CURRENT RELEASE 1994 A drinkable style in the old-fashioned way. It is about up-front fruit and benign tannins. The nose has raspberry aromas plus leaf characters. The palate is medium-bodied with sweet berry flavours and these are followed by gentle tannins on a soft finish. It is great with a straightforward spag' bol'.

QUALITY ♛♛♛♛
VALUE ★★★½
GRAPES grenache, cabernet sauvignon
REGION Barossa Valley, SA
CELLAR ↓ 1
ALC./VOL. 13.0%
RRP $9.90

Bazzani Cabernet Shiraz Dolcetto

The wines from Bazzani (which started life as Warrenmang) are not afraid to march to the beat of a different drum. Viva la difference, it is refreshing to watch house styles developing.
CURRENT RELEASE 1994 Very much skewed towards Italy. This is a very drinkable wine with a refreshing tartness. The colour is dark ruby and the nose has dried-fruit aromas and tart raspberries. The medium-bodied palate is a mix of sweet and sour fruit flavours. The finish is dominated by acid with a dusting of oak. Try it with salami and olives.

QUALITY ♛♛♛♛
VALUE ★★★
GRAPES cabernet sauvignon, shiraz, dolcetto
REGION Pyrenees, Vic.
CELLAR ↓ 3
ALC./VOL. 12.0%
RRP $19.00

Best's Cabernet Sauvignon

QUALITY ♥♥♥♥
VALUE ★★★½
GRAPES cabernet sauvignon
REGION Great Western, Vic.
CELLAR 2–7+
ALC./VOL. 14.0%
RRP $19.30

Best's have been more famous in the past for shiraz than cabernet – they didn't have any cabernet planted until the block near the front gate, in 1981. Maker Simon Clayfield.
Previous outstanding vintages: '88, '91
CURRENT RELEASE 1993 Typical of Best's style, this is very fresh, slow-developing and fruit-driven. The nose shows aromatic raspberry, mulberry and blackcurrant notes with a touch of leafiness. The palate is fiery and time is needed to tame an exuberantly youthful astringency. Cellar, then serve with braised lamb shanks.

Best's Pinot Noir

QUALITY ♥♥♥♥
VALUE ★★★
GRAPES pinot noir
REGION Great Western, Vic.
CELLAR 4
ALC./VOL. 13.5%
RRP $15.45

Pinot meunier has been grown at Best's since the 1860s, but varietal pinot noir didn't arrive till the 1990s.
Previous outstanding vintages: '92
CURRENT RELEASE 1994 Cherry-like fruit is very much to the fore here, with down-played oak and not especially strong varietal definition. The nose has bright cherry fruit, and the palate adds a touch of vanilla. Could build more gamey pinot characters with age. Serve with pasta.

Black Jack Cabernet Merlot

Not something you find in a casino but the winery takes its name from a local road that takes its name from a sailor who jumped ship in the gold rush. Makers Ian McKenzie and Ken Pollock.

CURRENT RELEASE 1993 Amazing nose with an aroma like blackberry cordial. The colour also fills the bill with extreme density. The palate offers sweet blackberry fruit that is matched by black tea-like tannins. There is also plenty of grip. Try it with a steak and kidney pudding.

QUALITY ?????
VALUE ★★★★
GRAPES cabernet sauvignon, merlot
REGION Bendigo, Vic.
CELLAR 2–8
ALC./VOL. 13.8%
RRP $18.00

CURRENT RELEASE 1994 Typical of the district, this is a concentrated wine that doesn't stint on tannin. The colour is deep ruby and the nose has loads of spice and berry aroma. The palate is medium-bodied with cherry and plum flavours and there is a ferrous flavour on the finish. It also has plenty of black tea-like tannin on the finish. It needs time; try it with hare stew.

QUALITY ????
VALUE ★★★★
GRAPES cabernet sauvignon, merlot
REGION Bendigo, Vic.
CELLAR 3–6
ALC./VOL. 14.7%
RRP $18.00

Black Jack Shiraz

A black jack is many things including a large generous beer drinking cup and something you use to cosh people with.
Previous outstanding vintages: '93
CURRENT RELEASE 1994 A big but civilised wine with loads of flavour. The colour is dark and the nose has rich berry aromas, spice and perfume. The palate is rich with dark cherry and licorice flavours and there are well-integrated tannins on a long finish. It drinks quite well now; try it with a steak sandwich.

QUALITY ?????
VALUE ★★★★½
GRAPES shiraz
REGION Bendigo, Vic.
CELLAR 6
ALC./VOL. 14.3%
RRP $18.00

Bleasdale Bremerview Shiraz

QUALITY ♟♟♟♟
VALUE ★★★★
GRAPES shiraz
REGION Langhorne Creek, SA
CELLAR 🍾 2–6
ALC./VOL. 13.5%
RRP $16.50

New labels for this company and hopefully the old label depicting the sailing ship HMS *Buffalo* now resides in Davy Jones's locker. Maker Michael Potts.
CURRENT RELEASE 1993 An intense wine that has a slightly porty and very plummy nose. The palate is full-on plum and there is some regional softness but this is quickly swamped by new American oak on a very firm finish. It goes well with steak and eggs.

Bleasdale Frank Potts Cabernet Malbec Merlot

QUALITY ♟♟♟♟♟
VALUE ★★★★½
GRAPES cabernet sauvignon 67%, malbec 28%, merlot 5%
REGION Langhorne Creek, SA
CELLAR 🍾 6
ALC./VOL. 13.0%
RRP $19.00 🍷

Bleasdale was established in 1850 and up to now nothing much has changed since then. This is their entree into modern winemaking. Maker Michael Potts.
CURRENT RELEASE 1992 Bordeaux blend from the river flats, this impressive wine offers lots of structure and flavour. The colour is an intense ruby and the nose has strong blackberry aromas. The palate is a mix of blackberries, spices and herbs with a salty tang. There is some heavy metal American oak on a protracted tannic finish. Decanting will open it up; try with a casserole of kid.

Bleasdale Mulberry Tree Cabernet Sauvignon

QUALITY ♟♟♟♟
VALUE ★★★★
GRAPES cabernet sauvignon
REGION Langhorne Creek, SA
CELLAR 🍷 5
ALC./VOL. 13.5%
RRP $17.50

There is no indication about the significance of the name on the label but the new packaging looks pretty stylish.
CURRENT RELEASE 1993 A very well-made wine that expresses the regional character. The colour is mid-ruby and the nose smells of crushed berries. The medium-bodied palate is laden with berries and these team with some sympathetic oak on a chalky dry finish. It drinks well with osso bucco.

Blue Pyrenees Estate

This is the red wine from a company that can trace its roots back to the days when brandy was king in Australia. The vineyard was originally planted to that end but it has been completely redeveloped. Maker Vincent Gere.
Previous outstanding vintages: '82, '88, '90, '91
CURRENT RELEASE 1993 Rich wine from a rich year. There is a lovely integration of all components to make a typical cellar style. The colour is dense and the nose is a mix of berry and briar. The palate is full bodied with succulent fruit flavours which are married to dusty dry oak on a long finished. It goes very well with a saddle of venison.

QUALITY ♛♛♛♛
VALUE ★★★★
GRAPES cabernet sauvignon, merlot, shiraz
REGION Pyrenees, Vic.
CELLAR 🍷 5
ALC./VOL. 13.5%
RRP $24.00

Boston Bay Cabernet Sauvignon

Making wine in isolation is difficult. In this case the grapes are trucked to either the Barossa or Clare Valley.
CURRENT RELEASE 1993 The colour is a mid brick-red and the nose has strong mulberry and blackberry aromas plus a suggestion of green leaf. The palate is sweet with strong mulberry flavours and light spice characters. The finish shows some discreet wood and plenty of acid. There is cellar potential but it drinks well with a shepherd's pie.

QUALITY ♛♛♛♛
VALUE ★★★★
GRAPES cabernet sauvignon
REGION Eyre Peninsula, SA
CELLAR 🍷 5
ALC./VOL. 13.0%
RRP $17.50

Boston Bay Merlot

This vineyard was established in 1984 and the production is in the order of 2500 cases.
CURRENT RELEASE 1993 This is an interesting wine with mulberry and mulched leaves on the nose. The palate is medium-bodied with succulent berry flavours. There are plum and cherry flavours that are matched by subtle oak and gentle tannins. It drinks well now; try it with a lightly spiced standing rib roast.

QUALITY ♛♛♛♛
VALUE ★★★½
GRAPES merlot
REGION Eyre Peninsula, SA
CELLAR 🍷 4
ALC./VOL. 12.0%
RRP $17.50

Bowen Estate Cabernet Sauvignon

QUALITY ♟♟♟♟♟
VALUE ★★★★★
GRAPES cabernet sauvignon
REGION Coonawarra, SA
CELLAR ⬤ 2–8
ALC./VOL. 14.0%
RRP $21.00

The end of the Coonawarra terra rossa strip is laughingly called 'Coonawarra sud'. The grapes growing closer to Penola ripen about two weeks later than those in the north. Makers Doug and Emma Bowen.

Previous outstanding vintages: '84, '85, '86, '87, '88, '89, '90, '91, '92, '93

CURRENT RELEASE 1994 The Bowens manage great balance in their wines, and this is a very good example. The nose is loaded with spice, cassis and vanilla aromas. The palate is complex with great cherry-berry depth of flavour and cinnamon and clove spices. The finish shows some well-tailored oak and fine-grained tannins. The very positive grip makes it an ideal wine to accompany a game pie.

Bowen Estate Shiraz

QUALITY ♟♟♟♟♟
VALUE ★★★★★
GRAPES shiraz
REGION Coonawarra, WA
CELLAR ╏ 8
ALC./VOL. 14.0%
RRP $21.00

Best Shiraz

Bowen watchers, and there are many, will be surprised to know the Bowen family is now in their new home! The splendid house has been many years in the building because the money was usually spent on new winemaking equipment instead of bricks and brackets.

Previous outstanding vintages: '86, '87, '88, '89, '90, '91, '92

CURRENT RELEASE 1994 A very civilised style, slightly more cultured that the usual Bowen shiraz. The nose is spicy with sweet berry-fruit aromas. The medium to full-bodied palate is already very complex with sweet plum and cherry flavours and these are dusted with spice and a rumour of vanilla. The finish has fine-grained tannins and persistent grip. It is great with a designer steak sandwich.

Brands Family Reserve Cabernets

The last of the Mohicans ... this is the last of the line. The McWilliams marketers have decreed it should be deleted.
CURRENT RELEASE 1990 Like the old vine shiraz, this is always released with some bottle-age. It has an aged colour and a mellow mint/camphor bouquet that shows a lot of maturity. It's medium-bodied with a dry tannin finish and the aged characters are taking over the fruit. Drink it now, with aged cheddar.

QUALITY ▼▼▼▼
VALUE ★★★
GRAPES cabernet sauvignon 60%, cabernet franc 20%, merlot 20%
REGION Coonawarra, SA
CELLAR 2
ALC./VOL. 13.0%
RRP $21.90

Brands Laira Cabernet Sauvignon

More and more these days, cabernet sauvignon is talked about as being the great grape of Coonawarra. Maker Jim Brand.
CURRENT RELEASE 1994 A much improved cabernet, with more concentration than normally found at Laira. Deep purple-red hue, and a fine perfume which reveals stylish French oak, dark berries and mint. Compact, structured and graceful, this is impressive and a little more length is all that's needed. Roast beef here.

QUALITY ▼▼▼▼▼
VALUE ★★★★
GRAPES cabernet sauvignon
REGION Coonawarra, SA
CELLAR 8
ALC./VOL. 13.5%
RRP $16.90 $

Brands Laira Shiraz

Eric Brand, the founder of Brands Laira, was Owen Redman's brother-in-law, which gave him a good intro to winemaking.
CURRENT RELEASE 1994 An early-drinking shiraz of some charm and style. The colour is deep red-purple, the nose has sweet cherry and vanilla with mint and coconut aspects from fresh oak. It's mediumweight and smooth, and invites early consumption. Try it with duck.

QUALITY ▼▼▼▼
VALUE ★★★
GRAPES shiraz
REGION Coonawarra, SA
CELLAR 5
ALC./VOL. 12.0%
RRP $14.50 $

Brands Original Vineyard Shiraz

QUALITY 🍷🍷🍷🍷
VALUE ★★★
GRAPES shiraz
REGION Coonawarra, SA
CELLAR 🍾 2
ALC./VOL. 12.5%
RRP $21.90 🍾

Made from the produce of vines planted in 1896, which makes them centenarians this year. Maker Jim Brand.
CURRENT RELEASE 1990 Quite a lot of forward development here. The colour is medium brick-red and it has a complex bouquet of aged leathery, earthy characters with a hint of camphor. The taste is lean, smooth and mature. Ready to go, with aged hard cheeses.

Bremerton Lodge Cabernet Sauvignon

QUALITY 🍷🍷🍷
VALUE ★★★
GRAPES cabernet sauvignon
REGION Langhorne Creek, SA
CELLAR 🍾 3
ALC./VOL. 13.5%
RRP $14.00

Eventually the winemaking bug bights every grape grower. In this case the winemaker/proprietor, Craig Wilson was thus bitten. The production is around 2400 cases a year.
CURRENT RELEASE 1993 A very seductive nose that is all cabernet. The colour is a deep brick-red and the palate is medium-bodied with sweet cherry flavours and a hint of rust and Langhorne Creek earth. The finish is gentle with mellow tannins and soft oak. It goes well with a traditional braised steak.

Bridgewater Mill Millstone Shiraz

QUALITY 🍷🍷🍷🍷
VALUE ★★★★
GRAPES shiraz
REGION McLaren Vale, SA
CELLAR ⇌ 2–8
ALC./VOL. 14%
RRP $19.00

If you are ever up Bridgewater way in the Adelaide Hills, eat at the restaurant at the mill. MS believes it is one of the best in Australia. Maker Brian Croser.
CURRENT RELEASE 1993 Tuff Stuff. The wine is a youngster but in certain ways it is old-fashioned. It has a dense colour and a spicy nose. Plum flavours dominate the palate and there is a healthy background of spice. There is also loads of French oak on the finish. It needs cellaring but you can try it now with a venison pie.

Brokenwood Cabernet Sauvignon

Brokenwood started life as a hobby farm for moneyed professionals in Sydney who thought it would be cute to have a share in a winery and vineyard. These days it is a professional and serious business. Maker Iain Riggs.
Previous outstanding vintages: '91, '93
CURRENT RELEASE 1994 This is a United Nations effort as far as fruit sources are concerned and the construction work has paid dividends. The colour is textbook red-ruby and the nose is a delightful mix of cassis and leaf aromas. The palate is medium to full-bodied and there is ripe blackberry with a hint of chocolate flavour. The finish shows off some cedar oak and there are attractive astringent tannins. It will cellar well but you can try it now with roast lamb

QUALITY ♛♛♛♛♛
VALUE ★★★★★
GRAPES cabernet sauvignon
REGION Coonawarra, McLaren Vale, SA; Goulburn Valley, Vic
CELLAR 🍷 2–8
ALC./VOL. 13.0%
RRP $18.50

Brokenwood Graveyard Vineyard

There is nothing dead about this wine. This is a wine that drags the Hunter Valley into new realms of finesse and flavour. It is expensive and also hard to find.
Previous outstanding vintages: '83, '85, '86, '87, '88, '89, '90, '91, '93, '94
CURRENT RELEASE 1995 The low-yielding vines have paid dividends because of the concentration of flavour. It has a deep red/purple colour and the nose is spicy with some macerated plum aromas. The medium-bodied palate offers tangy plum flavours with attendant spice and the oak fits like the proverbial glove. There are fine-grained tannins on a concentrated finish. It is tough enough for smoked duck.

QUALITY ♛♛♛♛♛
VALUE ★★★★
GRAPES shiraz
REGION Hunter Valley, SA
CELLAR 🍷 3–9
ALC./VOL. 13.5%
RRP $35.00

Brown Brothers Everton

QUALITY ♟♟♟♙
VALUE ★★★★
GRAPES cabernet sauvignon 40%, merlot 32%, shiraz 16%, malbec 12%
REGION King Valley, Vic.
CELLAR 🍷 3
ALC./VOL. 13.0%
RRP $11.40

The Everton vineyard used to be a low-yield high-altitude vineyard for Brown Brothers during the 1960s. It fell into disrepair in the 1970s. The name lives on with this blend.
CURRENT RELEASE 1994 A very civilised blend with a deep brick-red colour and a raspberry accented nose. The palate is medium-bodied with ripe berry characters and these are attended by soft tannins and supple acid. It would go well with a basil and tomato pizza.

Brown Brothers Family Reserve Cabernet Sauvignon & Shiraz

QUALITY ♟♟♟♟
VALUE ★★★★
GRAPES cabernet sauvignon, shiraz
REGION King Valley, Vic.
CELLAR 🍷 3
ALC./VOL. 12.5%
RRP $18.50

Let's not corrupt the Mae West line about a 'hard man ...', it is good to find a mature wine available to the public. Genuine vintage wines are normally hard to find.
CURRENT RELEASE 1987 The colour is a deep brick-red and the nose has strong developed fruit aromas. The medium-bodied palate has sweet fruit flavours with a mellow texture. The oak has melded well and the finish is gentle yet supportive. It needs a medium-flavoured dish like a veal casserole.

Brown Brothers Family Selection Cabernet Sauvignon

QUALITY ♟♟♟♙
VALUE ★★★
GRAPES cabernet sauvignon
REGION King Valley, Vic.
CELLAR 🍷 3
ALC./VOL. 13.0%
RRP $17.80

The King Valley, Victoria, started life as one of Australia's premium tobacco-growing areas. In these days of political correctness it has swapped one vice for another.
CURRENT RELEASE 1994 It's made in the Brown Brothers way. It is a seamless style that is easy to drink. The colour is a deep crimson and the nose has sweet raspberry aromas with hints of chocolate. The medium-bodied palate has raspberry and blackberry flavours. The finish shows well-integrated oak. It is well balanced and ready to drink now. Try it with savoury mince.

Brown Brothers Family Selection Shiraz

'There's not a whole lot of shakin' goin' on' as far as this wine is concerned. This is a style that lacks conviction.

CURRENT RELEASE 1994 This is an austere style with as medium-ruby colour and plenty of spice on the nose. The palate is austere with black pepper and berry flavours. The finish shows oak and acid. Drink it now with steak and eggs.

QUALITY 🍷🍷🍷
VALUE ★★½
GRAPES shiraz
REGION King Valley, Milawa, Mystic Park, Vic.
CELLAR 🍾 3
ALC./VOL. 13.0%
RRP $14.05

Brown Brothers Family Selection Victoria Cabernet Sauvignon

The Family Selection is another way of saying cellar release. The wines that are cellared are usually marketed when they are near their peak. Maker John Brown Jr.

CURRENT RELEASE 1986 Age has been kind, the colour is a mid brick-red and the nose has a concentrated fruit juice aroma that is a consequence of cellaring. The palate is medium-bodied with sweet, succulent fruit and a hint of truffles. The finish retains some astringency. There is a fine crust so decant and serve with a mushroom risotto.

QUALITY 🍷🍷🍷🍷
VALUE ★★★★
GRAPES cabernet sauvignon
REGION north-east Vic.
CELLAR 🍾 3
ALC./VOL. 13.5%
RRP $19.00 🍾

Brown Brothers Tarrango

It probably seemed like a good idea at the time. To cross sultana with touriga, but given Australian consumers' propensity to ignore light-red styles, you have to ask, why bother?

CURRENT RELEASE 1995 The colour is a pale ruby and the nose has sweet raspberry aromas. The palate is light with sweet berry flavours that are matched by a soft acid on a clean finish. It could be served well chilled; try it with a terrine.

QUALITY 🍷🍷🍷
VALUE ★★★
GRAPES tarrango
REGION north-east Vic.
CELLAR 🍾 1
ALC./VOL. 12.0%
RRP $10.40

Browns of Padthaway Cabernet Sauvignon

QUALITY 🍷🍷🍷🍷
VALUE ★★★★
GRAPES cabernet sauvignon
REGION Padthaway, SA
CELLAR 🍾 4
ALC./VOL. 14.5%
RRP $14.00

This is a relative newcomer on the wine scene and as the name suggests it makes wines exclusively from Padthaway fruit. The wine was made at Rymill winery in Coonawarra. Maker John Innes.
CURRENT RELEASE 1994 The colour is a vibrant ruby/purple and the nose is a mix of blackberry and leaf aromas. The middleweight palate has intense blackberry fruit with hints of capsicum and spice. There are discreet oak overtures on the finish and some pleasant grip. It goes well with roast squab.

Buller & Son (R. L.) Beverford Cabernet Sauvignon

QUALITY 🍷🍷🍷🍷
VALUE ★★★½
GRAPES cabernet sauvignon
REGION Swan Hill, Vic.
CELLAR 🍾 3
ALC./VOL. 13.8%
RRP $13.50

The Buller family has two winery locations, one at Beverford near Swan Hill and the other at Rutherglen.
CURRENT RELEASE 1992 The colour is a deep brick-red and the nose has strong plum aromas. The palate is medium-bodied with sweet raspberry fruit flavours with a hint of spicy oak. The finish shows mildly astringent tannins and some discreet oak. It drinks well now with a casserole of kangaroo.

QUALITY 🍷🍷🍷🍷
VALUE ★★★½
GRAPES cabernet sauvignon
REGION Swan Hill, Vic.
CELLAR 🍾 4
ALC./VOL. 13.0%
RRP $13.50

CURRENT RELEASE 1993 A very enjoyable style that is rich, yet restrained. It has a deep ruby colour and the nose offers a hint of port plus capsicum aroma. The palate is rich with sweet raspberry and the finish shows some well-integrated oak and pleasant grip. It drinks well after two hours breathing; try it with a hearty casserole.

Buller & Son (R. L.) Mondeuse Shiraz

Mondeuse is a north-east Victorian speciality. It makes deeply coloured wines with plenty of tannin.
CURRENT RELEASE 1994 It has a deep-ruby colour and a fragrant nose showing plenty of red berries on a slightly porty background. The palate is rich with strong berry flavours and these are followed by typically grippy tannins. There is also evidence of fresh acid. It should cellar well; try it with roast squab.

QUALITY ♟♟♟♟
VALUE ★★★★
GRAPES mondeuse, shiraz
REGION not stated
CELLAR ➡ 2–6
ALC./VOL. 12.4%
RRP $19.50

Buller & Son (R. L.) Victoria Classic

Classic what? The level of alcohol? The lack of finesse? The lack of information about the varieties? The indifferent packaging? Never mind, it drinks well.
CURRENT RELEASE 1993 It is soft, supple and slippery. The colour is mid-ruby with some brick-red elements. The nose has porty overtones and the palate is juicy with some sweet berry flavours. These are offset by some modest tannin and discreet acid. It drinks well with barbecued lamb straps.

QUALITY ♟♟♟♟
VALUE ★★★½
GRAPES not stated
REGION not stated
CELLAR ↕ 3
ALC./VOL. 14.6%
RRP $10.00 Ⓢ

Calais Estates Reserve Shiraz

This is a very limited production number that won the people's choice prize at the '96 NSW Wine Awards. Maker Gary Reed.
Previous outstanding vintages: '93
CURRENT RELEASE 1994 A voluptuous, extra-ripe shiraz in a luscious style we seldom see from the Hunter. Liberal use of American oak adds a large dose of vanilla and chocolate to the aroma and the taste is rich and plummy with a twist of licorice. There are cinnamon/spice aspects too. A decadent shiraz to serve with rare kangaroo.

QUALITY ♟♟♟♟♟
VALUE ★★★★
GRAPES shiraz
REGION Hunter Valley, NSW
CELLAR ↕ 6+
ALC./VOL. 13.0%
RRP $30.00

Campbells Barkly Durif

QUALITY ♛♛♛♛♛
VALUE ★★★★
GRAPES durif
REGION Rutherglen, Vic.
CELLAR 🍾 2–7+
ALC./VOL. 13.0%
RRP $22.00 🍷

Rutherglen used to be known as Barkly in its early days and one of the main streets is Barkly St. Maker Colin Campbell.
Previous outstanding vintages: '92
CURRENT RELEASE 1993 This is a worthy follow-up to the startling debut vintage. The style is big and tannic, in keeping with the reputation of this local specialty grape. There are herbal stalky notes on the nose and a trace of oak. Big flavour and tannin to match, but the tannins are smooth and ripe and the wine has heaps of promise. We'd like to see it in two or three years. Serve with venison.

Campbells Rutherglen Durif

QUALITY ♛♛♛♛
VALUE ★★★½
GRAPES durif
REGION Rutherglen, Vic.
CELLAR 🍷 5
ALC./VOL. 13.6%
RRP $18.00 🍷

Campbells, a family-owned winery, celebrated its 125th anniversary in 1995. This is one of its regular mature releases under the Classic Regional Style label. Maker Colin Campbell.
CURRENT RELEASE 1988 Very idiosyncratic wine and the claim of 'regional style' is no lie! The colour is aged medium brick-red, the nose brings forth descriptors such as porty, burnt, creosote and sump oil. It is undeniably made from very ripe, hot-climate grapes and is a big, gutsy wine with strong tannins and no pretence to elegance. Serve with game casserole.

Campbells Silverburn Red

QUALITY ♛♛♛
VALUE ★★★
GRAPES shiraz, durif, cabernet sauvignon, merlot
REGION Rutherglen, Vic.
CELLAR 🍷 3
ALC./VOL. 12.9%
RRP $11.00

Silverburn is one of the Campbell clan's original vineyards at Rutherglen. The brand is a new one, inspired by the proposed EC agreement to phase out generic names like Chablis and Graves. Maker Colin Campbell.
CURRENT RELEASE 1994 The colour is nice and deep; the nose is minty and shows some rather green oak together with herbal fruit. It's a light to middleweight with a very soft finish. A basic quaffer which could be drunk with meatballs.

Canobolas-Smith Alchemy

The name of this winery combines the name of the owners – the Smith family – with the mountain on whose lower slopes they planted their vines in 1986. Maker Murray Smith.
Previous outstanding vintages: '93
CURRENT RELEASE 1994 This a serious red, with structure and ripeness which belie the chilly climate. While the nose is at first subdued, there is excellent concentration of colour and flavour, finishing with abundant firm tannins. As it airs, more of the ripe blackcurrant fruit flavours are revealed. Try it with barbecued Illabo lamb.

QUALITY ♀♀♀♀♀
VALUE ★★★★½
GRAPES cabernet sauvignon, cabernet franc, merlot, shiraz
REGION Orange, NSW
CELLAR ↦ 2–10+
ALC./VOL. 13.5%
RRP $17.00 (cellar door)

Cape Jaffa Cabernet Sauvignon

The label design reflects a nautical theme, conjuring images of explorer Nicolas Baudin, who gave Cape Jaffa its name. You can see the sea from the vineyard. Maker Ralph Fowler.
CURRENT RELEASE 1994 Smoky, briary, dark berry nose, with a touch of tomato sauce aroma. There's some extractiveness on the finish and the tannins could be softer. Goes better with food: try gourmet bangers. A respectable inter-region blend, but watch out for the '95.

QUALITY ♀♀♀
VALUE ★★½
GRAPES cabernet sauvignon
REGION Coonawarra 60%, Mount Benson 40%, SA
CELLAR ▯ 4
ALC./VOL. 13.5%
RRP $18.00 (cellar door)

CURRENT RELEASE 1995 From 100 per cent Mount Benson fruit, this is an exciting omen for the region. There are fresh blackcurrant and mulberry perfumes, stylish oak support and some of the leafier aspects that remind of nearby Coonawarra. Good concentration and length, pleasing fruit sweetness and harmony. A graceful cabernet to serve with pink lamb.

QUALITY ♀♀♀♀♀
VALUE ★★★½
GRAPES cabernet sauvignon
REGION Mount Benson, SA
CELLAR ▯ 6+
ALC./VOL. 13.0%
RRP $19.30

Cape Mentelle Shiraz

QUALITY	🍷🍷🍷🍷
VALUE	★★★½
GRAPES	shiraz
REGION	Margaret River, WA
CELLAR	🍾 3–10+
ALC./VOL.	14.0%
RRP	$19.30

Shiraz is a variety that is not strongly represented at Margaret River. Perhaps the current shiraz boom will see some more vines planted there. Maker John Durham.

Previous outstanding vintages: '83, '86, '87, '88, '89, '90, '91, '92, '93

CURRENT RELEASE 1994 Tannin is the major feature of this year's Mentelle shiraz. It's got a terrific kick in the finish. Colour is as rich and purple as ever, the nose shows gamey, meaty/spicy complexities and the tannin coats the mouth, leaving the tastebuds crying out for hearty oxtail stew. One for the cellar.

Cape Mentelle Zinfandel

QUALITY	🍷🍷🍷🍷
VALUE	★★★½
GRAPES	zinfandel
REGION	Margaret River, WA
CELLAR	🍾 5
ALC./VOL.	14.0%
RRP	$19.30

It's damning with faint praise to observe that this is the best varietal zinfandel in Australia. There are very few others. Makers John Durham and David Hohnen.

Previous outstanding vintages: '81, '82, '84, '88, '90, '91, '92, '93

CURRENT RELEASE 1994 This seems lighter in weight than usual, elegant and not so spicy. The nose shows a big, sweet raspberry aroma of impressive intensity. It's light on the oak, lean and gentle in the mouth with controlled tannin to finish. Serve with gourmet hamburgers.

Capel Vale Merlot

QUALITY	🍷🍷🍷🍷?
VALUE	★★★★
GRAPES	merlot
REGION	south-west coastal, WA
CELLAR	🍾 2–8
ALC./VOL.	13.0%
RRP	$19.30

This is Capel Vale's third attempt at this varietal, with grapes from their own Capel vineyard. Maker Rob Bowen.

CURRENT RELEASE 1994 A truly excellent full-bodied merlot with concentrated fruit and fine, firm tannins that need time to soften. Lots of guts, big finish, and promises to repay cellaring. The only reservation is a greenish tomato-bush aspect in the nose. Drink with beef bordelais.

Capel Vale Shiraz

Capel is the name of the nearest town, and the winery and vineyard are about an hour north of the Margaret River region. Maker Rob Bowen. Previous outstanding vintages: '93
CURRENT RELEASE 1994 A pleasant but rather simple nose shows cherry and strawberry scents with an overtone of cough mixture. The taste is fruity and sweet with subtle wood and some tannin extractiveness on the finish. Try it with saddle of hare.

QUALITY 🍷🍷🍷
VALUE ★★½
GRAPES shiraz
REGION south-west coastal & Mt Barker, WA
CELLAR 🍾 6
ALC./VOL. 13.5%
RRP $19.30 Ⓢ

Cassegrain Chambourcin

Chambourcin is a rare and intriguing grape which adds more variety to the winemaker's palette. Maker John Cassegrain.
CURRENT RELEASE 1995 A flirtatious hussy with a flamboyant purple colour. Deep raspberry fruit dances a sophisticated routine with toasty oak on the bouquet. Soft, round and fleshy, with fruit-sweetness and real drinkability. Goes well with duck.

QUALITY 🍷🍷🍷🍷
VALUE ★★★★
GRAPES chambourcin
REGION Hastings Valley, NSW
CELLAR 🍾 3
ALC./VOL. 12.2%
RRP $14.50

Cassegrain Five Mile Hollow Red

This is a 'fruit salad' style blended from five varieties. You could say it's John (ex-Tyrrell's) Cassegrain's Long Flat Red.
CURRENT RELEASE 1995 A quaffing, dry red with a slightly feral gamey nose which cleaned up with airing. It's light-medium in weight with some toasty oak and a coconutty, grainy tannin finish. Very good everyday house red. Serve with kangaroo.

QUALITY 🍷🍷🍷🍷
VALUE ★★★½
GRAPES shiraz, pinot noir, chambourcin, cabernet sauvignon, merlot
REGION Hastings Valley, NSW
CELLAR 🍾 4
ALC./VOL. 11.8%
RRP $12.50

Cassegrain Shiraz

QUALITY ♛♛♛♕
VALUE ★★★
GRAPES shiraz
REGION Hastings Valley, NSW
CELLAR 🍾 5
ALC./VOL. 12.1%
RRP $16.00

Like the Hunter Valley, the Hastings does not produce high-baumé reds every year. Hence the cool, peppery character of this shiraz.
CURRENT RELEASE 1994 Excellent deep red-purple hue prepares you for a vibrant youngster. The nose is a riot of crushed black pepper, green peppercorns and other spices. The taste is middleweighted, lean and gamey with gentle tannin and pulls up a trifle short. Would team with venison.

Castle Crossing Chambourcin

QUALITY ♛♛♛
VALUE ★★★★
GRAPES chambourcin
REGION Sunraysia, Vic.
CELLAR 🍾 1
ALC./VOL. 12.0%
RRP $6.95 Ⓢ

Chambourcin is a little-known French hybrid which has fired the imagination of a small band of Australian winemakers. It makes a red with very intense colour. Maker Bob Shields.
CURRENT RELEASE 1995 The Allambie Wine Company has turned this unusual grape to a very fresh, estery red whose aromas are unusual but fascinating. It's herbal and cherry-like in a somewhat pinot-like guise. Light to middleweight palate, soft and easy to quaff young. Terrific pasta wine.

Chain of Ponds Cabernet Sauvignon

Chain of Ponds has a nice ring to it ... and it actually exists. It's a place in the Adelaide Hills near Gumeracha.

CURRENT RELEASE 1993 A lovely up-front cabernet that drinks well right now. It is quite aromatic with some leafy cabernet aromas and toasty nutmeg/spicy oak. The palate is neat, compact and elegantly structured with a supple tannin grip and a definite finish. A very promising early effort. Suits stuffed pig's trotters.

QUALITY 🍷🍷🍷🍷
VALUE ★★★½
GRAPES cabernet sauvignon
REGION Adelaide Hills, SA
CELLAR 🍾 6+
ALC./VOL. 13.0%
RRP $26.00

CURRENT RELEASE 1994 Not as accessible or immediately charming as the '93, this vintage has a fine, dark hue and is quite solid, with more of the greenish cabernet flavours apparent. There is deep blackcurrant flavour on the palate with leafy undertones and it needs more time to mellow. Cellar, then serve with rare beef.

QUALITY 🍷🍷🍷🍷
VALUE ★★★½
GRAPES cabernet sauvignon
REGION Adelaide Hills, SA
CELLAR ⟼ 2–5+
ALC./VOL. 13.0%
RRP $26.00

Chambers Cabernet Sauvignon

Bill Chambers is the fifth generation of his family to own and operate their small winery. His son Stephen is studying wine science with a view to continuing the tradition.

CURRENT RELEASE 1991 Very much a regional style – very ripe and fruit-sweet on the tongue, it has stacks of earthy, fungal, dried-herb regional character in the bouquet and is quite tannic on the finish. The flavours are savoury and mellow, showing some age development. Drink with comfort food, such as steak and kidney pie.

QUALITY 🍷🍷🍷
VALUE ★★★½
GRAPES cabernet sauvignon
REGION Rutherglen, Vic.
CELLAR 🍾 5+
ALC./VOL. 13.6%
RRP $15.00 🍾

Chambers Rosewood Shiraz

QUALITY 🍷🍷🍷🍷
VALUE ★★★★
GRAPES shiraz
REGION Rutherglen, Vic.
CELLAR 🍾 4
ALC./VOL. 12.4%
RRP $15.00

Winemaker Bill Chambers says that contrary to popular belief, Rutherglen reds aren't always monsters. This one is living proof.
CURRENT RELEASE 1994 An elegant, spicy, peppery cooler-year style of shiraz, which is tight, lean and compact on the palate. It is understated and very, very drinkable. Try it young with roast duck.

Chapel Hill Cabernet Sauvignon

QUALITY 🍷🍷🍷🍷🍷
VALUE ★★★★★
GRAPES cabernet sauvignon
REGION McLaren Vale 73%, Coonawarra 27%, SA
CELLAR 🍾 10+
ALC./VOL. 13.5%
RRP $21.00

Year in, year out, Pam Dunsford's Chapel Hill reds are among McLaren Vale's best. Her cabernet is a two-region blend which harks back to the great Mildara reds of the 1950s.
Previous outstanding vintages: '88, '89, '90, '91, '92, '93
CURRENT RELEASE 1994 Simply wonderful red wine! The colour is deep red-purple, the nose is voluminous mint, coconut, toasty oak and berries. Lots happening here! Rich, full-bodied, smooth and decadent, it has lovely fruit, flesh and concentration. Irresistible with char-grilled beef fillet.

Chapel Hill Reserve

QUALITY 🍷🍷🍷🍷🍷
VALUE ★★★★
GRAPES cabernet sauvignon 67%, shiraz 33%
REGION McLaren Vale 67%, Coonawarra 33%, SA
CELLAR ⇌ 12 +
ALC./VOL. 13.5%
RRP $35.00

This is Pam Dunsford's top wine of the vintage, a cellar special that demands time. Dunsford's McLaren Vale grapes are sourced from some of the district's best vineyards, and the Coonawarra cabernet for this one comes from the Blarney Block.
CURRENT RELEASE 1992 Lock this one away for a few years; it's rather heavily timbered but should turn into a more balanced wine with age. It has all the right ingredients: stacks of rich flavour, smoothness, savoury wood-driven flavour complexities and supple but persistent tannins. If you drink it young, decant and breathe for a couple of hours first.

Chapel Hill Shiraz

Chapel Hill has its own 5-ha. vineyard at Kangarilla. This wine comes from Kangarilla and Blewitt Springs. Maker Pam Dunsford.
Previous outstanding vintages: '90, '91, '93
CURRENT RELEASE 1994 A rich, smooth wine with plenty of oak, smelling smoky and toasty with plums and berries. A fresh young shiraz which can only improve with time. Drink with beef casserole.

QUALITY ♛♛♛♛♝
VALUE ★★★★
GRAPES shiraz
REGION McLaren Vale, SA
CELLAR 🍾 6+
ALC./VOL. 13.5%
RRP $17.60

Charles Melton Grenache

Graeme 'Charlie' Melton is one of the individuals who can be credited with inspiring the grenache renaissance.
Previous outstanding vintages: '93
CURRENT RELEASE 1994 This is good now but will be great when the oak settles further into the wine. At present the coconutty, toasty American oak is assertive. The wine has body and plenty of grip, fullness and length. There is a nice oak/fruit harmony in the mouth and it has the makings of a lovely bottle in three or four years. Drink with saddle of hare.

QUALITY ♛♛♛♛
VALUE ★★★★
GRAPES grenache
REGION Barossa Valley, SA
CELLAR 🍾 6+
ALC./VOL. 14.5%
RRP $16.00 (cellar door)

Charles Melton Rose of Virginia

Charlie Melton doesn't make white wines, but this is his surrogate white. It's also a very handy cash-flow earner.
CURRENT RELEASE 1996 Very much in the maker's usual style: deeply coloured for a rosé without sweetness and the dryness of the finish accentuated by a trace of tannin. Just after bottling it was already looking good, with raspberry/candy fruit and promising to taste even better with six months or so in bottle. Serve with antipasto and a mild chill.

QUALITY ♛♛♛♛
VALUE ★★★½
GRAPES grenache
REGION Barossa Valley, SA
CELLAR 🍾 2
ALC./VOL. 12.0%
RRP $12.00 (cellar door)

Charles Sturt University Limited Release Cabernet Shiraz

QUALITY ♀♀♀♀
VALUE ★★★½
GRAPES cabernet sauvignon, shiraz
REGION Coonawarra, SA & Heathcote, Vic.
CELLAR 🍷 6+
ALC./VOL. 13.0%
RRP $16.40

Rodney Hooper buys grapes from wherever he chooses to make his limited release wines, which are invariably good. This dual gold-medallist intelligently combines Heathcote shiraz with Coonawarra cabernet.
CURRENT RELEASE 1993 Ripe, blackberry-like cabernet dominates the blend at this point, with a twist of leafiness adding to the aromatic lift. In the mouth it has some pepperiness and lively acid, excellent depth of fruit flavour and shows potential to cellar well. Goes great with beef wellington.

Chateau Reynella Basket Pressed Cabernet Sauvignon

QUALITY ♀♀♀♀
VALUE ★★★½
GRAPES cabernet sauvignon
REGION McLaren Vale, SA
CELLAR ➡ 1–8
ALC./VOL. 13.5%
RRP $19.00 Ⓢ 🍷

Roll out the barrel, and wheel out the basket press ... this is symptomatic of a general industry revival of old-fashioned red winemaking techniques. Maker Steve Pannell and team.
Previous outstanding vintages: '88, '90, '91, '92
CURRENT RELEASE 1993 Slightly bizarre meaty, animal characters with a minty aspect, all reflecting a generous complement of charry American oak. Improves as it breathes to have attractive spicy aromas, and although the palate seems disjointed, bottle-age should bring it together. Try venison.

Chateau Reynella Basket Pressed Shiraz

QUALITY ♀♀♀♀
VALUE ★★★
GRAPES shiraz
REGION McLaren Vale, SA
CELLAR ➡ 2–6+
ALC./VOL. 14.5%
RRP $19.30 Ⓢ 🍷

Under David O'Leary, the basket press was revived at Hardys and his successor Steve Pannell continues the tradition. The vines that grow this wine were planted in the '30s.
CURRENT RELEASE 1993 Very intense gamey, peppery, meaty nose with lively cool-year varietal character, and the palate has plenty of stuffing but is slightly bitter on the finish. Ample depth and weight, and it should come good in the cellar. Then drink with game pie.

Chateau Tahbilk Shiraz

Tahbilk celebrated its 135th anniversary in 1995, and the distinguished history of this atmospheric property is now enshrined in the excellent Len Evans Museum at the winery.
Previous outstanding vintages: '71, '76, '80, '82, '85, '86, '90, '92
CURRENT RELEASE 1993 A most attractive Tahbilk, showing cherry-plum fruit, elegance and balance. Typically fruit-driven, it has relatively gentle tannins and ready drinkability. The harsh tannins of some of the vintages of yesteryear are nowhere in sight. Goes well with beef bordelais.

QUALITY 🍷🍷🍷🍷
VALUE ★★★★½
GRAPES shiraz
REGION Goulburn Valley, Vic.
CELLAR 🍾 6+
ALC./VOL. 13.0%
RRP $12.80 Ⓢ 🍾

Chateau Xanadu Cabernet Sauvignon

Xanadu are putting a lot of effort into their cabernets lately, not least on price. The Reserve is over $40 and this one's topped $20.
CURRENT RELEASE 1994 The nose shows dominant oak and this is reflected in the grippy tannin astringency of the palate. There are aromas of dried herbs and walnut, and good depth of fruit underneath it all. Has the makings of a fine bottle of cabernet. Cellar, then serve with roast beef and a rich demi-glaze.

QUALITY 🍷🍷🍷🍷
VALUE ★★★½
GRAPES cabernet sauvignon
REGION Margaret River, WA
CELLAR ⟶ 2–8+
ALC./VOL. 13.5%
RRP $23.30 🍾

Chateau Xanadu Featherwhite

Xanadu's Swiss winemaker Jurg Muggli sells most of this to Switzerland, where they love the style – it's similar to a local rosé made from wooded pinot noir, similarly barrel-fermented and given a malolactic treatment.
CURRENT RELEASE 1994 Light, developed, smoked salmon-pink colour. The nose has some oak plus developed characters giving it a savoury edge that follows through to the palate. It's quite different to fruity Australian-style rosés. The palate is dry, with strength and finish. It could be served with bouillabaisse.

QUALITY 🍷🍷🍷
VALUE ★★★
GRAPES cabernet sauvignon
REGION Margaret River, WA
CELLAR 🍾 1
ALC./VOL. 13.0%
RRP $16.00

Chatsfield Shiraz

QUALITY 🍷🍷🍷🍷
VALUE ★★★★
GRAPES shiraz
REGION Mount Barker, WA
CELLAR 1–7+
ALC./VOL. 12.9%
RRP $16.90

The Mount Barker region of WA is one of the most exciting areas for cool-climate shiraz. Here, they can grow a spicy style which has fullness and great charm.
CURRENT RELEASE 1993 Slight development in the colour, and the nose has a graphite/peppery note and lightly handled wood. A big, gutsy wine with lots of extract, tannin and flavours of licorice and plum. The mid-palate is soft and tannin chimes in on a forceful finish. Try it with Irish stew.

QUALITY 🍷🍷🍷🍷🍷
VALUE ★★★★½
GRAPES shiraz
REGION Mount Barker, WA
CELLAR 1–8+
ALC./VOL. 13.0%
RRP $16.90

CURRENT RELEASE 1994 This is a lovely wine, stylishly fruit-driven and sweet on the palate with licorice and sweet berry flavours. The bouquet has green peppercorn and a little as-yet unintegrated coconut oak. Well balanced, smooth and long in the mouth. A year or two and it will be even better. Casserole here.

Coldstream Hills Pinot Noir

QUALITY 🍷🍷🍷🍷🍷
VALUE ★★★½
GRAPES pinot noir
REGION Yarra Valley, Vic.
CELLAR 3
ALC./VOL. 12.5%
RRP $23.00 ⓢ

Pinot is the raison d'etre of Coldstream Hills, if not its bread and butter. Although it's a smallish winery, it produces more premium pinot noir table wine than anyone else in Australia, which is no small feat.
Previous outstanding vintages: '91, '92, '94
CURRENT RELEASE 1995 While not as outstanding as the '94, this is a very smart pinot and typical of the maker's style. Medium-light purple-red, it has a fresh, ripe cherry/strawberry fruit-led nose, with lightly handled spicy oak providing support. Delicious sweet pinot flavour, smooth and easy drinking, with light tannins and excellent varietal definition. Char-grilled salmon here.

Coldstream Hills Reserve Cabernet Sauvignon

Can it be that the Yarra Valley is Bordeaux and Burgundy rolled into one? Better known for its pinot, Coldstream is playing fine tunes with cabernet too.
Previous outstanding vintages: '92
CURRENT RELEASE 1994 True to house style, this is an aromatic, fine-boned cabernet which features stylish cedary oak. The wood combines with blackcurrant regional fruit to give a sweetly perfumed nose, and the palate is complex, flavour-packed and oh-so classy. Goes well with pink lamb and pesto.

QUALITY 🍷🍷🍷🍷̧
VALUE ★★★★
GRAPES cabernet sauvignon
REGION Yarra Valley, Vic.
CELLAR 🍾 8+
ALC./VOL. 13.5%
RRP $30.00

Coldstream Hills Reserve Pinot Noir

Since 1990, James Halliday has been bottling the best of his pinot and chardonnay under a Reserve label. Around 15 to 20 per cent of the total production, they are reserve wines in the truest sense of the word.
Previous outstanding vintages: '87, '88, '91, '92
CURRENT RELEASE 1994 A stunner to challenge the great '91. Deep coloured, showing dominant toasty/cedary French oak in its youth, and excellent fruit concentration in the mouth. Power-packed, with tight, firm tannins and a big finish, this is an exciting pinot. The flavour lingers long and it teams well with Peking duck.

QUALITY 🍷🍷🍷🍷🍷
VALUE ★★★★
GRAPES pinot noir
REGION Yarra Valley, Vic.
CELLAR 🍾 6
ALC./VOL. 13.5%
RRP $32.00

Coriole Lloyd Reserve Shiraz

The wine was named after Coriole's founder Hugh Lloyd. The family still owns and operates the winery, with Mark Lloyd managing.
Previous outstanding vintages: '89, '90, '91, '92
CURRENT RELEASE 1993 The 70-year-old vines have done their thing. Although the nose shows strong and slightly unintegrated American oak, with lashings of coconut and mint, there is a mass of sweet ripe fruit to taste and the structure is smooth, round and full flavoured. The overall impression is of great class – a pleasure to drink. Suits pepper steak.

QUALITY 🍷🍷🍷🍷̧
VALUE ★★★★
GRAPES shiraz
REGION McLaren Vale, SA
CELLAR 🍾 10
ALC./VOL. 14.0%
RRP $25.00

Cowra Estate Shiraz Cabernet

QUALITY ♛♛♛
VALUE ★★★
GRAPES shiraz, cabernet sauvignon
REGION Cowra, NSW
CELLAR 🍾 3
ALC./VOL. 13.0%
RRP $15.50

The pioneer vineyard in Cowra was established by Tony Grey in 1973 and now has 72 ha. of vines. It has no winery but there is a place for visitors to try the wines.
CURRENT RELEASE 1994 The colour is a trifle on the light side and the aromas are likewise a tad pedestrian with simple cherry and lightly leafy aspects. The weight is light to medium, the tannins soft, making the wine a drink-now proposition. Spaghetti bolognese here.

Craiglee Shiraz

QUALITY ♛♛♛♛⁕
VALUE ★★★★
GRAPES shiraz
REGION Sunbury, Vic.
CELLAR 🍾 12+
ALC./VOL. 13.3%
RRP $20.00 (cellar door) 🍾

Pat Carmody is actually producing less wine these days, due to his ongoing feud with planning and environment authorities, who would like him to rip up his vineyard. This would be a tragedy as it produces great shiraz.
Previous outstanding vintages: '80, '84, '85, '86, '88, '90, '91, '92
CURRENT RELEASE 1993 Intense peppery/spicy/cherry fruit and low-key oak are the hallmarks of Craiglee and they are here in abundance. The structure is tight and refined, with puckering tannins and a focused, dry finish. The profile is serious and the youthful grip is very firm, suggesting short-term cellaring would be of benefit. Drink with duck confit.

QUALITY ♛♛♛♛⁕
VALUE ★★★★½
GRAPES shiraz
REGION Macedon, Vic.
CELLAR 🍾 12+
ALC./VOL. 14.0%
RRP $22.50

CURRENT RELEASE 1994 A bigger, richer wine than the '93 and according to Pat Carmody, more central Victorian in structure. The usual superb deep purple colour and intensely pepper/spicy cool-grown shiraz aromas are there in full glory. The cherry/spice palate flavours are elegant and long, yet with definite tannin on a firm, dry finish. Very stylish and will be long-lived. Serve with rare kangaroo.

Cullen Cabernet Sauvignon Merlot

Cullen's is without doubt one of the most exciting winemakers in an exciting region, producing wines of real substance and longevity the hard way – with no shortcuts. Maker Vanya Cullen. Previous outstanding vintages: '84 '86, '90, '91, '92

CURRENT RELEASE 1993 A magnificent wine, hauntingly perfumed with cedar, dark berries, sandalwood and mint. The palate has terrific power, concentrated flavour with fruit and wood seamlessly harmonised, culminating in a big finish of great length. Very classy stuff! Try it with beef wellington.

QUALITY ΨΨΨΨΨ
VALUE ★★★★½
GRAPES cabernet sauvignon, merlot, cabernet franc
REGION Margaret River, WA
CELLAR 2-12+
ALC./VOL. 13.0%
RRP $28.25

CURRENT RELEASE 1994 Very dark purple-red colour and cedary, spicy nose reveals long wood-maturation. There's masses of tannin demanding cellaring. Flavours of walnut and dark berry are lurking beneath the oak and tannin with some ripe, licorice undercurrents. A very powerful cabernet to cellar, then serve with aged hard cheeses.

QUALITY ΨΨΨΨΨ
VALUE ★★★★
GRAPES cabernet sauvignon 60%, merlot 30%, cabernet franc 10%
REGION Margaret River, WA
CELLAR 2-10+
ALC./VOL. 13.0%
RRP $28.25

Cullen Pinot Noir

Winemaker Vanya Cullen doesn't muck around when it comes to red wines – she goes for the max every time. This pinot is on an altogether more serious plane than most others in Australia. Previous outstanding vintages: '93

CURRENT RELEASE 1995 An Aussie DRC, dare we say! This is a simply outstanding pinot. Its depth and concentration are truly in the big league. The colour is very deep, the nose rich in chocolate, vanilla, caramel notes with a twist of volatile acid and lots of other nice things. The palate reveals rich cherry and berry flavours encased in an ample envelope of supple tannins. Glorious power and length. A triumph! Drink from 1997, with duck.

QUALITY ΨΨΨΨΨ
VALUE ★★★★★
GRAPES pinot noir
REGION Margaret River, WA
CELLAR 1-6+
ALC./VOL. 13.5%
RRP $28.00

Dalfarras Shiraz

QUALITY	▼▼▼▼
VALUE	★★★★
GRAPES	shiraz
REGION	central Vic.
CELLAR	2–6
ALC./VOL.	12.0%
RRP	$14.50

Support this label and you are going to become familiar with the art of Rosa Dalfarras. We've seen worse. Rosa is the wife of maker Alister Purbrick.

CURRENT RELEASE 1993 A restrained style that should open up with further bottle-age and breathing. The colour is a deep crimson and the nose has blackberry aromas tinged with spice. The palate is constrained with muted blackberry fruit but there is also complexity thanks to the American oak. The finish has fine-grained tannins. Try it with pink lamb.

Dalwhinnie Pyrenees Shiraz

QUALITY	▼▼▼▼▼
VALUE	★★★
GRAPES	shiraz
REGION	Pyrenees, Vic.
CELLAR	5–15
ALC./VOL.	14.0%
RRP	$80 (Case lots only)

For those who dare with brave wallets. This is a very limited release and is recorded here to alert readers that such a wine exists and they should join the waiting list for next year.

CURRENT RELEASE 1992 The colour shows a typical Pyrenees intensity – deep purple/indigo. The nose offers a strong hint of lemon grass and Vietnamese mint. The palate is substantial with intense blackberry fruit mingled with spices. These are matched by a black tea-like astringent finish. There are lashings of grip and it will cellar well. It needs a substantial dish like a game pie.

Darling Park Cabernet Merlot

QUALITY	▼▼▼▼
VALUE	★★★½
GRAPES	cabernet sauvignon, cabernet franc, merlot
REGION	Mornington Peninsula, Vic.
CELLAR	4
ALC./VOL.	12.8%
RRP	$18.00

This winery/vineyard was established in 1986 at Red Hill by John and Delys Sergeant. Maker Kevin McCarthy (consultant).

CURRENT RELEASE 1993 An elegant style that has a mix of fruits on the palate. The nose offers redcurrant fruit aromas plus tobacco and cigar box smells. The palate is a contest between cherry and raspberry flavours and there is a leaf component in the mix. The finish is dominated by astringent acid. It is fine with pink lamb and mint sauce.

David Traeger Shiraz

David Traeger did yeoman's service at Mitchelton before striking out on his own accord with a label featuring his name. It has all the hallmarks of becoming a good ol' wine boy.

CURRENT RELEASE 1993 The nose is a bit gamey with a background of plums and spice. The colour is dense and the palate is rich with developed plum flavours. The oak slips into the picture with gentle tannins. It is easy to drink; try it with lamb shanks.

QUALITY ♛♛♛
VALUE ★★★
GRAPES shiraz
REGION Nagambie, Vic.
CELLAR ◗ 4
ALC./VOL. 11.5%
RRP $15.00

David Wynn Cabernet Sauvignon

This is another wine in the David Wynn range made to provide value for money. The grapes can be sourced from regions other than the home vineyard. Maker Adam Wynn.

CURRENT RELEASE 1994 This is a well-made wine of considerable elegance. The nose has a strong blackcurrant component and that is the major flavour on the palate. The wood combines well to make for an astringent finish. It is very well balanced and drinks accordingly. Try it with barbecued pork in a mango sauce.

QUALITY ♛♛♛♛
VALUE ★★★★
GRAPES cabernet sauvignon
REGION Eden Valley, SA
CELLAR ◗ 4
ALC./VOL. 12.7%
RRP $14.00

David Wynn Patriarch Shiraz

Named after the saviour of Coonawarra and a very thorough gent, David Wynn died in his garden after a Sunday lunch and a couple of glasses of good wine. Apparently his end was as dignified as his life. Maker Adam Wynn.
Previous outstanding vintages: '92, '93

CURRENT RELEASE 1994 The fruit comes from old vines and the wine shows typical depth of flavour. The colour is deep and the nose is rich with abundant ripe plum and spice aromas. The bulky palate has plenty of flesh. There are ripe plum flavours saturated with spices and pepper. French oak adds grip and tannin to the finish. It drinks well with savoury mince on toast (a joke David Wynn would have enjoyed).

QUALITY ♛♛♛♛⸮
VALUE ★★★★
GRAPES shiraz
REGION Barossa & Eden Valley, SA
CELLAR ◗ 6
ALC./VOL. 13.0%
RRP $23.00

David Wynn Pinot Noir

QUALITY	♛♛♛
VALUE	★★★
GRAPES	pinot noir
REGION	Eden Valley, SA
CELLAR	🍷 2
ALC./VOL.	13.0%
RRP	$12.00

Could this be the off-cuts from the famed Mountadam pinot noir? If so, it is a very pleasant drink at an affordable price.

CURRENT RELEASE 1994 This is a soft, drinkable wine with obvious varietal character. The nose is vinous with strong cherry aromas. The palate has sweet strawberry flavours and these are backed by some modest tannins on a clean finish. You could contemplate chilling the wine. The best accompaniment is char-grilled tuna with wild rice.

De Bortoli Yarra Valley Cabernet Sauvignon

QUALITY	♛♛♛♛
VALUE	★★★★
GRAPES	cabernet sauvignon
REGION	Yarra Valley, Vic.
CELLAR	← 2–7
ALC./VOL.	13.0%
RRP	$19.90

If you are Yarra Valley bound and in need of sustenance around lunch-time you could do no better than eat at the De Bortoli restaurant which is top flight by any estimation. Maker Steve Webber. Previous outstanding vintages: '88, '90, '91

CURRENT RELEASE 1993 A tough little number that needs breathing to open up. The colour is intense and the nose, while herbal, also promises the wood that follows. The palate has intense blackberry plus hints of herbs. The finish displays some black tea-like tannins and powerful grip. It goes well with char-grilled kangaroo.

De Bortoli Yarra Valley Pinot Noir

QUALITY	♛♛♛♛?
VALUE	★★★★
GRAPES	pinot noir
REGION	Yarra Valley, Vic.
CELLAR	🍷 6
ALC./VOL.	13.0%
RRP	$19.00

Tilting at windmills? Most Yarra Valley wineries have pinot noir as some sort of grail. Happily in most cases they seem to be coming close to grasping the chalice. Maker Steve Webber.

CURRENT RELEASE 1994 This is a very convincing wine that has substance and flavour. The colour is a medium-ruby and the nose has strawberry and cherry aromas with a hint of truffle and earth. The palate has a mouth-filling quality and there are some lush berry flavours that are matched with well-integrated oak. It drinks well now and is crying out for succulent pink lamb with rosemary and mint.

De Bortoli Yarra Valley Shiraz

Shiraz is a rare commodity in the Yarra Valley but judging by the consistent results achieved by De Bortoli it is difficult to understand why this is so.

Previous outstanding vintages: '89, '90, '91, '92
CURRENT RELEASE 1993 No beg pardons here. The wine has an intense deep purple colour. The nose displays fully ripe plums, spices and ferment aromas. The palate is complex and rewarding with abundant varietal character plus pepper and spice. The finish displays well-tuned oak and plenty of grip. Great balance, so put it alongside doner kebab.

QUALITY ♛♛♛♛
VALUE ★★★★½
GRAPES shiraz
REGION Yarra Valley, Vic.
CELLAR → 2–8
ALC./VOL. 13.5%
RRP $20.30

Deakin Estate Cabernet Sauvignon

This wine contains some ruby cabernet – a variety bred for hot, dry climates by Professor Olmo, who crossed cabernet sauvignon and carignan. In days of yore it was known as Sunnycliff. Maker Mark Zeppel.

CURRENT RELEASE 1995 The colour is medium purple-red and the nose shows vanillan oak plus berry and earthy aromas turning slightly gamey. It tastes lean and somewhat short with some dominant oak character, but there is good flavour and it's excellent value for money. Try it with gourmet hamburgers.

QUALITY ♛♛♛
VALUE ★★★★
GRAPES cabernet sauvignon 85%, ruby cabernet 15%
REGION Murray Valley, Vic.
CELLAR ↓ 3
ALC./VOL. 12.0%
RRP $8.50

Delamere Pinot Noir

QUALITY ♛♛♛
VALUE ★★★
GRAPES pinot noir
REGION Pipers Brook, Tas.
CELLAR 🍷 2
ALC./VOL. 13.3%
RRP $23.00

Richard Richardson can never be accused of making middle-of-the-road wines. His style is determinedly individual, and sometimes he hits the heights.
Previous outstanding vintages: '90
CURRENT RELEASE 1994 This is a grunge pinot noir! The colour is medium-depth red, the nose shows developed gamey, slightly animal, earthy characters that reflect idiosyncratic winemaking. There is a vegetal side to the flavour, and the palate is lean and austere. It calls for food. Try char-grilled octopus.

Delatite Devil's River

QUALITY ♛♛♛♛
VALUE ★★★½
GRAPES cabernet sauvignon, merlot
REGION Mansfield, Vic.
CELLAR 🍷 5
ALC./VOL. 12.8%
RRP $16.50

Delatite winery was founded in 1982 after the Ritchie family of growers decided to turn their hand to winemaking. Prior to that the grapes were sold to Brown Brothers.
CURRENT RELEASE 1994 The colour is a vibrant ruby and the nose has an intense eucalypt and menthol character. The medium-bodied palate has sweet raspberry flavour and this is balanced by a woody finish with vanilla flavours. With all that mint it goes well with lamb.

Delatite Dungeon Gully

QUALITY ♛♛♛♛
VALUE ★★★
GRAPES merlot, malbec
REGION Mansfield, Vic.
CELLAR 🍷 2
ALC./VOL. 13.0%
RRP $16.50

What's going on in them thar Mansfield Hills? Bit of D&D under the shadow of Mount Buller? What with 'devils, dungeons, dead men et al' should there be some leather in the cabernet? Maker Ros Ritchie.
CURRENT RELEASE 1994 A curious blend that makes for an interesting drink. The wine has a medium-ruby colour with purple robes. The nose is very cherry-berry with a hint of boiled lollies. The palate is sweet with attractive berry fruit and this is balanced by mild tannins and some clean acid. It goes well with a rabbit stew (if you can find the rabbits).

Delatite Pinot Noir

This winery produces in the order of 12 000 cases per year and the cellar door would have one of the best views in the country.
CURRENT RELEASE 1994 As impressive as ever, the wine has made little progress since the last review. There is a hint of mint on the nose and that offers sweet strawberry and meaty-fruit characters. There are also plum and cherry flavours which are matched by strong acid and a firm tannin grip. Great with duck.

QUALITY ████▌
VALUE ★★★★½
GRAPES pinot noir
REGION Mansfield, Vic.
CELLAR 🍾 3 +
ALC./VOL. 14.0%
RRP $17.40

Domaine Cabernet Sauvignon

This is the top cuvée of Peter Althaus's Stoney vineyard at Campania in the Coal River Valley. Althaus is a refugee from the computer rat-race.
CURRENT RELEASE 1993 Fruit, fruit and more fruit. In fact you might wonder that it's a bit too fruity and, as the French say, not vinous enough. Electric purple hue, fresh raw blackcurrant aroma with some crushed-leaf overtones, and a slightly monotone but lushly fruited palate. Cellar, then serve with a good Tassie washed-rind cheese such as Red Square.

QUALITY ████
VALUE ★★½
GRAPES cabernet sauvignon
REGION Coal River Valley, Tas.
CELLAR 🍾 2–7+
ALC./VOL. 12.5%
RRP $38.00

Dromana Estate Cabernet Merlot

The label shows a stained-glass panel in the door of the homestead at Dromana Estate. It depicts a brain forming the thought of the vinification process. Makers A. B. O'Connor and G. J. Crittenden.
CURRENT RELEASE 1993 For all the alcohol this remains very much a cool-climate style. It has a pronounced leafy/herbal quality on the nose. The palate is medium-bodied with a rather thin texture but there is also an intensity of blackberry flavour. There are supple tannins on a long finish. It should cellar well but it drinks well with a warm salad of quail.

QUALITY ████
VALUE ★★★½
GRAPES cabernet sauvignon 90%, merlot 10%
REGION Mornington Peninsula, Vic.
CELLAR 🍾 2–10
ALC./VOL. 14.0%
RRP $22.00

Dromana Estate Pinot Noir

QUALITY ♛♛♛♛♕
VALUE ★★★★
GRAPES pinot noir
REGION Mornington Peninsula, Vic.
CELLAR 🍷 6
ALC./VOL. 14.0%
RRP $20.00

Colour is seldom a reliable guide to this variety, those with lighter colours quite often exhibit spring-steel backbones. Maker Garry Crittenden. Previous outstanding vintages: '91
CURRENT RELEASE 1995 A light-coloured but full-volume wine with plenty of punch. The nose is a vortex of spice, leaf and berry aromas. The palate appears to be medium-bodied but builds in the mouth with berry flavour and a warmth of alcohol. The finish shows fine-grained tannins and strong acid. It drinks well now but will cellar; try it with baked squab.

Eaglehawk Shiraz Merlot Cabernet

QUALITY ♛♛♛
VALUE ★★★½
GRAPES shiraz, merlot, cabernet sauvignon
REGION McLaren Vale & Clare Valley, SA
CELLAR 🍷 3
ALC./VOL. 12.5%
RRP $10.90 ⓢ

Eaglehawk is a Wolf Blass brand that emanates from the old Quelltaler winery at Watervale. Since Blass bought it, the name has progressed from Quelltaler to Eaglehawk to Black Opal and now back (mercifully) to Quelltaler! Maker David O'Leary.
CURRENT RELEASE 1994 This is a somewhat nondescript wine with herbal aromas and hints of blackcurrant. It has adequate intensity for the money and is good value when it's discounted to $7.95. The finish has good grip and length. Serve it with barbecued sausages.

Elderton Cabernet Sauvignon

QUALITY ♛♛♛♛♛
VALUE ★★★★½
GRAPES cabernet sauvignon
REGION Barossa Valley, SA
CELLAR 🍷 8+
ALC./VOL. 14.0%
RRP $19.00

This is based on the original vines in the company's Nuriootpa vineyard, which are over 50 years old.
Previous outstanding vintages: '92, '93
CURRENT RELEASE 1994 This is the epitome of the sweet, rich, sunny Barossa style that's winning hearts all over the world. Excellent deep purple-red colour. Sweet rich blackcurrant cabernet fruit with oak and tannin aplenty but in fine harmony. Good depth and concentration. Impressive stuff, a real lip-smacker. Try it with roast beef.

Elderton Command Shiraz

Your wish is my command, says the very marketing-orientated Neil Ashmead. This flagship red gets three years in oak, one in bottle.
CURRENT RELEASE 1992 One for the wood lovers. Pungent, assertive oak in the coconut, vanilla and toast spectrum dominates. There's almost a rancio long-term wood-matured character. It does have plenty of intensity and weight with a lingering finish. But whether it will ever come into balance is a moot point. Serve with mild Indian curry.

QUALITY ♛♛♛♛
VALUE ★★★
GRAPES shiraz
REGION Barossa Valley, SA
CELLAR ➡ 2–6+
ALC./VOL. 14.5%
RRP $26.50 $

Elderton Merlot

If the USA is any guide, we will all be swimming in merlot before too long. Maker James Irvine and Neil Ashmead.
CURRENT RELEASE 1994 'Not a wine for the faint-hearted', warns the back label. But never fear, this is a harmless and sassy drink. Deep hue; rich berry and vanilla oak nose; fleshy, chunky palate with alcohol warmth and lashings of tannin from liberal oak. Should be a crowd-pleaser, and the vanillan oak should be more harmonious in a year.

QUALITY ♛♛♛♛
VALUE ★★★
GRAPES merlot
REGION Barossa Valley, SA
CELLAR ▯ 4+
ALC./VOL. 14.0%
RRP $23.00

Elderton Shiraz

If ever there was proof the Barossa and shiraz are made for each other, it is at Elderton where they seem to achieve voluptuous richness with great regularity.
Previous outstanding vintages: '86, '88, '90, '91, '92, '93
CURRENT RELEASE 1994 This is like coming home. Lashings of sweet ripe fruit are the feature. The alcohol is high and there is sweet flavour and supple tannin galore but no hint of portiness. The nose has classic spicy/gamey shiraz character and the oak is well judged. A blinder of a shiraz to serve with tandoori lamb.

QUALITY ♛♛♛♛♛
VALUE ★★★★
GRAPES shiraz
REGION Barossa Valley, SA
CELLAR ▯ 8 +
ALC./VOL. 14.0%
RRP $17.70

Evans & Tate Margaret River Shiraz

QUALITY ♟♟♟♝
VALUE ★★★
GRAPES shiraz
REGION Margaret River, WA
CELLAR 🍾 6+
ALC./VOL. 13.0%
RRP $24.60

E & T was established by John and Toni Tate, who have handed most of the day-to-day running over to their lively son, Franklin. Maker Brian Fletcher.

CURRENT RELEASE 1993 This is a big, rich, soft wine smelling of pungent pepper/spice and gamey aromas. The spiciness continues throughout the palate and there's good depth of flavour, with a soft finish that falls away slightly. Drinks well with pepper steak.

Fire Gully Cabernet Merlot

QUALITY ♟♟♟♝
VALUE ★★★
GRAPES cabernet sauvignon, cabernet franc, merlot
REGION Margaret River, WA
CELLAR 🍾 4
ALC./VOL. 13.0%
RRP $20.20

This is the second label for Pierro, which denotes the grapes were not estate-grown but from neighbouring vineyards in the district. Maker Dr Mike Peterkin.

CURRENT RELEASE 1994 This is an elegant wine that has attractive structure. The nose has spicy aromas and berry characters. The medium-bodied palate has cherry and berry flavours. There are vanilla flavours and hints of toast on the finish. It drinks well now with a game and mushroom risotto.

Forest Hill Cabernet Sauvignon

QUALITY ♟♟♟♝
VALUE ★★★½
GRAPES cabernet sauvignon
REGION Mount Barker, WA
CELLAR 🍾 4
ALC./VOL. 12.0%
RRP $14.65

This vineyard was the original experimental plot for the Mount Barker region. These days it is owned and expanded by Vasse Felix. Maker Clive Otto.

CURRENT RELEASE 1993 This is a cool-climate number with a botanical twist (that is leafy characters). The nose is leafy with varietal fruit aromas like cassis and cherry. The palate is a middleweight with cherry and blackberry flavours and there are dusty dry characters on the finish. It goes well with veal shanks.

Fox Creek Shiraz

Sparky Marquis and his parents-in-law Helen and Jim Watts run this 34-ha. vineyard at Willunga. This wine won Marquis the title of Bushing King at the local wine show in '95, which was good timing as it was his debut wine, immediately putting Fox Creek on the map.
CURRENT RELEASE 1994 A massive wine, terrifically concentrated, rich and powerful, with almost purple/black hue, plenty of oak and opulently ripe, plummy fruit. A gutsy, tannic wine with great potential for the cellar. Team it with pork spare ribs in plum sauce.

QUALITY ♛♛♛♛♛
VALUE ★★★★½
GRAPES shiraz
REGION McLaren Vale, SA
CELLAR 🍾 10+
ALC./VOL. 14.6%
RRP $18.00 (cellar door)

Freycinet Cabernet Sauvignon

The vineyard was founded in 1980 by Geoffrey Bull who made his money from abalone diving. The annual production is in the order of 4000 cases. Previous outstanding vintages: '91, '93
CURRENT RELEASE 1994 The cool climate origins are obvious thanks to a leafy cigar-box nose with hints of toast. There is sweet, ripe, raspberry fruit flavours on the palate which are garnished by some tobacco character. The finish is dry and astringent with fine-grained tannins and medium grip. It serves well with smoked lamb cutlets.

QUALITY ♛♛♛♛
VALUE ★★★
GRAPES cabernet sauvignon
REGION east coast, Tas.
CELLAR 🍾 5
ALC./VOL. 13.4%
RRP $35.00

Freycinet Pinot Noir

This vineyard is on the east coast of Tasmania and it has been ideally located in a manner to make maximum use of the sunshine. Maker Geoffrey Bull.
Previous outstanding vintages: '91, '92, '93, '94
CURRENT RELEASE 1995 A very youthful style with a fresh strawberry nose and a hint of bubblegum character. The medium-bodied palate has concentrated strawberry flavours and hints of dark cherry plus a touch of sap. The finish shows off some clean acid. It goes well with char-grilled tuna on a red capsicum salsa.

QUALITY ♛♛♛♛
VALUE ★★★
GRAPES pinot noir
REGION east coast, Tas.
CELLAR 🍾 3
ALC./VOL. 13.0%
RRP $35.00

Galah Wine Clare Valley Shiraz

QUALITY	🍷🍷🍷🍷🍷
VALUE	★★★★★
GRAPES	shiraz
REGION	Clare Valley, SA
CELLAR	2–10+
ALC./VOL.	14.4%
RRP	$15.00 (mail order)

Don't laugh when you see the label: this is seriously good stuff. The fruit comes off Wendouree's 'young' vines – the 60-year-old whippersnappers. Maker Stephen George. Previous outstanding vintages: '92

CURRENT RELEASE 1994 A marvellously fine perfume of spices, earth and berries teases the senses and the palate does not disappoint. Big and very tannic, built for the long haul, this baby has tremendous intensity and power, mouth-coating tannin and is concentrated in every regard. The finish seems endless. A great wine. Cellar, then serve with spicy sausages.

Garry Crittenden Barbera

QUALITY	🍷🍷🍷🍷
VALUE	★★★
GRAPES	barbera
REGION	King Valley, Vic.
CELLAR	4
ALC./VOL.	13.5%
RRP	$18.00

The grapes were grown by former tobacco farmer Arnie Pizzini in the King Valley, which has become a goldmine for Italian grape varieties.
CURRENT RELEASE 1994 A youthful, fruity style that some may find a bit callow. The nose has bituminous character perhaps from the oak, and plenty of soft berry fruit which runs through the soft tannin palate. Could be better in a year or two. Drink with roast kid.

Garry Crittenden Granaccia

QUALITY	🍷🍷🍷🍷
VALUE	★★★
GRAPES	grenache
REGION	not stated
CELLAR	3
ALC./VOL.	14.0%
RRP	$18.00

Dromana Estate's proprietor is one very enterprising vigneron, and his latest kick is Italian varietals, for which he sources fruit from far and wide. Granaccia is the Sicilian name for grenache.
CURRENT RELEASE 1994 A powerful, spirity alcoholic wine with deep purple hue, stalky, licorice nose and rich, chunky palate. Not a lot of finesse, but a ballsy over-ripe style whose key asset is in-your-face flavour. Try it with spicy pasta siciliana.

Garry Crittenden Nebbiolo

This is the great grape of Barolo and Barbaresco, in Piedmont. The wine has similarities to a Piedmontese wine, too. Grower Fred Pizzini. Maker Garry Crittenden.
CURRENT RELEASE 1994 Interesting wine and a genuine alternative to cabernet and shiraz. The colour is of modest depth, the nose has an unusual combination of chocolatey, gamey and raspberry aromas, turning to cassis on the palate and finishing with a surprising grip. Drink with osso bucco.

QUALITY ♆♆♆♆
VALUE ★★★½
GRAPES nebbiolo
REGION King Valley, Vic.
CELLAR 🍷 5+
ALC./VOL. 13.5%
RRP $18.00 🍾

Geoff Merrill Mount Hurtle Shiraz

A Geoff Merrill moustache comes free with every bottle, but it might take a while to find it. Tip: it's not necessarily on the label.
CURRENT RELEASE 1993 This is a lightish, straightforward, ready-drinking shiraz with smoky, meaty and light cherry aromas. It is clean and lively in the mouth without great depth. The finish is soft and easy, with light tannin. Try it with mushroom risotto.

QUALITY ♆♆♆
VALUE ★★★
GRAPES shiraz
REGION McLaren Vale, SA 59%, Victoria 41%
CELLAR 🍷 3
ALC./VOL. 13.0%
RRP $16.00

Geoff Merrill Who Cares? The Reds

Who cares about the name of a wine? I do! says Geoffrey Merrill, from under his Merv Hughes moustache.
CURRENT RELEASE 1994 This is a decent quaffing dry red, with lightish medium-red hue, fresh straightforward cherry-fruit aroma and a simple fruity, herbal taste, without appreciable oak. For everyday drinking.

QUALITY ♆♆♆
VALUE ★★★½
GRAPES grenache 90%, shiraz 10%
REGION McLaren Vale, SA
CELLAR 🍷 2
ALC./VOL. 14.0%
RRP $13.00 ⓢ

Giaconda Pinot Noir

QUALITY ♟♟♟♟
VALUE ★★★½
GRAPES pinot noir
REGION Beechworth, Vic.
CELLAR 🍾 4
ALC./VOL. 13.0%
RRP $29.80

The entire allocation for the NSW wholesaler is something like 15 cases! It doesn't touch the sides. Maker Rick Kinzbrunner.
Previous outstanding vintages: '90, '91, '92
CURRENT RELEASE 1994 Developed medium-light red/brick-red colour; marked stalky characters with vegetable and sappy aromas. The structure is very good: intense flavour, lively and leanish with plenty of persistence. A complex pinot style to serve with beef carpaccio.

Glenara Cabernet Sauvignon Merlot Cabernet Franc

QUALITY ♟♟♟♟
VALUE ★★★★
GRAPES cabernet sauvignon 65%, merlot 22%, cabernet franc 13%
REGION Adelaide Hills, SA
CELLAR 🍾 5+
ALC./VOL. 13.5%
RRP $17.00 🍾 ☺

In the good ol' days, this wine might have been called Cabernets or just Cabernet, but now the law requires spelling it out. Either that or dream up a name like Pyrus or Alexanders.
CURRENT RELEASE 1993 A serious red in a serious bottle (tall, deep punt, etc.). The nose has blackcurrants and toasty oak, with some jammy overtones, while the palate has good depth of rich, ripe flavour which lingers well. There's generous use of oak and the wine would cellar well. Serve with satays.

Glenara Shiraz

QUALITY ♟♟♟♟
VALUE ★★★★
GRAPES shiraz
REGION Adelaide Hills, SA
CELLAR ⇌ 1–6+
ALC./VOL. 15.0%
RRP $17.00 🍾 ☺

Organic vineyards are very scarce in this country and although there's a big demand for organic wine in Europe it's still a small niche market here.
CURRENT RELEASE 1993 Remarkably alcoholic and solidly built wine for such a cool region. The nose is herbal, minty and fruit-driven, and the palate is peppery, quite ruggedly structured with a warm alcohol finish and some bitter extraction. Plenty of weight and length. A real surprise packet. Serve it with osso bucco.

Goundrey Reserve Shiraz

WA's Mount Barker region is continuing to excel at elegant, spicy shiraz. This is one of the best. Maker Brenden Smith.
Previous outstanding vintages: '85, '87, '91, '92
CURRENT RELEASE 1994 Glowing red-purple hue; marvellously deep, well-defined pepper/spice aromas beautifully integrated with subtle oak. The palate is intensely cool-climate, with tightly focused flavours, elegance and balance. A stylish wine indeed, to serve with cassoulet.

QUALITY 🍷🍷🍷🍷
VALUE ★★★★
GRAPES shiraz
REGION Great Southern, WA
CELLAR 🍾 5+
ALC./VOL. 13.0%
RRP $18.00

Gramp's Grenache

Following the trend to rediscover grenache in the Barossa, Orlando has produced this commendable effort from vines around its base at Rowland Flat.
CURRENT RELEASE 1994 A classic grenache and a lovely wine that can be enjoyed young. Typical sweet floral grenache nose, aromatic and showing high ripeness and alcohol. The taste is jammy and almost sweet, very fruit-driven and supple. Delicious with English cheeses.

QUALITY 🍷🍷🍷🍷
VALUE ★★★★
GRAPES grenache
REGION Barossa Valley, SA
CELLAR 🍾 4
ALC./VOL. 14.0%
RRP $14.00 Ⓢ

Grant Burge Filsell Shiraz

Burge's cellar-door sales and office are beside Jacob's Creek at Rowland Flat, but he makes his wines in the old Basedow winery in Tanunda. He sold the Basedow brand last year to Terry Hill.
CURRENT RELEASE 1994 This is a shade lighter than previous editions, the dominant factor at time of tasting being rather sharp coconutty oak. The oak has a lot of toastiness, and the finish has balance and softness. A pleasant middle-rank shiraz to drink with smoked lamb.

QUALITY 🍷🍷🍷🍷
VALUE ★★★
GRAPES shiraz
REGION Barossa Valley, SA
CELLAR 🍾 4
ALC./VOL. 13.5%
RRP $19.30

Grant Burge Hillcot Merlot

QUALITY ♛♛♛♛
VALUE ★★★★
GRAPES merlot 90%, cabernet sauvignon 10%
REGION Barossa Valley, SA
CELLAR 🍾 5
ALC./VOL. 13.5%
RRP $15.30

Merlot is currently the darling variety in the US, and since we tend to ape their trends, it will probably take off here too. Maker Grant Burge.
CURRENT RELEASE 1993 A marked coconutty aroma betrays the presence of American oak, and the same sweet vanilla character flows through the wine. It is richly flavoured, chunky and full – more about oak than merlot varietal character, but a damn good drink with a venison chop.

Grant Burge Meshach Shiraz

QUALITY ♛♛♛♛
VALUE ★★½
GRAPES shiraz
REGION Barossa Valley, SA
CELLAR ➾ 4–8+
ALC./VOL. 14.0%
RRP $36.00

This is a 'Let's go for the jugular!' style. Meaning it is the richest fruit Mr Burge can find, infused with as much oak as he dares. Opinion is divided on whether the mark is overstepped.
Previous outstanding vintages: '88, '90
CURRENT RELEASE 1992 One for the lumber lovers. The nose is all aggressive coconutty, resiny oak and the taste is huge and grippy, with some harshness. There's guts aplenty, but the question is whether it will ever overcome the assault of the killer barrels. Don't touch it for at least two more years. Then give it plenty of air and serve with spicy sausages.

Green Point Pinot Noir

QUALITY ♛♛♛♛
VALUE ★★★½
GRAPES pinot noir
REGION Yarra Valley, Vic. 100%
CELLAR 🍾 4
ALC./VOL. 13.5%
RRP $19.80

This is the only red table wine produced by Domaine Chandon, entirely from Yarra Valley grapes. It is sold mostly ex-winery, where it is very good value at $14.
CURRENT RELEASE 1995 Tasted as a barrel sample, this had good deep colour and rich spicy, cherry aromas. There was plenty of weight on the palate and the flavour filled the mouth. It can be expected to pick up a bit more oak before its release in September '96. A good match for roast pigeon.

Grosset Gaia

Gaia is the mythical earth-mother of ancient Greek legend, reflecting the environmentally sound principles Jeffrey Grosset follows in the vineyard. Previous outstanding vintages: '90, '91, '92, '93 CURRENT RELEASE 1994 Absolutely marvellous wine. It has power yet subtlety, the oak is there but doesn't intrude, the mid-palate is all about blackcurrants and other dark berries, supported by assertive but supple tannins. The end impression is of a dense, profound wine of great length and cellaring potential. Serve with mature cheese, such as an aged Italian Reggiano.

QUALITY ♟♟♟♟♟
VALUE ★★★★★
GRAPES cabernet sauvignon 80%, cabernet franc 15%, merlot 5%
REGION Clare Valley, SA
CELLAR 🍾 10+
ALC./VOL. 13.5%
RRP $24.00

Grosset Piccadilly Pinot Noir

This is just a hatful – the back label declares 250 cases – which is just enough to start a feeding frenzy and a headache for the wholesalers. Previous outstanding vintages: '93, '94 CURRENT RELEASE 1995 Very fine wine, although perhaps a shade lighter than the '94. The colour is medium red-purple and the nose airs to bring up strawberry and sappy nuances. There is delicious pinot flavour, the fine strawberry fruit supported by discreet oak, and the balance is impeccable. A top drink with tuna sashimi.

QUALITY ♟♟♟♟♟
VALUE ★★★★
GRAPES pinot noir
REGION Adelaide Hills, SA
CELLAR 🍾 4
ALC./VOL. 13.5%
RRP $25.00

Hanging Rock Victoria Shiraz

This is going out on a viticultural limb, the vineyard at Macedon would be one of the coolest in the land and the climate must sorely test the patience of this variety. Maker John Ellis.
CURRENT RELEASE 1994 Intense pepper and cool-climate characters are the key to this wine. It has a vibrant colour and pepper and blackberry on the nose. The palate is medium-bodied with blackberry, dark cherry and loads of spice. There is a lift of vanillan oak on the finish. It is a young style that needs time. It goes with aged cheddar.

QUALITY ♟♟♟♟♟
VALUE ★★★★
GRAPES shiraz
REGION Macedon, Vic.
CELLAR ⟶ 3–6
ALC./VOL. 12.5%
RRP $18.00

RED WINES

Happs Merlot

QUALITY ♛♛♛♛♚
VALUE ★★★★
GRAPES merlot
REGION Margaret River, WA
CELLAR 🍷 5
ALC./VOL. 12.6%
RRP $15.00 (cellar door)

Ex-teacher Erl Happ has an unusual winery-cum-pottery workshop at his Yallingup property at the far north end of Margaret River.

CURRENT RELEASE 1992 This is a lovely velvety merlot that shows how hard Erl Happ has worked to improve his vineyard over the years. The nose has complex gamey and over-ripe plummy scents reminiscent of Pomerol, and the concentrated fruit has an intriguing spiciness. Fleshy, high-extract and smooth. Try it with saddle of hare.

Hardys Bankside Grenache

QUALITY ♛♛♛♛
VALUE ★★★★½
GRAPES grenache
REGION McLaren Vale, SA
CELLAR 🍷 5
ALC./VOL. 14.5%
RRP $13.00

Grenache is making a comeback of tidal wave proportions. People have rediscovered the flavour of the grape variety, which puts the emphasis on fruit. Maker David O'Leary (now with Mildara Blass).

CURRENT RELEASE 1993 There has been little change since the last review. Deep colour and a strong raspberry nose. There is concentrated berry flavours with plum, cherry and raspberry with the addition of coffee and vanilla oak. It's a bit of a hunk with plenty of tannin grip. It drinks well with some robust food like hare sausages.

Hardys Bankside Shiraz

QUALITY ♛♛♛♛
VALUE ★★★★
GRAPES shiraz
REGION McLaren Vale, SA
CELLAR 🍷 4
ALC./VOL. 14.5%
RRP $13.00 ⓢ

Bankside is an important icon in the Hardy ethos. It was the original cellars that were burnt down in 1905. Maker David O'Leary.

CURRENT RELEASE 1993 There is evidence of some bottle development. The nose has a strong varietal aroma with spices and meaty characters. The palate is tight with intense plum flavours plus pepper spice. Oak makes for a firm finish with plenty of grip. It goes well with venison sausages.

Hardys Eileen Hardy

As ever this is the top of the BRL Hardy totem. It has a distinguished history and it is named after the matriarch of the Hardy clan. Maker David O'Leary.
Previous outstanding vintages: '70, '71, '75, '79, '81, '82, '86, '87, '88, '89, '90, '91
CURRENT RELEASE 1992 Since the last review (*1995/ 96 Guide*), little has changed. The colour is a deep ruby with purple highlights. The nose is spicy with ripe plum aromas. The palate is rich and says 'shiraz' to us. The solid-plum flavours are laced with spice. There is a forceful finish with plenty of grip and fine-grained tannin. Try it with a rich dish like a game pie.

QUALITY ♛♛♛♛♛
VALUE ★★★★
GRAPES shiraz
REGION McLaren Vale, Clare Valley, Padthaway, SA
CELLAR ▬ 3–15
ALC./VOL. 13.5%
RRP $26.00

CURRENT RELEASE 1993 Rich as ever, this wine struts its stuff with an impressive depth of flavour. The nose is an amalgam of ripe berries, herbs and spices dusted with pepper. The palate offers solid plum and blackberry flavours and some rather forward oak that calls the tune on the finish. It needs time in the bottle to overcome adolescence but it is fine now with a robust game and wild mushroom pie.

QUALITY ♛♛♛♛♛
VALUE ★★★★
GRAPES shiraz
REGION McLaren Vale, Clare Valley, Padthaway, SA
CELLAR ▬ 4–12
ALC./VOL. 14.5%
RRP $27.00

Hardys Nottage Hill Cabernet Shiraz

It's getting harder to find a decent drink under $10. Here's one that is reliable in the role of an everyday tipple.
CURRENT RELEASE 1994 Soft and cheerful with no demands on the palate. The nose has soft berry aromas and a hint of spice. The palate is simple but also generous with clean berry-fruit flavours and there is gentle tannin on the finish. Take it to a barbecue but avoid the burnt chops.

QUALITY ♛♛♛
VALUE ★★★
GRAPES cabernet sauvignon, shiraz
REGION McLaren Vale, SA
CELLAR ▯
ALC./VOL. 13.0%
RRP $8.80 ⓢ

Hardys Padthaway Cabernet Sauvignon

QUALITY 🍷🍷🍷🍷
VALUE ★★★★
GRAPES cabernet sauvignon
REGION Padthaway, SA
CELLAR 🍾 7
ALC./VOL. 14.0%
RRP $15.00

This is a relatively new label in the BRL Hardy portfolio. Before it was minted the fruit was used for blending across the company range of reds.
CURRENT RELEASE 1993 An iron fist in a velvet glove. The nose has strong berry aromas plus a hint of vanillan oak. The medium-bodied palate hides the alcohol. There are sweet berry flavours and a touch of vanilla. The finish struts its stuff with fine-grained tannins and plenty of grip. It is a wine that goes well with lamb shanks.

Hardys R R Traditional Dry Red

QUALITY 🍷🍷🍷
VALUE ★★★½
GRAPES not stated
REGION not stated
CELLAR 🍾
ALC./VOL. 13.0%
RRP $7.50 $

Just what makes this wine 'traditional' is a bit hard to fathom. It is an affordable soft easy-drinking style.
CURRENT RELEASE 1995 There is a reasonable amount of flavour here. The nose is floral with a hint of gunsmoke. The palate has straightforward berry flavour and the finish is soft. It's just the thing for snorkers, rollers and mash.

Hardys Thomas Hardy Cabernet Sauvignon

QUALITY 🍷🍷🍷🍷
VALUE ★★★★
GRAPES cabernet sauvignon
REGION Coonawarra, SA
CELLAR 🍾 2–7
ALC./VOL. 13.5%
RRP $27.00

What a terrible label for such a fine wine, it looks like a bargain barrel special when in fact it is the running mate for the Eileen Hardy label.
Previous outstanding vintages: '89, '90
CURRENT RELEASE 1991 Still a brooding wine that is reluctant to open up. (Romantics should anthropomorphise and think of a Heathcliff-type character.) It has a nose offering ripe fruit with some cedar aromas. The palate is flavoured by blackberries with a hint of licorice. There are firm tannins and stern oak on a long finish. It needs more time, then try it with steak and kidney.

Hay Shed Hill Cabernet Sauvignon

There is a pretty smart new winery with a 120 tonne capacity on the property. At the moment the production is around 5000 cases.

CURRENT RELEASE 1994 This is an intense style with evidence of some heavy extraction. The nose has briar and blackberry aromas and the palate offers some muted blackberry flavours which are followed by some firm tannins that are just a touch stalky. The French oak on the finish dominates. It needs time in the bottle; try it with mutton bird.

QUALITY ♛♛♛♜
VALUE ★★★½
GRAPES cabernet sauvignon
REGION Margaret River, WA
CELLAR ➡ 2–7
ALC./VOL. 13.0%
RRP $18.00

Hay Shed Hill Pinot Noir

There is a pretty mean looking pitchfork on the label which impales a grape leaf. The presentation is pretty classy all the way down to the long cork. Maker Peter Stanlake.

CURRENT RELEASE 1995 The colour is impressive being a deep ruby and the nose is sappy with touches of cherry. The palate is slightly austere with some muted strawberry flavours which are dominated by French oak. It is a very dry style that would drink well with a rich dish like devilled kidneys.

QUALITY ♛♛♛♜
VALUE ★★★½
GRAPES pinot noir
REGION Margaret River, WA
CELLAR 🍾 4
ALC./VOL. 13.6%
RRP $19.00

Heggies Merlot

New line and it is clearly being given the Roller (Rolls Royce) treatment. Sexy dark bottle, cut-down label and flash capsule. At least the wine lives up to the new suit of clothes. Maker Brian Walsh.

CURRENT RELEASE 1992 A tough style with a smoky rose garden aroma on the nose. The medium-bodied palate has cherry and mulberry flavours. The finish is very astringent with fine-grained tannins and plenty of grip. It needs time but with the present level of tannin it goes well with smoked kangaroo.

QUALITY ♛♛♛♛
VALUE ★★★★
GRAPES merlot
REGION Eden Valley, SA
CELLAR ➡ 2–6
ALC./VOL. 13.0%
RRP $21.00

Heggies Pinot Noir

QUALITY ♛♛♛♛
VALUE ★★★½
GRAPES pinot noir
REGION Eden Valley, SA
CELLAR 🍷 4
ALC./VOL. 13.5%
RRP $20.50

This location should be well suited to the production of quality pinot noir. It is cool and late ripening.
CURRENT RELEASE 1994 There is a bit of dash and eccentric character here. The nose is a mix of mushrooms and truffles with a touch of earth. The palate has cherry/berry characters and slightly meaty qualities. The finish is dry with subtle oak. It goes well with char-grilled quail.

Henschke Abbott's Prayer

QUALITY ♛♛♛♛♛
VALUE ★★★★
GRAPES cabernet sauvignon, merlot
REGION Adelaide Hills, SA
CELLAR 🍷 8
ALC./VOL. 13.5%
RRP $33.00

This was the star of last year's Guide. Obviously the Abbot has had his hands pressed together yet again, because the impressive style continues to flourish. According to MS this is also a rake's prayer.
Previous outstanding vintages: '89, '90, '91, '92, '93
CURRENT RELEASE 1994 Very impressive with a Bordeaux-like structure but an Australian heart. The nose is exquisite with a seductive mix of fresh berries and classy oak. The palate is finely balanced with lively redcurrant flavours that have a smooth and supple flavour. The finish is where the Bordeaux-style asserts itself. It is dry, chalky and grippy. A bonza style with loads of potential, try it with casseroled kid, Spanish style.

Henschke Cyril Henschke Cabernet Sauvignon

Cyril Henschke (1924–79) was one of Australia's foremost winemakers. That mantle has been easily inherited by son Stephen in league with viticulturist wife, Prue.
Previous outstanding vintages: '81, '86, '88, '90, '91, '92
CURRENT RELEASE 1993 Right in the groove with all the richness we've come to expect from this label. The colour is intense and the nose has a wonderful array of plum, blackberry, licorice and spice aromas. Blackberry is the main flavour on the palate and there is also a licorice note. These are coupled with some elegant oak and very fine-grained tannins that offer length and grip. There is an impressive grandeur and it will mature for many years. Try it now with medallions of venison.

QUALITY ♛♛♛♛♛
VALUE ★★★★★
GRAPES cabernet sauvignon 88%, cabernet franc 7%, merlot 5%
REGION Eden Valley, SA
CELLAR 2–8
ALC./VOL. 14.5%
RRP $36.00

Henschke Hill of Grace

Perhaps the second Australian wine icon after Grange and the price makes it a rich person's sport. But it is a very rare wine that comes from vines planted in 1860 (pre-phylloxera). The yield is naturally small, keeping the wine a rare commodity in high demand.
Previous outstanding vintages: '82, '86, '88, '89, '90, '91
CURRENT RELEASE 1992 As glorious and mysterious as ever! The colour is mid to dark-ruby and the nose is an exotic mix of coffee, berries, earth and licorice. The palate has poise, there are strong shiraz flavours, plus abundant spice. The oak is graceful, adorning the fruit with fine-grained tannins. There is also a coffee and vanilla flavour on the finish. It is beautifully balanced and is beaut with a seasoned rolled loin of lamb.

QUALITY ♛♛♛♛♛
VALUE ★★★★
GRAPES shiraz
REGION Eden Valley, SA
CELLAR 2–10
ALC./VOL. 14.1%
RRP $80.00

Henschke Keyneton Estate

QUALITY ♟♟♟♟
VALUE ★★★½
GRAPES shiraz, cabernet, malbec
REGION Eden and Barossa Valleys, SA
CELLAR 🍷 3
ALC./VOL. 13.8%
RRP $21.00

There is a sad story to the Keyneton district. It was pioneered by Henry Evans in the 1840s and when he dropped off the twig, his wife turned tea-total and up-rooted his vines.
Previous outstanding vintages: '93
CURRENT RELEASE 1995 This triple blend from two areas has a mid-ruby colour. There is a strong cherry-berry aroma with a hint of lolly shop smells. The palate is medium-bodied with succulent red-berry flavours. These are followed by some gentle oak that helps support the fruit but doesn't preclude the wine for immediate consumption. Try it with oxtail broth.

Henschke Lenswood Giles Pinot Noir

QUALITY ♟♟♟♟
VALUE ★★★★
GRAPES pinot noir
REGION Adelaide Hills, SA
CELLAR 🍷 4
ALC./VOL. 13.5%
RRP $33.00

High-altitude and cool-climate Lenswood is shaping up as one of Australia's premium regions for producing pinot noir when used to make a table wine.
CURRENT RELEASE 1995 The colour is pale but the wine doesn't lack flavour. The nose is strong on strawberry aroma and there is also a waft of lolly smells. The palate has reasonable weight with strawberry and cherry leading the flavour band. It is very clean and the feral pinot characters are absent. The finish is well balanced with obvious acid. It drinks well now; try it with a rabbit stew.

Henschke Mount Edelstone

Edelstone means 'noble stone' but in this case the mount is studded with noble vines that produce noble wine.
Previous outstanding vintages: '78, '80, '84, '86, '88, '90, '91, '92, '93
CURRENT RELEASE 1994 A little less bulky than recent releases but still with that concentrated fruit character. The colour is medium-ruby and the nose has strong berry aromas with a hint of briar. The palate has strong raspberry flavours with a background of licorice. The oak slips into the picture with a quiet entrance and the finish has fine-grained tannins that linger. It drinks well now; try it with rare roast beef and Yorkshire pud.

QUALITY ♛♛♛♛♛
VALUE ★★★★
GRAPES shiraz
REGION Eden Valley, SA
CELLAR 🍾 7
ALC./VOL. 13.0%
RRP $33.00

Heritage Estate Shiraz

The time is coming when the sub-regions of the Barossa will become a significant marketing tool. For example the back label notes this wine comes from Kalimna. Maker Steve Hoff.
CURRENT RELEASE 1994 An almost elegant style that has been to Weight Watchers. The nose has plum and ripe berry aromas. The palate is medium-bodied and the main flavour is plum with other berries bringing up the rear. Discreet American oak fills out a dry finish. It drinks well now; try it with salt bush mutton.

QUALITY ♛♛♛♛
VALUE ★★★★
GRAPES shiraz
REGION Barossa Valley, SA
CELLAR 🍾 6
ALC./VOL. 12.5%
RRP $14.50

Hickinbotham Mornington Peninsula Merlot

QUALITY 🍷🍷🍷🍷
VALUE ★★★½
GRAPES merlot
REGION Mornington Peninsula, Vic.
CELLAR 🍾 6
ALC./VOL. 12.5%
RRP $22.00

The silhouette on the label is getting smaller and smaller. MS had a theory it was Peter Gunn but who is old enough to remember that TV show? Maker Andrew Hickinbotham.

CURRENT RELEASE 1993 Here's a merlot with attitude. It is not brawny but it does have a steel backbone. The nose offers rose-water aromas and the palate is a mix of cherry and raspberry flavours. The finish has excellent tannin grip. The elegance makes it suitable for pink lamb fillets with Middle Eastern spices.

Hill Smith Estate Cabernet Sauvignon Shiraz

QUALITY 🍷🍷🍷🍷?
VALUE ★★★½
GRAPES cabernet sauvignon, shiraz
REGION Eden Valley, SA
CELLAR 🍾 6
ALC./VOL. 12.5%
RRP $14.00

In the words of the Peggy Lee song, 'Is that all there is?' This label has never seemed to reach full potential. Much vaunted cool-climate location seems to be the eternal bridesmaid that has the very occasional fling resulting in brilliance.

CURRENT RELEASE 1992 A lean style that is more about winemaking than fruit. The colour is medium-ruby with berry aroma and vinous qualities on the nose. The palate is lean with soft redcurrant flavours. American oak struts its stuff on the finish which is a bit like the tail wagging the dog. It is great with smoked lamb loin chops.

QUALITY 🍷🍷🍷?
VALUE ★★★½
GRAPES cabernet sauvignon, shiraz
REGION Eden Valley, SA
CELLAR 🍾 4
ALC./VOL. 12.5%
RRP $15.75

CURRENT RELEASE 1993 Cool-climate stuff putting the emphasis on elegance. The nose has raspberry aromas plus hints of green leaf. The medium-bodied palate has a mix of blackberry and raspberry flavours and these are joined by some well-integrated oak. The finish displays fine-grained tannins and balanced grip. It goes well with lamb shanks.

Hillstowe Buxton Cabernet Merlot

This is a McLaren Vale blend that is made by the Laurie family who are based in historic Hahndorf in the Adelaide Hills.
CURRENT RELEASE 1993 This is a well-made wine that captures regional characters. It is soft and earthy with succulent fruit aromas on the nose. The palate is medium-bodied with sweet raspberry and cherry flavours that are wedded to well-integrated oak. It drinks well with veal shanks.

QUALITY ????
VALUE ★★★★
GRAPES cabernet sauvignon 85%, merlot 15%
REGION McLaren Vale, SA
CELLAR 3
ALC./VOL. 13.5%
RRP $17.00

Hillstowe Carey Gully Pinot Noir

This wine was made from grapes grown in the Adelaide Hills using carbonic maceration (fermentation in uncrushed whole bunches).
CURRENT RELEASE 1993 The colour is a pale brick-red and the nose is spicy with strong berry aromas and a hint of herbs. The medium-bodied palate offers slightly tart cherry flavours and there is acid and fine-grained tannin on the finish. It drinks well now; try it with a veal casserole.

QUALITY ????
VALUE ★★★
GRAPES point noir
REGION Adelaide Hills, SA
CELLAR 3
ALC./VOL. 13.5%
RRP $24.00

Hillstowe Hoddles Pinot Noir

The grapes came from a vineyard which was planted by David Paxton in the Yarra Valley. It was acquired by BRL Hardy.
CURRENT RELEASE 1993 This is a medium-bodied wine with plenty of flavour. It has a sappy nose and a pale brick-red colour. The palate is reserved with reluctant strawberry and cherry flavours. There is strong acid and dusty oak tannins on the finish. It drinks well now; try it with a smoked ham omelette.

QUALITY ????
VALUE ★★½
GRAPES pinot noir
REGION Yarra Valley, Vic.
CELLAR 3
ALC./VOL. 13.5%
RRP $18.00

Hollick Coonawarra

QUALITY ♀♀♀♀
VALUE ★★★★
GRAPES cabernet sauvignon 82%, merlot 15%, cabernet franc 3%
REGION Coonawarra, SA
CELLAR 🍷 4
ALC./VOL. 13.5%
RRP $18.00

Hollick continue to field their own generic which is an entertaining blend that sells at a fair price. Maker Pat Tocaciu.
Previous outstanding vintages: '84, '88, '90, '91, '92
CURRENT RELEASE 1993 An elegant wine, yet this one is bigger than the usual. The nose is leafy with an underscore of blackberry aromas. Blackberry is the main flavour on a sweet, complex palate. It is followed by fine-grained tannins on a pleasantly astringent finish. It is just the wine for barbecued marinated lamb straps.

QUALITY ♀♀♀♀♀
VALUE ★★★★★
GRAPES cabernet sauvignon, merlot, cabernet franc
REGION Coonawarra, SA
CELLAR 🍷 7
ALC./VOL. 13.9%
RRP $18.50

CURRENT RELEASE 1994 Perhaps the best yet and a convincing argument for a Coonawarra blend. It is rich and well balanced. The nose has blackberry and spice aromas. The palate weighs in with plums and blackberry flavours and there is fine-grained tannin with an astringent grip on the finish. It drinks well now and shows perfect balance. Try it with a rich rabbit stew.

Hollick Ravenswood

QUALITY ♀♀♀♀♀
VALUE ★★★★
GRAPES cabernet sauvignon
REGION Coonawarra, SA
CELLAR 🍷 8
ALC./VOL. 13.5%
RRP $45.00

This is the full banana for the Hollick stable. It is a limited release that is only produced when the vintage conditions yield fruit of sufficient quality. Maker Patrick Tocaciu.
Previous outstanding vintages: '88, '89, '90, 91
CURRENT RELEASE 1992 As ever this is superior wine at a wallet-withering price. The colour is intense and the nose has strong blackberry and mulberry aromas with a suggestion of toasty oak. The palate is rich with full-on berry fruit flavours with hints of chocolate and mint. The finish shows some classy new American oak with a fair bit of charring. It is a very neat package and because everything fits together so well it drinks well now. Try it with lamb shanks.

Hollick Terra Red

This is a drink-now, serve by-the-glass at those bistros that are cool in terms of being seen. It is also a style that can get down and dirty in your local pub.
CURRENT RELEASE 1994 This is a very attractive fruit-salad style that has flavour and drinkability. There is spice and ripe berry fruit on the nose. The palate has blackberry flavours with some fleshy malbec characters and just a hint of tartness. The finish is astringent with acid and oak teaming to clean up the palate. It drinks well with osso bucco.

QUALITY ♛♛♛♛
VALUE ★★★★
GRAPES shiraz, malbec, cabernet sauvignon
REGION Coonawarra, SA
CELLAR 🍾 3
ALC./VOL. 13.0%
RRP $13.90

Houghton Cabernet Sauvignon

The Houghton winery is located near Perth and BRL Hardy have lavished much care and attention on the original homestead and the grounds. Maker Paul Lapsley.
CURRENT RELEASE 1993 It has gained some complexity since the last review. The colour is deep ruby and there are berry and leaf aromas on the nose. The medium-bodied palate is quite complex with blackberry and briar flavours and these are matched by some soft tannins and balanced acidity on the finish. It goes well with lamb fillets on a bed of angel hair pasta.

QUALITY ♛♛♛♛
VALUE ★★★★½
GRAPES cabernet sauvignon
REGION Frankland River, Margaret River, Mount Barker, WA
CELLAR 🍾 3
ALC./VOL. 12.5%
RRP $11.50

Houghton Cygnet

Young swan from the Swan Valley made from early picked (young) cabernet sauvignon – guess so. This is a new line and it is hard to peg it as a style. Rosé or light red? Maker Paul Lapsley.
CURRENT RELEASE 1995 The colour is a deep pink and the nose is full of vibrant berry aromas with a hint of leaf. The palate has a hint of sweetness and the berry character has a tart edge. Crisp acid adds the balance. It could be served well chilled; try it with antipasto.

QUALITY ♛♛♛♛
VALUE ★★★½
GRAPES cabernet sauvignon
REGION Frankland River, Gingin, WA
CELLAR 🍾
ALC./VOL. 10.0%
RRP $9.90

Ingoldby Cabernet Sauvignon

QUALITY ♟♟♟♟♟
VALUE ★★★★★
GRAPES cabernet sauvignon
REGION McLaren Vale, SA
CELLAR 🍾 10+
ALC./VOL. 12.5%
RRP $12.60 ⓢ

Ingoldby has a proud reputation for producing gut-busting McLaren Vale reds. This was vinified by previous owner Walter Clappis and bottled by the new owner, Mildara.

CURRENT RELEASE 1994 Serious dark colour introduces a lovely rich, chunky, typically regional red with lush sweet fruit, tremendous body and a tannin grip to match. It lingers for ages on the after-palate and although unmistakeably cabernet, there's no hint of leafiness. It discounts to $10.95 – extraordinary value! Serve with venison.

Ingoldby Grenache

QUALITY ♟♟♟♟
VALUE ★★★★
GRAPES grenache
REGION McLaren Vale, SA
CELLAR 🍾 3
ALC./VOL. 12.0%
RRP $13.00

Ingoldby has always been noted for characterful reds. Now it's now part of the Mildara Blass fold, fans will be watching in hope that the style won't be watered down.

CURRENT RELEASE 1994 This is a lean, savoury style with obvious cedary oak and a slightly short finish. There's plenty of drying tannin and elegant spicy flavour. A pleasing, lighter interpretation of grenache in contrast to the over-the-top styles predominating today. Try it with pigeon.

Ingoldby Shiraz

QUALITY ♟♟♟
VALUE ★★★
GRAPES shiraz
REGION McLaren Vale, SA
CELLAR 🍾 4
ALC./VOL. 13.0%
RRP $15.00 ⓢ

Desperate for high-quality red grapes, Mildara Blass took over Ingoldby in 1995, adding to its belt of South Australian scalps in a year which took in Andrew Garrett, Garrett Family and Tolleys Pedare.

CURRENT RELEASE 1993 Fresh, uncomplicated aromas of cherry, berry and mint lead into a straightforward, fruit-driven style of shiraz which lacks a little concentration but provides decent current drinking. Seems a tad ordinary compared to the Ingoldby reds of recent memory. Drink with hamburgers.

James Irvine Grand Merlot

Jim Irvine is a leading consultant winemaker whose name has been linked with many successful South Australian wines over the years. He has a small wine company based in Eden Valley.

CURRENT RELEASE 1992 A puzzling wine: it doesn't come up well in blind tastings but, boy, does it taste good when you settle down with a glass or two! Volatility is noticeable, but as all Grange followers know a little VA often does no harm, and can even be an asset. This merlot is rich and powerful enough to cope. With prolonged breathing it gives more and more. A concentrated merlot with a very complex vinous bouquet, hinting at blackberry jam and licorice. Rich and savoury in the mouth with a very long finish, firmed by tight tannins. A fascinating red (with great packaging) which we've scored on sensual pleasure rather than clinical quality.

QUALITY ★★★★★
VALUE ★★★
GRAPES merlot
REGION Eden Valley, SA
CELLAR 8+
ALC./VOL. 13.5%
RRP $54.00

Jamieson's Run

This marque was given a big boost in its early years when it won the Jimmy Watson Trophy. It hasn't looked back and sales continue to climb. Can be found at $12.95. Maker Gavin Hogg. Previous outstanding vintages: '86, '88, '90, '91, '93

CURRENT RELEASE 1994 Nice deep colour and a noseful of ripe berries, crushed leaves and cassis, with some obvious coconutty oak. Regional Coonawarra identity shines through and the mediumweight palate has mild tannins and a soft finish. A drink-now style; goes with roast lamb and mint sauce.

QUALITY ★★★★
VALUE ★★★★
GRAPES shiraz, cabernet sauvignon, merlot, cabernet franc
REGION Coonawarra, SA
CELLAR 5
ALC./VOL. 12.5%
RRP $15.60

Jane Brook Cabernet Merlot

QUALITY ▼▼▼▽
VALUE ★★★
GRAPES cabernet sauvignon 85%, merlot 15%
REGION Middle Swan Valley, WA
CELLAR 🍷 4
ALC./VOL. 12.2%
RRP $14.50

Labelling has never been a Western Australian strong point. Here is another example of a dull effort that is no doubt beloved by the proprietors but dies on the dinner table.

CURRENT RELEASE 1994 There is an Italian quality on the nose which smells of dried cherries and mixed dried fruits. The medium-bodied palate has dark cherry flavours plus a hint of raspberry. French and American oak add grip to the finish. It drinks well with goulash.

Jim Barry McCrea Wood Cabernet Malbec

QUALITY ▼▼▼▼
VALUE ★★★
GRAPES cabernet sauvignon, malbec
REGION Clare Valley, SA
CELLAR 🍷 5
ALC./VOL. 13.5%
RRP $22.85

This is a traditional Clare Valley blend that was pioneered by Wendouree cellars. It is good to see the style continue in the hands of another maker.

CURRENT RELEASE 1994 This is a rich, ripe and sumptuous wine that offers malbec softness and a cabernet spine. It is a big wine that retains elegance. There is a strong fruit character on the nose and the palate is soft and lush. The main flavour is blackberry and the mouth-filling texture makes the wine almost chewy. The oak floats in like a falling veil adding a dry quality to the finish. It is great with a steak and mushroom casserole.

Jim Barry McCrea Wood Shiraz

McCrea Wood is not oak from Scotland. In 1970 Jim Barry purchased 70 acres of vineyard in the Armagh area from Duncan McCrea Wood. Maker Mark Barry.

CURRENT RELEASE 1993 A rich wine with a deep colour and a strong varietal nose. There are plums, blackberries and spice on the nose while the palate displays typical Clare Valley abundance. This is followed by some subtle oak and a gentle grip on the finish. Just the thing for a warming lamb and barley casserole.

QUALITY ★★★★½
VALUE ★★★★
GRAPES shiraz
REGION Clare Valley, SA
CELLAR 4
ALC./VOL. 14.0%
RRP $20.00

CURRENT RELEASE 1994 This is a rich extracted style that offers soft fruit and robust tannin. The nose has plums and spice aromas. The palate has soft-fruit flavours with a hint of pressings character. There is also pepper and spice. The finish shows deft use of oak that adds balance and vanilla flavour. It drinks well as a youngster; try it with liver and bacon.

QUALITY ★★★★½
VALUE ★★★
GRAPES shiraz
REGION Clare Valley, SA
CELLAR 6
ALC./VOL. 13.0%
RRP $22.85

Jimmy Watson's Cabernet Shiraz

Here's a wine from the Mildara Blass group made for the Watson Family who run a wine bar in Carlton, Melbourne. Said bar was founded by Jimmy Watson but this wine has nothing to do with the Jimmy Watson Memorial Trophy. Large parts of the wine industry think this is a size 12 right in the sacred rump of that unholy cow. Not so, the only conjunction is Jim who founded the bar and died, thus the trophy.

CURRENT RELEASE 1994 This is a soft, drinkable wine made for bistros. The colour shows youthful vibrancy and the nose is full of ripe plums. The palate has loads of sweet berry character and there is a dusting of oak which gives a gentle grip. It can be served with an osso bucco.

QUALITY ★★★★
VALUE ★★★½
GRAPES cabernet sauvignon, shiraz
REGION Barossa Valley, Padthaway, SA
CELLAR 3
ALC./VOL. 13.0%
RRP $12.50

Kangaroo Island Trading Company Cabernet Merlot

QUALITY 🍷🍷🍷🍷
VALUE ★★★
GRAPES cabernet franc 45%, cabernet sauvignon 30%, merlot 25%
REGION Kangaroo Island, SA
CELLAR ➡ 2–8+
ALC./VOL. 13.5%
RRP $18.00

Caj Amadio, of Chain of Ponds, has several hectares of vines at Cygnet River and believes Kangaroo Island has great potential for wine. This is the fourth release of this label.
CURRENT RELEASE 1994 Very dense, dark blackish-red colour and an unusual nose of raspberry jam and green herbs. The effect is quite exotic; the palate is better but forbiddingly tannic with harsh astringency and it's unready just now. Cellar, then serve with marinated buffalo fillet.

Karina Vineyard Cabernet Merlot

QUALITY 🍷🍷🍷🍷
VALUE ★★★
GRAPES cabernet sauvignon, 5% merlot
REGION Mornington Peninsula, Vic.
CELLAR 🍷 4+
ALC./VOL. 12.5%
RRP $17.50

Time may yet prove this district too cool for cabernet, although pinot noir and whites do impress. Maker Graeme Pinney.
CURRENT RELEASE 1994 This is a lean, cool-grown cabernet with some Ribena-like characters in the bouquet, a little tannin and a touch of austerity on the finish. Could build more complexity with a year or two's cellaring. Try it with corned beef and white sauce.

Karriview Pinot Noir

QUALITY 🍷🍷🍷🍷
VALUE ★★★½
GRAPES pinot noir
REGION Lower Great Southern, WA
CELLAR 🍷 4+
ALC./VOL. 13.5%
RRP $25.00

This is only the fifth vintage from this tiny 2-ha. vineyard at Denmark. It's a property with great promise. Maker John Wade.
Previous outstanding vintages: '93
CURRENT RELEASE 1994 The colour is deceptively light and the nose shows lovely perfumes of strawberry, cherry and sappy/fungal accents. The taste is intense and lean with quite high acid, which makes it rather sharp solo but excellent with the right food. Try raw tuna with Le Puy lentils and wasabe. Magic!

Katnook Estate Cabernet Sauvignon

Katnook did an unusual manoeuvre a few years ago when, following a disastrous 1993 harvest, it sold its main vineyard to Southcorp and began planting a new one, the results of which are eagerly awaited in the district.
Previous outstanding vintages: '90, '91
CURRENT RELEASE 1992 Tasted in January '96, this was unbelievably oaky, and difficult to enjoy at that stage. A year or two in the cellar may help. It was better with food but the dominant flavour tends to be raw, grippy coconut/toasty oak. Try it with pink lamb cutlets.

QUALITY 🍷🍷🍷
VALUE ★★½
GRAPES cabernet sauvignon
REGION Coonawarra, SA
CELLAR 2–8
ALC./VOL. 13.5%
RRP $30.00

Kay's Amery Cabernet Sauvignon

This family winery produces 6500 cases a year, of which the reds are outstanding. Maker Colin Kay.
CURRENT RELEASE 1993 Typically gutsy stuff from this traditional Vales producer. Dense colour, lashings of coconut/toasty oak, and earthy regional character. The wine may not have a lot of subtlety but it makes up for that with intensity and bigness of sweet fruit and tannin. Serve with a hearty beef casserole.

QUALITY 🍷🍷🍷🍷
VALUE ★★★★
GRAPES cabernet sauvignon
REGION McLaren Vale, SA
CELLAR 7+
ALC./VOL. 13.0%
RRP $18.00

Kay's Amery Shiraz

McLaren Vale has the runs on the board as one of Australia's best shiraz regions. These days they're picking the grapes super-ripe and making blockbusters.
CURRENT RELEASE 1994 Subdued cherryish, lightly spicy nose, very much a fruit style: soft in the middle, leanish yet persistent. There are peppery varietal notes on the palate with some cherry and vanilla on the finish. The flavours grow in the mouth and the tannins are supple. Try it with wiener schnitzel.

QUALITY 🍷🍷🍷🍷
VALUE ★★★★
GRAPES shiraz
REGION McLaren Vale, SA
CELLAR 8
ALC./VOL. 13.7%
RRP $18.00

Kay Brothers Amery Block 6 Shiraz

QUALITY ♛♛♛♛
VALUE ★★★½
GRAPES shiraz
REGION McLaren Vale, SA
CELLAR ☛ 2–8+
ALC./VOL. 14.9%
RRP $22.50

The label, which is a blast from the past in itself, tells us the grapes were hand-picked from 101-year-old vines. Kay's celebrated their centenary in 1990.
Previous outstanding vintages: '90, '91, '92
CURRENT RELEASE 1993 This can be a rustic, slightly feral red and in years like '93 it may lack elegance, although the generosity of flavour and tannin does much to make up for it. This has a rich colour, strong oaky elements in the cinnamon/spicy nose, and a lot of licorice on the palate. A red with grunt which holds its alcohol well. Try it with beef rissoles.

Killerby Shiraz

QUALITY ♛♛♛♛
VALUE ★★★
GRAPES shiraz
REGION south-west coastal, WA
CELLAR ☛ 1–5+
ALC./VOL. 13.6%
RRP $17.60

The Killerby wines, sourced from a 16-ha. planting near Bunbury, grow in quality and consistency year by year. Maker Matt Aldridge.
Previous outstanding vintages: '90, '93
CURRENT RELEASE 1994 They've really gone for the doctor with this one: a massive wine with heaps of extract, plenty of alcohol and robust, jammy flavours. The nose has gamey shiraz scents with dried-herb and spice notes. Not a lot of finesse, but the raunchy flavours are generous and it should keep well. Serve with lambs fry.

Kingston Estate Merlot

QUALITY ♛♛♛♛
VALUE ★★★★½
GRAPES merlot
REGION Riverland, SA
CELLAR 🍷 5+
ALC./VOL. 12.5%
RRP $9.60

Kingston Estate is a new brand from the Moularadellis family at Kingston-on-Murray. They are selling very good wines at most affordable prices.
CURRENT RELEASE 1994 A smooth, rich red scented with dark berry and coconutty oak. It offers more if decanted and aired for several hours – the chocolate, vanilla and cherry flavours opening up on the palate. A high-quality red from an unfashionable area and at this price, it deserves to be taken very seriously. Good with pizza.

Kingston Estate Shiraz

The Riverland is hardly Mecca for shiraz lovers, but in capable hands shiraz can make a respectable, lighter-bodied early drinking red. Maker Bill Moularadellis.
CURRENT RELEASE 1993 Medium-light red-purple colour and a nose of meaty, earthy, slightly animal shiraz character. This leads into a light-bodied, low-tannin, ready-drinking style which has some Italianate earthy/autumnal savoury flavours. Drink now, with rissoles.

QUALITY ♥♥♥
VALUE ★★★½
GRAPES shiraz
REGION Riverland, SA
CELLAR 🍾 2
ALC./VOL. 13.0%
RRP $10.00

Kingston Reserve Shiraz

Again, this is not an area where you'd expect to find a winery marketing an aged shiraz, but Kingston Estate is no ordinary winery.
CURRENT RELEASE 1991 This is developing at a rate of knots, but it's a surprise packet, showing attractive mellow, fully-mature aged characters at five years old. The colour is medium brick-red, the nose has sweet licorice and black-olive scents with a touch of portiness. The palate is very mellow and attractively aged with a dry tannin finish. Drink up now, with aged cheese.

QUALITY ♥♥♥♥
VALUE ★★★★
GRAPES shiraz
REGION Riverland, SA
CELLAR 🍾
ALC./VOL. 13.5%
RRP $17.00

Koppamurra Cabernet Merlot

There is some argument over whether the district will be called Koppamurra, or Naracoorte Ranges (as Koppamurra Wines hopes) or something else. This is the area's original vineyard, in what looks like becoming an important region.
CURRENT RELEASE 1994 The lovely deep purple-red hue mirrors the character and quality of the wine. There are toasty oak, dark berry and briary complexities and the fruit has good concentration and extract, despite a slight dip in the middle. It should reward cellaring. Try it with pepper steak.

QUALITY ♥♥♥♥
VALUE ★★★★½
GRAPES cabernet sauvignon 50%, cabernet franc 22%, merlot 28%
REGION Naracoorte Ranges, SA
CELLAR 🍾 6+
ALC./VOL. 13.2%
RRP $11.00 (cellar door)

Krondorf Shiraz Cabernet

QUALITY ♛♛♛♛
VALUE ★★★★½
GRAPES shiraz, cabernet sauvignon
REGION McLaren Vale & Barossa Valley, SA
CELLAR 🍷 5
ALC./VOL. 12.5%
RRP $11.00 Ⓢ

This is arguably the best value for money drinking red in the Mildara Blass portfolio, at just $8.95 discounted. It puts a strong case for the traditional cab-shiraz blend, which has been largely supplanted by cab-merlots. Maker Nick Walker.
CURRENT RELEASE 1994 Nice deep colour and a strong bouquet of toasty oak and dark berry scents. There's surprising weight and richness in the mouth, with generous plum flavours and a long, warm finish that carries a satisfying grip. Terrific value. Serve with beef kebabs.

Laanecoorie

QUALITY ♛♛♛♛♝
VALUE ★★★★½
GRAPES cabernet sauvignon, cabernet franc, merlot
REGION Maryborough, Vic.
CELLAR ⇀ 2–8
ALC./VOL. 13.0%
RRP $17.00

The name means 'the land of the big kangaroo' and the new label provides a cute visual game. The vineyard owner, John McQuilten, when not smoking and tending vines is a Labor Party heavy. Maker John Ellis (contract).
CURRENT RELEASE 1993 This is a tri-part blend that shows all the exuberance of youth. The colour is a deep garnet and the nose is zesty with fresh berry aromas and plenty of spicy oak. The palate is quite tight at first but loosens up with breathing. There are redcurrant and blackberry fruit flavours which are followed by fresh oak and a substantial tannin grip. It's a youngster and how could you go past what is depicted on the label.

Lakes Folly Cabernets

The first Lakes Folly was foot-trod with Dr Max playing encouragement in the form of Zorba the Greek on an old upright piano. Things have changed somewhat but the spirit continues. Maker Stephen Lake.
Previous outstanding vintages: '72, '87, '89, '91, '92, '93
CURRENT RELEASE 1994 Very Bordeaux in style but like one from a leaner year. The nose has great complexity, and there are berries, cedar and briar patch aromas. The palate is lean and constrained. It has a blackberry base and there is plenty of spice. The finish has a dry with a chalky quality. It needs time; try it with rabbit and mushroom pie.

QUALITY ♛♛♛♛♛
VALUE ★★★½
GRAPES cabernet sauvignon, shiraz, petit verdot, merlot
REGION Hunter Valley, NSW
CELLAR 🍷 6
ALC./VOL. 13.0%
RRP $32.00

Lark Hill Cabernet Merlot

Lark Hill is looking more to warmer vineyards on the western side of the Canberra region to source its cabernet. The flavours are riper there. Maker Sue Carpenter.
CURRENT RELEASE 1993 Leafy cool-grown fruit aromas together with classy French oak. The profile is lean rather than rich, tightly structured with fine, firm tannin on the finish. A stylish, elegant red to serve with teppanyaki beef.

QUALITY ♛♛♛♛
VALUE ★★★★
GRAPES cabernet sauvignon, merlot
REGION Canberra district, NSW
CELLAR 🍷 8+
ALC./VOL. 13.0%
RRP $16.00 (cellar door)

Lark Hill Pinot Noir

The Canberra district should be a prime site for pinot, being cool and continental. Makers Sue and David Carpenter.
CURRENT RELEASE 1995 Gamey to the point of being risqué when first poured, this Burgundian-style pinot breathes to show a more agreeable bouquet and very attractive flavour. Soft, easy drinking, low on tannin, it's a pinot of good balance and length. Try it with char-grilled tuna.

QUALITY ♛♛♛♛
VALUE ★★★★
GRAPES pinot noir
REGION Canberra district, NSW
CELLAR 🍷 2
ALC./VOL. 13.0%
RRP $14.00 (cellar door)

Leasingham Bin 56 Cabernet Malbec

QUALITY ♛♛♛♛
VALUE ★★★★
GRAPES cabernet sauvignon 85%, malbec 15%
REGION Clare Valley, SA
CELLAR 🍷 4
ALC./VOL. 13.5%
RRP $15.00

This enduring bin number was selected as the best red blend in last year's *Guide*. It has a long and distinguished history that dates back to the legendary Mick Knappstein. Maker Richard Rowe.

Previous outstanding vintages: '71, '72, '75, '78, '80, '81, '84, '88, '90, '92, '93

CURRENT RELEASE 1994 After last year's extravaganza this wine is a little demure which probably reflects the vintage. The nose has coffee and berry aromas. The palate is medium-bodied with a fleshy character thanks to the malbec. There are blackberry flavours and some dusty oak characters. Supple tannins complete the finish. It drinks well with confit of duck.

Leasingham Bin 61 Shiraz

QUALITY ♛♛♛♛♛
VALUE ★★★★★
GRAPES shiraz
REGION Clare Valley, SA
CELLAR 🍷 10
ALC./VOL. 14.0%
RRP $14.50

This is one of the most consistent wines on the market. The objective of capturing Clare Valley richness in a balanced wine seems routine at this winery. Maker Richard Rowe.

Previous outstanding vintages: '90, '91, '92, '93

CURRENT RELEASE 1994 The style seems to be carved in stone, toasty oak and sweet plum fruit weave their magic. The colour is dark and the nose has elements of toast and ripe berry aromas. The aforementioned palate is a duet of wood and fruit and the finish has fine-grained tannins and positive grip. It drinks well with lamb satays.

Leasingham Classic Clare Cabernet Sauvignon

This is the other 'classic' in the red range. It was introduced to mark the centenary of the winery in 1991.
Previous outstanding vintages: '91, '92
CURRENT RELEASE 1993 The wine is in the process of throwing a crust, so some of the early bumptious qualities have yielded to time. The nose has strong berry aromas plus cedar oak. The palate has fined down a tad but blackberry still dominates. The tannins on the finish are quite graceful making the wine approachable now. Try it with rare beef and Yorkshire pud.

QUALITY ★★★★
VALUE ★★★★
GRAPES cabernet sauvignon
REGION Clare Valley, SA
CELLAR 8
ALC./VOL. 13.0%
RRP $21.00

Leasingham Classic Clare Shiraz

Unlike most wines so labelled it's possible to see some 'classic' qualities in this wine. This is the top of the range for this Clare winery that is part of the BRL Hardy group.
Previous outstanding vintages: '91, '92
CURRENT RELEASE 1993 Not much progress since the last review as far as bottle development is concerned. It remains a tightly structured wine. The nose is spicy with a hint of mint. The palate is a mixture of blackberry and plum flavours. There is obvious vanillan oak on the finish. It is a powerful yet elegant wine. Try it with minted lamb.

QUALITY ★★★★
VALUE ★★★★½
GRAPES cabernet sauvignon
REGION Clare Valley, SA
CELLAR 9
ALC./VOL. 13.5%
RRP $21.00

Leconfield Coonawarra Cabernet

QUALITY ♛♛♛♛♛
VALUE ★★★★★
GRAPES cabernet sauvignon, merlot, cabernet franc, petit verdot
REGION Coonawarra, SA
CELLAR 🍷 8
ALC./VOL. 13.5%
RRP $20.00

Last year's model was awarded Best Cabernet Sauvignon in this *Guide*. This one comes close to emulating the feat; it is a classy wine maintaining a high standard. Maker Ralph Fowler.
Previous outstanding vintages: '80, '82, '88, '90, '91, '92, '93
CURRENT RELEASE 1994 Great effort from a fractious vintage. The nose is a mix of blackberry and tobacco leaf. The palate confirms this with similar flavours. It is medium-bodied with depth and complexity. The berry fruit is very satisfying and the oak intermingles in a quite hypnotic effect. There is plenty of fine-grained tannin and good grip. It will cellar but you can drink it now. Try it with doner kebab.

Leeuwin Estate Art Series Cabernet Sauvignon

QUALITY ♛♛♛♛♛
VALUE ★★★★½
GRAPES cabernet sauvignon
REGION Margaret River, WA
CELLAR ⇌ 2–8
ALC./VOL. 13.5%
RRP $29.00

This is the top of the totem for this marque. The object is to capture the essence of the variety and the region. Maker Bob Cartwright.
Previous outstanding vintages: '79, '82, '87, '89, '91
CURRENT RELEASE 1992 Very sophisticated wine with great elegance and style. The colour is intense and the nose has blackberries, toasty oak and spices. The medium-bodied palate has rich blackberry flavours, hints of chocolate, vanilla and spice. The oak is superbly tailored to the fruit. There is a long astringent finish with fine-grained tannins and positive grip. It will cellar well but you can drink it now with venison sausages.

Leeuwin Estate Prelude Cabernet Sauvignon

Leeuwin started life with the crosshairs of its sight focused on the top shelf. The wines were always meant to be expensive. Prelude evolved to make the label accessible to most of us and give consumers a preview of things to come.
CURRENT RELEASE 1991 An accessible wine that has the benefit of bottle-age. It has a complex nose and the palate displays sweet concentrated raspberry flavours with a hint of leaves. There is discreet oak and a warmth of alcohol on the finish. It drinks well now; try it with a beef casserole.

QUALITY ????
VALUE ★★★
GRAPES cabernet sauvignon
REGION Margaret River, WA
CELLAR 4
ALC./VOL. 14.0%
RRP $19.50

Lengs & Cooter Grenache

Pardon us, the back label states 'this is a wine made to be enjoyed!' How many wines are made to be suffered? Proprietors Karel Lengs and Colin Cooter.
CURRENT RELEASE 1995 The wine was made from fruit from 50-year-old vines. The colour is a medium-ruby and there is a warm raspberry nose. The palate continues the raspberry theme and the berry character is sweet. The finish has a warmth of alcohol. It could be served chilled and it would be great with savoury mince on toast.

QUALITY ????
VALUE ★★★½
GRAPES grenache
REGION Clare Valley, SA
CELLAR 2
ALC./VOL. 15.5%
RRP $14.50

Lengs & Cooter Shiraz

This is a small outfit making small amounts of hand-crafted wines. Their marketing efficiency is somewhat below their winemaking talents, so you'll have to seek them out.
CURRENT RELEASE 1994 A Chuck Norris style that really beats you up but is a bit simple in the process. It's all about potential. Given time in the cellar the assertive tannins will soften. The colour is dense and the nose is packed full of pepper and spice. The palate is very potent with deep plum flavours, pepper and spice. Tannin rules the finish; try it with wild boar.

QUALITY ????
VALUE ★★★½
GRAPES shiraz
REGION Clare Valley, SA
CELLAR 4–8
ALC./VOL. 13.8%
RRP $18.50

Lenswood Vineyard Pinot Noir

QUALITY ♥♥♥♥♥
VALUE ★★★★★
GRAPES pinot noir
REGION Adelaide Hills, SA
CELLAR ▮ 6
ALC./VOL. 13.0%
RRP $28.00

Could the Lenswood district become the high citadel for Australian pinot noir? The way this marque and its neighbours are shaping it may well be ... Maker Tim Knappstein.
Previous outstanding vintages: '91, '92, '93
CURRENT RELEASE 1994 A lovely wine as usual, with a cherry-red colour and a nose offering berries plus hints of meat. The palate is complex with a velvety texture. It has cherry and raspberry flavours which are married to fine-grained tannins on a persistent finish. It is a wine with backbone substantial enough to handle a beef and red wine casserole.

Lillydale Vineyards Cabernet Merlot

QUALITY ♥♥♥♥
VALUE ★★★½
GRAPES cabernet sauvignon, merlot
REGION Yarra Valley, Vic.
CELLAR ⊂⊐ 2–6
ALC./VOL. 13.0%
RRP $14.50

A by-product of the McWilliams takeover here is that prices have dropped to some of the lowest in the Yarra Valley.
CURRENT RELEASE 1994 This is a heavily worked wine that seems to miss the target slightly, but not for want of trying. The colour is dark and the nose is ripe and chocolatey with a lot of high-toast oak and a certain porty note. There's a big clout of tannin and the finish is tough. It's all about structure rather than fruit; maybe time will bring the elements together.

Lillydale Vineyards Pinot Noir

QUALITY ♥♥♥♥
VALUE ★★★★
GRAPES pinot noir
REGION Yarra Valley, Vic.
CELLAR ▮ 2
ALC./VOL. 12.0%
RRP $14.50

The Yarra Valley is making a strong case for becoming the leading Australian region for pinot. McWilliams have owned Lillydale Vineyards since 1994. Maker Alex White.
CURRENT RELEASE 1995 This could be the best Lillydale pinot yet. The colour is a rather light shade of brick-red, but the nose has definite varietal spicy, cherry-pip aromas showing authentic fruit with well-handled oak. The palate is soft and sappy, with character and length, and the aftertaste has an appealing gaminess. Try it with beef carpaccio.

Lindemans Hunter River Reserve Shiraz Bin 8200

Is nothing sacred? The label designers must be in mortal danger at the prospect of falling off their wallets. The old label was hardly a masterpiece, but it had been around for decades and was as familiar as a pair of comfortable slippers.
Previous outstanding vintages: '59, '65, '67, '68, '73, '79, '80, '83, '86, '87
CURRENT RELEASE 1991 This is a developed style with loads of Hunter character. The nose shows mature concentrated fruit aromas plus a hint of leather. The plate is rich and chewy with plum and blackberry fruit flavours. There are also regional signatures of leather and earth. The finish has soft tannins and sweet charred-oak characters. It drinks well with a classic lamb and barley casserole.

QUALITY ♉♉♉♉?
VALUE ★★★★
GRAPES shiraz
REGION Hunter Valley, NSW
CELLAR 🍾 10
ALC./VOL. 12.5%
RRP $22.50

Lindemans Limestone Ridge

Limestone Ridge is a vineyard in Coonawarra on some of the richest terra rossa soil on the strip. It has been the birthplace for distinguished wines. Maker Greg Clayfield.
Previous outstanding vintages: '82, '86, '88, '90, '91
CURRENT RELEASE 1992 A rather flat style that has changed little since the last review. The coconut and toast of the oak is still there but has become subdued somewhat. The fruit is starting to peek through the wooden curtain. There is still plenty of tannin grip on the finish. Try it with rare beef.

QUALITY ♉♉♉?
VALUE ★★½
GRAPES shiraz, cabernet sauvignon
REGION Coonawarra, SA
CELLAR 🍾 5
ALC./VOL. 13.0%
RRP $28.00

Lindemans Nyrang Shiraz

QUALITY ♛♛♛♛
VALUE ★★★½
GRAPES shiraz
REGION not stated
CELLAR 🍾 2
ALC./VOL. 13.0%
RRP $10.40 Ⓢ

'Suicide is painless, it brings on many changes ...' Why this old label hasn't self-immolated is a moot point. It continues to seesaw between greatness and mediocrity.
CURRENT RELEASE 1994 A decent red at a decent price. The colour is dense and the nose has a ripe plum and vinous aroma. The plum theme is continued on the palate. Soft tannins grace a modest finish. It is ready to drink; stick it beside an Irish stew.

Lindemans Padthaway Cabernet Merlot

QUALITY ♛♛♛♛
VALUE ★★★★
GRAPES cabernet sauvignon, merlot
REGION Padthaway, SA
CELLAR 🍾 3
ALC./VOL. 13.5%
RRP $14.50

One of the serious problems in the Padthaway district is a rising salinity due to the irrigation needed for the vines. It will be interesting to watch how viticulturists solve the problem.
CURRENT RELEASE 1994 This is a very drinkable wine that doesn't break the bank. It has a strong blackberry nose with a dusting of spice. The palate is a mix of plums, spice and cherry flavours. The finish contributes sweet vanillan oak flavours and gentle tannins. It drinks well now with lamb chops with rosemary.

Lindemans Pyrus Classic Release

Lindemans, which is part of the Southcorp group, has an admirable policy of cellaring distinguished vintages and re-releasing them as 'classics'. Pyrus is a regular candidate. Maker Greg Clayfield.

CURRENT RELEASE 1985 This was a Jimmy Watson Trophy winner in 1986. The colour is still youthful and the nose has an extracted Ribena character. The palate is full-on blackberry and concentrated fruit-juice flavours. The tannin is soft yet there is sufficient grip. It drinks very well. Decant and enjoy with pink lamb in a reduction sauce.

QUALITY 🍷🍷🍷🍷🍷
VALUE ★★★★
GRAPES cabernet sauvignon, merlot, malbec, cabernet franc
REGION Coonawarra, SA
CELLAR 🍾 2
ALC./VOL. 12.5%
RRP $36.00

CURRENT RELEASE 1992 This is a fine-boned style that reflects the nature of the vintage. The nose has strong cassis aromas plus evidence of new oak and a whisper of herbs. The palate is medium-bodied with blackberry and mulberry fruit flavours and these are followed by some dominant oak on a gently astringent and grippy finish. It should be decanted to avoid the crust. Try it with roast turkey.

QUALITY 🍷🍷🍷🍷🍷
VALUE ★★★½
GRAPES cabernet sauvignon, merlot, malbec, cabernet franc
REGION Coonawarra, SA
CELLAR 🍾 4
ALC./VOL. 13.0%
RRP $28.00

Lindemans St George Cabernet Sauvignon

St George is named after Major General Hinton St George, one of the 'wine doctors' (a la Dr Henry Lindeman). Today it is a discrete vineyard on the terra rossa strip. Maker Greg Clayfield. Previous outstanding vintages: '86, '88

CURRENT RELEASE 1992 Little change since last year. The wine remains fine-boned and lean. It has an intense ruby colour and there is obvious oak as well as fruit on the nose. The palate has cassis and dark cherry flavours. The finish is astringent and long. Decant and try it with squab.

QUALITY 🍷🍷🍷🍷
VALUE ★★★
GRAPES cabernet sauvignon
REGION Coonawarra, SA
CELLAR 🍾 2–6
ALC./VOL. 12.5%
RRP $28.00

Madfish Bay Premium Dry Red

QUALITY ▼▼▼▼
VALUE ★★★
GRAPES pinot noir, cabernet franc, merlot
REGION various, WA
CELLAR 🍾 2
ALC./VOL. 13.5%
RRP $15.30

The label features a picture of a turtle rendered in a traditional Australian Aboriginal rock-painting style. Made by John Wade at Howard Park.
CURRENT RELEASE 1994 Spicy, gamey bouquet with lots of leafy herbaceousness and some nice cedary oak. The cabernet blackcurrants follow through to the mouth, where there is very intense, lively flavour with some bitter tannins on the finish. Needs food: serve it with barbecued pork sausages.

Majella Shiraz

QUALITY ▼▼▼▼
VALUE ★★★★
GRAPES shiraz
REGION Coonawarra, SA
CELLAR 🍾 6
ALC./VOL. 13.5%
RRP $19.00

Brian 'Prof' Lynn has been a prominent grapegrower in Coonawarra for over 25 years. He recently decided to get with the strength and start a label of his own.
Previous outstanding vintages: '91, '92
CURRENT RELEASE 1993 Shades of Peppermint Pattie! This elegant red has an intense pepperminty nose dominating fresh lifted aromatics. The palate is also lively with plenty of wood (although not as much as the previous vintage), the flavours are highly attractive, and linger well with grip and balance. Should go well with wild duck.

Massoni Red Hill Pinot Noir

QUALITY ▼▼▼▼
VALUE ★★★
GRAPES pinot noir
REGION Mornington Peninsula, Vic.
CELLAR 🍾 2
ALC./VOL. 13.0%
RRP $29.00

Ian and Sue Home now own this wine company, which was begun by Melbourne restaurateurs Leon and Vivienne Massoni.
CURRENT RELEASE 1995 Nice wine, with good middle-palate sweetness and sappy as well as ripe, sweet berry aromas. Vanillan oak also chimes in strongly, with a touch of gaminess for good measure. The colour is light but there's plenty of appealing flavour. Drink now, with tuna sashimi.

Maxwell Ellen Street Shiraz

From its name you'd think this vineyard was right in the nerve centre of McLaren Vale, kerbed and guttered and all. In fact Ellen Street is a country road. Maker Mark Maxwell.
CURRENT RELEASE 1993 A big, hefty, solid citizen, without much varietal definition but plenty of guts and tannin to spare. Could be cellared with confidence. A fine match for civet of hare.

QUALITY 🍷🍷🍷🍷
VALUE ★★★★
GRAPES shiraz
REGION McLaren Vale, SA
CELLAR 🍾 5
ALC./VOL. 13.5%
RRP $12.95 (cellar door)

McWilliams Hanwood Cabernet Sauvignon

The Hanwood Barrel is one of the less forgettable sights of the wine world, in the class of the big merino at Goulburn and the big pineapple at Nambour.
CURRENT RELEASE 1994 This is starting to show some age already. It's a medium brick-red colour and has a developed plummy nose with a little earthiness. The taste is light and simple, with again more mellow than fresh-fruity flavours. Try it with barbecued snags.

QUALITY 🍷🍷🍷
VALUE ★★★
GRAPES cabernet sauvignon
REGION Riverina, NSW
CELLAR 🍾 1
ALC./VOL. 12.0%
RRP $9.40

Meadowbank Vineyard Cabernet

This is a vineyard north of Hobart that is part of a large mixed farming property. It grows some of the best wool in the country and also produces essential oils. Maker Greg O'Keefe.
CURRENT RELEASE 1994 A very convincing style and obviously the fruit was properly ripe. The colour is impressive deep red-purple. The nose is rich with strong blackberry, tobacco-leaf aromas. The palate is complex with sweet blackberry and dark cherry flavours tinged with spice. The oak on the finish is very sympathetic with substantial tannin grip. It drinks well with venison sausages.

QUALITY 🍷🍷🍷🍷
VALUE ★★★★
GRAPES cabernet sauvignon
REGION Derwent Valley, Tas.
CELLAR 🍾 5
ALC./VOL. 13.0%
RRP $22.00

Milburn Park Grenache

QUALITY ♛♛♛
VALUE ★★★
GRAPES grenache
REGION Sunraysia, Vic.
CELLAR 🍾 1
ALC./VOL. 13.0%
RRP $11.50 Ⓢ

This is one of the many brands of the Alambie Wine Co. from the Sunraysia. They are a high-tech outfit doing good things with hot-area fruit. Maker Bob Shields.

CURRENT RELEASE 1995 This soft, fruity young quaffer has a medium-light red colour and sweetly floral grenache nose, uncomplicated by oak. The palate is light-bodied, pleasantly fruity and a tad short, but it's a serviceable pasta wine.

Mildara Alexanders

QUALITY ♛♛♛♛
VALUE ★★★½
GRAPES cabernet sauvignon, malbec, merlot
REGION Coonawarra, SA
CELLAR 🍾 5
ALC./VOL. 12.5%
RRP $28.00 Ⓢ 🍾

This is the top of the Mildara tree, released with some maturity and quite a different style to the White Label Cab or Robertson's Well.
Previous outstanding vintages: '85, '86, '87, '88, '90

CURRENT RELEASE 1991 Still the current release, but it has developed some from last year's note. The colour is red to brick-red, the bouquet shows strong coffee grounds from the oak and developed plum and leather overtones, with just a hint of mint. It drinks smoothly, the flavour gentle and mellow with savoury rather than fruity flavours, plenty of oak and a soft finish. Try it with kassler.

Mildara Church Hill Shiraz Cabernet Merlot

QUALITY ♛♛♛
VALUE ★★★½
GRAPES shiraz, cabernet sauvignon, merlot
REGION McLaren Vale, Coonawarra, SA & Sunraysia, Vic.
CELLAR 🍾
ALC./VOL. 12.0%
RRP $10.00 Ⓢ

Why Church Hill? Perhaps Mildara is angling for the altar-wine market.

CURRENT RELEASE 1994 A decent light-bodied quaffer that won't offend. The nose is lightly spicy with some plum and the taste is soft and shows some shiraz spice. It is a basic drinking red at a better than average price, dipping as low as $6.95, which is seriously good value. Suits picnics.

Mildara Coonawarra Cabernet Sauvignon

Mildara keeps bringing out new labels, but this is still the one that offers the most thrills. It has a long and glorious history. Maker Gavin Hogg. Previous outstanding vintages: '63, '71, '76, '79, '80, '86, '88, '90, '91, '93
CURRENT RELEASE 1994 A worthy follow-up to the great '93, this is a wine of sublime flavour and depth, a profound blackcurrant bouquet, ripe and complex, with good background oak and rich, almost luscious palate flavour. It is the very essence of Coonawarra and strongly recommended. Pink lamb is a must.

QUALITY ♟♟♟♟♟
VALUE ★★★★★
GRAPES cabernet sauvignon
REGION Coonawarra, SA
CELLAR 10+
ALC./VOL. 13.0%
RRP $20.00 Ⓢ

Mitchell Growers (The) Grenache

The growers in this case were Hague and Walton, and the back label gives them credit. Maker Andrew Mitchell.
Previous outstanding vintages: '94
CURRENT RELEASE 1995 This is a stunner and bound to get the party swinging. Fresh, estery young grenache aromas without obvious oak: grapey, spicy, plum and licorice. A whopper. Some will find this just TOO big, but even if you're not a size queen, you have to admit it's an impressive wine. Try it with civet of hare.

QUALITY ♟♟♟♟♟
VALUE ★★★★½
GRAPES grenache
REGION Clare Valley, SA
CELLAR 4
ALC./VOL. 14.5%
RRP $16.50

Mitchell Peppertree Vineyard Shiraz

It's a happy coincidence: shiraz is an often-peppery wine and there's a pepper tree in the middle of the vineyard. Maker Andrew Mitchell. Previous outstanding vintages: '84, '86, '87, '90, '91, '92, '93
CURRENT RELEASE 1994 A blood and thunder wine that tries hard to be more. It is very fresh and youthful in every respect, with rather assertive tannin extractiveness that needs time to soften. Have they overdone it? Time will tell. Put it away for a couple of years, then serve with spicy sausages.

QUALITY ♟♟♟♟
VALUE ★★★
GRAPES shiraz
REGION Clare Valley, SA
CELLAR 2–7+
ALC./VOL. 14.0%
RRP $17.90

RED WINES

Mitchelton Chinaman's Bridge Merlot

QUALITY ♛♛♛♛
VALUE ★★★½
GRAPES merlot
REGION King Valley, Vic.
CELLAR 🍷 5
ALC./VOL. 13.5%
RRP $16.00 Ⓢ

The label features a colourful (some would say garish) rendition of an old wooden bridge across the Goulburn near Mitchelton. Maker Don Lewis.
CURRENT RELEASE 1994 A leap forward from the '93, this is a lovely drinking merlot with a nose of red berry and oak, the palate deep and rich with fleshy blackberry concentration and positive tannins, very focused on the middle palate. Drink with beef and blackcurrant demi-glaze.

Mitchelton Print Label Cabernet Merlot

QUALITY ♛♛♛♛♛
VALUE ★★★★
GRAPES cabernet sauvignon, merlot
REGION Yarra Valley, Pyrenees, Strathbogie Ranges, Vic.
CELLAR 🍷 2–10+
ALC./VOL. 13.5%
RRP $24.00 🍷

Winemaker Don Lewis has really upped the ante with his reds in recent years. While he's been casting his net increasingly wide for superior grapes, the vineyards around the winery are now being upgraded too.
CURRENT RELEASE 1993 This is exciting stuff: deep dense purple-red hue; rich oaky/dark berry concentrated aromas; rich, weighty, powerful flavour and impressive persistence. Shows much better structure than the Mitchelton reds of the '80s.

Mitchelton Victoria Reserve Shiraz

QUALITY ♛♛♛♛♛
VALUE ★★★★
GRAPES shiraz
REGION mainly Pyrenees & Heathcote, Vic.
CELLAR 🍷 1–10+
ALC./VOL. 13.5%
RRP $23.35 Ⓢ 🍷

This range has been through something of an identity crisis, with the names Reserve and Victoria being used interchangeably, and the gold Reserve lettering almost impossible to read.
CURRENT RELEASE 1993 A wine with plenty of stuffing. There are rich, ripe, minty/dark berry flavours aplenty and no sign of green or peppery herbaceous notes. Full-bodied, sweetly plummy fruit, good concentration and grip. Shows the dominant hallmarks of the Pyrenees component. Scrumptious shiraz to have with wild duck.

Montana Cabernet Sauvignon Merlot

Montana is grafting a lot of the cabernet sauvignon in its vast Marlborough vineyards over to merlot, which ripens more reliably in the cool climate.
CURRENT RELEASE 1994 A fair current-drinking red, with some briary characters but without too much green fruit. The merlot gives it a smooth, supple middle. It has no great depth but is lean, dry and pleasant enough with a gourmet hamburger.

QUALITY ♀♀♀
VALUE ★★★
GRAPES cabernet sauvignon, merlot
REGION Marlborough, NZ
CELLAR 🍾 1
ALC./VOL. 12.0%
RRP $12.00

Montana Saints Cabernet Merlot

According to chief winemaker Peter Hubscher, this is the first red that shows the influence of Montana's association with the distinguished Bordeaux house, Cordier.
CURRENT RELEASE 1994 The colour is nice and deep, the nose is soft, ripe and non-leafy. The flavour is bigger and richer than we are used to seeing from Montana, with good length. The palate is well structured with soft but persuasive tannins and a little warmth, which is a rare thing in Kiwi cabernets. Real progress here. Drink with New Zealand lamb.

QUALITY ♀♀♀♀
VALUE ★★★½
GRAPES cabernet sauvignon, merlot
REGION Hawkes Bay, NZ
CELLAR 🍾 3
ALC./VOL. 12.5%
RRP $15.00 ⓢ

Montana Timara Cabernet Merlot

This is viewed by Montana as its competitor for Jacob's Creek, and it's interesting to note that half of the cabernet grapes in the current release are Australian.
CURRENT RELEASE *non-vintage* A soft, light-bodied, very drinkable red which has more than a smattering of warm-grown Aussie character in its chocolatey overtones. There are also light spicy notes and some earthy berry flavours, but mercifully no greenness. Take it to a barbecue.

QUALITY ♀♀♀
VALUE ★★★½
GRAPES cabernet sauvignon, merlot
REGION New Zealand & Australia
CELLAR 🍾 1
ALC./VOL. 12.0%
RRP $8.00

Moondah Brook Cabernet Sauvignon

QUALITY ▼▼▼▼⁄
VALUE ★★★★½
GRAPES cabernet sauvignon
REGION Darling Ranges, WA
CELLAR 🍾 6
ALC./VOL. 13.0%
RRP $15.00

WA is full of babbling brooks, which in the eastern states would be termed creeks. Moondah is part of the BRL Hardy/Houghton group. Maker Paul Lapsley.

CURRENT RELEASE 1993 This label is coming up in the world. The price is on the ascent and, happily, so is the quality. It's an excellent full-bodied, complex cabernet with lashings of toasty oak and some minty, leafy aspects together with blackberry flavours. The palate is rich and strong, with good firm tannin spine. Length and structure beyond its station. Roast veal here.

Moss Wood Cabernet Sauvignon

QUALITY ▼▼▼▼⁄
VALUE ★★★★
GRAPES cabernet sauvignon, merlot, cabernet franc
REGION Margaret River, WA
CELLAR 🍾 10+
ALC./VOL. 13.0%
RRP $27.00 🍾

Keith and Clare Mugford have taken Moss Wood onwards and upwards since founders Bill and Sandra Pannell sold it to them in the mid '80s. Moss Wood Cabernet is one of the country's most eagerly sought reds.

Previous outstanding vintages: '75, '76, '83, '85, '86, '90, '91, '92

CURRENT RELEASE 1993 A high-ranking Moss Wood which drinks beautifully now but has a great future for the patient cellarer. Rich cherry, raspberry cabernet fruit, cracked pepper and light-oak scents greet the nose. There's excellent concentration and power with berries and garden mint in a fruit-driven palate. Delicious with rare roast beef.

Mount Avoca Cabernet

Mount Avoca was started by Melbourne stockbroker John Barry and his architect wife Arda in 1970. Today their son Matt is also involved. Cabernet is one of their strengths.
CURRENT RELEASE 1993 This is a thumper, showing the strong tannins typical of the district. The colour is very dense, the nose strong on toast and vanilla from oak. It should gather more complexity with age, and will undoubtedly keep well, but can be enjoyed already with a hearty steak.

QUALITY 🍷🍷🍷🍷
VALUE ★★★½
GRAPES cabernet sauvignon
REGION Pyrenees, Vic.
CELLAR 🍾 10
ALC./VOL. 13.0%
RRP $19.00

Mount Avoca Shiraz

These wines have a pungent gaminess that polarises tasters. Some like it, some don't. Decanting and airing can help.
CURRENT RELEASE 1993 The first impression is of a whole cupboardful of spices: clove, nutmeg, cinnamon and pepper. Gamey notes creep in later. The fruit outpunches the wood, and there is a lot of it. Sweet, ripe and smoothly tannic, it can be drunk now with casseroled rabbit.

QUALITY 🍷🍷🍷🍷🍷
VALUE ★★★★½
GRAPES shiraz
REGION Pyrenees, Vic.
CELLAR 🍾 7+
ALC./VOL. 13.0%
RRP $14.00

Mount Benson Vineyards Cabernet Sauvignon

Former crayfisherman Bill Wehl was the first to grow grapes in the emerging Mount Benson region. The vines were planted in 1989 and the wines are made at Brands Laira.
CURRENT RELEASE 1993 The vineyard's second vintage yielded a promising wine: deeply coloured with coconut and walnut oak aromas over dark berry varietal fruit, and good fruit sweetness in the mouth. A touch of mint, mediumweight and decent length. Try it with duck.

QUALITY 🍷🍷🍷🍷
VALUE ★★★½
GRAPES cabernet sauvignon
REGION Mount Benson, SA
CELLAR 🍾 5
ALC./VOL. 13.0%
RRP $15.00 (cellar door)

Mount Helen Cabernet Sauvignon Merlot

QUALITY ♉♉♉♉⚆
VALUE ★★★★½
GRAPES cabernet sauvignon, merlot
REGION Strathbogie Ranges, Vic.
CELLAR 🍷 8
ALC./VOL. 12.5%
RRP $19.00

This vineyard high in the Strathbogie Ranges used to part of the Tisdall plantings. It was a pioneering venture that now belongs to the Mildara Blass group. Maker Toni Stockhausen.
CURRENT RELEASE 1991 This is a very elegant cool-climate style from a high-altitude vineyard. The nose has developed fruit aromas and wafts of cedar. The palate has strong blackberry fruit flavours and the softness of merlot provides padding for the cabernet skeleton. The tannin on the finish is well integrated and lingering. It has developed well. Try it with casseroled kid.

Mount Ida Shiraz

QUALITY ♉♉♉♉♉
VALUE ★★★★★
GRAPES shiraz
REGION Heathcote, Vic.
CELLAR 🍷 8
ALC./VOL. 13.0%
RRP $18.00 Ⓢ

This vineyard was originally planted by the artist Leonard French. These days it is part of the Mildara Blass empire. Maker Toni Stockhausen. Previous outstanding vintages: '91
CURRENT RELEASE 1992 This is an example of God's-own shiraz country and what can happen with a good winemaker. The colour is deep and the seductive nose has strong fruit aromas and lots of pepper. The depth of fruit is outstanding, it is rich and concentrated with plum and cherry flavours. There is also evidence of bottle-age development. The tannins on the finish are dry and coating. It drinks well now and needs a dish with robust flavours. Try it with kidneys in a light mustard sauce.

Mount Langi Ghiran Shiraz

Big changes are happening at 'Langi', with new plantings and new partners. The '93 won our Penguin award for best shiraz in last year's *Guide*, and the '94 is right up there with it. Maker Trevor Mast.
Previous outstanding vintages: '84, '86, '88, '89, '90, '91, '92, '93
CURRENT RELEASE 1994 Another humdinger from Masty. Very deep, dark purple-red; high-fidelity cool-climate shiraz aromas of pepper and spices, and the palate again has spice galore but also sweeter, riper notes of cherry and plum. It's a typical Langi fruit-driven style with the oak playing second fiddle. A lovely wine to drink now or over the next decade or more, with game meats.

QUALITY 🍷🍷🍷🍷🍷
VALUE ★★★★★
GRAPES shiraz
REGION Grampians, Vic.
CELLAR 🍾 12+
ALC./VOL. 13.5%
RRP $23.35

Mount Pleasant Old Paddock & Old Hill Shiraz

Maurice O'Shea founded Mount Pleasant in 1921 and McWilliams bought into it in the 1930s. Long-serving winemaker is Phil Ryan.
CURRENT RELEASE 1990 Mount Pleasant reds are very much a house style, the hallmarks being forward development, brownish colour, earthy non-fruity aromas and savoury taste. Great if you like that sort of thing. This has more depth than most, with intensely regional earth and old leather smells, heaps of Hunter character, and smooth, supple, dry flavours. A food wine – try it with mature cheddar.

QUALITY 🍷🍷🍷🍷
VALUE ★★★
GRAPES shiraz
REGION Hunter Valley, NSW
CELLAR 🍾 2+
ALC./VOL. 11.5%
RRP $20.30

Mount Trio Pinot Noir

QUALITY ♘♘♘♘
VALUE ★★★½
GRAPES pinot noir
REGION Mount Barker, WA
CELLAR 🍾 2
ALC./VOL. 13.0%
RRP $15.00

This is the private brand of Plantagenet's winemaker Gavin Berry and his partner Gill Graham. They have a vineyard in the Porongurup Range, near Albany. Maker Gavin Berry.

CURRENT RELEASE 1994 The colour is medium-light purple-red, the bouquet distinctly pinoid with strawberry/cherry and slightly gamey characters. There's just a whisper of oak, nice slinky pinot texture and a trace of astringency on the finish. It drinks well with Thai-style beancurd and oyster sauce.

Mountadam Pinot Noir

QUALITY ♘♘♘♘♘
VALUE ★★★★
GRAPES pinot noir
REGION Eden Hills, SA
CELLAR 🍾 5
ALC./VOL. 13.0%
RRP $28.00

This is a very impressive winery high in the Eden Hills. It's God's own country and could be the place for the great pinots of Australia. Winemaker Adam Wynn is one of the leaders in the field.

Previous outstanding vintages: '89, '90, '91, '93

CURRENT RELEASE 1994 A very good complex style that has indisputable varietal credentials. The colour is a deep ruby and the nose has a complex mix of cherry, wood, briar and smoke aromas. The palate is medium-bodied with strong dark cherry flavours and a hint of truffles. The finish has strong acid and oak making it robust and a good cellar proposition. It also drinks well now; try it with roast pheasant.

Mountadam The Red

Adam Wynn is one of the most qualified and talented winemakers in the land, so if he wants to make wine as if it was a Superman movie, who are we to argue.
Previous outstanding vintages: '89, '90, '91
CURRENT RELEASE 1992 This is a cellar style that gives the impression of being over-worked. The nose is vinous with some rose-petal and berry aromas. The palate is quite tight with some elegant fruit, cherry and raspberry flavours that are a little flat and are wedded to well-integrated oak on a classically Bordeaux-ish finish. It should cellar well. Try it with veal shanks in a rich reduction sauce.

QUALITY ▼▼▼
VALUE ★★
GRAPES cabernet sauvignon 50%, merlot 50%
REGION Eden Hills
CELLAR 2–6
ALC./VOL. 12.5%
RRP $35.00

Ninth Island Pinot Noir

Pretty unwooded pinot noir could be a coming style. This second label from Pipers Brook takes its name from one of the islands off the north coast of Tasmania.
CURRENT RELEASE 1995 This is a very drinkable style with a pretty pink colour. The nose has strawberry and cherry smells with a background of spice. The medium-bodied palate has sweet berry flavours with cherry and raspberry flavours. There has been no wood treatment so acid carries the finish. It goes well with pan-fried sardines and could be served chilled.

QUALITY ▼▼▼▽
VALUE ★★★
GRAPES pinot noir
REGION northern Tas.
CELLAR 1
ALC./VOL. 12.9%
RRP $15.00

Ninth Island Rosé

How long before Australians understand that this is a great summer style and it isn't sissy to drink pink wine?
CURRENT RELEASE 1995 The colour has onion-skin and pink hues. The nose offers sweet-berry aromas plus some leaf smells and a hint of lantana. The palate is quite substantial with plenty of berry flavours and the wine really scores with a very dry finish. It can be served chilled. Try it with doner kebab.

QUALITY ▼▼▼▼
VALUE ★★★★
GRAPES cabernet franc, merlot
REGION northern Tas.
CELLAR ▯
ALC./VOL. 12.9%
RRP $11.00

Ninth Island Tamar Cabernets

QUALITY ????
VALUE ★★★½
GRAPES cabernet sauvignon 50%, cabernet franc 50%
REGION Tamar Valley, Tas.
CELLAR 🍷 3
ALC./VOL. 12.9%
RRP $16.50

Take One: The Pipers Brook cooking label. Take Two: The Pipers Brook affordable label. Take Three: The Pipers Brook label for wines made from non-vineyard fruit. Cut! Maker Andrew Pirie.

CURRENT RELEASE 1994 Accentuate the positive and eliminate the negative – the leafy herbal qualities of this wine can be exploited with a dish like pink lamb. It has a leafy nose and a palate that shows plenty of green herbal qualities. The medium-bodied palate has raspberry/blackberry flavours and these are matched by a dusty dry finish that has persistent astringency.

Normans Lone Gum Shiraz Cabernet

QUALITY ???
VALUE ★★★
GRAPES shiraz, cabernet sauvignon
REGION Murray Valley, SA
CELLAR 🍷 1
ALC./VOL. 13.0%
RRP $9.90

The huge gum in question is protected by the National Trust. It is an enigmatic river red gum that stands alone in the vineyard 9 kms from the nearest river.

CURRENT RELEASE 1995 The colour is a pale garnet and the nose has soft berry aromas. The palate is light to medium-bodied with sweet raspberry fruit flavours. Soft oak makes for a gentle finish. It is a quaffing style that would go well at a barbecue with some spare ribs.

Notley Gorge Pinot Noir

QUALITY ????
VALUE ★★★★
GRAPES pinot noir
REGION northern Tas.
CELLAR 🍷 4
ALC./VOL. 12.6%
RRP $19.00 (cellar door)

This is a small vineyard at Glengarry in Tasmania with a production of around 1800 cases per annum. Makers Doug Bowen, Andrew Hood (consultant).

CURRENT RELEASE 1993 A very well-made wine that expresses plenty of varietal character. The colour is a deep crimson and the nose has strong berry aromas. The palate is a mix of cherry and strawberry flavours and these are framed by well-integrated tannin on a mildly grippy finish. It drinks well now, try it with spaghetti carbonara.

Oakridge Estate Cabernet Merlot

Oakridge is one of the younger Yarra wineries, established in 1982. This wine used to be labelled Quercus and plays second fiddle to the reserve cabernet sauvignon.
CURRENT RELEASE 1993 The colour shows some early development and the nose is dominated by a gunsmoke character. The taste is rich and velvety, smooth and very much in drinking mode. Try it with Lebanese lamb giros.

QUALITY ▼▼▼▼
VALUE ★★★½
GRAPES cabernet sauvignon, merlot
REGION Yarra Valley, Vic.
CELLAR 3
ALC./VOL. 13.6%
RRP $16.00

Orlando Jacaranda Ridge Cabernet Sauvignon

There aren't any hills at Coonawarra, so a ridge is the next best thing to give their brand names a lift. This is Orlando's flagship cabernet.
Previous outstanding vintages: '88, '89, '90, '91
CURRENT RELEASE 1992 A rather unyielding Jacaranda with serious tannins and latent flavours. Put it in the cellar: at present it's showing cedary oak on the nose and the palate is dominated by solid astringency. Will probably never reveal the charms of the '91, but time will surely mellow it. Drink with steak.

QUALITY ▼▼▼▼
VALUE ★★½
GRAPES cabernet sauvignon
REGION Coonawarra, SA
CELLAR 2-7+
ALC./VOL. 13.0%
RRP $35.00 ⓢ

Orlando Lawson's Shiraz

Padthaway is noted more for white wines, but as the vines mature winemakers are mapping the vineyards and isolating special plots which yield outstanding red grapes.
Previous outstanding vintages: '88, '90, '91, '92
CURRENT RELEASE 1993 Typical Lawson's concentration here, aided and abetted by lashings of coconutty oak. It's undeniably massive and generously flavoured, but somewhat stolid and forbidding. Will take years to mellow into an attractive drink. Lawson's is still a wine in search of a style.

QUALITY ▼▼▼▼
VALUE ★★½
GRAPES shiraz
REGION Padthaway, SA
CELLAR 2-8+
ALC./VOL. 13.5%
RRP $35.00 ⓢ

Orlando Russet Ridge Cabernet Sauvignon

QUALITY ♥♥♥⚬
VALUE ★★★½
GRAPES cabernet sauvignon, shiraz, merlot
REGION Coonawarra, SA
CELLAR 🍾 5
ALC./VOL. 12.5%
RRP $15.50 ⓢ

This brand was developed a couple of years ago and the '91 was the first release. It offered good value right from the start. It seems to be a style that drinks best young. Maker Phil Laffer and team.
Previous outstanding vintages: '91, '92
CURRENT RELEASE 1993 The oak's been toned down and the emphasis is on minty/berry Coonawarra fruit, with a whisper of coconutty oak. Not a complex wine, it's a leaner style with a touch of astringency on the finish which doesn't stop it being drink-now. Try kidneys.

Orlando St Hugo Cabernet Sauvignon

QUALITY ♥♥♥♥⚬
VALUE ★★★★
GRAPES cabernet sauvignon
REGION Coonawarra, SA
CELLAR 🍾 8
ALC./VOL. 13.5%
RRP $24.00 ⓢ

Hugo Gramp was head of Orlando when he died in a famous air crash near Melbourne in the 1940s. This wine commemorates him.
Previous outstanding vintages: '82, '86, '88, '90, '92
CURRENT RELEASE 1993 Another lovely St Hugo, very approachable now but with medium-term ageing potential. Minty/berry regional fruit aromas with raspberry and leafy accents. A smooth red with gentle tannins, to drink with pink lamb fillet.

Osborne's Pinot Noir

QUALITY ♥♥♥
VALUE ★★★
GRAPES pinot noir
REGION Mornington Peninsula, Vic.
CELLAR 🍾 3
ALC./VOL. 13.0%
RRP $21.00

New winery and label from Merricks in Victoria. The products may be difficult to find in your local bottle shop so contact cellar door.
CURRENT RELEASE 1994 A light elegant style that drinks well now. The colour is a medium-ruby and the nose has strong cherry aromas. There is plenty of sweet berry characters on the strawberry flavoured palate and the finish displays plenty of acid. It can be served with barbecued pink lamb straps.

Paringa Estate Pinot Noir

They are trying hard to make the definitive Mornington pinot. There are lots of winemaking tweaks being used to increase the complexity. Previous outstanding vintages: '92, '93, '94
CURRENT RELEASE 1995 The colour is a mid-ruby and the nose is savoury with cherry and plum aromas. The palate is medium-bodied with fairly intense cherry flavours and hints of spice. There is also a silky texture to the fruit. Fine-grained tannin rounds out the finish. It is well balanced with excellent grip. Try it with quail and mushroom risotto.

QUALITY ♛♛♛♛
VALUE ★★★
GRAPES pinot noir
REGION Mornington Peninsula, Vic.
CELLAR 🍾 5
ALC./VOL. 12.5%
RRP $28.00

Parker Estate Terra Rossa First Growth

Cheeky name, sensational quality. Up to and including 1994 this was made at Leconfield by Ralph Fowler. Later vintages will be made elsewhere, so it's a case of wait and see. Previous outstanding vintages: '88, '90, '91
CURRENT RELEASE 1993 This is a mightily impressive red wine: concentrated colour and flavour, powerful berry fruit and cedary oak give a lovely perfume laced with peppermint and leafy high notes. Perfect ripeness, great charm and intensity with gentle but positive tannins and an overall impression of great harmony. Big future. Drink with aged cheddar.

QUALITY ♛♛♛♛♛
VALUE ★★★½
GRAPES cabernet sauvignon, merlot, cabernet franc
REGION Coonawarra, SA
CELLAR ⇌ 1–12+
ALC./VOL. 13.0%
RRP $45.00

Pauletts Cabernet Merlot

Here's a good example of a very experienced winemaker teasing the best from a reluctant vintage that didn't really want to ripen properly.
CURRENT RELEASE 1994 Elegant wine that has loads of grace. The vinous nose has strong berry aromas and the palate offers sweet cherry flavours that are dusted with spice. Although the wine spent 18 months in small oak, the wood remains restrained; however, the finish is long. It should cellar well but drink it now and it goes well with bratwurst on a tomato salsa.

QUALITY ♛♛♛♛
VALUE ★★★★
GRAPES cabernet sauvignon 70%, merlot 30%
REGION Clare Valley, SA
CELLAR 🍾 5
ALC./VOL. 13.0%
RRP $14.95

Pauletts Shiraz

QUALITY ♛♛♛♛
VALUE ★★★★
GRAPES shiraz
REGION Clare Valley, SA
CELLAR 🍷 6
ALC./VOL. 13.0%
RRP $14.95

Great place to visit for both the hospitality and the view. This would be an ideal place for a restaurant. Maker Neil Paulett.
CURRENT RELEASE 1994 Stylish wine with great varietal expression. The colour is a vibrant ruby and the nose has loads of spice and ripe-fruit aromas. The medium-bodied palate has sweet berry flavours plus loads of spice. The oak treatment is neatly tailored to the weight of fruit. It drinks well now with marinated lamb fillets.

Pendarves Cabernet Merlot Malbec

QUALITY ♛♛♛♛
VALUE ★★★★
GRAPES cabernet sauvignon, merlot, malbec
REGION Hunter Valley, NSW
CELLAR 🍷 6
ALC./VOL. 12.5%
RRP $19.00

If you could bottle zeal, Dr Phillip Norrie could out-produce Mildara Blass when it comes to the cause of wine and health. Phil is also the proprietor of a small vineyard and in drought-stricken times he has been known to water his vines by hand.
CURRENT RELEASE 1994 The nose has full berry aromas and the colour is a very healthy ruby purple. The palate is medium-bodied and there are attractive zesty raspberry fruit flavours. Each component plays its part and oak graces the finish. There is an attractive lift of spice and fine-grained tannins on the finish. It needs more time in the bottle but you can drink it now with smoked kangaroo.

Penfolds Bin 128 Coonawarra

This is the only Penfolds bin number to remain faithful to its regional roots. The rest are promiscuous blends from several regions in an attempt to make a cellar style.
Previous outstanding vintages: '71, '78, '80, '82, '86, '88, '90, '91
CURRENT RELEASE 1993 Although there are some regional echoes the overall character is that of a Penfolds wine. There is a deep colour and the ripe-plum aromas are accentuated by some toasty oak characters. The palate has attractive depth and the major flavour is plum with pepper and spices. The finish shows typical high-toned oak and enthusiastic grip. It drinks well with a rich cassoulet.

QUALITY 🍷🍷🍷🍷🍷
VALUE ★★★★½
GRAPES shiraz
REGION Coonawarra, SA
CELLAR 🍾 8
ALC./VOL. 13.5%
RRP $16.00 ⓢ

Penfolds Bin 389 Cabernet Shiraz

Used to be known as 'poor man's Grange' but at the current Grange prices make that 'pauper's Grange'. It also was usually made only from Barossa and Magill material, but these days it is a United Nations cellar style.
Previous outstanding vintages: '66, '71, '80, '83, '86, '87, '90, '91, '92
CURRENT RELEASE 1993 Tough stuff, this wine is very reluctant so show fruit at the moment. The colour is deep crimson and the nose has the usual toasty aroma plus a hint of blackberry. The palate is restrained and dominated by oak. There is muted blackberry flavour underneath high-toned American oak. The finish is grainy with astringent tannins. It needs time, try it with a char-grilled T-bone and all the trimmings.

QUALITY 🍷🍷🍷🍷
VALUE ★★★★
GRAPES cabernet sauvignon, shiraz
REGION Padthaway, Barossa Valley, Coonawarra, McLaren Vale, SA
CELLAR ↣ 3–10+
ALC./VOL. 13.5%
RRP $20.50

RED WINES

Penfolds Bin 407 Cabernet Sauvignon   CHRISTMAS '96

QUALITY ♘♘♘♘
VALUE ★★★★
GRAPES cabernet sauvignon
REGION McLaren Vale, Coonawarra, Padthaway, SA
CELLAR 🍾 8
ALC./VOL. 13.5%
RRP $20.00

This bin number came into being a few years back to plug a price gap between Bin 389 and Bin 707. It was an instant hit. Maker John Duval (and a cast of thousands).
Previous outstanding vintages: '90, '91, '92
CURRENT RELEASE 1993 This is an approachable wine with lots of classic cabernet features. The nose has strong blackberry aroma and there is a hint of toasty oak as well as tobacco. The palate continues the blackberry theme and there are some suggestions of green stalk characters under the toasty oak. It is a typical Penfolds style and it goes well with rack of pink lamb.

Penfolds Bin 707 Cabernet Sauvignon

QUALITY ♘♘♘♘♘
VALUE ★★★★
GRAPES cabernet sauvignon
REGION Coonawarra, Padthaway, Adelaide Hills, SA
CELLAR 🍾 2–10
ALC./VOL. 13.5%
RRP $55.00

According to folklore the bin number was a consequence of an executive day-dreaming while looking out the window at the (then) Tempe HQ of Penfolds when a Boeing 707 was taking off from Mascot airport. This is denied by Penfolds, but the timing fits the story.
Previous outstanding vintages: '64, '76, '80, '83, '84, '86, '87, '90, '91, '92
CURRENT RELEASE 1993 This is a typical example. The nose has strong blackberry aromas and there are suggestions of mint, toasted wood and cedar. The palate has been fully worked with extracted blackberry fruit that has joined with the classy oak. It is an exotic mixture of flavours and the finish shows off some new oak and plenty of tannin grip. It needs time; at the moment venison medallions are appropriate.

Penfolds Clare Estate

The 120-ha. site was selected by the late Max Schubert with help from Mick Knappstein. Part of the planting is being organically managed with a view to specialised export.
Previous outstanding vintages: '93
CURRENT RELEASE 1994 Not as fleshy or opulent as we've come to expect, which probably reflects the nature of the vintage. The nose is vinous with some dusty oak, The medium-bodied palate has blackcurrant flavours which are supported by French oak. The finish shows off fine-grained tannins and considerable grip. It goes well with barbecued lamb straps.

QUALITY ♛♛♛♛
VALUE ★★★★
GRAPES merlot, malbec, cabernet sauvignon, cabernet franc
REGION Clare Valley, SA
CELLAR 🍷 4
ALC./VOL. 13.0%
RRP $17.50 ⓢ

Penfolds Grange

The icon of Aussie wine, which is fast becoming irrelevant to most wine lovers. In the past 12 months it's become the prey of frenzied collectors both local and overseas. The auction market has gone berserk and retailers don't help by continuing to raise the retail price.
Previous outstanding vintages: '52, '53, '55, '62, '63, '66, '71, '76, '83, '86, '88, '90
CURRENT RELEASE 1991 Market hysteria is a strange thing and Grange silliness is inspired more by love of money than love of wine. The market has embraced the '91 as it did the '90, because it's just as good. If anything it's more classical, showing perhaps less fruit and opulence in youth but more structure. The famous twinge of volatility is back, and it has all the concentration and massive, forceful, oaky, tannic savouriness that becomes classic Grange old leather, truffles, earth and dried-fruit complexity with age. Keep at least five years then serve with aged hard cheeses.

QUALITY ♛♛♛♛♛
VALUE ★★½
GRAPES shiraz 95%, cabernet sauvignon 5%
REGION Barossa Valley, McLaren Vale, SA
CELLAR ⟶ 5–15+
ALC./VOL. 13.6%
RRP $195–$250

Penfolds Kalimna Bin 28

QUALITY ♗♗♗♗
VALUE ★★★½
GRAPES shiraz
REGION Barossa Valley, Padthaway, McLaren Vale, SA
CELLAR 3–8
ALC./VOL. 13.5%
RRP $16.50

One of the difficult questions is whether to include wine we know won't be available when this book is published. Our retail contacts tell us the Penfolds range is in very short supply and unlikely to be available late in the year. Hopefully readers have some wines in the cellar so these entries will still be of service. To leave them out is unthinkable.

Previous outstanding vintages: '82, '83, '86, '87, '88, '90, '91, '92

CURRENT RELEASE 1993 Very much a cellar style that shows the variety to advantage. The colour is deep ruby and the nose has plum and spice aromas. The medium-bodied palate has slightly subdued fruit flavours. Plum is the main component and there is also a hint of earth. The finish shows some chalky dry characters plus a vanillan lift. It needs time in the bottle. Try it with devilled kidneys.

Penfolds Magill Estate Shiraz

QUALITY ♗♗♗♗♗
VALUE ★★★★
GRAPES shiraz
REGION Coonawarra, SA
CELLAR 2–8
ALC./VOL. 13.0%
RRP $35.90

The Magill vineyard was the cradle of Grange and playground for Max Schubert. These days the price looks relatively benign. Maker John Bird.

Previous outstanding vintages: '83, '86, '87, '88, '89, '90, '91

CURRENT RELEASE 1992 This says Penfolds shiraz to us. The colour is deep and the nose has plum and vanilla spice aromas. The palate is complex and chewy. It is medium to full bodied and there is blackberry and spice in abundant quantity. The finish shows off some extravagant tannin and loads of grip. It needs a rich dish like quail ravioli in a reduction sauce.

Penfolds Old Vine Shiraz Grenache Mourvedre

Young Charlie Melton has a lot to answer for. He popularised the unpopular grape varieties and even the large companies are leaping on the band wagon.
CURRENT RELEASE 1993 A richer style with a good mix of fruit and oak. The colour is dense and the nose has toast and berry aromas. The palate is full of sweet raspberry fruit flavours and these are attended by toasty oak flavours on a finish that has plenty of tannin. It needs decanting and a hearty casserole to set it off properly.

QUALITY ♛♛♛♛
VALUE ★★★
GRAPES shiraz, grenache, mourvedre
REGION Barossa Valley, SA
CELLAR 4
ALC./VOL. 13.5%
RRP $18.00

Penfolds St Henri

This style was originally invented by John Davoren as a reaction to Grange. The latest model sees the addition of cabernet sauvignon; however, the wine was matured in the traditional 2000-litre casks.
Previous outstanding vintages: '76, '80, '82, '83, '85, '86, '87, '89, '90
CURRENT RELEASE 1992 As ever it is a rich and slightly old-fashioned wine. The nose is a mix of dressed leather and ripe fruit aromas. The palate has succulent ripe fruit with the emphasis on cherry and plum. There is also an earthy grace note. The oak is supportive but not intrusive; however, the finish is long with some satisfying grip. It is just the wine for a hearty winter casserole.

QUALITY ♛♛♛♛
VALUE ★★★
GRAPES shiraz, cabernet sauvignon
REGION McLaren Vale, Barossa, Coonawarra, Padthaway & Clare Valley, SA.
CELLAR 6
ALC./VOL. 13.5%
RRP $25.00

RED WINES

Penley Estate Cabernet Sauvignon

QUALITY	🍷🍷🍷🍷🍷
VALUE	★★★★½
GRAPES	cabernet sauvignon
REGION	Coonawarra, SA
CELLAR	🍾 10+
ALC./VOL.	14.0%
RRP	$38.00 🍾

Best Red Wine

One glance at the packaging tells you the stuff inside is going to taste good. Kym Tolley has a large new vineyard in Coonawarra and plans to be self-sufficient in grapes very soon.
Previous outstanding vintages: '90, '91, '92
CURRENT RELEASE 1993 This has Coonawarra written all over it, and a certain kinship with Penfolds, for whom Kym Tolley used to work. Lush blackcurrant cabernet fruit well married to stylish toasty oak, hints of walnut and lashings of sweet berries. A proudly oak-driven style with oodles of class to go with the swish bottle. Try it with pink lamb.

Penley Estate Hyland Shiraz

QUALITY	🍷🍷🍷🍷
VALUE	★★★
GRAPES	shiraz
REGION	Coonawarra, SA
CELLAR	🍾 3+
ALC./VOL.	13.5%
RRP	$16.20

Winemaker Kym Tolley's mother was a Penfold, and his grandfather used the surname Penfold Hyland, hence the name of this nostalgic wine.
CURRENT RELEASE 1993 An easy-going soft, rich red with chocolatey overtones to its cherry, plummy fruit. There is well-rounded berry/chocolate flavour on the palate, assisted by some vanillan oak, and the finish is very soft. Drink now with barbecued hamburger.

Pepper Tree Wines Merlot

This Hunter-based company has connections with Coonawarra. It is a progressive get-up-and-go concern with Chris Cameron as chief winemaker. Maker Chris (Hopper) Archer.

CURRENT RELEASE 1995 This is a killer merlot with loads of grunt. The medium-ruby colour tells fibs because it hides the richness to follow. The palate has succulent cherry and raspberry flavours which are mingled with vanilla and spice. The palate is rich with strong American oak and fine-grained tannins. There is also a warmth of alcohol and a slippery texture. It needs a big dish like garlic snails.

QUALITY ♛♛♛♛♛
VALUE ★★★
GRAPES merlot
REGION Coonawarra, SA
CELLAR 🍷 8
ALC./VOL. 14.6%
RRP $40.00

Petaluma Coonawarra

For MS, Petaluma red wines have been a vexed question – perhaps he expects too much – putting Petaluma on too lofty a pedestal. Perhaps the ever-impatient Shield should wait until some of the wines mature. Makers Brian Croser, Andrew Hardy.

Previous outstanding vintages: '79, '82, '86, '87, '88, '90, '91

CURRENT RELEASE 1993 He of little faith, this is a softer version with a higher proportion of merlot. The nose has ripe fruit aromas plus hints of toasty oak. The palate is ample and mouth-filling with raspberry and blackberry flavours. There is also a trace of anise (possibly from the wood treatment). The finish is fine-tuned by oak and grippy tannin. It drinks quite well now. Try it with rare roast beef.

QUALITY ♛♛♛♛♛
VALUE ★★★★
GRAPES cabernet sauvignon, merlot
REGION Coonawarra, SA
CELLAR 🍷 10
ALC./VOL. 13.0%
RRP $38.00 🍷

Petaluma Coonawarra Merlot

QUALITY ♢♢♢♢♢
VALUE ★★★★½
GRAPES merlot
REGION Coonawarra, SA
CELLAR ⬌ 2–8+
ALC./VOL. 13.5%
RRP $38.00

Brian Croser is watching the Coonawarra boundary debate with interest, as part of his merlot (67 per cent in 1993) comes from his Sharefarmers vineyard, which is likely to find itself on the wrong side of the line.
Previous outstanding vintages: '90, '91, '92
CURRENT RELEASE 1993 Vies with the '91 as the best under this label yet, and a good advertisement not only for Sharefarmers but also for Petaluma's (manual) viticultural practices. Youthful deep purple colour – a Petaluma trademark; ripe blackberry and dark chocolate aromas with a faint hint of crushed leaves. The palate has very good concentration and length and fine, firm tannin structure. A superb merlot to cellar and bring out later with hard cheeses.

Peter Lehmann Cabernet Sauvignon

QUALITY ♢♢♢♢♢
VALUE ★★★★★
GRAPES cabernet sauvignon
REGION Barossa Valley, SA
CELLAR ▮ 8
ALC./VOL. 13.5%
RRP $17.00

In the Barossa Valley cabernet sauvignon is emerging as a poor cousin to shiraz. However, in certain years it can rise to the occasion and steal the crown. Maker Andrew Wigan.
Previous outstanding vintages: '92, '93
CURRENT RELEASE 1994 A very fine wine that has both Barossa richness and finesse. The nose is full-on fruit with loads of blackberry aroma. Blackberry is the major flavour on the palate and there are touches of chocolate and vanilla. The oak is well integrated and provides a raft for the fruit. The fine-grained tannins on the finish are elegant but firm. It is a style that will improve with cellaring. T-bone steak and mushrooms are just the ticket.

Peter Lehmann Clancy's Gold Preference

Named after Clancy of the Overflow, this wine has been a great exercise in brand building. It won the Gold Penguin in one of the earlier *Guides*.
Previous outstanding vintages: '88, '89, '91
CURRENT RELEASE 1994 Very much a cellar style that was made to be drunk early. The nose has strong berry aromas with a touch of wood. The palate is rich with sweet berry fruit flavours and a touch of spice. The finish shows some discreet oak and soft tannins. It is the perfect accompaniment for pasta with a meat sauce.

QUALITY ▼▼▼▼
VALUE ★★★★
GRAPES shiraz, cabernet sauvignon, merlot
REGION Barossa Valley, SA
CELLAR 🍷 3
ALC./VOL. 13.5%
RRP $14.15

Peter Lehmann Mentor

The Lehmann marketeers are always looking for names for their wine styles. These days the legendary Peter Lehmann would be flat out finding a mentor. It is a role he naturally assumes by dint of decades of experience and achievement. Maker Andrew Wigan.
CURRENT RELEASE 1991 Does Bordeaux come to the Barossa? Never, but some of the components are there. The nose is laden with fruity berry aromas and the palate is rich and sweet. Cherry and raspberry are the main fruit flavours and they are supported by well-integrated oak. It drinks well now, try it with a rich cassoulet.

QUALITY ▼▼▼▼▼
VALUE ★★★★★
GRAPES cabernet sauvignon 61%, malbec 22%, shiraz 12%, merlot 5%
REGION Barossa Valley, SA
CELLAR 🍷 5
ALC./VOL. 13.5%
RRP $25.00

CURRENT RELEASE 1992 Gentle and complex wine that shows the benefit of bottle-age and careful blending. The colour is deep red and the nose has strong berry aromas and some smoky wood. The palate is soft but chewy with loads of berry fruit and a well-integrated oak component. The finish shows good-mannered French and American oak. It drinks well now with veal shanks.

QUALITY ▼▼▼▼⁞
VALUE ★★★★½
GRAPES cabernet sauvignon 71%, malbec 15%, shiraz 10%, merlot 4%
REGION Barossa Valley, SA
CELLAR 🍷 4
ALC./VOL. 13.0%
RRP $25.00

Peter Lehmann Shiraz

QUALITY ♛♛♛♛♛
VALUE ★★★★½
GRAPES shiraz
REGION Barossa Valley, SA
CELLAR 🍷 6
ALC./VOL. 14.0%
RRP $14.15

This is the Barossa's mother lode and few companies make it much finer than this. The price has taken a hike since last year but so have many other wines.
Previous outstanding vintages: '92, '93
CURRENT RELEASE 1994 As ever it is an opus of richness. The colour is an inviting dark plum and the nose is full of spice and ripe berries. The palate is succulent with some chewy textures and ripe-plum flavours. The oak sneaks in the back door adding grip. It is well balanced so it drinks well now. Try it with goose sandwiches.

Pewsey Vale Cabernet Sauvignon

QUALITY ♛♛♛♛
VALUE ★★★★
GRAPES cabernet sauvignon
REGION Eden Valley, SA
CELLAR 🍷 4
ALC./VOL. 12.0%
RRP $13.20

Pewsey Vale was originally established in 1847 by Joseph Gilbert. The Hill Smith clan revived the property and vineyard in 1961 with the object of producing quality riesling. Red wines were to follow.
CURRENT RELEASE 1994 Cool climate almost to a fault, but sophistication wins the day. The nose has ripe berry smells on a woody background. The middleweight palate has sweet blackberry flavours with a touch of leaf character. The finish is a mix of tannin and acid and it lingers long. It is a style that is suited to Italian food like osso bucco.

Pibbin Wines Pinot Noir

This winery was established in 1992. The cellar door is located in an 1890 cottage and there is bed and breakfast accommodation available. Maker Roger Salkeld.

CURRENT RELEASE 1993 There is a slightly feral/armpit character to the nose that would be much loved in France. There are also minty characters on both the nose and the palate. The major flavour is cherry and there is firm evidence of fine-grained tannin on a grippy finish. It needs a robust dish, try it with squab.

QUALITY 🍷🍷🍷🍷
VALUE ★★★½
GRAPES pinot noir
REGION Southern Vales, SA
CELLAR 🍾 3
ALC./VOL. 13.5%
RRP $17.00

CURRENT RELEASE 1994 The colour is a mid to light-ruby and the nose has fleshy, meaty aromas plus hints of berries. The palate is light to medium-bodied. The emphasis is on spice rather than fruit. There are light strawberry flavours. The acid on the finish adds an astringent dimension. It drinks well now, try it with baked quail.

QUALITY 🍷🍷🍷
VALUE ★★★
GRAPES pinot noir
REGION Adelaide Hills, SA
CELLAR 🍾 3
ALC./VOL. 13.6%
RRP $17.00

CURRENT RELEASE 1995 The colour is a very delicate pink and the nose has meaty pinot noir aromas plus a hint of fresh berries. The palate is fairly neutral with just a hint of strawberry and the finish shows some very positive acid. It should be served well chilled. Try it with a warm salad of yabbies.

QUALITY 🍷🍷🍷🍷
VALUE ★★★
GRAPES pinot noir
REGION Adelaide Hills, SA
CELLAR 🍾 3
ALC./VOL. 12.5%
RRP $17.00

Pierro Pinot Noir

This is one of the better presented wines from WA. Many Western Australian labels lack finesse when it comes to art design and quality. Maker Dr Mike Peterkin.

CURRENT RELEASE 1994 The colour plays the wine false. It is more powerful than the pale brick-red would suggest. There is a strong strawberry aroma on the nose and that is the major flavour on the palate. It also has loads of strong grip on the finish which tends to dominate. It goes well with pan-fried quail.

QUALITY 🍷🍷🍷
VALUE ★★½
GRAPES pinot noir
REGION Margaret River, WA
CELLAR 🍾 4
ALC./VOL. 12.5%
RRP $24.80

Pikes Clare Valley Shiraz

QUALITY 🍷🍷🍷🍷
VALUE ★★★★
GRAPES shiraz
REGION Clare Valley, SA
CELLAR 🍾 2–8
ALC./VOL. 13.5%
RRP $16.50

Proprietor Neil Pike is a Clare valley identity who founded his own winery with a little help from brother Andrew (who belongum Penfolds) and produces around 10 000 cases a year. Maker Neil Pike.

CURRENT RELEASE 1994 Vibrant colour and lively zest in this healthy bawling baby of a wine. The nose has plum and coffee oak aromas. The palate is tight blackberry flavours laced with coffee and high-toned oak. The finish is very dry with lots of oak. It needs time, try it with crumbed bangers and mash.

Pipers Brook Pellion Pinot Noir

QUALITY 🍷🍷🍷🍷🍷
VALUE ★★★★
GRAPES pinot noir
REGION Pipers Brook, Tas.
CELLAR 🍾 3
ALC./VOL. 12.3%
RRP $24.00

This is the jewel in the Tasmanian crown and it has been thus since the planting of the vineyard in 1974. Proprietors Andrew and Sabrina have a scholarly bent, hence the classical reference. Maker Andrew Pirie.

CURRENT RELEASE 1994 A wine that is ready to go but also blessed with entertaining complexity. The colour is dark cherry-red and there are raspberries and cherry flavours on the palate. These are laced with spice and the finish has fine-grained tannin and natural acidity. It is bella with pink lamb with a mint sauce.

Pirramimma Cabernet Sauvignon

QUALITY 🍷🍷🍷🍷
VALUE ★★★★
GRAPES cabernet sauvignon
REGION McLaren Vale, SA
CELLAR 🍾 3
ALC./VOL. 13.0%
RRP $15.65

This vineyard/winery was established in 1892 and today it produces around 40 000 cases and is expanding into the hills above McLaren Vale. Maker Geoff Johnson.

CURRENT RELEASE 1992 Good honest stuff that shows plenty of regional character. The colour is a deep crimson and the nose offers strong blackberry fruit aromas. There is also a hint of iron tonic flavour which gives way to soft tannins and a gentle finish. It drinks well with a Yorkshire hot pot.

Plantagenet Pinot Noir

Gavin Berry has continued the reputation John Wade established for Plantagenet. His skills even extend to the most fickle grape of all.
Previous outstanding vintages: '90, '91, '92, '93
CURRENT RELEASE 1994 Another great success for this marque, a quite burgundian pinot with cherry, gamey and burnt-sugar characters and a silky, almost oily, glycerol-rich texture. Terrific with barbecued field mushrooms in herbs and olive oil.

QUALITY 🍷🍷🍷🍷
VALUE ★★★
GRAPES pinot noir
REGION Mount Barker, WA
CELLAR 🍾 2
ALC./VOL. 13.5%
RRP $22.50

Plantagenet Shiraz

Plantagenet owner Tony Smith is an English migrant who can trace his lineage back to the royals of that name. Maker Gavin Berry.
Previous outstanding vintages: '76, '77, '83, '84, '85, '88, '90, '91, '92, '93
CURRENT RELEASE 1994 The alcohol strength has jumped but the wine still shows typical Plantagenet character. The nose is intensely peppery with a certain vegetable overtone and the French oak is stylish and discreet. In the mouth it has lovely fruit sweetness and smoothness with elegant weight. A distinctive style. Serve with pepperpot stew.

QUALITY 🍷🍷🍷🍷
VALUE ★★★
GRAPES shiraz
REGION Mount Barker, WA
CELLAR 🍾 8+
ALC./VOL. 14.5%
RRP $22.50

Port Phillip Estate Reserve Pinot Noir

This vineyard is owned by Melbourne QC Jeffrey Sher and his wife Diana. The wine is made by local pinot exponent Lindsay McCall of Paringa Estate.
CURRENT RELEASE 1995 It's won two gold medals and we can see why: this is a delightful pinot and more evidence that pinot is part of the Peninsula's future. The colour has good depth and the nose has complex smoky, gamey and sappy pinot/oak interactions. The palate has tremendous depth of lush fruit, good richness and surprising tannin astringency. Perfect with roast duck.

QUALITY 🍷🍷🍷🍷🍷
VALUE ★★★★½
GRAPES pinot noir
REGION Mornington Peninsula, Vic.
CELLAR 🍾 5
ALC./VOL. 13.0%
RRP $18.00 (cellar door)

Best Pinot Noir

Preece Cabernet Sauvignon

QUALITY ♘♘♘♘
VALUE ★★★★
GRAPES cabernet sauvignon
REGION mainly Goulburn & King Valleys, Vic.
CELLAR 🍷 5+
ALC./VOL. 13.0%
RRP $14.65 ⓢ

Winemaking legend Colin Preece was in retirement from his role as Seppelt's winemaker at Great Western when he consulted on the establishment of Mitchelton.
CURRENT RELEASE 1994 Like the current chardonnay release, this is a step up from the previous vintage. The colour, aroma and flavour all show good concentration of stylish berry fruit flavours and sensitive use of quality oak. The '94 also reflects a better season than '93. Drinks well with lamb.

Prentice LeRoy's Blend

QUALITY ♘♘♘♘
VALUE ★★★★
GRAPES mourvedre, grenache, shiraz
REGION not stated
CELLAR 🍷 4
ALC./VOL. 13.0%
RRP $18.00

Neil Prentice is well known in Melbourne wine and cafe circles. He has taken a passionate hobby into a serious business.
CURRENT RELEASE 1994 Inspired by Chateauneuf du Pape and it comes very close in style. The colour is mid-ruby and the nose has plum, berry and spice aromas. The palate is complex with plum and cherry flavours and the finish confirms the balance and adds grip. Very good with a game pie.

Primo Estate Adelaide Shiraz

QUALITY ♘♘♘♘
VALUE ★★★★
GRAPES shiraz
REGION Adelaide Plains, SA
CELLAR 🍷 3
ALC./VOL. 13.0%
RRP $16.50

The maker continually manages to produce fine wines from the hot lands of the Adelaide plains. In this case traditional techniques like open fermenters have been used. Maker Joe Grilli.
CURRENT RELEASE 1994 Civilised style that shows admirable expression of fruit characters and a deft use of oak. The colour is a deep brick-red and the vinous nose has plenty of berry aromas. The palate is medium-bodied with cherry and raspberry flavours. Well-tuned oak adds structure to a balanced finish. It drinks well now with marinated lamb fillets.

Prince Albert Pinot Noir

This vineyard was established in 1975 by Bruce Hyett and it is devoted to the production of pinot noir only. It produces 600 cases a year. At cellar door you can buy the unfiltered version of the current release. Maker Bruce Hyett.
CURRENT RELEASE 1994 The colour is a medium-ruby with a hint of brick-red. The nose has dark cherry and strawberry aromas plus a hint of mint. The medium-bodied palate has sweet berry flavours which are backed by some well-mannered French oak on a lingering finish. It is great with a mushroom risotto.

QUALITY ♛♛♛♛
VALUE ★★★★
GRAPES pinot noir
REGION Geelong, Vic.
CELLAR 🍷 6
ALC./VOL. 13.0%
RRP $19.00

Red Hill Estate Pinot Noir

If your forte is méthode champenoise, there is little doubt there will be a chardonnay and pinot noir table wine lurking at the back of the winery. Most makers can't resist the temptation. Maker Jenny Bright (viticulturist John Runting).
CURRENT RELEASE 1994 A typical regional style that is easy to drink. The nose offers cherry and violet aroma. The palate continues the cherry flavours plus adds some stewed plums. The finish shows plenty of backbone and fine-grained tannins. It drinks well now, try it with a squab pie.

QUALITY ♛♛♛♛
VALUE ★★★★
GRAPES pinot noir
REGION Mornington Peninsula, Vic.
CELLAR 🍷 4
ALC./VOL. 12.5%
RRP $21.00

Red Rock Pinot Noir

Still they come: this is a new vineyard from a new area. The Otway Ranges are south-east of Melbourne.
CURRENT RELEASE 1995 A pleasant debut with good varietal character. The colour is a pale cherry-red and the nose is full of strawberry aroma with a hint of perfume. The light-bodied palate has sweet strawberry flavours and there is clean acid on the finish. Try it with char-grilled ocean trout.

QUALITY ♛♛♛
VALUE ★★★
GRAPES pinot noir
REGION Otway Ranges, Vic.
CELLAR 🍷 2
ALC./VOL. 11.5%
RRP $20.00

Redbank Sally's Paddock

QUALITY ♛♛♛♛
VALUE ★★½
GRAPES cabernet sauvignon, shiraz, cabernet franc, malbec, merlot
REGION Pyrenees, Vic.
CELLAR 🍷 2–6
ALC./VOL. 12.0%
RRP $32.45

Named after the proprietor's wife, Sally Robb, this has always been an individual style with an eclectic mix of grape varieties. Maker Neill Robb. Previous outstanding vintages: '80, '81, '82, '86, '88, '90, '91, '92

CURRENT RELEASE 1994 A lean style that is not without charm. The nose is complex with pepper, spice and plum aromas. The palate has a slight green-fruit character with lots of pepper and spice. The main flavour is plum. Acid is the major component on the finish which is long and astringent. It goes well with bratwurst sausages.

Redgate Cabernet Sauvignon

QUALITY ♛♛♛♛
VALUE ★★★★
GRAPES cabernet sauvignon 95%, cabernet franc 5%
REGION Margaret River, WA
CELLAR 🍷 6
ALC./VOL. 13.2%
RRP $19.00

The name Redgate comes from a nearby beach where the SS *Georgette* foundered 101 years before the vineyard was planted.

CURRENT RELEASE 1993 This is a typical regional cabernet sauvignon. It has a leafy cassis nose with a hint of rose petals, the palate is intense with ripe cherry flavours that are framed by American oak. The finish shows off some toasty vanillan oak and grippy tannins. It drinks well after breathing. Try it with a rare eye fillet steak.

Redgate Cabernet Sauvignon Reserve

QUALITY ♛♛♛♛♛
VALUE ★★★★½
GRAPES cabernet sauvignon
REGION Margaret River, WA
CELLAR 🍷 2–6
ALC./VOL. 13.3%
RRP $29.00

This company was founded in 1976 by Bill Ullinger and his son Paul. It is located 3 kms from the Indian Ocean. Maker Andrew Forsell.

CURRENT RELEASE 1993 Very Margaret River in terms of style. It is one of the better examples with a deep red/garnet colour. The nose is a mixture of blackberry, cigar box and leaf aromas. The palate is concentrated with sweet blackberry flavours and dark cherry. There is a strong leaf and herbal character that makes the transition to an oaky finish. The tannin supplies plenty of grip. It can be served now with roast squab.

Redgate Pinot Noir

Still they come, sharpening lances to tilt at the pinot windmill. This one has had a considerable amount of winemaking effort during its construction.

CURRENT RELEASE 1993 The colour is a mid-ruby and the nose has some succulent berry aromas with hints of earth. The palate is sweet with strong cherry flavours and there is a hint of truffle character. The finish is dominated by acid. It drinks well now and goes nicely with lamb shanks.

QUALITY ????
VALUE ★★★½
GRAPES pinot noir
REGION Margaret River, WA
CELLAR ▮ 3
ALC./VOL. 12.8%
RRP $19.00

Redman Cabernet Sauvignon

Redman only make red wines in the belief that 'every white wine would be a red if it had a choice'. Fair enough.

CURRENT RELEASE 1994 Very young and fit wine that has far to go. It has a vinous nose with some primary ferment aromas and strong cherry smells. The middleweight palate is dominated by sweet fruit, particularly blackcurrant and cherry and there is a hint of mint. The oak makes for a tinder dry finish with fine-grained tannins. It goes well with a rare char-grilled steak.

QUALITY ????
VALUE ★★★★
GRAPES cabernet sauvignon
REGION Coonawarra, SA
CELLAR ▮ 5
ALC./VOL. 12.5%
RRP $19.00

Redman Cabernet Sauvignon Merlot

As a piece of history, the Redman family sold Rouge Homme (Frog for Redman) to Rothmans (which owned Lindemans) in the 1960s and moved just up the road to found Redman.

CURRENT RELEASE 1992 The nose tells porky pies. It is bursting with ripe, almost jammy fruit aromas. The palate is quite elegant and almost austere with reluctant raspberry fruit flavours. American oak on the finish supplies a vanillan lift and there is pleasing grip. It goes well with meatloaf.

QUALITY ????
VALUE ★★★
GRAPES cabernet sauvignon, merlot
REGION Coonawarra, SA
CELLAR ▮ 3
ALC./VOL. 13.0%
RRP $19.00

Redman Coonawarra Shiraz

QUALITY ♥♥♥♪
VALUE ★★★★
GRAPES shiraz
REGION Coonawarra, SA
CELLAR 🍷 3
ALC./VOL. 13.0%
RRP $12.50 Ⓢ

In days of yore this used to be known as a 'claret.' It was always the wine in the portfolio that was made for early drinking. Makers Bruce and Malcolm Redman.

CURRENT RELEASE 1994 A very drinkable style that has regional integrity and excellent fruit. The nose is a mix of spice and cherry-fruit aromas. The palate continues the cherry theme and there is discreet oak on a well-balanced finish. It is great with gnocchi and a meat sauce.

Renmano Chairman's Selection Cabernet Sauvignon

QUALITY ♥♥♥♥
VALUE ★★★★
GRAPES cabernet sauvignon
REGION Riverland, SA
CELLAR 🍷 3
ALC./VOL. 13.0%
RRP $11.00 Ⓢ

Part of the BRL Hardy line-up and usually very good value for money. The packaging is a bit bush league so decanting can save you looking at the bottle. Maker Fiona Donald.

CURRENT RELEASE 1994 Very healthy colour of bright ruby and the nose is full of berry and cherries. The palate is quite rich with succulent berry flavours and the oak has been well tailored to give support to the fruit and adds grip to the balanced finish. It drinks well now and it goes a treat with steak and eggs.

Renmano Chairman's Selection Shiraz

QUALITY ♥♥♥♥
VALUE ★★★★
GRAPES shiraz
REGION Riverland, SA
CELLAR 🍷 4
ALC./VOL. 13.0%
RRP $11.00 Ⓢ

Most chairpersons we know couldn't tell wine from cod liver oil. The notion of a chairperson choosing the wine is not encouraging but you can depend on this brand because the winemaker does all the selection.

CURRENT RELEASE 1994 A fine wine from commercial grapes in a mammoth winery. The nose is spicy with plum and coconut aromas. The palate is medium-bodied with ripe plum flavours that are supported by coconut oak on the dry finish. It is well balanced and ready to go. Try it with a traditional mince meat pie.

Ribbon Vale Cabernet Sauvignon

This small winery has an output of 3500 cases per year from a 7-ha. vineyard.
CURRENT RELEASE 1993 An authentic style that has spent 18 months in wood. The colour is deep and the nose has blackberry and oak aromas. The middleweight palate is quite hard with blackberry fruit and a strong oak influence. Oak is the taskmaster on the finish which is long and firm. It needs more time in the bottle. Try it with steak and kidney pie.

QUALITY ♛♛♛♝
VALUE ★★★½
GRAPES cabernet sauvignon
REGION Margaret River, WA
CELLAR ➡ 2–5
ALC./VOL. 13.0%
RRP $18.00

Ribbon Vale Cabernet Sauvignon Merlot

This vineyard was established in 1977 at Willyabrup. If you look at the map of southern Western Australia you'll notice most of the locations end in 'up'. The suffix means 'available fresh water' in the local Aboriginal dialect. Maker Mike Davies.
CURRENT RELEASE 1993 Someone has been over this with a spanner – it is very tight. The colour is deep red-purple and the nose is vinous. The palate is unyielding with firm fruit and a reluctant dark cherry flavour. Black tea-like tannins make for a very firm finish that is astringent and almost stalky. It responds to breathing and can be served with baked kid.

QUALITY ♛♛♛♝
VALUE ★★★½
GRAPES cabernet sauvignon 90%, merlot 10%
REGION Margaret River, WA
CELLAR ➡ 2–6
ALC./VOL. 13.0%
RRP $18.00

Richard Hamilton Grenache Shiraz

QUALITY 🍷🍷🍷🍷
VALUE ★★★★½
GRAPES grenache 60%, shiraz 40%
REGION McLaren Vale, SA
CELLAR 🍾 5
ALC./VOL. 13.5%
RRP $14.00

The grapes were grown in Burton's Vineyard (Burton Hamilton) which was planted in 1914. Old vines indeed. Maker Ralph Fowler.
Previous outstanding vintages: '93
CURRENT RELEASE 1995 A bit more serious than some of the surfers of the grenache tidal wave. This is old-fashioned in style but very youthful in character. The nose is savoury with spice and raspberry fruit aromas. The medium-bodied palate has sweet raspberry flavours with a hint of earth. The finish is dry and dusty and adds balance to the equation. It drinks well now with devilled kidneys.

Richard Hamilton Hut Block Cabernet Sauvignon

QUALITY 🍷🍷🍷🍷
VALUE ★★★★½
GRAPES cabernet sauvignon
REGION McLaren Vale, SA
CELLAR 🍾 3–8
ALC./VOL. 13.0%
RRP $15.35

The hut is real and it is rustic to the max. Funny they don't feature it on the label – everyone else would.
Previous outstanding vintages: '93
CURRENT RELEASE 1995 This wine is only a pup, it's still in nappies. The nose is inky with strong blackberry aromas on a ferric background (a regional characteristic). The palate has a middle like one of the authors, round and generous. Blackberry is the major flavour and there is a splash of spice. The finish shows youthful and slightly raw tannin with loads of grip. It needs time, try it with jugged hare.

Richmond Grove Barossa Shiraz

We are confused. Richmond Grove started life as a vineyard and winery named Hollydeen in the upper Hunter Valley. It was changed to Richmond Grove and acquired by Wyndham which in turn was acquired by Orlando. Now the name is applied to wines from South Australia. Makers Steve Clarkson, John Vickery.

CURRENT RELEASE 1993 The emphasis is on drinkability. The colour is a deep crimson and the nose is spicy with hints of leaf and herbs. There is plenty of sweet berry flavour on the relatively simple palate and discreet oak on the finish makes it a hot-to-trot style. Try it with a casserole of kid.

QUALITY ♥♥♥⁄
VALUE ★★★½
GRAPES shiraz
REGION Barossa Valley, SA
CELLAR 🍾 3
ALC./VOL. 12.0%
RRP $9.90 Ⓢ

Richmond Grove Coonawarra Cabernet Sauvignon

There are no boundaries to the Richmond Grove brand. The objective seems to be the production of affordable commercial wines.

CURRENT RELEASE 1993 A drinkable style with a herbal nose with hints of cigar box and berry fruit aromas. The palate has sweet cassis flavour and the finish is acid dominated with fine-grained tannin taking a back seat. It drinks well now, try it with pan-fried veal in a tomato sauce.

QUALITY ♥♥♥♥
VALUE ★★★★½
GRAPES cabernet sauvignon
REGION Coonawarra, SA
CELLAR 🍾 3
ALC./VOL. 13.0%
RRP $9.90 Ⓢ

Riddoch Coonawarra Cabernet Shiraz

This is the mid-range for the Katnook Winery. It has always stood for easy drinkability and good value. Maker Wayne Stehbens.

CURRENT RELEASE 1994 A young healthy wine that is very friendly on the palate. The colour is a bright red-purple. The nose is spicy with pepper, plum and ripe berry aromas. The palate is medium to full-bodied with ripe raspberry fruit flavours and these are tied to some well-mannered oak on a well-balanced finish. It drinks well with a seared T-bone steak, and don't forget the eggs.

QUALITY ♥♥♥♥
VALUE ★★★★
GRAPES cabernet sauvignon 56%, shiraz 44%
REGION Coonawarra, SA
CELLAR 🍾 5
ALC./VOL. 13.5%
RRP $13.00

Riddoch Run (The) Cabernet Sauvignon

QUALITY ♛♛♛♛♛
VALUE ★★★★★
GRAPES cabernet sauvignon
REGION Coonawarra, SA
CELLAR 🍾 10+
ALC./VOL. 14.2%
RRP $16.10

From the next vintage, this will revert to the Rymill brand. The winery and vineyard are owned by Peter Rymill, a direct descendant of the 'father of Coonawarra', John Riddoch.
Previous outstanding vintages: '91, '92
CURRENT RELEASE 1993 This powerful cabernet has a subdued nose which needs air to open up and reveal its best. Big volume of flavour, high alcohol, firm grip: a Charles Atlas kind of Coonawarra. The flavours are savoury and complex rather than fruity, and the huge finish lingers on and on. Try it with pot-au-feu. Great value.

Riddoch Run (The) Shiraz

QUALITY ♛♛♛♛½
VALUE ★★★★½
GRAPES shiraz
REGION Coonawarra, SA
CELLAR 🍾 10
ALC./VOL. 14.0%
RRP $14.50

Peter Rymill has recently erected a stunning winery which promises to be a new showpiece for the district. For many years he's been one of Coonawarra's biggest contract grapegrowers. Maker John Innes.
Previous outstanding vintages: '91, '92
CURRENT RELEASE 1993 A super-ripe, opulent style of Coonawarra shiraz, jam-packed with sweet, round, chunky fruit in the cherry/plum range, and embellished with licorice and spice. A complex but not oaky style to drink with steak and kidney pie.

Rochford Premier Pinot Noir

Rochford is the hobby of engineer Bruce Dowding, whose approach is far more professional than the average hobbyist. The pinot is exciting but the cabernet rather green. Previous outstanding vintages: '91, '92, '93
CURRENT RELEASE 1994 This is concentrated pinot in colour, nose and taste, but the acid is also rather high, making it very much a food wine. There are sappy, briary and vegetable notes to the bouquet and the palate is seriously powerful, but also somewhat astringent. Deep, long and structured, it should age well. Serve with veal sweetbreads.

QUALITY ♟♟♟♟⸮
VALUE ★★★½
GRAPES pinot noir
REGION Macedon, Vic.
CELLAR ⸺ 1–5+
ALC./VOL. 13.0%
RRP $28.00

Rosabrook Estate Cabernet Merlot

This Margaret River vineyard was established in 1980 on Rosa Brook Road. The CEO, Dan Pannell, is from a winemaking dynasty in these parts.
CURRENT RELEASE 1994 An attractive style with certain Italian leanings. The nose has plenty of berry aroma an hints of leaves and wood. The palate offers sweet blackberry fruit flavours with hints of leaves and spices. The finish is dry and there is ample dusty oak. It drinks well now with pork fillet in a mango sauce.

QUALITY ♟♟♟♟
VALUE ★★★★
GRAPES cabernet sauvignon 80%, merlot 20%
REGION Margaret River, WA
CELLAR ▯ 5
ALC./VOL. 13.8%
RRP $16.00

Rosabrook Estate Shiraz

QUALITY ♛♛♛♛
VALUE ★★★★
GRAPES shiraz
REGION Margaret River, WA
CELLAR 🍷 5
ALC./VOL. 13.1%
RRP $15.95

Slaughter House 5 – the cellar door is located in an old abattoir circa 1930. These days the red stuff is in the bottle. So it goes. Maker Dan Pannell.
CURRENT RELEASE 1994 A handy wine that drinks well now. The nose is plummy with wafts of leaves and spices. The palate is medium-bodied and dominated by ripe plum flavours lifted with spice. There are gripping tanins and acid on the finish which is long and dry. It drinks well with pork and white beans.

Rosemount Balmoral Syrah

QUALITY ♛♛♛♛♛
VALUE ★★★½
GRAPES shiraz
REGION McLaren Vale, SA
CELLAR ➤ 2–10
ALC./VOL. 13.2%
RRP $40.00

Balmoral is a suburb in Brisbane and the name of a property, circa 1852, owned by the Oatley family who also belongum Rosemount. Why they use syrah when shiraz would be perfectly adequate is probably a marketing foible. Maker Phil Shaw.
Previous outstanding vintages: '89, '90, '91, '92
CURRENT RELEASE 1993 Bold, brawny and buxom. The colour is a deep red-purple. The nose has developed fruit aromas plus spice and oak smells. The mouth-filling palate is a mix of blackberry and plums which are laced with lively spice. There is the usual regional length of palate and the finish supplies fine-grained tannin plus lingering acid. It has far to go, try it now with an aged bitey cheddar.

Rosemount Estate Shiraz Cabernet

This wine won the RAS Value Award in the 1996 Sydney show. Who are we to disagree?
CURRENT RELEASE 1995 A soft, flavoursome red which drinks well now. The colour is a deep ruby and the berry-scented nose has a leafy background. There is rich plum flavour on the palate and this is enlivened by herb flavours. The finish is soft, making the wine easy to drink. Great with pink lamb chops.

QUALITY 🍷🍷🍷🍷
VALUE ★★★★★
GRAPES shiraz, cabernet sauvignon
REGION various
CELLAR 🍾 3
ALC./VOL. 12.0%
RRP $9.95

Rosemount Rose Label McLaren Vale Shiraz

Beautiful label that features a stylised rendition of a rose that could well grace a poster for the opera *Carmen*. It seems set to be a very impressive part of the Rosemount portfolio. Maker Phil Shaw.
CURRENT RELEASE 1993 It is a synergy between McLaren Vale regional character and American oak. The colour is a deep crimson with purple highlights. The nose is dominated by vanilla and custard powder aromas from the oak. The palate is medium-bodied with attractive blackberry flavour with spices like clove and nutmeg. The finish brings down a solid American oak curtain.

QUALITY 🍷🍷🍷🍷
VALUE ★★★★
GRAPES shiraz
REGION McLaren Vale, SA
CELLAR 🍾 5
ALC./VOL. 13.0%
RRP $20.00

Rosemount Show Reserve Cabernet Sauvignon

The grapes for this wine come from a vineyard very close to the town of Penola. When it was planted it was supposed to be on the last available terra rossa soil. Somehow wine companies keep finding more. Maker Phil Shaw.
CURRENT RELEASE 1993 A tough little number that will only be tamed by bottle-age. It is typically Coonawarra down to the boot straps. The nose has strong blackberry aromas plus a hint of leaves. Blackberry is the major theme on the palate and there is also a hint of tobacco. The finish is astringent and a tad hard at present. It is tough enough for tea-smoked duck.

QUALITY 🍷🍷🍷🍷
VALUE ★★★★
GRAPES cabernet sauvignon
REGION Coonawarra, SA
CELLAR ⇒ 3–8
ALC./VOL. 13.5%
RRP $22.00

Salitage Pinot Noir

QUALITY ♛♛♛♛
VALUE ★★★
GRAPES pinot noir
REGION Pemberton, WA
CELLAR 🍾 1–5+
ALC./VOL. 13.9%
RRP $30.40

Pemberton/Manjimup is shaping up as a fine region for pinot. We just need to wind the clock forward to when the vines are more mature. Previous outstanding vintages: '93, '94
CURRENT RELEASE 1995 This has a light-medium purple-red colour which belies the wine's imposing structure. The aromas are of cherry and subtle oak, somewhat undeveloped. The palate carries a lot of tannin and the oaky astringency demands you drink it with food – at least while it's so young. It should reward cellaring.

Saltram Barossa Reserve Cabernet Sauvignon

QUALITY ♛♛♛♛♟
VALUE ★★★★
GRAPES cabernet sauvignon
REGION Barossa Valley, SA
CELLAR 🍾 4–15+
ALC./VOL. 14.0%
RRP $20.00

The Barossa Reserve label is a newie from Saltram, with a shiraz and a chardonnay also in the series. Maker Nigel Dolan.
CURRENT RELEASE 1994 Another blinder '94 red from Saltram. This is terrifically concentrated, a big mother with solid tannic structure and density. Its Schwarzenegger grip is obviously designed for the long haul. Leave it till at least 2000, and pair it with a hearty meat casserole.

Saltram Barossa Reserve Grenache

QUALITY ♛♛♛♛♟
VALUE ★★★★
GRAPES grenache
REGION Barossa Valley, SA
CELLAR 🍾 5
ALC./VOL. 13.8%
RRP $15.00

The label notes say grenache was once the most widespread grape variety in the Barossa. Right now it's having its Second Coming.
CURRENT RELEASE 1995 Sweet grapey, confectionery, typical ripe grenache nose, exuberantly fruit-driven and with a hint of spice. The palate has deep rich flavour of deliciously intense spiciness and rounds off with nice drying tannins. A classy grenache. Try it with rabbit casserole.

Saltram Mamre Brook Cabernet Shiraz

What is it about the name that gives us a warm, cosy feeling about suckling at the breast of old mother Barossa?
CURRENT RELEASE 1994 1994 was obviously a successful year for Saltram reds. This is shy and closed to sniff, but what a palate! There are toasty and spicy flavours, vaguely discernible among the tannin and tight-packed density of the wine. Much of the flavour is latent and it needs air. There's excellent concentration and backbone. Cellar, then serve with saddle of hare.

QUALITY ♙♙♙♙♟
VALUE ★★★★
GRAPES cabernet sauvignon 73%, shiraz 19%, malbec 8%
REGION Barossa Valley, SA
CELLAR ▬ 1–10+
ALC./VOL. 13.2%
RRP $17.70

Sandalford Cabernet Sauvignon

Sandalford owns the largest vineyard in the Margaret River region, and in recent times the quality of the wines has rocketed. Maker Bill Crappsley.
CURRENT RELEASE 1994 Now you're talking! Sandalford has joined the elite group of fine Margaret River cab makers with this lovely bottle of red. It has a deep colour, a strongly American oak influenced nose featuring coconut and vanilla, and a rich, full palate which packs a punch. The oak is cleverly used and the wine is full and satisfying on the finish. Serve with roast beef

QUALITY ♙♙♙♙♟
VALUE ★★★★½
GRAPES cabernet sauvignon
REGION Mount Barker, Margaret River, Swan Valley, WA
CELLAR ↑ 8+
ALC./VOL. 12.5%
RRP $18.50

Sandalford Caversham Cabernet Shiraz

This is the basic Sandalford red, a new line made from grapes grown in the Swan Valley, where the winery is located. Maker Bill Crappsley.
CURRENT RELEASE 1994 Fresh red-purple hue and vivid berry fruit characters on the nose. Light, straightforward leafy and berry taste, without much wood. The palate has a slight dip in the middle but it's very drinkable. Could also be kept with confidence as it has some tightness in structure. Goes well with Mongolian lamb.

QUALITY ♙♙♙
VALUE ★★★
GRAPES cabernet sauvignon, shiraz
REGION Swan Valley, WA
CELLAR ↑ 3+
ALC./VOL. 13.0%
RRP $12.00

Sandalford Shiraz

QUALITY 🍷🍷🍷🍷🍷
VALUE ★★★★
GRAPES shiraz
REGION Margaret River & Mount Barker, WA
CELLAR 🍾 8+
ALC./VOL. 13.0%
RRP $17.00

This won a gold medal at the '95 Mount Barker Show, one of the better-run regional wine competitions in Australia.
CURRENT RELEASE 1994 A beguiling fruit-driven shiraz with strong pepperminty nose and lashings of rich, ripe fruit. There's a liberal rejoinder of tannin to balance the sweet fruit on the finish. The mintiness is a thread that runs throughout. Drink with lamb and mint sauce.

Schinus Cabernet

QUALITY 🍷🍷🍷🍷
VALUE ★★★★
GRAPES cabernet sauvignon
REGION King Valley, Vic.
CELLAR 🍾 4
ALC./VOL. 13.5%
RRP $14.00 (cellar door)

The King Valley has proved a happy hunting ground for Garry Crittenden. The cabernet grapes comes entirely from there. You can buy this wine by the glass for $4 at the winery restaurant on the Mornington Peninsula.
CURRENT RELEASE 1994 Sweet, fresh, simple but lifted blackcurrant cabernet aromas, which translate to a smooth, accessible palate. It's medium-bodied, soft and supple with drink-now charm and moderate length. Try it with milk-fed veal.

Scotchmans Hill Pinot Noir

QUALITY 🍷🍷🍷🍷🍷
VALUE ★★★★
GRAPES pinot noir
REGION Geelong, Vic.
CELLAR 🍾 3
ALC./VOL. 13.0%
RRP $19.00

The Brownes of Scotchmans Hill have bought another Drysdale property called Spray Farm and they are bent on expanding. Maker Robin Brockett.
Previous outstanding vintages: '90, '91, '92, '93
CURRENT RELEASE 1994 Still one of the best pinots around, and doesn't cost the earth. Good depth of colour and a rich gamey burgundian bouquet that shows spicy cherry fruit and a stylish touch of oak. Sweet fruit on the complex palate is gentle but penetrating, with a smooth finish. Try it with beef carpaccio.

Seaview Cabernet Sauvignon

Seaview claims to have been the first to market a varietally labelled cabernet, the 1951 vintage. That makes this the 44th of the line. Maker Mike Farmilo.
CURRENT RELEASE 1994 A style which harks back to the friendly, smooth Seaview reds of yore. Deep of hue and rich of taste, it smells of toasty oak and ripe berryish fruit and the tannins are smooth but persistent. It's a gutsy full-bodied red for serving with rare kangaroo.

QUALITY ♛♛♛♛
VALUE ★★★★½
GRAPES cabernet sauvignon
REGION McLaren Vale, Coonawarra, Padthaway, SA
CELLAR 🍾 4+
ALC./VOL. 13.5%
RRP $12.00

Seaview Shiraz

Seaview is a burgeoning brand these days, the Southcorp marketers stacking the famous old name up with dry whites, sparkling wines and super-reserve labels. Maker Mike Farmilo.
CURRENT RELEASE 1993 A ready-drinking shiraz of easy drinkability but no major impact. Cassis, blackcurrant and mint reveal themselves to the nose and the taste is quite acid with a certain leanness. Should handle hamburgers well.

QUALITY ♛♛♛
VALUE ★★★
GRAPES shiraz
REGION McLaren Vale, SA
CELLAR 🍾 3
ALC./VOL. 13.0%
RRP $10.00

CURRENT RELEASE 1994 Smoky toasty nose from ripe fruit and nicely handled oak. Berry flavours in the mouth: rich, ripe and warm. A real crowd-pleaser which has more strength and oak than expected at the price. Serve with pork spare ribs.

QUALITY ♛♛♛
VALUE ★★★½
GRAPES shiraz
REGION McLaren Vale, SA
CELLAR 🍾 5
ALC./VOL. 13.5%
RRP $11.00

Seppelt Chalambar Shiraz

QUALITY 🍷🍷🍷🍷
VALUE ★★★½
GRAPES shiraz
REGION Great Western, Pyrenees, Geelong, Ovens Valley & Strathbogie Ranges, Vic.
CELLAR 🍾 5
ALC./VOL. 12.5%
RRP $14.60 $

Chalambar is the name of a hill at Ararat, near Great Western. It used to be a commercial red Burgundy style which Seppelt deleted for a while, then resurrected recently as part of the 'Victorian portfolio'.
CURRENT RELEASE 1993 Lovely cool-area shiraz aromatics – pepper, spices and berries – thoroughly tantalising. Elegant mediumweight palate which has subtle wood, softness and poise. Very appealing current drinking style. Try it with lamb kebabs.

Seppelt Dorrien Cabernet Sauvignon

QUALITY 🍷🍷🍷🍷🍷
VALUE ★★★★½
GRAPES cabernet sauvignon
REGION Barossa Valley, SA
CELLAR 🍾 10+
ALC./VOL. 13.0%
RRP $26.00 $ 🍾

Dorrien is a famous Seppelt vineyard on the Barossa Valley floor near Tanunda. Dorrien cabernet is only sold in the very best vintages. The '91 has won nine gold medals and two trophies. Maker Ian McKenzie and team.
Previous outstanding vintages: '80, '88, '90
CURRENT RELEASE 1991 Dense and chunky, this exciting cabernet will be a long-liver. A typical Barossa red, it is one of the better Dorriens we can remember. The nose is spicy, minty, ripe and earthy. There is some coconutty oak showing and the texture is rich and fleshy with plenty of extract and a good grip on the finish. Serve with venison cutlets.

Seppelt Drumborg Cabernet Sauvignon

The Seppelt individual vineyard reds have been repackaged in smart new dark labels and tall, elegant, heavy-glass bottles. They really look the part. Drumborg is a cool-climate vineyard in south-western Victoria.
CURRENT RELEASE 1991 This is obviously made from cool-grown grapes: elegance is the key word, with refined flavours, tightness and length. The nose shows cedar, berries and mint, and the palate is smooth and supple with a gentle balance, fine style and persistence. Could be the best Drumborg cab yet. Serve with pink lamb.

QUALITY ♛♛♛♛♛
VALUE ★★★★
GRAPES cabernet sauvignon
REGION Portland, Vic.
CELLAR 🍾 10+
ALC./VOL. 12.0%
RRP $26.00 Ⓢ

Seppelt Great Western Shiraz

Seppelt has been making outstanding shiraz from its old vines at Great Western since the early 1950s, when Colin Preece was in command. They are still among the great reds of Australia.
Previous outstanding vintages: '54, '62, '67, '71, '85, '86, '88
CURRENT RELEASE 1991 Colin Preece would have approved of this one! It's a great, rich, sensuous lump of a wine with deep, ripe licorice and spicy/berry flavours and a really drying tannin finish. The nose has dry, earthy regional characters and the wine, although formidably concentrated and tannic, is smooth, friendly and approachable at five years. The tannin is balanced by wonderful fruit sweetness. Enjoy it with game.

QUALITY ♛♛♛♛♛
VALUE ★★★★★
GRAPES shiraz
REGION Grampians, Vic.
CELLAR 🍾 10+
ALC./VOL. 13.5%
RRP $26.00 Ⓢ

Sharefarmers Vineyard Red

QUALITY ♀♀♀
VALUE ★★★
GRAPES malbec 38%, cabernet sauvignon 30%, merlot 19%, cabernet franc 13%
REGION Coonawarra, SA
CELLAR 🍾 4
ALC./VOL. 13.5%
RRP $14.50

Petaluma is making hay while it can here: the label says Coonawarra but the odds are stacked against them as the vineyard is on the wrong side of a critical boundary line. It's Petaluma's bistro-style red.

CURRENT RELEASE 1993 Very herbaceous green-leafy cabernet and malbec aromas dominate this wine. The palate has blackcurrant ripe cabernet flavours as well as length and grip, but the green mint taste is rather strong and the acid pronounced. OK quality, but a little raw for a restaurant wine.

Shottesbrooke Merlot

QUALITY ♀♀♀♀⟨
VALUE ★★★★½
GRAPES merlot
REGION McLaren Vale, SA
CELLAR 🍾 6
ALC./VOL. 13.0%
RRP $18.00

Things have got serious for proprietor/winemaker Nick Holmes. He started this label as a hobby and now he's producing 7000 cases and setting up his own winery.

CURRENT RELEASE 1995 This is a very convincing wine with great structure. The colour is a vibrant ruby and the nose is perfumed with plenty of spice. The palate is rich with sweet succulent raspberry and some capsicum flavours. Oak takes a back-seat role making for an elegant finish. It is a well-balanced wine that drinks well now. Try it with rabbit casserole.

St Hallett Faith Shiraz

QUALITY ♀♀♀♀
VALUE ★★★★
GRAPES shiraz
REGION Barossa Valley, SA
CELLAR 🍾 5+
ALC./VOL. 12.5%
RRP $16.00

O come all ye faithful! The name of St Hallett's new second-string shiraz, while it refers to the Faith Lutheran school next door to the Faith vineyard, has the ring of preacher Bob McLean addressing his flock about it. A non-export label.

CURRENT RELEASE 1994 Very different style to the Old Block. A leaner, less-oaky, earthy and lightly spicy shiraz of elegance and structure. It has less opulence but good length and balance. Drink with rare barbecued veal.

St Hallett Gamekeeper's Reserve

Bob McLean is a dedicated brand-builder. This is the running-mate of the Poacher's Reserve white.
CURRENT RELEASE 1995 This is a very flavoursome drink-now red, soft and spicy with some crushed black pepper character and lightly handled oak. For easy drinking while young, with quail and mushrooms.

QUALITY 🍷🍷🍷🍷
VALUE ★★★★
GRAPES shiraz, grenache, mourvedre, touriga
REGION Barossa Valley, SA
CELLAR 🍾 3
ALC./VOL. 13.0%
RRP $12.00

St Hallett Old Block Shiraz

Bob McLean and Stuart Blackwell are holding Old Block for an extra three months' bottle-age before release: a smart move, as the oak is more integrated and the wine more ready. Maker Stuart Blackwell.
Previous outstanding vintages: '84, '86, '88, '90, '91, '92
CURRENT RELEASE 1993 The wine that put St Hallett on the world map is right on form in '93: dark colour, very concentrated chocolate, vanilla nose with a hint of pepper/spice; sweet, smooth, round and fleshy in the mouth. There is great depth and richness with high extract. Easy to make friends with now, but has a big future too. Try it with aged cheese such as Heidi gruyere.

QUALITY 🍷🍷🍷🍷🍷
VALUE ★★★★★
GRAPES shiraz
REGION Barossa & Eden Valleys, SA
CELLAR 🍾 1–10+
ALC./VOL. 13.5%
RRP $27.40 🍾

St Huberts Cabernet Merlot

Swiss migrant Hubert de Castella established a vineyard in the Yarra Valley in the 1860s. The current plantings went in a century later.
CURRENT RELEASE 1994 The colour is dense and dark, the nose closed until given ample breathing time. Tomato-bush and extractive notes give way to appealing blackcurrant cabernet fruit and toasty French oak. The tannin structure seems well suited to ageing and it should be a classic Yarra red in time. Serve with venison.

QUALITY 🍷🍷🍷🍷
VALUE ★★★½
GRAPES cabernet sauvignon, merlot
REGION Yarra Valley, Vic.
CELLAR 🍾 1–10
ALC./VOL. 12.9%
RRP $18.00

St Huberts Pinot Noir

QUALITY 🍷🍷🍷🍷
VALUE ★★★
GRAPES pinot noir
REGION Yarra Valley, Vic.
CELLAR 🍾 4
ALC./VOL. 11.5%
RRP $18.00

St Hubert was the patron saint of hunters, which is only half of the reason behind the name and insignia of this Yarra Valley winery. Maker Greg Traught.
CURRENT RELEASE 1995 This wine really 'came up' with breathing. The colour is typical medium-red-purple; the nose eventually showed attractive cherry fruit and spicy oak complexities. There's a trace of CO_2 and the palate has some depth and persistence. It's a wine that needs a little coaxing. Try it with carpaccio.

St Mary's Cabernet Sauvignon

QUALITY 🍷🍷🍷🍷
VALUE ★★★½
GRAPES cabernet sauvignon
REGION south-east SA
CELLAR ⊂= 2–8+
ALC./VOL. 13.0%
RRP $21.70

St Mary's is named as a tribute to Mother Mary MacKillop, who is more than halfway to being Australia's first saint. She taught in a school at nearby Penola, long long time ago.
CURRENT RELEASE 1994 This shows the quality of the soil out at St Mary's, which is arguably as good as the terra rossa strip. Impressive fruit concentration, appealing cabernet flavour, not as grassy as the '93 and although the oak stands out a bit and it could use a little more polish, this is a very good drink. Try it with venison cutlets.

St Mary's Shiraz

QUALITY 🍷🍷🍷🍷🍷
VALUE ★★★★½
GRAPES shiraz
REGION south-east SA
CELLAR ⊂= 1–10+
ALC./VOL. 13.8%
RRP $16.60

Founder Barry Mulligan has Tyrrell's as a partner in this newish vineyard, 18 km west of the main Coonawarra strip. It looks like being left out of the official Coonawarra region, but Mulligan is lobbying hard to be included.
CURRENT RELEASE 1994 This is a big, ultra-ripe style that you don't often see at Coonawarra, an arresting wine which proves the vineyard's ability to achieve high baumés. Dark hue and masses of flavour in the plum, licorice and vanilla spectrum. Rich, chunky, full-bodied – a superb wine with a huge finish. Try it with marinated buffalo fillet.

Stoney Vineyard Cabernet Sauvignon

Stoney began life in 1973, thanks to George Park. The tiny vineyard has exploded in size under the tutelage of Swiss couple, Peter and Ruth Althaus.
CURRENT RELEASE 1994 A raw, purple, baby wine with a future. All it needs is a few years in a quiet place. The nose shows undeveloped, slightly unfinished berry and blackcurrant aromas, the palate has brash fruit and crisp cool-climate acid, finishing with firm tannin astringency. Cellar, then serve with venison.

QUALITY ♛♛♛♛
VALUE ★★★½
GRAPES cabernet sauvignon, 5% cabernet franc
REGION Coal River Valley, Tas.
CELLAR ➟ 2–7
ALC./VOL. 12.5%
RRP $19.00

Stonier's Cabernet

This won its category in the Sydney International Top 100 in 1995. The grapes came from the Stonier, Dexter and Elgee Park vineyards. Maker Tod Dexter.
CURRENT RELEASE 1993 Good colour, and the nose shows an unusual combo of cherry essence and vanilla. The palate is light-medium in weight and carries a raspberry fruit flavour. It's very soft and easy to drink now, with wiener schnitzel.

QUALITY ♛♛♛
VALUE ★★½
GRAPES cabernet sauvignon 85%, cabernet franc, merlot 15%
REGION Mornington Peninsula, Vic.
CELLAR ▯ 3
ALC./VOL. 13.5%
RRP $19.00

Stonier's Reserve Cabernet

In size of crush (if not design of winery) Brian Stonier's probably has the edge as the Mornington Peninsula's major winery.
Previous outstanding vintages: '88, '90, '91
CURRENT RELEASE 1992 Subdued briary, earthy and oaky scents with some green-leaf. There is more body than the standard wine, but it is similarly soft with mild, smooth but drying tannin and will probably not reward more than a year or two's cellaring. Drink with beef stroganoff.

QUALITY ♛♛♛♛
VALUE ★★½
GRAPES cabernet sauvignon, cabernet franc, merlot
REGION Mornington Peninsula, Vic.
CELLAR ▯ 4
ALC./VOL. 13.5%
RRP $30.00

Stonyfell Metala Original Plantings Shiraz

QUALITY ♞♞♞♞♞
VALUE ★★★★★
GRAPES shiraz
REGION Langhorne Creek, SA
CELLAR 🍷 15+
ALC./VOL. 13.5%
RRP $24.00 🍷

A special release made from grapes off the Old Block and Cellar Block planted in 1891 and 1894 respectively. In other words, the vines are all centenarians. Maker Nigel Dolan.

CURRENT RELEASE 1994 A smashing red wine! Very deep purple-red hue; dense spicy, earthy berry aromas with fruit as the dominant force. Tremendous concentration on the palate: big and ripe, very rich flavour and grippy, mouth-coating tannins. Chocolate and vanilla-smothered berries. An absolute stunner. This is one of the great finds of the year. Grab some!

Stonyfell Metala Shiraz Cabernet

QUALITY ♞♞♞♞
VALUE ★★★★
GRAPES shiraz 70%, cabernet sauvignon 30%
REGION Langhorne Creek, SA
CELLAR 🍷 8+
ALC./VOL. 13.5%
RRP $14.00 ⓢ 🍷

Stonyfell is a family-owned independent vineyard at Langhorne Creek from which Saltram has been taking grapes for many long years.
Previous outstanding vintages: '71, '83, '84, '86, '92, '93

CURRENT RELEASE 1994 Back on form since the '92, after a change of winemaker, and the '94 continues the revival. Deep colour; coconutty oak and stalky, minty aromas lead into a robust style with some firm tannin astringency. A mouth-puckering finish brings back nostalgic memories of Metalas of old. Sweet, ripe, gutsy; a top vintage. Try it with steak.

Taltarni Cabernet Sauvignon

At Taltarni they tend to do all things well and aim for consistency rather than flash-in-the-pan brilliance. As solid as the line up is, it would be great to see a spectacular standard-bearing red. Previous outstanding vintages: '78, '79, '81, '82, '84, '86, '88, '90

CURRENT RELEASE 1992 The wine has developed considerably since the last review. It is now a pussy cat, open, friendly and playful. The colour is a mid-garnet and the nose has dusty oak and cassis aromas. The palate is soft with fresh raspberry flavours and there is well-integrated French oak on a sanguine finish. It goes well with tandoori lamb.

QUALITY ♛♛♛♛
VALUE ★★★
GRAPES cabernet sauvignon 87%, merlot 9%, cabernet franc 4%
REGION Pyrenees, Vic.
CELLAR 🍷 3
ALC./VOL. 13.0%
RRP $19.50

CURRENT RELEASE 1993 **The age of reason has dawned, this is a very elegant wine that offers restrained power.** There are smoky oak and raspberry aromas on the nose. The palate has a tight structure and raspberry and blackberry flavour. The finish is very French with a chalky feel, fine-grained tannin and lingering astringency. It goes well with escargot in garlic butter.

QUALITY ♛♛♛♛♛
VALUE ★★★★½
GRAPES cabernet sauvignon, cabernet franc, merlot, malbec
REGION Pyrenees, Vic.
CELLAR 🍷 3–7
ALC./VOL. 13.6%
RRP $20.50 🍷

Best Cabernet Sauvignon

Taltarni Merlot

QUALITY 🍷🍷🍷🍷
VALUE ★★★½
GRAPES merlot 96%, cabernet franc 4%
REGION Pyrenees, Vic.
CELLAR 🍾 5+
ALC./VOL. 13.6%
RRP $20.00

For the record MS once worked for Taltarni as roving sales lunatic at large. He gave up the job to give writing a go. Many people wished he kept his day job.

CURRENT RELEASE 1992 Little change since last year and while it shows a completeness of style it could be criticised for lacking varietal character. The nose is a mix of plum, earth and spice. The palate has cherry and raspberry flavours as well as a tart character and a tinge of musk. The oak supports rather than intrudes on the finish. It drinks well now; try it with a hearty casserole.

QUALITY 🍷🍷🍷🍷
VALUE ★★★★
GRAPES merlot
REGION Pyrenees, Vic.
CELLAR 🍾 5
ALC./VOL. 13.6%
RRP $20.00

CURRENT RELEASE 1993 Big oak opening on the nose, in fact oak dominates. When you pull back the wooden curtain there are rose perfume and spice aromas on the nose. The palate is medium-bodied with strong cherry flavours and there is plenty of the scene-stealing oak on the finish which is dry and grainy. It should cellar well; try it with goulash.

Taltarni Shiraz

QUALITY 🍷🍷🍷🍷?
VALUE ★★★★
GRAPES shiraz
REGION Pyrenees, Vic.
CELLAR 🍾 4
ALC./VOL. 12.5%
RRP $19.50

Having a proprietor from Bordeaux could mean shiraz is always having to say sorry. Not so – in reality this variety does very well for the marque. Previous outstanding vintages: '77, '81, '82, '84, '86, '88, '90, '91, '92

CURRENT RELEASE 1993 A lovely wine that captures the essence of the variety and the district. It's all about spice. The nose has pepper, spice and strong berry aromas. The finish sets it apart, avoiding the American oak cliche but adding fine-grained tannin and grip. It drinks well now with osso bucco.

Tamburlaine Cabernet Merlot Malbec

This wine is described as a 'vintage blend' which means it is a blend of two years or more. In this case it works well. Makers Greg Silkman and Mark Davidson.
CURRENT RELEASE *non-vintage* A very attractive wine that has complexity and power. The nose has a strong berry aroma on the nose plus a background of leather. The palate has sweet fruit flavours and there are vanillan American oak characters on the finish. It drinks well now and a rich oxtail dish is just the ticket.

QUALITY ♛♛♛♛
VALUE ★★★★
GRAPES cabernet sauvignon, merlot, malbec
REGION Hunter Valley, NSW
CELLAR 🍶 5
ALC./VOL. 12.9%
RRP $18.00

Tamburlaine The Chapel

This is the flagship and it is an unusual point of departure. Non-vintage and the blend is not stated. Brave stuff in a varietal and vintage-obsessed market.
CURRENT RELEASE *non-vintage* Interesting and individual style. The nose has chocolate and earth overtones with berries. The palate is medium-bodied with a chewy texture. There are berry flavours plus hints of truffles. American oak dominates the finish which is chalky, dry and long. It is good with a steak and kidney pie.

QUALITY ♛♛♛♛
VALUE ★★★
GRAPES not stated
REGION Hunter Valley, NSW
CELLAR ➖ 2–6
ALC./VOL. 12.6%
RRP $20.00

Tarrawarra Pinot Noir

The original winemaker, David Wollan, has now departed for rich, wine-related computer fields but the winery continues much in the way of his original blueprint. Maker Michael Kluczko. Previous outstanding vintages: '88, '90, '91, '92
CURRENT RELEASE 1993 The style is now firmly fixed. The colour is a deep ruby and the nose has truffle and cherry aromas. The main flavour is dark (wild) cherry and there is a lot of background spice. French oak gets top billing on the finish. Grip and structure are the things that set the wine apart. Try it with a steak and kidney pudding.

QUALITY ♛♛♛♛♛
VALUE ★★★★★
GRAPES pinot noir
REGION Yarra Valley, Vic.
CELLAR 🍶 6
ALC./VOL. 13.0%
RRP $28.00

Tatachilla Cabernet Sauvignon

QUALITY ♛♛♛♛
VALUE ★★★★
GRAPES cabernet sauvignon
REGION McLaren Vale, Langhorne Creek, SA
CELLAR 🍷 5 +
ALC./VOL. 13.5%
RRP $17.60

Much traditional winemaking (open fermenters) goes into the wines under this label which is meant to revive the glory days of McLaren Vale reds.
CURRENT RELEASE 1994 This is a very vibrant style with loads of character. It has a deep colour and a rich nose full of blackberry aromas. The full-bodied palate has rich blackberry flavour and there is plenty of dry tannin on a vibrant finish. It should cellar well.

Tatachilla Foundation Shiraz

QUALITY ♛♛♛♛♛
VALUE ★★★★½
GRAPES shiraz
REGION McLaren Vale, Langhorne Creek, Padthaway, SA
CELLAR 🍷 10
ALC./VOL. 14.0%
RRP $20.00 🍷

This wine commemorates the founder of the Tatachilla label, Cyril Pridmore, who started the winery in 1901. The fruit is sourced from three areas when you'd expect a straight McLaren Vale.
CURRENT RELEASE 1994 Big wine with lots to recommend it. The colour is deep and the nose has strong shiraz aromas plus spice. The palate has great depth with ripe plum and berry characters. These are laced with spice. American oak adds astringent tannins to a grippy finish. It drinks well with pink lamb chops.

Tatachilla Merlot

QUALITY ♛♛♛
VALUE ★★★
GRAPES merlot
REGION McLaren Vale, Barossa Valley, SA
CELLAR 🍷 2
ALC./VOL. 13.5%
RRP $17.60

There has been much effort expended on this label over many years. In the late 1950s it was a power in the land. It finally seems set to regain that status.
CURRENT RELEASE 1994 Straight merlot from a McLaren Vale winery is an unusual release. In this case the wine is interesting but the nose is a tad disconcerting. The nose is earthy with damp undergrowth smells. The palate has intense berry flavours and these are matched by fine-grained tannin on a lingering finish. It drinks well with pink lamb fillets.

Te Mata Coleraine Cabernet Merlot

Te Mata was an old Hawkes Bay winery which the energetic chairman of the New Zealand Wine Institute, John Buck, resurrected in 1978. Maker Peter Cowley.
Previous outstanding vintages: '82, '85, '90, '91
CURRENT RELEASE 1994 New Zealand's most famous red upholds its reputation with a stylish, elegant wine that shows nice ripe fruit in the dark berry/cedar spectrum, avoiding greenness. The palate has modest grip and smooth berry flavours, ending with lovely mouth perfumes. Drink it with NZ venison.

QUALITY ♛♛♛♛♛
VALUE ★★★½
GRAPES cabernet sauvignon, merlot, cabernet franc
REGION Hawkes Bay, NZ
CELLAR 🍾 8+
ALC./VOL. 13.0%
RRP $32.00

Thistle Hill Cabernet Sauvignon

This Mudgee vineyard has been certified as 'organic' by the National Association for Sustainable Agriculture in Australia (NASAA). Maker David Robertson.
CURRENT RELEASE 1992 The deep brick-red colour shows some evidence of bottle-age and the nose offers mellow warm-fruit aromas and gentle oak. The palate is a case of arrested development. It is young and taut with deep blackberry fruit flavours and lots of acid and oak on the finish. It has attractive grip and goes well with a rump steak with mushroom sauce (which is hardly organic health food).

QUALITY ♛♛♛♛
VALUE ★★★★
GRAPES cabernet sauvignon
REGION Mudgee, NSW
CELLAR 🍾 4
ALC./VOL. 13.0%
RRP $14.40 ✪

Thistle Hill Zinfandel

QUALITY ♥♥♥♥
VALUE ★★★★
GRAPES zinfandel
REGION Orange, NSW
CELLAR 🍾 1
ALC./VOL. 14.0%
RRP $12.00

'Zin's the thing wherein to catch the conscience of the king.' Sorry about that, but this is a very heady wine.
CURRENT RELEASE 1995 The colour is a bright crimson and there is a burst of berry and spice aromas. The palate is sweet and succulent with raspberry and tobacco flavours, and plenty of zesty acid. It is a lively style that is entertaining to the last drop. It would not be a sin to slightly chill this zin. Try it with Turkish food.

Tim Adams Cabernet Sauvignon

QUALITY ♥♥♥♥
VALUE ★★★★
GRAPES cabernet sauvignon
REGION Clare Valley, SA
CELLAR 🍷 2–6
ALC./VOL. 13.0%
RRP $16.50

In spite of his relative youth Tim Adams is one of the Clare Valley's most experienced winemakers. He served his apprenticeship under the legendary Mick Knappstein (uncle of Tim K.) at the Leasingham winery.
CURRENT RELEASE 1994 This is a restrained style (in T. Adams terms) which reflects the nature of the vintage. The colour has the usual regional density and the nose has blackberry and spice aromas. The palate is tight with reluctant fruit flavours, redcurrant and blackberry flavours are in evidence and the oak has integrated well. It is a good wine to match with doner kebab.

Tim Adams (The) Fergus

QUALITY ♥♥♥♥½
VALUE ★★★★½
GRAPES grenache
REGION Clare Valley, SA
CELLAR 🍾 5
ALC./VOL. 14.0%
RRP $21.00

Full marks to Tim Adams. In their headlong rush to get a grenache on to the market some makers are forgetting the quality aspect. This wine captures the essence of the grape.
Previous outstanding vintages: '94
CURRENT RELEASE 1995 This is a lovely wine with a deep ruby colour and a nose loaded with ripe raspberry fruit aromas and a hint of mint. The palate is succulent with sweet ripe berry flavours and a chewy texture. This is supported by some sympathetic oak on a dry finish. It drinks like a dream and it is great with pan-fried quail.

Tim Adams Shiraz

Shiraz and Clare Valley sing a convincing song even in a difficult vintage. Here's an example of the variety transcending the conditions to deliver the goods.
CURRENT RELEASE 1994 There is an impressive impact from the concentration of fruit. The colour is deep and the nose has crushed mulberry aromas dusted with pepper. The palate has concentrated fruit flavours at the blackberry/mulberry end of the spectrum. The oak is well tailored and there are fine-grained tannins on a persistent finish. It would go well with a possum pie.

QUALITY 🍷🍷🍷🍷
VALUE ★★★★½
GRAPES shiraz
REGION Clare Valley, SA
CELLAR 🍾 10
ALC./VOL. 13.5%
RRP $15.50

Tim Gramp Shiraz

Interesting label, a stairway to infinity theme. Tim Gramp is descended from the family that founded Orlando. He started his own label in 1991
Previous outstanding vintages: '91, '92, '93
CURRENT RELEASE 1994 POW! This wine is almost too rich, if that's possible. The nose warns of the danger to follow. It is sweet and spicy with ripe plum, cinnamon and vanilla aromas. The palate floods the mouth with chunky plum flavours which are counter-balanced by soft dusty oak that adds a vanilla component. It is a very sensuous wine with a slippery mouthfeel. The finish is quite soft yet satisfying. It is perfect for a seasoned meatloaf.

QUALITY 🍷🍷🍷🍷
VALUE ★★★★½
GRAPES shiraz
REGION McLaren Vale, SA
CELLAR 🍾 5
ALC./VOL. 15.0%
RRP $19.00

Tim Knappstein Cabernet Merlot

QUALITY ♀♀♀♀̵
VALUE ★★★
GRAPES cabernet sauvignon, merlot
REGION Clare Valley, SA
CELLAR ▮ 3
ALC./VOL. 13.5%
RRP $20.00

This is the fighting brand for the marque and it looks as if the Mildara Blass group will continue to strap on the boxing gloves for the Clare Valley.
CURRENT RELEASE 1994 The colour is a rich Clare ruby and the nose has leafy, berry and black tea aromas. The middleweight palate is full of crushed berry flavours and these are mixed with a leafy green character. The finish is tinder dry and just a little winter green character slips in. It needs a dish like rare beef to set it off.

Tim Knappstein Cabernet Sauvignon

QUALITY ♀♀♀♀♀̵
VALUE ★★★★
GRAPES cabernet sauvignon
REGION Clare Valley 54%, Adelaide Hills 46%, SA
CELLAR ▮ 8
ALC./VOL. 13.5%
RRP $19.50

Tim Knappstein has parted company with the Clare enterprise but leaves his name behind. He is now at Lenswood but this wine would have been made almost exclusively by him.
CURRENT RELEASE 1993 Very stylish wine that shows pedigree. The colour is deep crimson and the nose offers blackberry and herbal notes. The same is encountered on the palate and the depth of fruit is impressive. The finish has plenty of fine-grained tannins and loads of grip. It should cellar well. Try it with rare kangaroo fillets.

Tim Knappstein The Franc

QUALITY ♀♀♀♀
VALUE ★★★★
GRAPES cabernet franc
REGION Clare Valley, SA
CELLAR ▮ 4
ALC./VOL. 13.5%
RRP $16.00

Legend has it that wine writer Phillip White (Adelaide *Advertiser*) suggested at a tasting that this wine had enough character to be bottled as a solo item. Tim Knappstein took him at his word.
CURRENT RELEASE 1994 The colour is vibrant and the nose has an assault on the nose with rose-petal and violet aromas. It smacks of the forbidden garden. The palate has sweet mulberry fruit and there is also a hint of spice. The tannin is surprisingly firm and there is extra length than you would normally find in the variety. Try it with steamed duck. (White was right!)

Tisdall Cabernet Merlot

The winery at Tisdall was originally a dairy/cheese factory and the cellar door was transferred to the historic port of Echuca (yes, this was a loading point of the Murray paddle steamers). Maker Toni Stockhausen.
CURRENT RELEASE 1995 Very drinkable and affordable wine with a strong blackberry aroma. This is the main flavour on the palate and there is also some spice. The finish shows substantial tannin. It is a style that satisfies and goes well with a designer hamburger.

QUALITY ♛♛♛♛
VALUE ★★★★
GRAPES cabernet sauvignon, merlot
REGION Echuca, Vic.
CELLAR 🍷 4
ALC./VOL. 13.0%
RRP $11.00

Tisdall Shiraz Cabernet

In a few years wine buyers will be asking, 'Who was or what is a Tisdall?' For the record, he was Dr Peter Tisdall, a local GP in the Cobram/Echuca region who had a vast wine vision that he put into practice. It was sold to Mildara Blass.
CURRENT RELEASE 1994 This is a good value drop with plenty of flavour. The colour is a bright ruby and the nose has strong plum and dusty oak aromas with hints of pepper. The medium-bodied palate is dominated by sweet raspberry fruit flavour and leaf characters. The oak on the finish is discreet, making it very drinkable. It is good with lamb chops.

QUALITY ♛♛♛♛
VALUE ★★★★
GRAPES shiraz, cabernet sauvignon
REGION Echuca, Vic.
CELLAR 🍷 4
ALC./VOL. 13.0%
RRP $11.00 ⓢ

Tollana TR 16 Shiraz

QUALITY ♛♛♛♛
VALUE ★★★★
GRAPES shiraz
REGION Eden Valley, SA
CELLAR 5
ALC./VOL. 13.5%
RRP $15.00 $

This is the sleeper in the Southcorp stable, always well made and usually good value. Don't tell too many people, let's just share the secret. Maker Neville Falkenberg.

Previous outstanding vintages: '82, '84, '87, '88, '90, '91

CURRENT RELEASE 1992 A thoroughly civilised wine with lots of regional finesse. The colour shows no sign of bottle-age, it remains intense. The nose has ripe plum aromas plus a hint of vanilla. The palate has mediumweight and sweet-plum flavours. The oak adds an extra dimension, and there is vanilla and grip from the fine-grained tannins. It drinks well with pink lamb chops.

Tollana TR 222 Cabernet Sauvignon

QUALITY ♛♛♛♛♛
VALUE ★★★★½
GRAPES cabernet sauvignon
REGION Adelaide Hills, Eden Valley, SA
CELLAR 6
ALC./VOL. 13.0%
RRP $16.50 $

Bin 222 has taken to the hills (see region). This bin number was made famous by Wolfgang Blass when he worked there in the late 1960s.

Previous outstanding vintages: '82, '84, '87, '88, '90, '91, '92

CURRENT RELEASE 1993 A very polished wine with loads of flavour. The colour is a deep ruby and the nose is an interesting mix of mint, chocolate, vanilla and berries. The palate has a strong blackberry flavour and there are also hints of mint and chocolate. Pleasant grip rounds out the finish. It drinks well now; use it your favourite way to cook beef.

Trentham Estate Ruby Cabernet

Ruby Cabernet is a cross between carignan and cabernet sauvignon, bred by H.P. Olmo at Davis University, California. There are 470 ha. planted in Australia.
CURRENT RELEASE 1995 The nose has a strong berry smell and the colour is bright ruby. The palate is light to medium-bodied and there is an abundant berry flavour which is matched by a slight stalky character. French oak dries up the finish and adds moderate grip. It would be fine with a venison osso bucco.

QUALITY ♛♛♛♛
VALUE ★★★½
GRAPES ruby cabernet
REGION Murray Valley, NSW
CELLAR 3
ALC./VOL. 13.5%
RRP $9.90

Trinity Ridge Merlot Noir

Forgive the confusion, this label is part of Barossa Ridge Wine Estate in Tanunda. And for a second thing, what is a merlot noir? Black merlot perhaps? According to the back label it is 'the little blackbird' when allowed to ripen properly. Maker Marco Litterini.
CURRENT RELEASE 1995 This is a rich style that has abundant fruit. The nose has strong berry/rose-petal aromas. There is also lots of spice. The palate is quite firm but there is also a level of sweetness and attractive berry flavours. The finish has drying tannins that linger long. It is tough enough to handle liver and bacon.

QUALITY ♛♛♛♛
VALUE ★★★★
GRAPES merlot
REGION Barossa Valley, SA
CELLAR 2–6
ALC./VOL. 13.0%
RRP $17.50

Tuck's Ridge Cabernet Sauvignon

This label is like a dragster, it came from nowhere in 1993 and seemed to reach full speed in terms of market penetration in record time.
CURRENT RELEASE 1993 An elegant wine that has a strong oak influence. The nose has a strong coffee and toast aroma. The palate offers sweet blackberry flavours with a lilt of spice. The finish has solid grip and plenty of fine-grained tannins. It drinks well with savoury lamb chops.

QUALITY ♛♛♛♛
VALUE ★★★★
GRAPES cabernet sauvignon
REGION Mornington Peninsula, Vic.
CELLAR 4
ALC./VOL. 12.5%
RRP $18.60

Tuck's Ridge Pinot Noir

QUALITY ♛♛♛♝
VALUE ★★★
GRAPES pinot noir
REGION Mornington Peninsula, Vic.
CELLAR 🍷 3
ALC./VOL. 12.0%
RRP $20.40

This vineyard is large by Mornington Peninsula standards. It stands at 25 ha. and much of the fruit is sold to large producers in other regions. Maker Daniel Green.

CURRENT RELEASE 1995 An affable style that is easy to like. The colour is a light ruby and the nose is very pungent. Loads of strawberry, leather and truffle aromas. The palate is soft with a medium body. There are strawberry flavours on the palate and surprisingly strong grip weakens the finish. It would go well with pasta and a mushroom sauce.

12 Acres Pinot Shiraz

QUALITY ♛♛♝
VALUE ★★½
GRAPES pinot noir 75%, shiraz 25%
REGION Goulburn Valley, Vic.
CELLAR 🍷 1
ALC./VOL. 11.0%
RRP $12.00

Why do wine writers get gun-shy when they see a blend like this on a label? It seems to go against natural lore but there is no law against it.

CURRENT RELEASE 1995 The nose is earthy with some strawberry aroma lurking underneath. The palate is medium-bodied with sweet strawberry flavours that are quickly swamped by some pressings-like tannins. The finish is very firm. It is right beside a designer burger.

12 Acres Shiraz

QUALITY ♛♛♛
VALUE ★★★
GRAPES shiraz
REGION Goulburn Valley, Vic.
CELLAR 🍷 4
ALC./VOL. 13.0%
RRP $15.00

Somehow 4.8 hectares wouldn't sound the same. This is a small winery founded in 1986 by Peter and Jana Prygodicz at Bailieston near Shepparton in Victoria.

CURRENT RELEASE 1994 This is a very rustic style with a powerful nose that has some funky oak qualities plus plenty of plum aromas. The palate is medium-bodied with ripe berry flavours and spices. These are followed by an iron fist of tannin on a lingering finish. It drinks now and would go with a casserole of beef.

Tyrrell's Brokenback Shiraz

Another example of a mature wine being marketed. Blessed be the Tyrrell tribe because they give folks without a cellar a chance to enjoy a wine at its peak.

CURRENT RELEASE 1990 This is a classic Hunter with a deep brick-red colour. The nose has scented leather, mature fruit and hints of earth. The palate is rich and chewy with ripe plums and plenty of mouthfeel. There is firm astringency and grip on the finish. It drinks well now; try it with a mushroom risotto.

QUALITY ★★★★½
VALUE ★★★★½
GRAPES shiraz
REGION Hunter Valley, NSW
CELLAR 3
ALC./VOL. 12.4%
RRP $20.00

Tyrrell's Old Winery Cabernet Merlot

Another in the range of drinkable reds from the Tyrrell's winery. For decades there have been rumours that Tyrrell's was about to be snapped up by one of the large conglomerates. Don't hold your breath, Tyrrell's are doing fine.

CURRENT RELEASE 1995 Big fruit on the nose and palate. It is a real softie that drinks without an argument. The colour is medium-ruby and the nose has sweet berry aromas. The palate is medium-bodied with sweet fruit flavours and the tannins on the finish are soft yet satisfying. It drinks well with an honest meat pie.

QUALITY ★★★★
VALUE ★★★★
GRAPES cabernet sauvignon, merlot
REGION Hunter Valley, NSW
CELLAR 3
ALC./VOL. 13.5%
RRP $12.00 $

Tyrrell's Old Winery Pinot Noir

The Old Winery range is Tyrrell's economy line and that's not necessarily damning with faint praise. These days it is getting harder to find an affordable drink.

CURRENT RELEASE 1995 The colour is brick-red and there is a sappy quality on the nose. Underneath you'll smell strawberries and cherries. The medium body has sweet berry flavours and there is discreet wood and lingering acid on the finish. It drinks well and think about a gentle chill in summer. Try it with marinated barbecued lamb straps.

QUALITY ★★★½
VALUE ★★★★
GRAPES pinot noir
REGION Hunter Valley, NSW
CELLAR 3
ALC./VOL. 13.0%
RRP $12.00 $

Tyrrell's Show Reserve Shiraz Cabernet

QUALITY 🍷🍷🍷🍷⸲
VALUE ★★★★½
GRAPES shiraz 65%, cabernet sauvignon 35%
REGION Hunter Valley, NSW; Coonawarra, SA
CELLAR 🍾 8
ALC./VOL. 12.5%
RRP $20.00

The Show Reserve is one of the many labels in a sometimes confusing Tyrrell's portfolio. The labels tend to look pretty much the boring same and you need to read a lot of fine print. Never mind, aged wines are always welcome.

CURRENT RELEASE 1991 Hands across the continent in this cross-area blend with grapes from two significant regions. The colour is intensely deep and the nose shows some bottle development with mature fruit aromas. The palate is still very firm with blackberry flavours and there is plenty of tannin on the finish which shows some positive grip. It is a big wine that needs big food. Try it with mature cheddar.

Valley of Vines (Red Blend)

QUALITY 🍷🍷🍷⸲
VALUE ★★★
GRAPES merlot, cabernet franc, cabernet sauvignon, petit verdot.
REGION Barossa Valley, SA
CELLAR 🍾 4
ALC./VOL. 13.0%
RRP $18.00 🍾

This is the label for Barossa Ridge Wine Estate that was established in 1987 by Marco and Dianne Litterini. This first release is a left-handed Bordeaux blend.

CURRENT RELEASE 1993 The nose has strong berry aromas and an earthy background. The palate is medium-bodied with sweet raspberry flavour and there are gentle tannins on the soft finish. It drinks well now and goes perfectly with a steak and mushroom pie.

Vasse Felix Cabernet Sauvignon

This was one of the pioneering vineyards in Margaret River with an establishment date of 1967. It is now a 35-ha. vineyard.

CURRENT RELEASE 1994 Very regional style with an emphasis on elegance and length. The nose is a mix of blackberry and leaf aromas. The middleweight palate has blackberry flavours and some herbal notes. Well-tuned oak makes for a long astringent finish. It drinks well now and cellaring will reward. Have it with smoked lamb loin chops.

QUALITY ▼▼▼▼▼
VALUE ★★★★
GRAPES cabernet sauvignon
REGION Margaret River, WA
CELLAR ← 1–6
ALC./VOL. 13.5%
RRP $26.45

Vasse Felix Classic Dry Red

Regular readers will know that MS in particular rails against the use of the word 'classic' on a label. What makes a wine a classic? The Leyland P 76 could have been described as a classic lemon of a motorcar.

CURRENT RELEASE 1994 The wine has a green herbal quality plus berry aromas on the nose. The palate offers rich dark cherry flavours and there are well-integrated oak flavours on the finish. The tannin is fine-grained and imparts some solid grip. It is a wine to drink now; try it with devilled kidneys.

QUALITY ▼▼▼▼
VALUE ★★★★
GRAPES cabernet sauvignon, merlot
REGION Margaret River, WA
CELLAR ▮ 3
ALC./VOL. 13.5%
RRP $16.95

Vasse Felix Shiraz

QUALITY ★★★★★
VALUE ★★★★
GRAPES shiraz
REGION Margaret River, WA
CELLAR 2–8
ALC./VOL. 13.5%
RRP $27.70

This is one of the jewels in the Margaret River crown. It is quite sizeable in local terms with a production of 25 000 cases. Maker Clive Otto.

CURRENT RELEASE 1994 Very attractive style that would give any local cabernet a run for its money. The nose has spices, pepper and plums. The palate is complex with layers of flavour including plum, berries spices and cracked pepper. The finish has impressive oak integration and generous tannin grip. It has great length and balance. Try it with a venison pie.

Wa-de-Lock Pinot Noir

QUALITY ★★★
VALUE ★★½
GRAPES pinot noir
REGION Gippsland, Vic.
CELLAR 1
ALC./VOL. 12.5%
RRP $14.65

Gippsland has come to world notice for its pinot, especially Bass Philip and Briagolong. This is estate-grown near Maffra and was made by proprietor Graeme Little.

CURRENT RELEASE 1995 This is a light-bodied pinot with a pale colour, and lacks intensity on nose and palate, which suggests dilution in the vineyard. It's not a bad substitute for a light beaujolais style or a fuller rosé. Try it with Singapore noodles.

Wandin Valley Estate Ruby Cabernet

Ruby cabernet is a hybrid of cabernet sauvignon and the southern French variety, carignan. It's not widely grown but is supposed to make better wine than cabernet sauvignon in hot climates.

CURRENT RELEASE 1994 A most attractive lighter-style, fruit-driven red with perfumes of redcurrants and raspberries, with a light shading of leafiness. It is lean and refined with positive, drying tannins. Serve with lamb satays.

QUALITY 🍷🍷🍷🍷
VALUE ★★★½
GRAPES ruby cabernet
REGION Hunter Valley, NSW
CELLAR 3+
ALC./VOL. 11.5%
RRP $13.50 (cellar door)

Warramate Cabernet Sauvignon

This is one of the early vineyards in the Gruyere district of the Yarra Valley. It is wedged between Coldstream Hills and Yarra Yering. Maker Jack Church.

CURRENT RELEASE 1993 It says Yarra Valley to us. The nose is a mix of coffee, blackberry and leaf. The palate is light to medium-bodied. Raspberry and green leaf flavours are dominant and there is some well-mannered oak on a balanced finish. It drinks well now and pasta in a meat sauce is just the ticket.

QUALITY 🍷🍷🍷🍷
VALUE ★★★
GRAPES cabernet sauvignon
REGION Yarra Valley, Vic.
CELLAR 4
ALC./VOL. 12.5%
RRP $21.00

Warrenmang Estate Shiraz

Warrenmang is run by the Bazzani family, experienced restaurateurs. It's no surprise they also have an excellent restaurant at the vineyard.

CURRENT RELEASE 1994 This is a lovely big lump of a wine; the colour is dense purple-red and the nose is ripe berries, mint and cedary oak. The palate has great depth of sweet, ripe fruit and nicely balanced wood, giving a deep and fleshy taste that finishes with measured grip and style. Typical of its region. Try it with lamb and mint sauce.

QUALITY 🍷🍷🍷🍷
VALUE ★★★★
GRAPES shiraz
REGION Pyrenees, Vic.
CELLAR 10
ALC./VOL. 13.5%
RRP $20.00

Water Wheel Cabernet Sauvignon

QUALITY 🍷🍷🍷🍷
VALUE ★★★★
GRAPES cabernet sauvignon
REGION Bendigo, Vic.
CELLAR 🍾 1–7
ALC./VOL. 13.5%
RRP $13.70

The Cumming family produce cherries and tomatoes for the fresh fruit market, as well as wine from the extensively revived vineyards first planted in 1972. The wines are always value for money. Maker Peter Cumming.
Previous outstanding vintages: '90, '91, '92
CURRENT RELEASE 1994 Typical of the maker, this is a very grapey, fruit-driven wine which could benefit from a couple of years in bottle to build some vinous character. It has the makings of a superb bottle: perfumed minty, mulberry/blackberry aromas with lifted American oak. It's busting out with sweet fruit and surprisingly smooth already. Deep flavour, supple and seductive. Give it a year or two, then serve with a casserole.

Wellington Pinot Noir

QUALITY 🍷🍷🍷🍷
VALUE ★★★½
GRAPES pinot noir
REGION Tasmania
CELLAR 🍾 3
ALC./VOL. 12.3%
RRP $17.00

Tasmania would seem to be the right place to plant pinot noir for both sparkling wine base and table wine. This is another example of the latter which shows the depth of flavour possible.
CURRENT RELEASE 1995 A fresh style with a light cherry-red colour. The nose has a sweet berry aroma on a meaty background. The palate has sweet strawberry and cherry flavours and there are soft tannins on an acid-driven finish. It drinks well now; try it with a kid casserole.

Wendouree Shiraz

The vines at Wendouree are truly old, although you won't find any Old Vine boasts on the labels. The shiraz is off 1919 plantings. Maker Tony Brady.
Previous outstanding vintages: '83, '86, '90, '91, '92
CURRENT RELEASE 1994 Dry spicy, earth and walnutty aromas dominate this dense, fleshy shiraz, and the word savoury occurs again and again. The flavour is dense and high-extract, with layers of flavour and tannin. It is smooth despite the tannin and will live for ages. A Clare classic to serve with saddle of hare.

QUALITY ♛♛♛♛♝
VALUE ★★★★
GRAPES shiraz
REGION Clare Valley, SA
CELLAR ⇌ 2–10+
ALC./VOL. 13.3%
RRP $20.00 (cellar door)

Wendouree Shiraz Malbec

If there's a winery that epitomises all the good things about traditional Clare reds, it would have to be Tony and Lita Brady's Wendouree.
Previous outstanding vintages: '83, '86, '90, '91, '92
CURRENT RELEASE 1994 This is a big, rustic wine that is typical Wendouree and makes no compromises. It smells of ripe plum and licorice with a hint of iodine. The palate reveals vanilla and chocolate as well, and the shape is solid, round and generous, with a firm finish. Serve with osso bucco.

QUALITY ♛♛♛♛
VALUE ★★★★
GRAPES shiraz 80%, malbec 20%
REGION Clare Valley, SA
CELLAR ⇌ 2–10+
ALC./VOL. 13.5%
RRP $18.00 (cellar door)

Wendouree Shiraz Mataro

While mataro has recently become trendy, Wendouree never abandoned it. This is a winery where tradition transcends fashion.
Previous outstanding vintages: '83, '86, '90, '91, '92
CURRENT RELEASE 1994 The nose is very peppery, like crushed peppercorns, and there are other spices as well. It's a fruit-driven style with lashings of tannin and a dry, savoury palate. A wonderful red with excellent structure and plenty of legs. Good with barbecued beef fillet.

QUALITY ♛♛♛♛♝
VALUE ★★★★½
GRAPES shiraz 90%, mataro 10%
REGION Clare Valley, SA
CELLAR ⇌ 1–10+
ALC./VOL. 12.8%
RRP $16.00 (cellar door)

Wetherall Cabernet Sauvignon

QUALITY ♛♛♛♛
VALUE ★★★★
GRAPES cabernet sauvignon
REGION Coonawarra, SA
CELLAR 🍷 5
ALC./VOL. 13.0%
RRP $15.00 (cellar door)

The Wetheralls have been growing Coonawarra grapes for many years, only recently branching out into winemaking. Maker Michael Wetherall. Previous outstanding vintages: '92
CURRENT RELEASE 1993 This is a real charmer, easy to appreciate and full of fun. The nose shows minty coconutty American oak and sweet-berry regional fruit. It's smooth, sweet and fruity to the palate, easy to drink right now, with lamb fillets and pesto.

Wetherall Shiraz

QUALITY ♛♛♛♝
VALUE ★★★★
GRAPES shiraz
REGION Coonawarra, SA
CELLAR 🍷 4+
ALC./VOL. 12.5%
RRP $13.00 (cellar door)

Wetheralls' cellar door sales is slap bang in the middle of the terra rossa strip, with a very decent restaurant next door called the Hermitage.
CURRENT RELEASE 1993 Very much a wood-driven shiraz, richly scented with toasty oak and medium-bodied, smooth and ready to drink, although it won't shy at a few years in the cellar. Made with the restaurant market firmly in mind. Try it with rissoles.

Wignalls Pinot Noir

QUALITY ♛♛♛♝
VALUE ★★½
GRAPES pinot noir
REGION Great Southern, WA
CELLAR 🍷 1
ALC./VOL. 14.0%
RRP $25.40

Ex-vet Bill Wignall carved out a big name for pinot noir right from the start, although they are very much wines for early drinking and have tended to fade fast. Maker John Wade.
Previous outstanding vintages: '91, '92
CURRENT RELEASE 1994 Quite a complex bouquet shows plenty of gaminess and a definite volatile lift. The palate is quite deep but acidic, tight and lean, and it needs food. Try it with barbecued quails.

Wild Duck Creek Duck Muck

This wouldn't win any awards for slick marketing, but there's something humble and homely about the name – and the duck footprints that wander across the label. Makers David Anderson and David McKee.
CURRENT RELEASE 1994 This is a blood-and-thunder rendition of Heathcote shiraz. It has an impenetrable purple-red colour and gutsy, aggressive, tannic pressings palate that gives no beg-pardons. Intense cherry and mint aromas. Not a wine for the faint-hearted. Needs to be handcuffed and cellared for at least two years, then serve with buffalo fillet.

QUALITY ♛♛♛♛⁂
VALUE ★★★★
GRAPES shiraz 90%, cabernet sauvignon 10%
REGION Heathcote, Vic.
CELLAR ⇨ 3–10
ALC./VOL. 15.0%
RRP $25.00

Willows (The) Cabernet Sauvignon

Peter Scholz's daytime job is as a winemaker at Peter Lehmann. The Willows is a family affair, with brother Michael in charge of the vines.
Previous outstanding vintages: '91
CURRENT RELEASE 1993 This is somewhat firmer than the shiraz. The nose has leafy and blackcurrany varietal fruit and the palate is supple, rich and big with lots of tannin and a little astringency. A generous red that could use a year or two more to soften. Then drink with osso bucco.

QUALITY ♛♛♛⁂
VALUE ★★★½
GRAPES cabernet sauvignon
REGION Barossa Valley, SA
CELLAR ⇨ 1–6+
ALC./VOL. 13.5%
RRP $16.00

Willows (The) Shiraz

The Scholz family have been medical doctors for generations; now they ply their public with a different kind of tonic. Maker Peter Scholz.
Previous outstanding vintages: '91
CURRENT RELEASE 1992 Very much a Barossa babe: very deep red-purple colour and rich vanilla, chocolate and berry flavours. The wine is soft and cuddly with gentle tannins, and slips down easily. It would be a treat with venison cutlets.

QUALITY ♛♛♛♛
VALUE ★★★★
GRAPES shiraz
REGION Barossa Valley, SA
CELLAR 🍾 6+
ALC./VOL. 14.0%
RRP $14.50

Wirra Wirra Angelus Cabernet Sauvignon

QUALITY 🍷🍷🍷🍷⸱
VALUE ★★★★
GRAPES cabernet sauvignon
REGION McLaren Vale & Coonawarra, SA
CELLAR 🍷 2–8+
ALC./VOL. 13.5%
RRP $25.50

Named thus because of the church bell installed at the winery, which used to hang outside St Ignatius, Norwood. The Angelus is a bellwether (sorry) for the Vales and is only made in the top years, the bell years.
Previous outstanding vintages: '90, '91, '92, '93
CURRENT RELEASE 1994 Another lovely big, juicy red under this extremely reliable label. Overt cedary French oak, sweet blackberries and almost a hint of jam. Lovely fruit concentration, positive tannins and supportive oak. Will richly repay a year or two before drinking. Needs pink Illabo lamb.

Wirra Wirra Church Block

QUALITY 🍷🍷🍷⸱
VALUE ★★★
GRAPES cabernet sauvignon, shiraz, merlot
REGION McLaren Vale, SA
CELLAR 🍷 5

This is W2's bistro red, a ready-drinker which can also take some age. Maker Ben Riggs.
CURRENT RELEASE 1994 Earthy regional nose together with some spice and subtle vanilla/coconut American oak. Soft and fleshy, with a little tannin on the finish to give it an air of authority. Drinks well with shish kebabs.

Wirra Wirra Original Blend

QUALITY 🍷🍷🍷🍷⸱
VALUE ★★★★
GRAPES grenache 70%, shiraz 30%
REGION McLaren Vale, SA
CELLAR 🍷 4
ALC./VOL. 14.0%
RRP $18.00

Winemaker Ben Riggs says grenache needs to be very ripe to give good flavour, hence 14–14.5% is common in grenache these days.
Previous outstanding vintages: '93, '94
CURRENT RELEASE 1995 A scrumptious mouthful of red. Concentrated pepper and berry flavours, fruit uppermost and only the merest hint of wood. Deep, full, rich palate with typical ripe grenache opulence yet structure as well. Drink with Lebanese lamb.

Wirra Wirra RSW Shiraz

Robert Strangways Wigley may have been Greg Trott's model. The founder of the original Wirra Wirra, he is supposed to have been a celebrated character.
Previous outstanding vintages: '92, '93
CURRENT RELEASE 1994 A lovely big lump of a wine, stacked with licorice, plum and sweet spicy notes from fully ripened grapes. The texture is voluptuous, and it needs a little time to build more complexity. Serve with game.

QUALITY ♀♀♀♀
VALUE ★★★
GRAPES shiraz
REGION McLaren Vale, SA
CELLAR 1-6
ALC./VOL. 14.0%
RRP $22.00

Wolf Blass Black Label Cabernet Shiraz

When Blass won three Jimmy Watsons on the trot with this wine it put him on the map. It's truly one of the great red wines of Germany . . . oops! I mean Australia. Price range: $42–$52. Maker John Glaetzer.
Previous outstanding vintages: '73, '74, '75, '78, '80, '82, '83, '84, '86, '87, '89, '91
CURRENT RELEASE 1992 Excellent colour: a deep dark red-purple robe. Marvellous depth and complexity here, like a splendid dark fruit cake it has a multitude of vanilla, coconut, camphor and rich plum/raisin fruit nuances. Lots of oak but all in superb harmony. Lush, flavour-packed, great length. Probably at its best now. Serve with aged cheeses.

QUALITY ♀♀♀♀♀
VALUE ★★★★
GRAPES cabernet sauvignon, shiraz
REGION Langhorne Creek, Barossa & Eden Valleys, McLaren Vale, Clare, SA
CELLAR 6
ALC./VOL. 13.0%
RRP $52.00 Ⓢ

Wolf Blass Brown Label Classic Shiraz

'No wood, no good' is the Blass philosophy, and this has always had lashings of it. With some bottle-age, the effect is a distinctive savoury style of shiraz.
Previous outstanding vintages: '88, '89, '90, '91, '92
CURRENT RELEASE 1993 This is typical of the style, although maybe a tad lighter than usual. Sweet, spicy, leafy nose with a trace of aniseed/mint. The mid-palate is sweet and rich with aged mellow flavours of considerable complexity. Truly a classic both of the maker and variety, drinking beautifully now with osso bucco.

QUALITY ♀♀♀♀?
VALUE ★★★★
GRAPES shiraz
REGION Eden Valley, McLaren Vale & Clare, SA & Hunter Valley, NSW
CELLAR 7
ALC./VOL. 13.5%
RRP $21.35 Ⓢ

Wolf Blass Red Label

QUALITY ▼▼▼
VALUE ★★★
GRAPES various
REGION various
CELLAR 🍾 2
ALC./VOL. 12.5%
RRP $12.65 ⓢ

Colour blind? Don't worry about it. The label tells you what colour it is! Wolf Blass colour coded his wines, then sat back and watched them sell like hotcakes. Red Label is the bottom rung on the ladder – what the marketers like to call 'entry level'.

CURRENT RELEASE 1994 Decent, drink-now red that is as reliable as the day is long. This one shows fairly forward development, with a slightly aged colour and a soft, mellow bouquet. The taste is gently leafy, smooth and round, and goes well with satays.

Wolf Blass Yellow Label Shiraz Cabernet

QUALITY ▼▼▼▼
VALUE ★★★★
GRAPES shiraz, cabernet sauvignon
REGION Langhorne Creek, Barossa and Eden Valleys, Clare, SA
CELLAR 🍾 5
ALC./VOL. 12.5%
RRP $14.75 ⓢ

Wolf's first red wine was released under a yellow label that was the forerunner of the current one, back in 1966. Those first vintages set a style that continues unchanged. Maker John Glaetzer.

CURRENT RELEASE 1994 Typical of the brand, this is a forward ready-drinking style which is well-rounded and slips down a treat with no need for cellaring. Sweet ripe plum and licorice nose; soft, warm, shirazzy palate with a gentle finish. Goes well with shepherd's pie.

Woodstock The Stocks Cabernet Sauvignon

QUALITY ▼▼▼▼
VALUE ★★★½
GRAPES cabernet sauvignon
REGION McLaren Vale, SA
CELLAR 🍾 5+
ALC./VOL. 13.5%
RRP $22.50 ⓢ

Each year the best Woodstock red wine is bottled as The Stocks, a name which refers to the rather nasty instrument of torture to be found in the grounds of the winery. Maker Scott Collett. Previous outstanding vintages: '91

CURRENT RELEASE 1993 Softness, smoothness and generosity of flavour are the keywords here. There may not be sharply defined cabernet character, but the wine is very friendly and loaded to the gunnels with deep chocolate, vanilla and berry flavours that linger well. Drink with pink lamb and pesto.

Wynns Cabernet Shiraz Merlot

We lament the passing of the original label design: the new label preserves the essential elements but we preferred the old one. Why can't marketers leave things alone? It wasn't broken, so why fix it?
CURRENT RELEASE 1993 It's difficult to mistake this for any other region than Coonawarra – elegant crushed leaf and blackcurrant aromas come bounding out of the glass. A very charming, soft wine designed for bistros and the drink-now clientele. Smooth, easy drinking, without great length or distinction. Goes well with lamb yeeros.

QUALITY ♛♛♛♕
VALUE ★★★½
GRAPES cabernet sauvignon, shiraz, merlot
REGION Coonawarra, SA
CELLAR 🍷 5
ALC./VOL. 13.5%
RRP $14.20

Wynns Coonawarra Estate Cabernet Sauvignon

In the better vintages the 'black label' represents superior value for money, and 1993 is such a vintage. Maker Peter Douglas.
Previous outstanding vintages: '62, '76, '82, '85, '86, '88, '90, '91
CURRENT RELEASE 1993 A superb wine, especially considering the large quantity produced. Slightly more leafy and less tannic than the John Riddoch, it is outstanding value with a dash of cedary oak, showing serious structure and length. Delicious with aged beef fillet.

QUALITY ♛♛♛♛♛
VALUE ★★★★
GRAPES cabernet sauvignon
REGION Coonawarra, SA
CELLAR 🍷 10+
ALC./VOL. 13.7%
RRP $20.00 Ⓢ

Wynns John Riddoch Cabernet Sauvignon

QUALITY ♛♛♛♛♛
VALUE ★★★½
GRAPES cabernet sauvignon
REGION Coonawarra, SA
CELLAR ▬ 3–14+
ALC./VOL. 13.5%
RRP $54.00 ⓢ

This is one of the handful of wines that carry the premium banner for the Coonawarra 'A' team. Recent years have seen the price escalate alarmingly.
Previous outstanding vintages: '82, '86, '87, '88, '90, '91
CURRENT RELEASE 1993 Praise the Lord and pass the decanter! This is heaven in a bottle. Even more powerful and focused than the black label, it's a profound red wine, tightly packed and richly tannic with lashings of well-integrated oak and massive sweet fruit on the mid-palate. Put it away for seven years and you'll have a great Australian wine. (Then drink with aged cheddar.)

Wynns Michael Shiraz

QUALITY ♛♛♛♛♛
VALUE ★★★½
GRAPES shiraz
REGION Coonawarra, SA
CELLAR ▬ 6–16+
ALC./VOL. 13.0%
RRP $54.00 ⓢ

The name changes from hermitage to shiraz this year. This wine scooped the 1996 Sydney Wine Show, pulling in three trophies, but copped a lot of press flak later for being heavy on timber. Maker Peter Douglas.
Previous outstanding vintages: '55, '90, '91
CURRENT RELEASE 1993 Sure, it's kinda splintery right now, but it's still a babe (in the woods?) and you'd be wasting your $54 to open it today. Cellar it and time will swallow that oak up. The wine is fearfully concentrated and massively powerful, with virtually none of the lighter peppery shiraz aromatics but all plums, cherries and licorice, layered with coconut and vanilla from the oak. Abundant tannin firms up the incredibly long finish. Bring it out in 2002 with a prime rib roast of beef.

Wynns Shiraz

The name changes from hermitage, and you might have to hunt for it this year: the quantity was drastically reduced, by about a third, from the plentiful '93 vintage.
Previous outstanding vintages: '86, '88, '90, '91, '93
CURRENT RELEASE 1994 Strict selection has produced a wine that's right up to the usual Wynns quality: rich, oaky, chocolatey, smoother than the '93 but lively, intense and drinks nicely now, with rare beef.

QUALITY ★★★★½
VALUE ★★★★½
GRAPES shiraz
REGION Coonawarra, SA
CELLAR 8
ALC./VOL. 13.5%
RRP $14.00 $

Yalumba Bush Vine Grenache

In the Barossa, old bush vines grow the best grenache, hence the name of this revival wine. Production is very limited. Maker Simon Adams and team.
CURRENT RELEASE 1994 Coffee grounds are the dominant aroma here, with vanilla, dark chocolate and other rich, sweet fruit smells. The taste is rustic, even feral, with grainy tannins and a smooth finish. Not a wine of elegance, but that's grenache for you. Very tasty all the same, especially when served with venison pie.

QUALITY ★★★★
VALUE ★★★★½
GRAPES grenache
REGION Barossa Valley, SA
CELLAR 4
ALC./VOL. 13.0%
RRP $13.00 $

Yalumba Family Reserve Cabernet Merlot

Merlot is the fashion red variety of the moment. It is supposed to fill out the mid-palate of cabernet and to soften a red for earlier drinkability. Maker Simon Adams and team.
CURRENT RELEASE 1994 This is something of a peppermint pattie: chocolate and mint combine on the bouquet and the taste is soft and rich with drying grainy tannins. The Langhorne Creek mint is quite assertive, if that's your bag. Try it with braised veal shanks.

QUALITY ★★★★
VALUE ★★★★½
GRAPES cabernet sauvignon 84%, merlot 16%
REGION Langhorne Creek 67%, Barossa Valley 23% & McLaren Vale 10%, SA
CELLAR 5
ALC./VOL. 13.5%
RRP $15.00 $

Yalumba Family Reserve Shiraz

QUALITY ♙♙♙♗
VALUE ★★★½
GRAPES shiraz
REGION Barossa & Eden Valleys, SA
CELLAR 🍷 4+
ALC./VOL. 13.0%
RRP $15.00 Ⓢ

The Family Reserve series is designed to reflect classic regions and the varieties for which they're famous. Where else to source shiraz but home base, the Barossa?
Previous outstanding vintages: '88, '90, '91, '92
CURRENT RELEASE 1994 Typically modern Barossa shiraz in that it smells of little but American oak at this point. A year or so in the cellar will set that to rights, for the wine has good flavour and body. Smooth and broad in the mouth, it has abundant earthy, chocolatey Barossa flavour and a soft finish. Drink with osso bucco.

Yalumba Galway Hermitage

QUALITY ♙♙♙♗
VALUE ★★★★
GRAPES shiraz
REGION Barossa Valley & McLaren Vale, SA
CELLAR 🍷 3
ALC./VOL. 13.0%
RRP $10.00 Ⓢ

Lt-Col. Sir Henry Galway was governor of South Australia from 1914–20. He was a friend of the Hill Smith family and they've named a wine after him since the 1940s.
Previous outstanding vintages: '88, '90, '92
CURRENT RELEASE 1994 Another top-value red under this reliable label. The '94 is a fruit-driven wine with a fresh nose of cherries and dark berries. It's light to medium-bodied, smooth and fruity with clean spicy flavours. Its intensity and length are unusual in its price bracket. Goes well with gourmet sausages.

Yalumba Oxford Landing Cabernet Shiraz

QUALITY ♙♙♙
VALUE ★★★★
GRAPES cabernet sauvignon, shiraz
REGION Riverland, SA
CELLAR 🍷 1
ALC./VOL. 12.5%
RRP $8.00 Ⓢ

Oxford Landing was a piece of crown land beside the Murray River near Waikerie, where drovers could stop and water their sheep on the way to the Adelaide markets.
CURRENT RELEASE 1994 Stalky cabernet and chocolatey, earthy warm-area characters, showing a fair amount of development for a two-year-old. Soft, easy-drinking with just a smidgin of tannin. Fair value; drink with lamb's fry.

Yalumba Menzies Cabernet Sauvignon

The red that caused Robert Menzies, the former PM, to exclaim that it was the finest Australian wine he'd tasted was neither Coonawarra nor pure cabernet, but a '60s Galway claret, then Yalumba's top wine. This wine commemorates the famous occasion.

CURRENT RELEASE 1992 The nose shows dominant coconut oak aroma, which should settle down with a year or so in bottle. There's also peppermint, vanilla and berry aromas, and the palate shows remarkable concentration and fleshy extract. Seems to pack more punch than earlier releases. Long finish with tannin aplenty. Try it with aged hard cheeses.

QUALITY ♆♆♆♆♇
VALUE ★★★½
GRAPES cabernet sauvignon
REGION Coonawarra, SA
CELLAR 🍷 6+
ALC./VOL. 13.0%
RRP $18.00 Ⓢ

Yalumba Octavius Shiraz

Sounds very ancient Rome, but this is much better than Falernian ever was. The name refers to the octaves – very small barrels – of unusually well-seasoned American oak that were used to mature the wine. Maker Brian Walsh and team. Previous outstanding vintages: '90, '91

CURRENT RELEASE 1992 Time to trot out that 'exercise in controlled power' line again! This is a whopper, and right up to the glass-staining concentrated hugeness of previous vintages. It is still enormously oaky but could yet find its balance, and, anyway, there's so much rich, ripe, sweet fruit on the palate that the oak issue pales into insignificance. Very assertive tannin grip to match, and should age superbly. Try three-year-old Heidi gruyère.

QUALITY ♆♆♆♆♆
VALUE ★★★½
GRAPES shiraz
REGION Barossa Valley, SA
CELLAR 🍷 2–8+
ALC./VOL. 14.1%
RRP $42.00

Yalumba The Signature Cabernet Shiraz

QUALITY ♛♛♛♛♛
VALUE ★★★★½
GRAPES cabernet sauvignon, shiraz
REGION Barossa Valley, Coonawarra, SA
CELLAR 🍾 10+
ALC./VOL. 14.0%
RRP $24.00 $

Best Red Blend/Other Variety

The Signature is a proud family tradition, which commenced with the 1962 Samuel's Blend, named (appropriately) after the founder. Each year commemorates a Yalumba stalwart, whose name appears on the back label.
Previous outstanding vintages: '62, '63, '66, '67, '75, '76, '81, '88, '90, '91
CURRENT RELEASE 1992 Continues the revival of this great line, which had a hiccup in the late '70s-early '80s. The '92 is a nostalgic wine, an old-fashioned style – rich and robust with earthy oaky aromas and a chunky, tannic, savoury palate that finishes with plenty of dark chocolate. Needs a good old-fashioned roast dinner.

Yarra Ridge Cabernet Sauvignon

QUALITY ♛♛♛♛♛
VALUE ★★★★
GRAPES cabernet sauvignon
REGION Yarra Valley, Vic.
CELLAR 🍾 8+
ALC./VOL. 12.5%
RRP $20.00 $

Mildara bought founder Louis Bialkower's remaining 50 per cent of Yarra Ridge during 1995. 1994 was an excellent year for Yarra cabernet. Maker Rob Dolan.
Previous outstanding vintages: '90, '91, '92
CURRENT RELEASE 1994 A very solid wine with some seemingly raisined fruit aromas, along with the more typical blackcurrants and crushed leaf. Concentrated licorice and dark berry flavours fill the mouth and linger long. The finish has good grip. Try it with rare kangaroo.

Yarra Ridge Merlot

QUALITY ♛♛♛♛
VALUE ★★★
GRAPES merlot
REGION Yarra Valley, Vic.
CELLAR 🍾 4
ALC./VOL. 13.0%
RRP $20.00 $

This pure merlot is not intended as an annual release, but only in the best vintages. It is mainly distributed to restaurants.
CURRENT RELEASE 1994 Leafy, briary, slightly stewy aromas and the greenish flavours follow through to the palate, where it's lean and tight, with a degree of elegance. Serve with rissoles.

Yarra Ridge Pinot Noir

While it doesn't scale the heights of some of the Yarra's other pinots, this has grown into one of the more important pinot brands in the country. Can be found as cheap as $16.95. Maker Rob Dolan.
CURRENT RELEASE 1995 A decent pinot without particularly exciting definition, showing a stewed cherry and spicy aroma and a full, smooth palate which does have some length to it. For drinking now. Try it with quail.

QUALITY ♛♛♛♖
VALUE ★★★½
GRAPES pinot noir
REGION Yarra Valley, Vic.
CELLAR 🍾 2
ALC./VOL. 13.0%
RRP $20.00 Ⓢ

Yarra Ridge Shiraz

This fruit comes from the Napoleoni vineyard, opposite St Huberts at Coldstream: one of the region's leading contract grapegrowers.
Previous outstanding vintages: '93
CURRENT RELEASE 1994 A most unusual style, with pronounced leathery, earthy character that takes us straight to the Hunter, as well as peppery cool-area aromas. The palate is elegant, savoury and balanced, and while it might lack a bit of power, it is a very appealing luncheon style. Serve with schnitzel.

QUALITY ♛♛♛♖
VALUE ★★★
GRAPES shiraz
REGION Yarra Valley, Vic.
CELLAR 🍾 5
ALC./VOL. 13.0%
RRP $20.00 Ⓢ

Yarra Yering Dry Red Wine No.1

Dr Bailey Carrodus is one of the true individuals of Australian wine. He does not engage in any promotions and is seldom seen outside his Yarra Valley property.
Previous outstanding vintages: '80, '81, '82, '86, '90, '91, '93
CURRENT RELEASE 1994 The ultra-low yields are evident in the density of the wine: concentrated colour and fleshy, high-extract palate with deep fruit and smooth tannins. The nose shows intense crushed-leaf and berry aromas of some complexity. This should age well as '94 was a top vintage. Cellar, then serve with pink lamb.

QUALITY ♛♛♛♛♖
VALUE ★★★★
GRAPES cabernet sauvignon, malbec, merlot, petit verdot
REGION Yarra Valley, Vic.
CELLAR ⇢ 3-12+
ALC./VOL. 13.0%
RRP $41.00

Yarra Yering Dry Red Wine No.2

QUALITY 🍷🍷🍷🍷🍷
VALUE ★★★★½
GRAPES 95% shiraz, viognier 5%
REGION Yarra Valley, Vic.
CELLAR 🍾 10+
ALC./VOL. 13.0%
RRP $41.00

Yarra Yering's 1973 vintage is claimed to have been the first commercial wine produced in the Yarra Valley since 1921. Maker Bailey Carrodus. Previous outstanding vintages: '80, '81, '87, '90, '91, '93

CURRENT RELEASE 1994 A great wine which stimulates and seduces. Rich meaty, spicy bouquet with ripe fruit characters and only a suggestion of pepper. The palate is sumptuous in the manner of a fine Cote Rotie: full, rich and complete. Fills the senses and leaves you wanting more. Try it with steak and kidney pie.

Yarra Yering Merlot

QUALITY 🍷🍷🍷🍷
VALUE ★½
GRAPES merlot
REGION Yarra Valley, Vic.
CELLAR 🍾 6+
ALC./VOL. 13.5%
RRP $173.00

Think of a number, any number ... When the first merlot was released, the price brought sideways glances of incredulity. It still does, but at least the wine is now very good.

CURRENT RELEASE 1994 The colour is deep purple-red and the nose is quite fetching, with green-olive, cherry and raspberry jam nuances. The palate is rich and fleshy with the vineyard's trademark concentration, silky and round with a slightly fumey aspect and alcohol warmth on a finish which is very long. Prefer the two Dry Reds, especially at the price. Strictly for those motivated by rarity.

Yarraman Road Cabernet Shiraz

QUALITY 🍷🍷🍷🍷
VALUE ★★★
GRAPES cabernet sauvignon, shiraz
REGION Hunter Valley, NSW
CELLAR 🍾 4+
ALC./VOL. 13.0%
RRP $22.00

Another small winery makes its debut, this time in the Upper Hunter, where there's been a steady – albeit modest – increase in winery numbers. Maker David Lowe.

CURRENT RELEASE 1994 A smooth, vanilla/chocolatey style showing plenty of wood, some blackberry fruit and, at this stage, no obvious Hunter character. A pleasant easy-drinking red, compact and elegant, and would team well with gourmet sausages.

Zema Estate Cabernet Sauvignon

This wine has been the mainstay of the estate's production. It is always reliable with a concentration of flavour.
Previous outstanding vintages: '84, '86, '88, '92
CURRENT RELEASE 1994 This is an intense wine with a deep red-purple colour and a herbal nose. There are also blackberry aromas and hints of oak. The palate is full of rich berry fruit and there is an attractive acid-oak balance on the finish. It is a wine with considerable length. It will cellar well; at the moment it drinks well with a hearty casserole.

QUALITY ♛♛♛♛♛
VALUE ★★★★½
GRAPES cabernet sauvignon
REGION Coonawarra, SA
CELLAR ⇨ 2–6
ALC./VOL. 13.0%
RRP $18.00

Zema Estate Cluny

Cluny is the name of a Coonawarra vineyard and this is the second release. It would be wrong not to mention the viticultural/winemaking contribution of Nick Zema.
CURRENT RELEASE 1994 A complex wine with a herbal nose and some undergrowth characters. The palate is medium-bodied with many fruit flavours acting on the palate. Raspberry and cherry are the major contributors and there is rich oak on the finish. It drinks well now; try it with a confit of duck

QUALITY ♛♛♛♛
VALUE ★★★★
GRAPES cabernet sauvignon 65%, merlot 15%, cabernet franc 10%, malbec 10%
REGION Coonawarra, SA
CELLAR 🍷 4
ALC./VOL. 12.9%
RRP $18.00

Zema Estate Family Selection

This is selected barrels for the best cabernet sauvignon that comes off a block which according to the proprietor Dimitrio Zema has, 'the best bludda red dirt in Coona – bludda – warra.' Dimitrio has a colourful turn of phase.
CURRENT RELEASE 1992 The nose is bludda marvellous. It has concentrated blackberry aromas and savoury oak. The palate is quite tight yet packed with flavour. It gives the impression of being a sleeping giant. There is beautifully crafted oak on a dry astringent finish. Coona – bludda – warra indeed! Try it with a casserole of duck.

QUALITY ♛♛♛♛♛
VALUE ★★★★½
GRAPES cabernet sauvignon
REGION Coonawarra, SA
CELLAR ⇨ 2–7
ALC./VOL. 13.4%
RRP $24.00

Zema Estate Shiraz

QUALITY ♛♛♛♛♛
VALUE ★★★★★
GRAPES shiraz
REGION Coonawarra, SA
CELLAR ← 3-8
ALC./VOL. 12.7%
RRP $15.95

Great little winery that makes great big wines. This is a cellar that reflects the enthusiasm and character of the proprietor and his family. Maker Matt Zema (Ken Ward, consultant).
Previous outstanding vintages: '84, '86, '88, '92
CURRENT RELEASE 1994 What a healthy young style, the colour is a vibrant ruby with purple robes. The nose is very fruity with hints of wood and mint. The palate is a middleweight with intense dark-plum flavours and lively spicy oak. There are black tea-like tannins on a long astringent finish. It is only a pup at the moment but it can handle a rich dish like jugged hare.

White Wines

Alkoomi Mount Frankland Early White

Merv and Judy Lange's Alkoomi vineyard produced some superb wines with Kim Hart as winemaker. There's been a change in recent times and Grant Mitchell is now on deck.

CURRENT RELEASE 1996 Tasted as a brand-new bottling, this has a pungent passionfruity nose and a trace of sweaty herbaceousness typical of the region. The yeast esteriness is still quite apparent. The flavour is lifted by a fair dose of residual sugar. Try it with a light fish curry.

QUALITY ♛♛♛
VALUE ★★★
GRAPES not stated
REGION Great Southern, WA
CELLAR 1
ALC./VOL. 12.0%
RRP $14.00 Ⓢ

All Saints Chardonnay

Things looked up while Neil Jericho was making the wine at All Saints, but now that he's moved on, there's a gaping hole.

CURRENT RELEASE 1994 This is a somewhat restrained style for Wahgunyah/Rutherglen. The colour is lightish yellow, the nose shows assertive cedary oak, and the finish is nicely arid. It has structure and hidden reserves of fruit. Expect it to fill out into a rich style fairly quickly. Serve with squab.

QUALITY ♛♛♛♛
VALUE ★★★★
GRAPES chardonnay
REGION Rutherglen, Vic.
CELLAR 5
ALC./VOL. 13.2%
RRP $16.50

All Saints Chenin Blanc

QUALITY ♟♟♟
VALUE ★★½
GRAPES chenin blanc
REGION north-east Vic.
CELLAR 🍾
ALC./VOL. 12.0%
RRP $13.80

Since the Brown Brothers bought All Saints the changes have been impressive. The grapes for this wine came from the neighbouring St Leonards vineyard, also Brown-owned.
CURRENT RELEASE 1995 Subdued, slightly dusty aromas and the wine lacks distinctive personality or intensity, the palate flavour being masked by sweetness. This is strictly tourist-bus fodder.

All Saints Late Harvest Semillon

QUALITY ♟♟♟♟♟
VALUE ★★★★
GRAPES semillon
REGION north-east Vic.
CELLAR 🍾 3
ALC./VOL. 10.0%
RRP $16.50 (375ml)

Winemaker Neil Jericho mastered stickies many years ago when he was working at Woorinen (remember them?) at Swan Hill.
CURRENT RELEASE 1995 Subdued apricot and peach aromas suggest a fairly light degree of botrytis infection. The palate is lusciously sweet and fruity, with low-alcohol lightness on the tongue and a deep, long, peach/nectarine flavour. A wine of real harmony. Try it with a fruit compote and cream.

All Saints Marsanne

QUALITY ♟♟♟
VALUE ★★★
GRAPES marsanne
REGION north-east Vic.
CELLAR 🍾 3
ALC./VOL. 13.0%
RRP $16.50

This was made by Neil Jericho, who presided over the new phase of winemaking at All Saints but departed in late 1995.
CURRENT RELEASE 1995 A decent commercial soft dry white. The fruit is appley and not especially distinctive, and the oak is only really apparent in the back label blurb, which means it's commendably subtle. Soft, round and fruity on the tongue, it does have some richness and length. Could team well with scallops à la nage.

Allandale Chardonnay

The Lower Hunter Valley was the cradle of the now-booming Australian chardonnay industry.
CURRENT RELEASE 1995 This is a typically rich, blowsy Hunter chardonnay with broad peachy/honey aromas coupled with nutty and straw overtones. The taste is very soft and round with some sweetness and it would be best served well chilled. Try it with chicken.

QUALITY ♷♷♷♸
VALUE ★★★
GRAPES chardonnay
REGION Hunter Valley, NSW
CELLAR 🍾 1
ALC./VOL. 13.5%
RRP $16.00

Allandale Semillon

Follow the Allandale Road out of Cessnock towards the vineyards and it will take you almost straight to Allandale winery. Maker Bill Sneddon.
CURRENT RELEASE 1995 Traditional early-picked Hunter semillon: light yellow colour; straw-like, earth and mineral aromas; lean, tight palate with fine fruit and a finish as dry as a bone. This will keep well, but if you drink it young, try pairing it with delicate fish.

QUALITY ♷♷♷♷
VALUE ★★★★
GRAPES semillon
REGION Hunter Valley, NSW
CELLAR 🍾 7
ALC./VOL. 11.9%
RRP $14.50

Allandale Semillon Sauvignon Blanc

Allandale is one of seven small wineries which have organised themselves into a Lower Hunter sub-region called Lovedale, named after the pioneering Love family.
CURRENT RELEASE 1994 Another lean, dry, savoury Hunter style without obvious sauvignon blanc varietal character. There are stalky and greenstick aromas along with the earth/straw regional aspects. The palate has intense straw/hay characters and an arid finish that calls out for food. Try it with yabbies.

QUALITY ♷♷♷♸
VALUE ★★★½
GRAPES semillon 80%, sauvignon blanc 20%
REGION Hunter Valley, NSW
CELLAR 🍾 3
ALC./VOL. 11.2%
RRP $14.50

Andrew Garrett Chardonnay

QUALITY ♥♥♥♥
VALUE ★★★★
GRAPES chardonnay
REGION McLaren Vale and Padthaway, SA
CELLAR 🍷 3
ALC./VOL. 13.0%
RRP $14.50 ⓢ

This discounts down to $10.95, a price-point where the Mildara group has several wines. Once upon a time $10 was seen as a barrier: people wouldn't pay a cent more. Now, those wines have moved up to $10.95 without consumer resistance.

CURRENT RELEASE 1995 This has a full yellow colour and a creamy barrel-fermented nose; subtle, smooth and very appealing. The palate is smooth and rounded with subtle oak and fine balance. There's a degree of richness and it's good value for money. A finer style to serve with crudités and aioli.

Andrew Garrett Sauvignon Blanc

QUALITY ♥♥♥♥
VALUE ★★★★
GRAPES sauvignon blanc
REGION Padthaway, SA
CELLAR 🍷 1
ALC./VOL. 12.5%
RRP $14.50 ⓢ

The Andrew Garrett winery is a picturesque place, with a lake, restaurant, motel and conference centre in its grounds. Maker Phil Reschke.

CURRENT RELEASE 1995 A very smart sauvignon: fresh gooseberry aromas with grassy notes, turning tropical on the finish. Fresh, crisp yet smooth and flavoursome with definite varietal character. A wine of quality and distinction. Try it with freshly shucked oysters.

Andrew Garrett Semillon

QUALITY ♥♥♥⟨
VALUE ★★★½
GRAPES semillon
REGION Padthaway, SA
CELLAR 🍷 2
ALC./VOL. 13.0%
RRP $12.90 ⓢ

The question on all McLaren Vale's lips is: will Andrew 'Phoenix' Garrett rise again and start another wine company? Mildara bought his first two.

Previous outstanding vintages: '90, '91, '92

CURRENT RELEASE 1995 Semillon is hardly Padthaway's star turn, but this is a worthy example. True to the maker's style it is clean and fresh, very competently made, with typical semillon lanolin/hand cream scent and a soft, rounded, faintly stalky taste. A green tang enlivens the finish. Serve with vegetarian foods.

Angove's Butterfly Ridge Colombard Chardonnay

New label here, and the butterfly has flown the coop. It's a little appreciated fact that Angove's is one of the biggest winemakers in Australia.

CURRENT RELEASE 1995 Greenish herbal, almost wormwood aromas and the palate is soft and seems low in acid, with a rather floppy lack of structure. Round and melony, it is clean, dry and well made. Excellent value at the price. Try it with crab cakes.

QUALITY 🍷🍷🍷
VALUE ★★★★
GRAPES colombard, chardonnay
REGION Renmark, SA
CELLAR 2
ALC./VOL. 12.5%
RRP $7.50 (S)

Annie's Lane Semillon

This fruit comes from the blessed patch of 60-year-old vines in front of the Quelltaler winery. They've produced great semillon as long as we can remember. This is a restaurant-only wine. Maker David O'Leary.

CURRENT RELEASE 1995 Full yellow, reflecting the use of oak. Barrel fermentation gives a smoky, toasty oak-led bouquet and the palate is soft and fruity with lively lanolin and lemon characters. A seamless wine that offers great value and will cellar well. Serve with buttery, lemony fish.

QUALITY 🍷🍷🍷🍷🍷
VALUE ★★★★★
GRAPES semillon
REGION Clare Valley, SA
CELLAR 5+
ALC./VOL. 13.0%
RRP $12.60

Antipodean

From Yalumba ... great package, great label. The challenge of wine marketing in the '90s is to dream up a great concept and give it an evocative name and a swish package. This is exhibit A.
Previous outstanding vintages: '94

CURRENT RELEASE 1995 More than just a pretty face. It's a grassy style with delicious flavour, balance and a winning combination of softness, richness and lively sauvignon tang. A lovely drink and while the label leads you to expect something truly exotic, it's really just a good example of the popular sauvignon/semillon genre. Try it with Nicoise salad.

QUALITY 🍷🍷🍷🍷½
VALUE ★★★½
GRAPES sauvignon blanc 49%, semillon 42%, viognier 9%
REGION Barossa, Clare & Eden Valleys, Angle Vale, SA; Yarra Valley, Vic.
CELLAR 2
ALC./VOL. 11.0%
RRP $16.00 (S)

Ashbrook Semillon

QUALITY ♟♟♟♟?
VALUE ★★★★
GRAPES semillon
REGION Margaret River, WA
CELLAR 🍾 1
ALC./VOL. 12.8%
RRP $15.00

Margaret River has a stamp of semillon all of its own, and what a contrast to the more trad Aussie style! Maker Brian Devitt.

CURRENT RELEASE 1995 Bright light yellow colour and intense grassy gooseberry aromas excite both the eye and the nose, and the taste does not disappoint. It's very lemony, crisp and bracing, more resembling sauvignon blanc perhaps but a delicious drink while young, with asparagus and shaved parmesan.

Balnaves Chardonnay

QUALITY ♟♟♟♟?
VALUE ★★★★½
GRAPES chardonnay
REGION Coonawarra, SA
CELLAR 🍾 3+
ALC./VOL. 13.0%
RRP $16.50 (cellar door)

Doug Balnaves, another Coonawarra viticulturalist turned wine producer, recently hired ex-Wynns winemaker Peter Bissell to head his new production team. There are 40 ha. of vines.

CURRENT RELEASE 1995 Lovely full-bodied chardonnay, rich and powerful, flowing with vanilla, cashew aromas and tropical/passionfruit flavours in the mouth. Plenty of fruit concentration and length, with a warm afterglow. Should go well with chicken and mango salad.

Bannockburn Chardonnay

QUALITY ♟♟♟♟♟
VALUE ★★★★½
GRAPES chardonnay
REGION Geelong, Vic.
CELLAR 🍾 5+
ALC./VOL. 14.0%
RRP $32.00

Fastidious and very French is the Bannockburn approach. All grapes are estate-grown and low-yields are paramount. The chardonnay is one of the most Burgundian in this country.

Previous outstanding vintages: '86, '87, '88, '90, '91, '92, '93

CURRENT RELEASE 1994 This is a tremendously complex wine with all the hallmarks of a fine Burgundy. Deep yellow colour; cedar, nuts and butter with peach fruit aromas all mixed up in a seamless melange of flavours. The taste is very rich, powerful and long. While it's terrific now it has a great future. Serve with roast pheasant.

Banrock Station Semillon Chardonnay

This is a new label from Kingston-on-Murray and the wines were made to drink now.

CURRENT RELEASE *non-vintage* The colour is a pale lemon yellow and the nose has overt citrus aromas. The medium-bodied palate has gentle citrus and gooseberry flavours. They are balanced by a crisp acid finish. It can be served well chilled; try it with a warm pesto chicken salad.

QUALITY ♥♥♥
VALUE ★★★
GRAPES semillon, chardonnay
REGION Riverland, SA
CELLAR 🍾
ALC./VOL. 12.0%
RRP $8.95

Banrock Station Unwooded Chardonnay

The back label bears repeating: 'It's simple really. You start with rich fertile soil. Into this you plant vine cuttings of noble pedigree. Nature adds water and sunlight. The vines bear fruit. The fruit is picked, crushed, fermented and aged. And then you drink it.' Now you know.

CURRENT RELEASE 1995 A fresh fragrant style with plenty of flavour. The nose offers melon and peach aromas and the rich palate offers melon and apricot. These are balanced by crisp acid on a lively finish. It can be served well chilled; try it with yabbies.

QUALITY ♥♥♥♥
VALUE ★★★★
GRAPES chardonnay
REGION Riverland, SA
CELLAR 🍾
ALC./VOL. 13.5%
RRP $8.95

Barratt Chardonnay

This winery was established in 1983 by Lindsay and Carolyn Barratt and the wines are made by various contract makers. Maker Jeffrey Grosset.

CURRENT RELEASE 1985 Very nutty nose where oak dominates and fruit chimes in with a little reluctance. The palate is chewy with grapefruit and peach flavours and there is also evidence of a major contribution from the oak. The finish is a mix of crisp oak and clean acid. It should be served with a medium chill. It would go well with tripe Italian style.

QUALITY ♥♥♥♥
VALUE ★★★½
GRAPES chardonnay
REGION Adelaide Hills, SA
CELLAR 🍾 6
ALC./VOL. 13.5%
RRP $ 24.00

Barwang Chardonnay

QUALITY 🍷🍷🍷🍷
VALUE ★★★★
GRAPES chardonnay
REGION Young, NSW
CELLAR 🍷 5
ALC./VOL. 13.5%
RRP $14.50

The hill tops of middle NSW have loads of viticultural potential, witness this vineyard and regions like Cowra. There is plenty of unused land that can be planted to vines. It could become the fruit bowl of Australia. Maker Jim Brayne.

CURRENT RELEASE 1995 Well-made authentic varietal style that has a classy wood treatment. The nose offers a mix of citrus, toast and peach aromas. The palate is complex with peach, melon and almond flavours attenuated by the American oak component on the finish which adds vanilla. French oak adds grip. It is a wine to serve near room temperature; try it with chicken and mushroom risotto.

Basedow Chardonnay

QUALITY 🍷🍷🍷🍷
VALUE ★★★★
GRAPES chardonnay
REGION Barossa Valley, SA
CELLAR 🍷 5
ALC./VOL. 13.8%
RRP $14.50

Following the corporate progress of this label is like trying to unravel a Le Carré spy novel. At last count it has been leased by Grant Burge to a distribution company. As long as the wines continue . . .

CURRENT RELEASE 1994 A big style that pitches oak against fruit and they call it a draw. The nose is woody but there is also underlying peach smells. The palate is big and rich with a mouth-filling quality. The main flavour is peach and this is quickly joined by oak which dominates the finish. There is no need to chill and it is big enough to deal with smoked meats.

Basedow Oscar's Tradition White Burgundy

Read semillon by any other name. Basedow was founded in 1896 so it will be doing the ton soon. Stand by for some spectacular wines (weather permitting). Maker Grant Burge.
CURRENT RELEASE 1995 Yankee Oak Rules OK! The nose is highly scented with coconut and Vietnamese mint aromas. The palate has a creamy texture with strong lemon and other citrus flavours. The finish shows dry dusty oak. Don't overchill and try it with milk fed veal.

QUALITY 🍷🍷🍷🍷
VALUE ★★★½
GRAPES semillon
REGION Barossa Valley, SA
CELLAR 🍾 4
ALC./VOL. 13.5%
RRP $12.00 Ⓢ

Bazzani Chardonnay Chenin Blanc

If you ever want a dirty weekend, even with your spouse, book into the Warrenmang resort where this wine is made. It is fabulous accommodation, great food and the hospitality from proprietor Luigi Bazzani is legendary. Maker Roland Kaval.
CURRENT RELEASE 1995 An unusual blend that probably won't start a trend but works as far as drinking is concerned. The nose is fruity with a hint of sherbet. The palate is a mix of sweet apple and peach flavours. It is full flavoured and the finish restores the balance with firm authority. Serve with a medium chill and try it with yabbies in a light chilli sauce.

QUALITY 🍷🍷🍷
VALUE ★★★
GRAPES chardonnay, chenin blanc
REGION Pyrenees, Vic.
CELLAR 🍾 1
ALC./VOL. 12.0%
RRP $14.50

Best's Chardonnay

Best's chardonnay is grown on a gravelly hillside above the winery, where the ever-present frost risk is avoided.
Previous outstanding vintages: '79, '81, '84, '89
CURRENT RELEASE 1995 This little trimmer is very finessy and doesn't betray its high alcohol strength. The colour is light yellow, the nose fruit-driven with melon, nectarine and cashew aromas, with a discreet overlay of cedary oak. The taste is refined and overtly fruity with a trademark note of passionfruit in the middle-palate. Try it with a minty Thai chicken salad.

QUALITY 🍷🍷🍷🍷🍷
VALUE ★★★★
GRAPES chardonnay
REGION Great Western, Vic.
CELLAR 🍾 5+
ALC./VOL. 14.0%
RRP $19.30

Best's Riesling

QUALITY ♙♙♙♙⟨
VALUE ★★★★½
GRAPES riesling
REGION Great Western, Vic.
CELLAR 🍷 10
ALC./VOL. 12.0%
RRP $13.50

Great Western is an under-rated riesling region and Best's has turned out some beauties over the years.
Previous outstanding vintages: '72, '81, '82, '85, '88, '90, '91, '92, '94
CURRENT RELEASE 1995 In youth this has doughy yeast esters which will give way to more floral and citrusy aspects with age. There is lime in the palate with a trace of sweetness and a little hardness that time may soften. There is rich, ripe fruit and good length. Chill well and serve with chicken and lychee salad.

Bethany Chardonnay

QUALITY ♙♙♙♙
VALUE ★★★★
GRAPES chardonnay
REGION Barossa Valley, SA
CELLAR 🍷 6
ALC./VOL. 13.5%
RRP $15.00

The Bethany winery is situated in a disused quarry under the shadow of Kaiser Stuhl in the Barossa Valley. It is the labour of love for the Schrapel family. Makers Geoff and Robert Schrapel.
CURRENT RELEASE 1995 No beg pardons here. The nose is a mix of peach and American oak aromas. The palate is a mix of raw peach and citrus flavours which are bolstered by exuberant American oak. It may do well in the cellar. Don't over chill and try with a traditional roast chook.

Bethany Selected Harvest Riesling

QUALITY ♙♙♙⟨
VALUE ★★★
GRAPES riesling
REGION Barossa Valley, SA
CELLAR 🍷 3
ALC./VOL. 9.5%
RRP $15.00

This style is developed by cordon pruning. Which means the fruit-bearing canes (cordons) of the vine are cut and the fruit is left to harden and dehydrate, thus concentrating the sugar.
CURRENT RELEASE 1995 As expected this is a rich style with a lemon-scented nose. The palate has a honeyed quality with lime and marmalade flavours that are balanced by clean acid on a lingering dry finish. The ferment was probably stopped to retain some sugar. It should be served well chilled; try it with confit of duck.

Bethany Semillon

There is a debate about whether to give semillon a wood treatment. In the Barossa it seems desirable but should it be French or American? It's an individual winemaking decision.

CURRENT RELEASE 1995 This one has an American oak treatment and it tends to lead the band. The nose has a caramel and talcum powder aroma (thanks to the oak). The palate shows some sweet fruit with gooseberry and peach flavours and the oak counter punches with a dusty dry finish and a vanillan oak lift. It should not be served too cold. Try it with pan-fried veal.

QUALITY ♥♥♥♥
VALUE ★★★★
GRAPES semillon
REGION Barossa Valley, SA
CELLAR 🍾 4
ALC./VOL. 12.5%
RRP $16.00

Bleasdale Sandhill Verdelho

Verdelho is a snake charmer of a variety. Just when a wine writer thinks he/she has the flavour nailed down, along comes another enigma to strike cobra-like doubt.

CURRENT RELEASE 1995 The dance of the seven veils, this example adds sweetness to the equation. The nose has tropical fruit aromas and there are tropical notes like pineapple and kiwi fruit on the sweet palate. This is balanced by some cohesive oak in a lingering dry finish. It can be served with a medium chill. Try it with a bowl of Singapore noodles.

QUALITY ♥♥♥♥
VALUE ★★★★
GRAPES verdelho
REGION Langhorne Creek, SA
CELLAR 🍾 6
ALC./VOL. 13.0%
RRP $13.50

Blue Pyrenees Chardonnay

QUALITY 🍷🍷🍷🍷
VALUE ★★★½
GRAPES chardonnay
REGION Pyrenees, Vic.
CELLAR 🍾
ALC./VOL. 13.0%
RRP $20.00

This label is continually lauded as a triumph, but its passage has not been smooth. At first it was ruled out of order because blue on a label was deemed to be confined to toilet product wrappers. This proves it ain't necessarily so.

CURRENT RELEASE 1995 No-holds barred style that makes use of both fruit and wood. The nose has powerful grapefruit aromas and cedar-like wood. The palate has a mouth-filling texture with grapefruit and melon flavours and these are followed by dry oak on a long persistent finish. It should not be served too cold. Try it with chicken and cheese tortellini.

Bluestone Bridge Chardonnay

QUALITY 🍷🍷🍷🍷
VALUE ★★★★
GRAPES chardonnay
REGION Macedon, Vic.
CELLAR 🍾 4
ALC./VOL. 12.5%
RRP $20.00

This is a brand new winery and the label reads like the liner notes on a locally produced CD that thanks friends and relatives. It has a certain naive charm. Makers Howard Bradfield and Juliana Smith.

CURRENT RELEASE 1995 A promising debut, this is a racing greyhound-style chardonnay. It is lean and muscly. The nose has melon, figs and toast aromas. The palate weighs in on the citrus end of the spectrum with grapefruit dominating. French and American oak are evident on the finish. Don't overchill and serve it with calamari in a light chilli sauce.

Boston Bay Chardonnay

This pioneering vineyard belongs to an impish character known as 'Fordie' who drinks in the front bar of the Exeter Hotel in Adelaide. Graham Ford is keen to establish the Eyre Peninsula as a wine-growing region. Maker David O'Leary (contract).
CURRENT RELEASE 1995 This is a big wine with loads of flavour. The nose is a mixture of grassy aromas and peach. The palate is mouth-filling with overt peach flavours and hints of guava and melon. There are also some buttery characters which are followed by a powerful finish that leaves coating oak in the mouth.

QUALITY ♛♛♛♛
VALUE ★★★★
GRAPES chardonnay
REGION Eyre Peninsula, SA
CELLAR 🍾 6
ALC./VOL. 12.8%
RRP $17.00

Boston Bay Riesling

Boston Bay is situated with sea views (you can chuck a rock into the water from the edge of the vineyard) near Port Lincoln on the Eyre Peninsula.
CURRENT RELEASE 1995 The nose says riesling to us. There is strong lime aroma and this is the dominant flavour on the palate. It is intense and the acid on the finish keeps things crisp and tidy. It can be served well chilled. Try it with Coffin Bay scallops in their shell with black bean sauce.

QUALITY ♛♛♛♛
VALUE ★★★★
GRAPES riesling
REGION Eyre Peninsula, SA
CELLAR 🍾 4
ALC./VOL. 10.7%
RRP $13.50

Bowen Estate Chardonnay

The estate was first established by Doug and Joy Bowen in 1972. It has built a formidable reputation for red wines but the chardonnay is not to be overlooked.
CURRENT RELEASE 1995 This is a very civilised style with some interesting flavours. The nose has lychee and melon aromas. The palate is restrained with a distinct citrus flavour and a background of peach. There is discreet wood on a dry finish. It should be served lightly chilled; try it with grilled barramundi.

QUALITY ♛♛♛♛
VALUE ★★★★
GRAPES chardonnay
REGION Coonawarra, SA
CELLAR 🍾 4
ALC./VOL. 12.5%
RRP $16.00

Boyntons of Bright Semillon

QUALITY ♛♛♛♛
VALUE ★★★★
GRAPES semillon
REGION Bright, Vic.
CELLAR 🍾 6
ALC./VOL. 12.0%
RRP $15.00

This is a small winery on the road to the snowfields in Victoria. It produces around 4800 cases a year. Maker Kel Boynton.

CURRENT RELEASE 1995 A pert style with some amusing characters. The colour is a lively bright yellow and the nose is full of herbs and straw. Gooseberry and herbal flavours dominate the palate and these are backed by some crisp acid on a fresh finish. It can be served well chilled; try it with sardines in beer batter.

Brands Laira Chardonnay

QUALITY ♛♛♛♛♛
VALUE ★★★★
GRAPES chardonnay
REGION Coonawarra, SA
CELLAR 🍾 3
ALC./VOL. 13.0%
RRP $16.90 Ⓢ

This Canberra trophy-winner was held back for extra bottle-age before release. Maker Jim Brand.

CURRENT RELEASE 1994 A true show pony: very rich oak and butterscotch malolactic bouquet, strong on vanilla and the palate shows excellent depth and richness. A very good wine of an unashamedly oaky style. Try it with any roasted poultry.

Brands Laira Family Reserve Chardonnay

QUALITY ♛♛♛♛♛
VALUE ★★★★
GRAPES chardonnay
REGION Coonawarra, SA
CELLAR 🍾 2
ALC./VOL. 12.5%
RRP $22.00

Family images are thought to be worth something in the marketing of wine, hence Brown Brothers, Drayton Family, Garrett Family, etc.

CURRENT RELEASE 1992 A beautifully developed chardonnay with deep golden colour and rich, opulent flavour. There's a multitude of different flavours including peach and quince and the oak has mellowed nicely into the fruit and aged characters. Serve with a ripe brie.

Brands Laira Riesling

Now owned by McWilliams, the Brand family holdings have been added to in large measure by the new owners. Several hundred hectares of new plantings will provide low-cost wine for McWilliams' inexpensive labels.

CURRENT RELEASE 1994 A rich, rather solid riesling which is starting to show bottle-age. Very dry and crisp, it has bracing acidity, a lime/lemon bouquet and a sherbety finish. Goes well with grilled swordfish.

QUALITY 🍷🍷🍷🍷
VALUE ★★★★
GRAPES riesling
REGION Coonawarra, SA
CELLAR 🍾 4
ALC./VOL. 11.0%
RRP $12.90 (S)

Brian Barry Jud's Hill Riesling

Brian Barry is one of the industry's most influential consultant winemakers, with a long record as a show judge and chairman. He's done much to raise winemaking standards and eradicate faults.

Previous outstanding vintages: '94

CURRENT RELEASE 1995 A lovely wine from a little-known producer, this has model fruit concentration and finesse. The colour is vibrant light yellow, the nose rich in fresh stone-fruit and tropical, slightly herbal aromas. The palate has very generous flavour and a lingering dry aftertaste. Serve with scallops à la nage.

QUALITY 🍷🍷🍷🍷🍷
VALUE ★★★★★
GRAPES riesling
REGION Clare Valley, SA
CELLAR 🍾 8
ALC./VOL. 12.7%
RRP $17.00

Bridgewater Mill Chardonnay

The house wines that went around the world. These wines are served in the restaurant but they are also the second label for the Petaluma group. Maker Brian Croser.

CURRENT RELEASE 1994 A refined tri-area blend that shows obvious evidence of barrel fermentation. It's almost a bit twee. The nose has peach, melon and wood aromas. The palate has a creamy barrel ferment texture and subdued peach and melon flavours. The finish shows some tightly fitting oak. It can be served with a medium chill; try it with a crab and noodle salad.

QUALITY 🍷🍷🍷🍷
VALUE ★★★★
GRAPES chardonnay
REGION Clare Valley, McLaren Vale, Adelaide Hills, SA
CELLAR 🍾 4
ALC./VOL. 13.5%
RRP $19.00

Bridgewater Mill Sauvignon Blanc

QUALITY ♛♛♛♛♕
VALUE ★★★★½
GRAPES sauvignon blanc
REGION Currency Creek, Coonawarra, Adelaide Hills, Clare Valley, SA
CELLAR 🍷 2
ALC./VOL. 12.0%
RRP $19.00

While the alcohol levels on the other wines under this label have been creeping up a bit, this wine continues to maintain a lower level.
CURRENT RELEASE 1995 An intense wine which captures the positive elements of the variety. The nose is a dervish of tropical fruit aromas. The palate continues the tropical theme and there is a gooseberry component. Plenty of acid on the finish makes for a refreshing drink. Try it with a ragout of char-grilled eggplant and capsicum drizzled in a special olive oil.

Brokenwood Chardonnay

QUALITY ♛♛♛♛♕
VALUE ★★★★½
GRAPES chardonnay
REGION McLaren Vale, SA; Cowra, Hunter Valley, NSW
CELLAR 🍷 6
ALC./VOL. 13.0%
RRP $18.50

Winemaker Iain Riggs is a lateral thinker: he doesn't believe in being a prisoner of a single vineyard so he sources fruit from several regions around Australia.
CURRENT RELEASE 1995 Loads of style in this well-crafted wine. There is nothing out of place and the proportions are near perfect. The nose has peach and wood aromas, and peach is the dominant flavour on the palate. The wood cuddles up to the fruit and makes for a dry lingering finish. It should be served lightly chilled. Try it with smoked cod with white sauce.

Brokenwood Cricket Pitch

QUALITY ♛♛♛♛♕
VALUE ★★★★½
GRAPES sauvignon blanc, semillon
REGION not stated
CELLAR 🍷 3
ALC./VOL. 13.0%
RRP $15.00

The name comes from an old parish map that shows the vineyard was once gazetted as the playing field of the Pokolbin district.
Previous outstanding vintages: '94, '95
CURRENT RELEASE 1996 Very young and fresh with loads of sauvignon blanc characters. There are grassy herbal aromas and the palate is substantial with generous fruit flavours and a hint of sweetness. There is some neat oak on the civilised finish. It is ready to go and can be served well chilled. Try it with pan-fried whiting.

Brokenwood Semillon

What started as a pinstriped commune goes from strength to strength. Brokenwood was founded in 1970 by a band of Sydney professionals who liked to get their hands dirty on weekends. Maker Iain Riggs.

CURRENT RELEASE 1995 A youthful style that shows potential. There is a strong citrus element to the nose plus a herbal background. Lemon flavour dominates the refreshing palate and crisp acid takes a bow on the finish. It can be served fairly well chilled and it goes well (believe it or not) with curried sausages.

QUALITY 🍷🍷🍷🍷
VALUE ★★★½
GRAPES semillon
REGION Hunter Valley, NSW
CELLAR 🍾 8
ALC./VOL. 11.0%
RRP $17.00

CURRENT RELEASE 1996 The colour is pale straw and the nose has a real hayshed aroma. There is plenty of freshly cut grass. The palate has a hint of honey and sweet gooseberry fruit. The finish shows some firm acid and has good length. Lots of potential here but chill well and try it with sushi.

QUALITY 🍷🍷🍷🍷🍷
VALUE ★★★★½
GRAPES semillon
REGION Hunter Valley, NSW
CELLAR 🍾 8
ALC./VOL. 11.0%
RRP $16.00

Brokenwood Unwooded Chardonnay

Depending on your point of view, unwooded chardonnay is a very interesting segue in flavour or like a salad without dressing or a kiss without a moustache.

CURRENT RELEASE 1996 Pale, young and fresh with a zesty lift on the finish. What else do you need to know? It is pitched at the citrus end of the chardonnay flavour spectrum and some tropical fruit flavours also creep in, adding a lift. The finish has crisp acid and there is a slight warmth of alcohol. It can be served well chilled; try it with tandoori chicken.

QUALITY 🍷🍷🍷🍷
VALUE ★★★★
GRAPES chardonnay
REGION Hunter Valley, NSW
CELLAR 🍾 3
ALC./VOL. 13.5%
RRP $15.00

WHITE WINES

Brookfields Sauvignon Blanc

QUALITY 🍷🍷🍷
VALUE ★★★
GRAPES sauvignon blanc
REGION Hawkes Bay, NZ
CELLAR 🍾 2
ALC./VOL. 11.5%
RRP $18.95

The winery/vineyard was established in 1937 in Hawkes Bay. The annual production is around 5000 cases. Maker Peter Robertson.

CURRENT RELEASE 1995 This is a restrained style made from grapes relatively low in sugar. The nose is grassy with hints of yeast. The medium-bodied palate has some tropical fruit characters plus gooseberry flavour. There is plenty of crisp acid on the dry finish. It can be served well chilled. Try it with Asian food.

Brown Brothers Dry Muscat Blanc

QUALITY 🍷🍷🍷
VALUE ★★★½
GRAPES muscat of Alexandria
REGION north-east Vic.
CELLAR 🍾
ALC./VOL. 12.0%
RRP $11.20

This is an interesting style that deserves a wider audience. It is a good seafood style at the right price.

CURRENT RELEASE 1995 It is a simple yet enjoyable style. The nose is very fragrant with typical muscat aromas. The palate has clean grape qualities with a hint of musk and these are followed by some very crisp acid. It should be served well chilled; try it with pan-fried whitebait.

Brown Brothers Family Reserve Chardonnay

QUALITY 🍷🍷🍷🍷
VALUE ★★★
GRAPES chardonnay
REGION King Valley, Vic.
CELLAR 🍾 4
ALC./VOL. 14.0%
RRP $23.00

The 'Family Reserve' part of the Browns' portfolio comes at an extra cost but it shows a step up in the level of quality and flavour. You also get bottle-age thrown in for good measure.

CURRENT RELEASE 1992 A rich style that is still doing a B&D number with wood. The colour is a bright green-gold and the nose is a mix of paw paw, peach and toasty oak. The palate has a buttery texture with full-on peach flavour and hints of grapefruit. Toasty oak fills out the finish and adds grip. It should be served lightly chilled. Try it with char-grilled tuna.

Brown Brothers Gewurztraminer

You could well ask why bother with this star-crossed variety. Yet is has a small following, particularly those who like to serve it with Asian food.
CURRENT RELEASE 1995 A very pungent style that shows a hint of cellulite. It is voluptuous and full flavoured. The nose is pungent with lychee, violets and spice aromas. The palate is dominated by gooseberry with hints of tropical fruit. There is soft acid on the finish. Chill it down and try it with Thai soup.

QUALITY 🍷🍷🍷🍷🍷
VALUE ★★★★★
GRAPES gewurztraminer
REGION King Valley, Vic.
CELLAR 🍾 2
ALC./VOL. 13.5%
RRP $14.50

Best White Blend/Other Variety

Brown Brothers Noble Riesling

John Brown senior recognised noble rot in the Milawa vineyard in the early '70s and made the prototype for this long-enduring and exciting style. Previous outstanding vintages: too numerous to mention
CURRENT RELEASE 1992 This wine is starting to show bottle development. The colour is golden amber and the nose has honey, caramel and vanilla aromas. The palate is rich with honeyed qualities, a hint of marmalade and an underscore of crisp lime/riesling flavours. There is fresh acid on the finish. It should be served well chilled with soft blue cheese.

QUALITY 🍷🍷🍷🍷🍷
VALUE ★★★½
GRAPES riesling
REGION Milawa, Vic.
CELLAR 🍾 4
ALC./VOL. 9.5%
RRP $31.00

Brown Brothers Rhine Riesling

No second guesses about the busiest cellar door in the land. The Brothers Brown do it very well and they handle tourist buses and mopeds with equal aplomb.
CURRENT RELEASE 1995 A straightforward wine that is easy to drink. The nose is a mix of citrus, pear and fennel aromas. The palate is all about keen lime flavour. Crisp acid adds zest to the finish. It should be served well chilled; try it with tempura vegetables.

QUALITY 🍷🍷🍷🍷
VALUE ★★★½
GRAPES riesling
REGION King Valley, Vic.
CELLAR 🍾 3
ALC./VOL. 12.5%
RRP $13.00

Brown Brothers Sauvignon Blanc

QUALITY 🍷🍷🍷🍷
VALUE ★★★½
GRAPES sauvignon blanc
REGION King Valley, Vic.
CELLAR 🍾 2
ALC./VOL. 12.0%
RRP $14.50

Yet another wine in the long line-up and again the fruit is drawn from King Valley. There remains the nagging question – has there ever been a great wine made from the fruit of said valley? Maker Roland Wahlquist.

CURRENT RELEASE 1995 Very pungent with heaps of lantana aroma on the nose. The colour is pale, almost leeched. The palate is pleasantly rich with a hint of sweetness and strong tropical fruit flavours. The finish shows some crisp acid. It should be served with a medium chill. Try it with crusty bread and extra virgin olive oil that has been infused with basil.

Brown Brothers Semillon

QUALITY 🍷🍷🍷🍷
VALUE ★★★★
GRAPES semillon
REGION north-east Vic.
CELLAR 🍾 3
ALC./VOL. 13.0%
RRP $14.00

Keeping track of the Brown Brothers' portfolio would take a computer that would rival 'deep thought' – here is another member of the huge clan.

CURRENT RELEASE 1993 More robust than your average Hunter, this wine is a mix of citrus and gooseberry. The nose has a distinct lanolin aroma as well as citrus. The palate lays on the gooseberry and there is discreet wood on a long finish. It can be served with a medium chill and it goes well with a Vietnamese country pancake.

Browns of Padthaway Chardonnay

QUALITY 🍷🍷🍷🍷
VALUE ★★★★
GRAPES chardonnay
REGION Padthaway, SA
CELLAR 🍾 2
ALC./VOL. 13.0%
RRP $14.00

Nothing to do with the brothers in Victoria. This family own the Glendon Park vineyard in Padthaway.

CURRENT RELEASE 1994 This is an unwooded style that shows plenty of varietal character. The nose offers fresh melon aromas and the palate continues with melon flavour. There is plenty of acid that adds refreshment on the finish. It can be served well chilled and it is very comfortable with smoked salmon.

Bullers Chenin Blanc

The grapes were grown near Swan Hill, Vic. The variety is a something of a lost cause but stalwart Bullers persist. Maker Richard Buller.
CURRENT RELEASE 1995 The colour is a pale lemon yellow and the nose has a heady mix of green apple, nutmeg and yeast aromas. The palate shows a hint of sweetness which is balanced by some tart acid which adds an attractive sweet and sour quality. It is a zesty mouth-cleansing wine that can be served well chilled. It is great with a ham sandwich.

QUALITY ♕♕♕♗
VALUE ★★★½
GRAPES chenin blanc
REGION Riverland, Vic.
CELLAR ↓ 2
ALC./VOL. 11.9%
RRP $12.50

Campbells Silverburn Dry White

There's a lot of Scottish pride around the Campbell establishment in Rutherglen. Why they call a creek (cool and wet) a burn (hot and fiery) is a mystery . . .
CURRENT RELEASE 1995 Beam me up, Scottie! This little lassie will do a highland fling around your palate. It's light and fruity, simple and easy-drinking, with faint grassy and berry aromas and a crisp acid finish. A general purpose quaffer to serve with seafood.

QUALITY ♕♕♗
VALUE ★★★
GRAPES semillon, sauvignon blanc
REGION Rutherglen, Vic.
CELLAR ↓
ALC./VOL. 11.7%
RRP $11.00 ⓢ

Canobolas-Smith Chardonnay

Cool-climate viticulture, this. Perched at 850 metres on the chilly slopes of Mount Canobolas, Murray and Toni Smith craft tiny quantities of intense wines.
Previous outstanding vintages: '93, '94
CURRENT RELEASE 1995 A crisp, tightly poised chardonnay with delicacy and subtle oak. The acid is crisp and tangy with underlying softness and a touch of 'sur lie' character. Very long finish and will improve with time. Try it with whitebait fritters.

QUALITY ♕♕♕♕
VALUE ★★★★
GRAPES chardonnay
REGION Orange, NSW
CELLAR ↓ 5
ALC./VOL. 13.4%
RRP $17.00 (cellar door)

Cape Jaffa Chardonnay

QUALITY ♛♛♛♛
VALUE ★★★½
GRAPES chardonnay
REGION Mount Benson, SA
CELLAR 🍾 2
ALC./VOL. 13.5%
RRP $16.50 (cellar door)

Cape Jaffa is in the exciting new Mount Benson region of south-west South Australia. It's a joint venture between the Hooper family, formerly of St Mary's, and Ralph and Debbie Fowler of Leconfield, Coonawarra.

CURRENT RELEASE 1995 A refined, fruit-dominant style of chardonnay, made by Ralph Fowler from Addison's vineyard – Cape Jaffa's next-door neighbour – while their own vines mature. It has a subdued nose, attractive delicacy and subtle flavour, with a soft but dry finish. Try it with prawns.

Cape Jaffa Sauvignon Blanc

QUALITY ♛♛♛♛
VALUE ★★★½
GRAPES sauvignon blanc 88%, semillon 12%
REGION McLaren Vale, SA
CELLAR 🍾 1
ALC./VOL. 13.5%
RRP $16.00 (cellar door)

While the Cape Jaffa vineyard is growing up, other people's grapes are used as a stop-gap. The vineyard is within sight of the sea and the Cape Jaffa lighthouse.

CURRENT RELEASE 1995 A light-bodied, delicate juicy style with fine tropical and cut-grass varietal fruit flavours and just a smidgin of wood from the barrel fermented component. Could use more intensity, but a good wine with a goat's cheese salad.

Cape Jaffa Semillon Sauvignon Blanc

QUALITY ♛♛♛♛♛
VALUE ★★★★
GRAPES semillon, sauvignon blanc
REGION McLaren Vale & Clare, SA
CELLAR 🍾 2
ALC./VOL. 12.5%
RRP $16.00

While the young vines at Cape Jaffa are coming into bearing, they buy fruit from other growers and sometimes other regions. Maker Derek Hooper.

CURRENT RELEASE 1996 Very pungent style: gooseberry and lantana, with a touch of the feline, and delicious depth of crisp, frisky fruit on the palate. Just the thing to serve with Nicoise salad.

Cape Jaffa Unwooded Chardonnay

Mount Benson is an emerging sub-region of the Limestone coast, which takes in Robe and Beachport in the south-east of SA. This is made from McLaren Vale grapes.

CURRENT RELEASE 1996 Very fresh, with slightly herbaceous, sauvignon blanc-ish scents and a vibrant, lively, fresh palate. There's a tonne of fruit in this and it's an excellent example of the unwooded style. Try it with antipasto.

QUALITY ♦♦♦♦
VALUE ★★★½
GRAPES chardonnay
REGION McLaren Vale, SA
CELLAR 🍾 3+
ALC./VOL. 12.5%
RRP $15.40

Capel Vale Chardonnay

Capel Vale blends from several WA regions these days, but this wine is from their own vines at Capel. Maker Rob Bowen.

CURRENT RELEASE 1994 A controversial wine, unusual ... but it grew on us. The bouquet is bizarre at first, with feral Burgundian smells of strong high-toast oak, 'sur-lie' characters and a vegetal edge to the fruit. It improved with extended breathing, and the combination of tropical fruit and oak flavours, and balance in the mouth were quite superb. It wouldn't do well in wine shows. A wine of character to serve with sweetbreads.

QUALITY ♦♦♦♦?
VALUE ★★★★
GRAPES chardonnay
REGION south-west coastal, WA
CELLAR 🍾 4+
ALC./VOL. 13.0%
RRP $21.00

Capel Vale CV Unwooded Chardonnay

It's arguable whether Australian drinkers had ever tasted true chardonnay flavour before the unwooded craze. Strange that it didn't happen sooner, because it's a more profitable wine to make without all the trimmings.

CURRENT RELEASE 1995 A pristine example of chardonnay varietal fruit: cashew nuts and peaches galore. Light, fruity, straightforward and a pleasure to sip. Happily, it avoids the slightly sweet finish of many of this style.

QUALITY ♦♦♦?
VALUE ★★★
GRAPES chardonnay
REGION south-west coastal, WA
CELLAR 🍾 2
ALC./VOL. 13.0%
RRP $16.00

Capel Vale Special Reserve Sauvignon Blanc

QUALITY ♛♛♛♛♛
VALUE ★★★★
GRAPES sauvignon blanc
REGION Pemberton, WA
CELLAR 🍾 2
ALC./VOL. 12.0%
RRP $21.50 Ⓢ

In 1995 winemakers Rob Bowen and Krister Jonsson had a batch of sauvignon blanc grapes so good they decided to release the wine separately, instead of putting it into their sauvignon blanc/semillon blend.

CURRENT RELEASE 1995 Dressed in an elegant black label, this high-quality white from the buzzy new cool-climate region of Pemberton has doughy, nutty and green-edged lemon/lime aromas. The fruit is deep and intense on the palate, and there's heaps of style and immediate appeal. Suits salads and seafood dishes.

Cassegrain Chardonnay

QUALITY ♛♛♛♛
VALUE ★★★
GRAPES chardonnay
REGION Hastings Valley, NSW
CELLAR 🍾 2
ALC./VOL. 12.2%
RRP $16.40

John Cassegrain and family developed this serious enterprise in the Hastings Valley at Port Macquarie in the early '80s. The Hastings grew wine in a previous life, last century.

CURRENT RELEASE 1995 Oak features prominently on the bouquet of this, the commercial Cassegrain chardonnay. Caramel and cedar aromas predominate and the taste is lively, crisp and intense with a hint of sweetness and good balancing acid. Try it with dolmades.

Cassegrain Five Mile Hollow Dry White

QUALITY ♛♛♛
VALUE ★★★
GRAPES semillon, verdelho, sauvignon blanc
REGION Hastings Valley, NSW
CELLAR 🍾
ALC./VOL. 11.0%
RRP $11.95 Ⓢ

Cassegrain is French for broken berries, which is exactly what they do to their grapes at vintage time. Maker John Cassegrain.

CURRENT RELEASE 1995 A light, fresh, simple dry white for everyday quaffing. The aroma is of dough and cashews, and it's very soft in the mouth. Try it with Caesar salad.

Cassegrain Fromenteau Reserve Chardonnay

According to the label, fromenteau is a 14th-century French name for the chardonnay grapevine. The Cassegrain family have a proud French family history.

CURRENT RELEASE 1993 Very much in the style of previous wines, this has a toasty, resiny bouquet from combined bottle-age and strong oak character. Buttery, nutty characters and some apricot notes also show in this lean and slightly austere style. Better with food: try creamy chicken boscaiola.

QUALITY 🍷🍷🍷🍷
VALUE ★★½
GRAPES chardonnay
REGION Hastings Valley, NSW
CELLAR 🍾 3
ALC./VOL. 12.7%
RRP $29.00

Castle Rock Chardonnay

The Porongurups are a few clicks out of Albany, the former whaling town on the southern WA coast.

CURRENT RELEASE 1994 The nose is dominated by butterscotch malolactic character and lots of toasty oak. The palate is full, smooth and again very buttery, giving it a Burgundy-like style. There is a high, grapefruit-like acidity and a touch of citrus peel on the finish. An unusual style. Try it with a rich paella.

QUALITY 🍷🍷🍷🍷
VALUE ★★★½
GRAPES chardonnay
REGION Great Southern, WA
CELLAR 🍾 2
ALC./VOL. 12.5%
RRP $18.70

Castle Rock Riesling

Castle Rock is the Diletti family's vineyard high in the Porongurup Range near Albany, WA. The wines are made locally under contract.

CURRENT RELEASE 1994 This is a shy, slow-ageing riesling with slatey/minerally cool-climate aromas and a tart lime juice palate, very crisp and lively with some Germanic overtones. More structure than fruit perhaps, but a good food wine. Try it with trout and hollandaise.

QUALITY 🍷🍷🍷🍷
VALUE ★★★½
GRAPES riesling
REGION Mount Barker, WA
CELLAR 🍾 5
ALC./VOL. 11.5%
RRP $15.80

Chain of Ponds Chardonnay

QUALITY 🍷🍷🍷🍷🍷
VALUE ★★★★½
GRAPES chardonnay
REGION Adelaide Hills, SA
CELLAR 🍾 4
ALC./VOL. 13.5%
RRP $25.00

The '94 vintage cleaned up the Adelaide Hills Wine Show before being voted the best chardonnay entered in the inaugural Boutique Wines of Australia in 1996.

CURRENT RELEASE 1994 A total stunner! This is a real surprise packet: very complex Burgundy-like flavours and rich, yet refined, palate structure. Buttery, vanillan and smoky, with oak and tropical fruit beautifully harmonised, and a finish that lingers long. Demands a three-star scallop dish.

QUALITY 🍷🍷🍷
VALUE ★★½
GRAPES chardonnay
REGION Adelaide Hills, SA
CELLAR ⇀ 1–4
ALC./VOL. 13.5%
RRP $25.00

CURRENT RELEASE 1995 This is a step or two behind '94, the sweaty, tea-leafy aromas reflecting a cool year and turning herbaceous in the palate. It is a simpler, lighter wine, and the finish shows some astringency and alcohol heat. It does have flavour and a few months more bottle-age may help. Try it with yabbies.

Chain of Ponds Riesling

QUALITY 🍷🍷🍷🍷
VALUE ★★★★
GRAPES riesling
REGION Adelaide Hills, SA
CELLAR 🍾 5+
ALC./VOL. 12.5%
RRP $14.00

Chain of Ponds streeted the first Boutique Wines of Australia judging in Sydney in May '96, taking home three trophies and an honourable mention. It's a vineyard going places.

CURRENT RELEASE 1994 This is a fine, pale-coloured, restrained, almost austere riesling which has mineral, slate and earth aromas rather than lifted floral aromas. In the mouth it is classically fine and dry yet intense, delicate and balanced. The finish is very neat and it's a wine we could drink a lot of. Suits fresh oysters.

Chain of Ponds Semillon

This 60-ha. Adelaide Hills vineyard, part-owned and managed by a builder named Caj Amadio, is turning out spectacular wines which are making heads turn.

CURRENT RELEASE 1994 Toasty, nutty, oak-influenced aromas shine out front in this stylish semillon. The palate is full and captivating, with richness and excellent depth. There's a little butteriness towards the pleasingly dry finish. Serious wine to drink with a chicken Caesar salad.

QUALITY ♛♛♛♛♜
VALUE ★★★★
GRAPES semillon
REGION Adelaide Hills, SA
CELLAR 🍾 5
ALC./VOL. 12.5%
RRP $17.00

CURRENT RELEASE 1995 Quite a different wine from the '94, this is leaner, with less overt fruit, a butterscotch malolactic character dominant in its youth. The acid is nevertheless pronounced and it could repay short-term cellaring. A wine to serve with seafood.

QUALITY ♛♛♛
VALUE ★★★
GRAPES semillon
REGION Adelaide Hills, SA
CELLAR 🍾 4+
ALC./VOL. 12.5%
RRP $17.00

Chapel Hill Reserve Chardonnay

Winemaker Pam Dunsford used to make these wines in an old (deconsecrated) church, before her flash new state-of-the-art winery was built.

CURRENT RELEASE 1995 This was still a baby at time of tasting, showing the delicacy of the 1995 vintage whites but promising to fill out with more time. The nose shows as-yet undeveloped grapefruity aromas and the palate is fresh, fruit-driven and fine, reflecting the style of Padthaway fruit more than McLaren Vale.

QUALITY ♛♛♛♜
VALUE ★★★
GRAPES chardonnay
REGION Padthaway and McLaren Vale, SA
CELLAR 🍾 5
ALC./VOL. 13.5%
RRP $17.70

Chapel Hill Unwooded Chardonnay

QUALITY ♟♟♟
VALUE ★★★
GRAPES chardonnay
REGION Padthaway, McLaren Vale, Angle Vale & Barossa Valley, SA
CELLAR 🍾 2
ALC./VOL. 12.5%
RRP $15.30

Pam Dunsford, the winemaker here, is a true individualist. Also a pioneer, she was Australia's first woman winemaking graduate, 20 years ago.

CURRENT RELEASE 1995 Delicate, light aromas of green peach and honeydew melon, simple, fruity and pleasant. The taste is much the same: soft, fruity and straightforward, with just a hint of sweetness. Good with most salads.

Charles Sturt University Limited Release Botrytis Semillon

QUALITY ♟♟♟♟︎
VALUE ★★★★
GRAPES semillon
REGION Griffith, NSW
CELLAR 🍾 2
ALC./VOL. 10.0%
RRP $16.40 (375ml)

Rod Hooper is a smart sourcer (sorcerer?) of grapes. Logically, the fruit for this sticky comes from sticky paradise, Griffith.

CURRENT RELEASE 1991 Here's a sweetie that's developing gracefully and isn't racing towards old-age like so many. The colour is full golden yet it retains freshness, with superb dried apricot, vanilla and honey characters and luscious sweetness. Excellent with baked apple tart.

Charles Sturt University Limited Release Chardonnay

QUALITY ♟♟♟♟︎
VALUE ★★★★
GRAPES chardonnay
REGION Cowra, NSW
CELLAR 🍾 5
ALC./VOL. 13.2%
RRP $16.40

This is the 10 000-case-brand marketed by the uni's Wagga campus, where they teach wine science and viticulture. Maker Rod Hooper. Previous outstanding vintages: '93, '94

CURRENT RELEASE 1995 A rich, complex barrel-fermented wine smelling of vanilla, peach and tropical fruits, soft and round in the mouth with a hint of sweetness. Although it had just been bottled, it won the public choice award at the 1996 Boutique Wines exhibition in Sydney. Should develop into a cracker.

Chateau Tahbilk Marsanne

Alister Purbrick has built this brand into a deceptively big-seller. Tahbilk has had marsanne in the ground since the '20s and one of the blocks, planted in 1927, may have the world's oldest marsanne vines.
CURRENT RELEASE 1995 Fragrant, herbal, slightly floral aroma with a touch of yeast-derived bread dough character in its youth. The palate is light-to-mediumweight, soft but lively, with a lemony aspect and has a richness and viscosity that is somewhere between riesling and chardonnay. It will build richness and honeysuckle character as it ages. Goes well with lemon sole.

QUALITY 🍷🍷🍷🍷🍷
VALUE ★★★★★
GRAPES marsanne
REGION Goulburn Valley, Vic.
CELLAR 🍾 5
ALC./VOL. 12.5%
RRP $13.00 Ⓢ

Chateau Xanadu Chardonnay

'For he on honey dew hath fed and drunk the milk of paradise ...' wrote Coleridge in his poem about Xanadu. Maker Jurg Muggli.
CURRENT RELEASE 1995 This is a finer style which shouldn't be served too cold. It comes up with airing, showing a straw/biscuity nose that's subdued in its youth. The palate is fine yet rich and has good intensity and mouth-filling qualities. The wood is nicely trimmed and it would benefit from cellaring. Serve with pasta and clam sauce.

QUALITY 🍷🍷🍷🍷
VALUE ★★★
GRAPES chardonnay
REGION 60% Margaret River, 40% Pemberton, WA
CELLAR ⇨ 1–4+
ALC./VOL. 13.5%
RRP $23.35

Chateau Xanadu Noble Semillon

This spent 10 months in oak, in quest of a world-class sauternes-like botrytis style.
CURRENT RELEASE 1993 The colour is deep developed yellow, the nose has a rather coarse resiny, sappy oak dominance, but the wine comes into its own in the mouth. It is rich and luscious with lots of sweetness and botrytised flavours of honey, apricot, vanilla and dried fruits. A complex, satisfying drink to serve with crème brûlée.

QUALITY 🍷🍷🍷🍷
VALUE ★★★
GRAPES semillon
REGION Margaret River, WA
CELLAR 🍾 2
ALC./VOL. 12.0%
RRP $20.00 (375ml)

Chateau Xanadu Secession

QUALITY ▼▼▼▼?
VALUE ★★★★
GRAPES semillon 40%, sauvignon blanc 30%, chenin blanc 30%
REGION Margaret River, WA
CELLAR 🍾 3
ALC./VOL. 13.0%
RRP $17.70

Xanadu is full of unusual ideas: this wine's name refers to the Viennese painters' secession of last century, although what this has to do with wine is not explained.
Previous outstanding vintages: '93, '94
CURRENT RELEASE 1995 Queensland secessionists will approve. The wine has an aromatic nose of grass and green-stick, and the taste is quite full yet crisp with abundant tropical fruit, smoothness, richness and impressive length. A generous wine that ends nicely dry. Try it with Queensland mud crab.

Chateau Xanadu Semillon

QUALITY ▼▼▼▼?
VALUE ★★★½
GRAPES semillon 85%, sauvignon blanc 15%
REGION Margaret River, WA
CELLAR 🍾 6
ALC./VOL. 13.5%
RRP $20.00

Best Semillon

Semillon in Margaret River has always impressed. Conor Laggan and Jurg Muggli give this a help along with a barrel fermentation in 60 per cent new oak.
CURRENT RELEASE 1995 This is a powerful semillon with serious drought-year concentration and length. The nose is unusual but appealing: smoky, green stick, herbaceous and tobacco notes. The wood handling is sensitive and the flavour intensity lingers long on the finish. Serve with char-grilled octopus.

Chimera Sauvignon Blanc Semillon

QUALITY ▼▼?
VALUE ★★★
GRAPES sauvignon blanc, semillon
REGION not stated
CELLAR 🍾
ALC./VOL. 11.5%
RRP $10.00

This is a new label, a joint venture between winewriter and vigneron James Halliday and Alister Purbrick, of Chateau Tahbilk.
CURRENT RELEASE 1995 The 'hologram' label is the wine's biggest asset. It's pale-hued, with shy aromas of bubblegum and estery fruit, and the taste is light, fairly tart and somewhat bland. Adequate at the price and could be paired with steamed dim sum.

Cloudy Bay Chardonnay

Marlborough is famous for its sauvignon blanc but chardonnay can be just as attractive, especially the full-frontal style with high alcohol and big malolactic influence. Maker Kevin Judd. Previous outstanding vintages: '92, '93
CURRENT RELEASE 1994 Seems slightly more subtle than previous years but with that trademark complexity of wonderful peach, honey, vanilla and tropical fruit characters. If you like your chardonnay to resemble a big bowl of fruit salad – this is your bag. Delicious now, with duck and mango salad.

QUALITY ♥♥♥♥♥
VALUE ★★★★
GRAPES chardonnay
REGION Marlborough, NZ
CELLAR 🍾 3
ALC./VOL. 14.0%
RRP $26.50

Cloudy Bay Sauvignon Blanc

The '95 Marlborough vintage was a harvest from hell, but the better makers managed to put together a good wine against the odds. Maker Kevin Judd.
CURRENT RELEASE 1995 Fresh and aromatic, showing the usual Cloudy Bay intensity and class. Aromas of green leaf, lemon/citrus, nettle and herbs fill the glass and there's good palate intensity to balance the crisp acid cut. The finish lingers remarkably well. Right up to its usual standard and ready to enjoy with fresh goat's milk cheese.

QUALITY ♥♥♥♥½
VALUE ★★★★
GRAPES sauvignon blanc
REGION Marlborough, NZ
CELLAR 🍾 2
ALC./VOL. 12.5%
RRP $18.00

Cockfighter's Ghost Semillon

This is a new vineyard owned by David Clarke of Poole's Rock. Legend has it that a horse named Cockfighter drowned in the creek there in mysterious circumstances and his ghost haunts the place. Maker Neil McGuigan.
CURRENT RELEASE 1995 A concentrated, drought-year wine with an intriguing aroma of dry twigs, mint and esters, which translates to lean, dry, lemon/lanolin flavours in the mouth. It's a classic style with good fruit weight and balance. Try it with flathead fish 'n' chips.

QUALITY ♥♥♥♥
VALUE ★★★½
GRAPES semillon
REGION Hunter Valley, NSW
CELLAR 🍾 5
ALC./VOL. 12.4%
RRP $15.50

Coldstream Hills Chardonnay

QUALITY ♊♊♊♊
VALUE ★★★
GRAPES chardonnay
REGION Yarra Valley, Vic.
CELLAR 🍾 5
ALC./VOL. 12.5%
RRP $21.75 ⓢ

Coldstream is a hugely successful winery these days. It has developed major new vine plantings to replace the Hoddles Creek grapes which it lost when BRL Hardy took over that vineyard. Makers James Halliday and Phil Dowell.
Previous outstanding vintages: '90, '91, '92, '94
CURRENT RELEASE 1995 A delicate wine in its youth, which promises to build character in the bottle although it seems 1995 is generally a light year for Victorian whites. Restrained cashew nut and tropical flavours with a touch of herbaceousness, very fruit-driven, fresh and vibrant reflecting a cool year. Try it with prosciutto melone.

Coldstream Hills Reserve Chardonnay

QUALITY ♊♊♊♊♊
VALUE ★★★★
GRAPES chardonnay
REGION Yarra Valley, Vic.
CELLAR 🍾 6
ALC./VOL. 13.5%
RRP $32.00

Coldstream chardonnays are built to mature slowly, relative to most Aussie chardonnays. There's no skin contact and little or no malolactic, both of which tend to 'hurry' chardonnay along. Hence they can be cellared.
Previous outstanding vintages: '86, '88, '90, '91, '92
CURRENT RELEASE 1994 An outstanding wine, to rival the '92 as Coldstream's best yet. Deep yellow; complex bouquet of cedar, toast and butter, showing lovely development but not overly oak reliant. Very intense, lively, finessed, with impressive power and length. A keeper, and marvellous with lobster.

Colonnade Chardonnay

QUALITY ♊♊♊♊
VALUE ★★★★
GRAPES chardonnay
REGION various
CELLAR 🍾 1
ALC./VOL. 12.5%
RRP $12.90

This is Domaine Chandon's cheaper still chardonnay, made from the tailles (hard pressings) of the sparkling wine grapes. Maker Wayne Donaldson and team.
CURRENT RELEASE 1994 This has an unusual nose of vanilla, honey and malt, starting to show some age development. The taste is lively, dry, firm on the finish and lingers well. It's good value drinking. Serve with corn fritters.

Coolangatta Estate Alexander Berry Chardonnay

Alexander Berry was a pioneer settler on the South Coast in 1822. Grown on Greg Bishop's 6-ha. vineyard at Berry.
Previous outstanding vintages: '94
CURRENT RELEASE 1995 The toasted/nutty oak was rather dominant in youth and some bottle-age may have moderated it by now. There's a lot of rather tart acid on the palate and again that gangly lack of harmony. Try it with chicken Kiev.

QUALITY 🍷🍷🍷
VALUE ★★★
GRAPES chardonnay
REGION south coast, NSW
CELLAR 🍾 1–4
ALC./VOL. 12.8%
RRP $14.00 (cellar door)

Coriole Chenin Blanc

Coriole persists with this unfashionable grape, usually with results much better than average. Maker Steve Hall.
CURRENT RELEASE 1995 Start with sherbety herbaceous fruit aromas; throw in a little grape sweetness and you've got a recipe for commercial sucess. The wine is fuller and richer than most chenins, and provided the sweetness does not offend, it's a pleasurable drop. Suits antipasto.

QUALITY 🍷🍷🍷
VALUE ★★★
GRAPES chenin blanc
REGION McLaren Vale, SA
CELLAR 🍾 1
ALC./VOL. 13.0%
RRP $14.20 Ⓢ

Cowra Estate Chardonnay

This vineyard, the original in Cowra, underwent major changes in 1995 with South African John Geber taking a controlling interest. He has big plans for the brand locally and overseas. Maker Simon Gilbert.
CURRENT RELEASE 1995 A very forward chardonnay (mature for its age) with a deep yellow hue, rich butterscotch, oak and peachy fruit bouquet, and a satisfying, mouth-filling flavour. Serious stuff and evidence that major improvements at this company go further than a new label.

QUALITY 🍷🍷🍷🍷½
VALUE ★★★★½
GRAPES chardonnay
REGION Cowra, NSW
CELLAR 🍾 3
ALC./VOL. 13.5%
RRP $15.50

Cullen Sauvignon Blanc

QUALITY ♆♆♆♆♆
VALUE ★★★★
GRAPES sauvignon blanc
REGION Margaret River, WA
CELLAR 🍾 5
ALC./VOL. 14.0%
RRP $25.00

Seventy per cent of this wine was barrel fermented, and the oak becomes more evident as the wine warms in the glass. If you don't want to smell oak, chill it harder. Maker Vanya Cullen.

CURRENT RELEASE 1995 An unusual style, showing smart French oak on the nose and great fruit concentration to match. The palate is tightly structured, fine and very long, with dryness but not austerity. All about structure and length, and could do interesting things with cellaring. Drink with a rich WA marron dish.

Currency Creek Sauvignon Blanc

QUALITY ♆♆♆♆♇
VALUE ★★★★
GRAPES sauvignon blanc
REGION Currency Creek, SA
CELLAR 🍾 2
ALC./VOL. 13.0%
RRP $16.00

The Tonkins' 60-acre Currency Creek vineyard is near the mouth of the Murray, between McLaren Vale and Langhorne Creek. They supply much of the fruit for Bridgewater Mill's sauvignon and there is a kinship of style.

CURRENT RELEASE 1995 A deliciously fine, tangy, crisp sauvignon with marked varietal character and excellent fruit depth on the palate – where so many are found wanting. It has delicacy and balance and is not propped up by sugar. An exemplary sauvignon. Serve with mussels.

Dalfarras Chardonnay

QUALITY ♆♆♆♆♇
VALUE ★★★★½
GRAPES chardonnay
REGION central Vic.
CELLAR 🍾 3
ALC./VOL. 13.5%
RRP $14.50

This label is one of the sleepers in the market. The wines tend to show more refinement than those from Chateau Tahbilk which is the other stable mate.

CURRENT RELEASE 1992 This wine has time on its side. The development means a rich green-gold colour and oak and peach aromas on the nose. The palate is quite complex with peach and citrus flavours intertwined with lees characters and wood components. The finish is dry and satisfying. It goes well lightly chilled with a mild chicken curry.

Dalfarras Marsanne

This is the other label (not second label) from the Chateau Tahbilk stable. In this case they break with tradition and give this variety some oak treatment. Maker Alister Purbrick.

CURRENT RELEASE 1993 The wood does good ... The colour is a mid gold and the nose has honeysuckle and gooseberry aromas. The palate is rich and complex with honeyed fruit and toasty oak flavours. The finish is dry with a successful mix of wood and acid. It should be served lightly chilled; try it with a Vietnamese country pancake.

QUALITY ♗♗♗♗♗
VALUE ★★★★½
GRAPES marsanne
REGION central Vic.
CELLAR 🍾 4
ALC./VOL. 13.0%
RRP $14.50

Dalfarras Rhine Riesling

Riesling from this neck of the woods isn't exactly a cause célèbre. It makes reasonable wines that sell for reasonable prices.

CURRENT RELEASE 1994 Starting to show some bottle-age, the colour is a mid-lemon yellow and the nose has a strong citrus aroma. The palate is lemon flavoured and the finish shows some clean acid. It drinks well now and can be teamed with a Thai fish curry. Serve very well chilled.

QUALITY ♗♗♗
VALUE ★★★
GRAPES riesling
REGION central Vic.
CELLAR 🍾 2
ALC./VOL. 12.0%
RRP $11.70

Darling Park Chardonnay

This is a Mornington Peninsula vineyard that has a small yet dynamic out-put. The cellar door features wood-fired oven tartes flambes – à la Alsace. Maker Kevin McCarthy.

CURRENT RELEASE 1995 This is a wood-driven style that comes down on the citrus end of the chardonnay spectrum. The nose is toasty and nutty with grapefruit aromas. The palate is medium-bodied with melon and peach flavours and there is ample evidence of barrel fermentation. The finish has strong toast and oak influence. It should be served with a medium chill; try it with crisply fried flounder.

QUALITY ♗♗♗♗
VALUE ★★★½
GRAPES chardonnay
REGION Mornington Peninsula, Vic.
CELLAR 🍾 5
ALC./VOL. 12.8%
RRP $19.00

White Wines

Darling Park Querida

QUALITY ▼▼▼
VALUE ★★½
GRAPES cabernet sauvignon, merlot, pinot grigio
REGION Mornington Peninsula, Vic.
CELLAR ▯
ALC./VOL. 12.0%
RRP $16.00

Dare I say it the packaging on this rosé style is straight out of a label designer or marketing man's wet dream. The label depicts the 'Fountain of Love' by Fargonard.
CURRENT RELEASE 1995 Strange blend that probably works a treat at cellar door. It has an onion skin blush and the nose offers heady perfume with a hint of varnish. The palate is light and slightly sweet and the finish is a tad coarse with a slightly stalky element. It needs to be served well chilled. Use it to pitch woo.

David Wynn Riesling

QUALITY ▼▼▼▼
VALUE ★★★★
GRAPES riesling
REGION Eden Valley, SA
CELLAR ▯ 3
ALC./VOL. 11.5%
RRP $12.00

This wine comes in a red wine bottle which is a point of packaging departure. Who cares if the wine drinks well? Maker Adam Wynn.
CURRENT RELEASE 1994 The wine is a big style with a strong aromatic nose plus a hint of kero. The palate has strong line flavours and there is plenty of acid on a tingling finish. It will develop with cellaring and can be served well chilled. Try it as a pre-dinner drink.

David Wynn Sauvignon Blanc

QUALITY ▼▼▼▯
VALUE ★★★½
GRAPES sauvignon blanc
REGION Eden Valley, SA
CELLAR ▯ 1
ALC./VOL. 12.5%
RRP $12.00

The total production for the Mountadam/David Wynn/Eden Ridge is a substantial 45,000 cases. It is made in a state-of-the-art modern winery.
CURRENT RELEASE 1994 Good varietal definition with this wine. It has a nose dominated by tropical fruit and gooseberry aromas. The palate continues with these flavours and there is also a grassy component. The finish is dominated by fresh acid. It drinks well with asparagus and you can chill to thrill.

David Wynn Unwooded Chardonnay

If there is a pioneer of unwooded chardonnay it would have to be Adam Wynn. He was well ahead of the folks in Mornington and other districts.

CURRENT RELEASE 1995 There is a potent lime and peach aroma on the nose. The palate has sweet peach, melon and grapefruit flavours and the acid completes the picture on the finish. The absence of wood means you can give it a big chill. Try it with seafood risotto.

QUALITY ♛♛♛♛
VALUE ★★★★
GRAPES chardonnay
REGION Eden Valley, SA
CELLAR 🍾 3
ALC./VOL. 12.5%
RRP $14.00

De Bortoli Noble One

'Night and day, you are the one.' This is the one, last year we gave it a gong as the best semillon. We could do the same this year but we like to share the wear. This is a remarkable label representing superior wines. Maker Darren De Bortoli.

Previous outstanding vintages: '82, '84, '87, '90, '91, '92

CURRENT RELEASE 1993 Right in the groove and groovin' high (if you'll excuse the jazz pun). The colour is a bright yellow-gold with green highlights. The nose has a mix of botrytis odours, ripe fruit and a lively acid lift. As ever the palate is complex with apricot, mixed dried fruits, marmalade and honey flavours. These are enhanced by some fresh acid on a cleansing finish. Serve very well chilled with smoked Atlantic salmon.

QUALITY ♛♛♛♛♛
VALUE ★★★★★
GRAPES semillon
REGION Riverina, NSW
CELLAR 🍾 10
ALC./VOL. 11.5%
RRP $22.00 (375 ml)

De Bortoli Yarra Valley Chardonnay

QUALITY ♛♛♛♛
VALUE ★★★★
GRAPES chardonnay
REGION Yarra Valley, Vic.
CELLAR 🍾 4
ALC./VOL. 13.0%
RRP $20.00

Expect to hear more of this wine, the Yarra Valley vineyard is expanding at a pace thanks to a constant demand for this wine. Maker Steve Webber.

CURRENT RELEASE 1995 This is a very well-made wine that has authentic varietal and regional characters. The nose offers strong peach and woodsmoke aromas. The palate is medium-bodied with sweet peach and melon flavours. The finish weighs in with very strong oak that really dries the mouth. It is almost astringent and shouldn't be served too cold. Try it with smoked turkey.

Delatite Chardonnay

QUALITY ♛♛♛♛
VALUE ★★★½
GRAPES chardonnay
REGION Mansfield, Vic.
CELLAR 🍾 4
ALC./VOL. 13.5%
RRP $18.20

This is an isolated vineyard under the shadow of Mount Buller. Judging by the bottled results there should be neighbouring vineyards by now. Maker Ros Ritchie.

Previous outstanding vintages: '90, '91, '93

CURRENT RELEASE 1994 Since the last review the wine is starting to show some bottle development. The nose is a mix of mango and toasty oak aromas. The palate has the expected peach and melon flavours and oak adds a nutty component to the long dry finish. It drinks well with a medium chill; try it with veal in a light cream sauce.

Delatite Dead Man's Hill Gewurztraminer

Down among the dead men ... Not a terribly alluring name and mishandling sees the variety leaving glass slippers on palace steps all over the land.
Previous outstanding vintages: '82, '86, '87, '93, '94
CURRENT RELEASE 1994 A very consistent style that errs on the side of elegance. It has a very fragrant nose with violets and rose-petal aromas. The palate has a distinct lychee flavour and this is balanced by some crisp acid on a refreshing finish. It is the crisp nature of the wine that sets it apart. Serve well chilled with smoked sausage.

QUALITY ♷♷♷♷♴
VALUE ★★★★½
GRAPES gewurztraminer
REGION Mansfield, Vic.
CELLAR 🍾 4
ALC./VOL. 12.5%
RRP $15.00

Delatite Sauvignon Blanc

Yet another release in what is a fairly broad portfolio from this winery that produces 12 000 cases a year.
CURRENT RELEASE 1995 The nose has strong herb and cut grass aromas. The palate packs a tropical fruit punch plus herbal qualities. This zesty fruit is balanced by assertive oak on a long finish. It can be served well chilled with oysters natural.

QUALITY ♷♷♷♷
VALUE ★★★★
GRAPES sauvignon blanc
REGION Mansfield, Vic.
CELLAR 🍾 3
ALC./VOL. 11.5%
RRP $15.00

Devil's Lair Chardonnay

This is the vineyard of brewing entrepreneur Philip Sexton, formerly of Redback and Matilda Bay. Smart man: he used beer to finance his wine industry foray. Maker Janice McDonald.
CURRENT RELEASE 1994 This is a masterful wine and a classic Margaret River style. Rich buttery aromas point to malolactic fermentation, but there's a complex melange of honey, toasty oak and other things reflecting barrel fermentation and lees-contact of very rich fruit. Very full-bodied with unctuous mouthfeel and ageing gracefully. Try it with char-grilled lobster.

QUALITY ♷♷♷♷♷
VALUE ★★★★
GRAPES chardonnay
REGION Margaret River, WA
CELLAR 🍾 3+
ALC./VOL. 14.5%
RRP $26.50

Dulcinea Vineyard Sauvignon Blanc

QUALITY ♛♛♛⸨
VALUE ★★★½
GRAPES sauvignon blanc
REGION Ballarat, Vic.
CELLAR ╏ 2
ALC./VOL. 12.0%
RRP $12.00

Theatre scholars will realise the connection with Man of La Mancha. It was chosen because 'only fools tilt at windmills'. Makers Simon Clayfield and Ron Stott (contract).

CURRENT RELEASE 1995 A very pungent style with a strong lychee and tinned pea aromas. The colour is very pale and the palate has strong herb and gooseberry flavours. There is crisp acid on the finish. It can be served well chilled. It goes well with white asparagus.

Evans & Tate 'Tate White'

QUALITY ♛♛♛⸨
VALUE ★★★
GRAPES chardonnay, grenache
REGION Swan Valley, WA
CELLAR ╏ 2
ALC./VOL. 13.0%
RRP $16.80

The company says this white wine was created 'to complement the unique cuisine of Western Australia', but do they mean goat's cheese, marron, venison or anchovies? It's a challenging blend of chardonnay and grenache. Maker Brian Fletcher.

CURRENT RELEASE 1995 A fuller colour betrays the oak component, which is very toasted and comes rocketing through on the bouquet, although it's less obvious in the mouth. The palate is soft and very agreeable with some breadth and depth to the flavour: very pleasing at the price. Serve with cold chicken.

Evans & Tate Two Vineyards Chardonnay

QUALITY ♛♛♛♛
VALUE ★★★½
GRAPES chardonnay
REGION various, WA
CELLAR ╏ 5
ALC./VOL. 13.0%
RRP $18.00 Ⓢ

This is the second-string chardonnay from E & T, and would cut the mustard with some makers' flagship bottlings. Maker Brian Fletcher.

CURRENT RELEASE 1995 A very tight-structured, intense wine with cashew nut, cedary aromas and great focus on its complex, structured palate. Still undeveloped, it has good potential for cellaring. Roast chicken here.

Fiddlers Creek Sauvignon Blanc

Another in the realm of great value for money. It is getting very difficult to find a drinkable wine and change out of $10.00.
CURRENT RELEASE 1995 Slightly toasty nose with some herbal reflections. The palate is mediumweight with gentle herbs and tropical fruit flavours. These are backed by some crisp acid on a clean dry finish. It can be served well chilled; try it with pan-fried whiting.

QUALITY 🍷🍷🍷
VALUE ★★★★
GRAPES sauvignon blanc
REGION Pyrenees, Vic.
CELLAR 🍾 1
ALC./VOL. 13.0%
RRP $8.00

Fiddlers Creek Semillon

There is a Fiddlers Creek in the Pyrenees region of Victoria. It is so named because some lucky miners hit pay dirt and broke out their fiddles. This wine is part of the Remy portfolio.
CURRENT RELEASE 1995 Big toasty nose with hints of gunsmoke. The palate is distinguished by a hint of sweetness and gooseberry flavours. The finish is dry and coating. It can be served with a medium chill; try it with KFC. The price is right.

QUALITY 🍷🍷🍷
VALUE ★★★½
GRAPES semillon
REGION Pyrenees, Vic.
CELLAR 🍾 1
ALC./VOL. 12.5%
RRP $8.00

Forest Glen Chardonnay

This is a cheapie brand from the Liquorland/ Vintage Cellars group, and comes with a swish label job. Pity it's a direct borrow from the Californian Forest Glen winery.
CURRENT RELEASE 1995 Pretty fair value at the price, but we wouldn't keep it longer than we had to. It's already very developed for a '95 and the palate, while it has quite a big framework, is hollow and astringent on the finish. Chill well and seve with barbecued octopus.

QUALITY 🍷🍷🍷
VALUE ★★★
GRAPES chardonnay
REGION Riverland, SA
CELLAR 🍾 1
ALC./VOL. 12.0%
RRP $10.00

Forest Hill Riesling

QUALITY 🍷🍷🍷🍷
VALUE ★★★★
GRAPES riesling
REGION Mount Barker, WA
CELLAR 🍾 4
ALC./VOL. 12.5%
RRP $14.65

This was the original experimental vineyard for the Mount Barker region, planted by the Department of Agriculture in 1965. It is now owned by Vasse Felix. Maker Clive Otto.

CURRENT RELEASE 1995 The colour is pale yellow and the nose is a full-on blast of crushed flowers and citrus oils. There is also a grace note of talcum powder. The palate has an intense lime quality and there is abundant acid, making for a very crisp finish, It can be served with a big cold hit and it is bella with freshly shucked oysters.

Four Sisters

QUALITY 🍷🍷🍷🍷
VALUE ★★★★
GRAPES sauvignon blanc, semillon
REGION not stated (Vic.)
CELLAR 🍾 2
ALC./VOL. 11.5%
RRP $12.50

Trevor and Sandy Mast have four daughters, hence this label. The artwork was done by one of the quartet. Maker Trev Mast.

CURRENT RELEASE 1995 A light and poised wine that was made for refreshing drinking. It works well with a fragrant herbal nose and a background of talcum powder. The medium-bodied palate is a mix of grass and gooseberry and the finish has crisp acid. It can be served well chilled and it is crying out for oysters natural.

Frankland Estate Rhine Riesling

QUALITY 🍷🍷🍷🍷
VALUE ★★★½
GRAPES riesling
REGION Great Southern, WA
CELLAR 🍾 4
ALC./VOL. 13.0%
RRP $14.70

Precisely who were the Franks? Only joking and no correspondence will be entered into. This is an enterprising estate that turns out 12 000 cases per annum.

CURRENT RELEASE 1995 A bold style that is quite rich and alcoholic. The nose is complex with a mix of pungent citrus and a hint of toast. The palate is powerful with lemon and grapefruit flavours and these are matched by some lively acid on a dry finish. It can be served well chilled. Seafood terrine goes well.

Frankland Estate Sauvignon Blanc

Judi Cullam and Barrie Smith's vineyard has produced some superb wines in its short history, despite a high turnover of winemakers.
CURRENT RELEASE 1995 This is a big, rich wine with stacks of flavour. It has a lifted nose without much grassiness but perhaps a trace of subtly handled oak. The powerful, lingering flavour finishes with some alcohol heat. Chill well and serve with mussels.

QUALITY ♛♛♛♛
VALUE ★★★½
GRAPES sauvignon blanc
REGION Lower Great Southern, WA
CELLAR 🍾 1
ALC./VOL. 14.0%
RRP $15.50

Freycinet Chardonnay

If there is a vinous apple of the Apple Isle's eye it would have to be chardonnay, which is well suited to its climatic conditions. This location will be producing some of the best examples on the island.
Previous outstanding vintages: '93, '94
CURRENT RELEASE 1995 This is a very polished style with complexity to the max. The colour is a pale yellow with green tinges. The nose is a mix of stone fruit and wood. The palate has plenty of peach, melon and grapefruit flavour which has been carefully wooded. The finish is dry with wood dominant. It shouldn't have its tripes chilled out; try it with char-grilled ocean trout.

QUALITY ♛♛♛♛♛
VALUE ★★★★
GRAPES chardonnay
REGION east coast, Tas.
CELLAR 🍾 6
ALC./VOL. 13.0%
RRP $26.50

Geoff Merrill Who Cares? The Whites

Merrill was bashing a ball around a golf course in frustration at being unable to think up a good brand-name. 'I'm sick of all this bullshit about labels. Who cares?' he cussed. 'It's the wine that matters!'
CURRENT RELEASE 1995 Delicate green grass/appley aromas to the fore in a crisp, light, pleasant quaffing dry white without apparent oak. Simple, fruity, round and easy to appreciate. Try it with Caesar salad.

QUALITY ♛♛♛
VALUE ★★★
GRAPES chenin blanc 66%, sauvignon blanc 34%
REGION McLaren Vale, SA
CELLAR 🍾
ALC./VOL. 12.0%
RRP $13.00 Ⓢ

Geoff Weaver Stafford Ridge Lenswood Chardonnay

QUALITY 🍷🍷🍷🍷
VALUE ★★★★
GRAPES chardonnay
REGION Adelaide Hills, SA
CELLAR 🍾 6+
ALC./VOL. 13.0%
RRP $19.00

Confucius he say, 'Wine with more than one name very confusing.' Mr Weaver should bite the bullet: is it Stafford Ridge or is it Geoff Weaver? Previous outstanding vintages. '90, '91, '93
CURRENT RELEASE 1994 Wowee! Is this passionfruity or what? The volume of tropical fruit aroma just swarms from the glass. Some might find it too much. The wine is very intense but light on its feet, again with tropical flavours in the mouth – soft, rounded, yet lively and with a nice note of honey throughout. Great balance and length. Try it with a duck and lychee green salad.

Gilberts Riesling

QUALITY 🍷🍷🍷🍷
VALUE ★★★★
GRAPES riesling
REGION Great Southern, WA
CELLAR 🍾 5
ALC./VOL. 11.8%
RRP $15.00

Yet more evidence that Mount Barker is a charmed spot to grow riesling. Jim and Bev Gilbert have their wines made at Plantagenet. Previous outstanding vintages: '90, '92
CURRENT RELEASE 1994 A different style of riesling, smelling fragrantly floral, with a hint of orange blossoms and bread-dough. The palate is crisp and delicate, tight and minerally. Good with crab cakes.

Glenara Unwooded Chardonnay

QUALITY 🍷🍷🍷
VALUE ★★★
GRAPES chardonnay
REGION Adelaide Hills, SA
CELLAR 🍾 2
ALC./VOL. 13.0%
RRP $15.00 ☻

The Verrall family are committed to growing their grapes organically on their Upper Hermitage property.
CURRENT RELEASE 1995 Attractive fruit character here, but the taste is a little sweeter than expected. Pristine youthful cashew/bread doughy aromas, sweet entry and then light, straightforward fruit flavour followed by a clean acid finish. Try with smoked eel pâté.

Goldwater Marlborough Chardonnay

The Goldwaters are headquartered on Auckland Harbour's Waiheke Island, but they made this one from Marlborough grapes (from a very good year).
CURRENT RELEASE 1994 Deep yellow hue; big lip-smacking butterscotch nose full of typical Kiwi chardonnay complexities (read full malolactic, barrel ferment and lees). It's a lovely, big, rich, voluptuous wine in the mouth, with some sweetness but also a warm, resonant finish, terrific fruit concentration and good backbone. Peaking now: slurp it with buttery grilled field mushrooms.

QUALITY ♛♛♛♛♛
VALUE ★★★★½
GRAPES chardonnay
REGION Marlborough, NZ
CELLAR 🍷 3
ALC./VOL. 14.0%
RRP $24.00

Goundrey Chardonnay

The wine market is littered with brands named after people who are no longer connected with them. This is one such.
CURRENT RELEASE 1994 A forward-developed wine, full gold in colour with a complex bouquet reflecting both bottle-age and Burgundian techniques. It's smoky, toasty and buttery. Notes of vanilla and honey creep into the palate. The structure is round and smooth with rich mouthfeel and good length. Lots happening here. Try it with a washed-rind cheese.

QUALITY ♛♛♛♛♛
VALUE ★★★½
GRAPES chardonnay
REGION Great Southern, WA
CELLAR 🍷 2
ALC./VOL. 14.0%
RRP $20.90

Goundrey Classic White

Jack Bendat is set to make a mark in the wine business: his five-year plan is to propel Goundrey to 100 000 cases.
CURRENT RELEASE 1995 A light, clean, fairly simple, quaffing dry white. The nose shows grassy and doughy aromas with a background of asparagus. It's light and gentle on the tongue, easy to appreciate and finishes soft and dry, if a tad short. Serve with fresh asparagus and butter.

QUALITY ♛♛♛
VALUE ★★★
GRAPES semillon, sauvignon blanc
REGION Great Southern, WA
CELLAR 🍷
ALC./VOL. 12.0%
RRP $14.00

Goundrey Reserve Riesling

QUALITY 🍷🍷🍷🍷
VALUE ★★★★
GRAPES riesling
REGION Great Southern, WA
CELLAR 🍾 4
ALC./VOL. 12.0%
RRP $16.00

Goundrey was purchased in 1995 by Perth businessman Jack Bendat. He has big plans for expansion. Maker Brenden Smith.

CURRENT RELEASE 1995 This is a very intense wine, impressing with spicy, doughy aromas with possibly a slight botrytis influence. The perfume is echoed in the mouth, where the structure is big and strong, intense and lively, finishing clean and dry. Needs strong food: try marron in a seafood sauce.

Goundrey Sauvignon Blanc

QUALITY 🍷🍷🍷🍷
VALUE ★★★★½
GRAPES sauvignon blanc
REGION Great Southern, WA
CELLAR 🍾 2
ALC./VOL. 11.5%
RRP $15.00

Goundrey began in 1971 when Mike and Alison Goundrey planted their first vines. They sold out last year to Perth radio-station owner Jack Bendat.

CURRENT RELEASE 1995 An excellent intensely grassy style – one for the hi-fi sauvignon enthusiasts. Pungent, crisp green aromas of New Zealand-like lantana and gooseberry. The palate is tangy and full of sparkle, but also manages to retain fullness and length. Impressive stuff to serve with mussel soup.

Goundrey Unwooded Chardonnay

Funny how trends start! Every winemaker within coo-ee pronounced unwooded chardonays dead before they'd had a chance, but they all made one just in case.

CURRENT RELEASE 1995 Won a gold in Canberra in late '95 but must have lost something in the intervening months. As it is, a decent if unexciting wine, starting to show obvious bottle-age; soft and easy on the tongue. Could be teamed with mushroom risotto.

QUALITY ♟♟♟
VALUE ★★★
GRAPES chardonnay
REGION Great Southern, WA
CELLAR ▯
ALC./VOL. 13.5%
RRP $14.00

CURRENT RELEASE 1996 This wine is redolent of the herbaceous and passionfruit scents of the earlier-picked chardonnays from this part of the world. There's a trace of user-friendly sweetness and the wine is soft, fruity, up-front and ready for glugging. Try it with cold crayfish salad.

QUALITY ♟♟♟♟
VALUE ★★★
GRAPES chardonnay
REGION Mount Barker, WA
CELLAR ▯ 2
ALC./VOL. 13.0%
RRP $14.00

Gramps Chardonnay

Johann Gramp was the guy who started it all for Orlando, back in the 1840s. His stentorian portrait still gazes over the Orlando team from the walls at Rowland Flat as they toil. Maker: Phil Laffer, Bernard Hickin and team.

CURRENT RELEASE 1995 A fairly broad, full-flavoured chardonnay featuring coconutty, dusty American oak, some buttery malolactic character and a trace of sweetness in the middle. Decent if uninspiring; could be teamed with KFC.

QUALITY ♟♟♟
VALUE ★★★
GRAPES chardonnay
REGION various, SA
CELLAR ▯ 1
ALC./VOL. 13.0%
RRP $14.00 ⑤

Green Point Chardonnay

QUALITY ♛♛♛♛♕
VALUE ★★★★
GRAPES chardonnay
REGION Yarra Valley, Vic.
CELLAR 🍾 3+
ALC./VOL. 13.5%
RRP $19.80

Green Point is the Yarra Valley grazing property purchased by Domaine Chandon in 1985, now the site of its vineyard and winery. The name is used for still wines and, in the UK, the bubbly as well. Maker Wayne Donaldson.

Previous outstanding vintages: '94

CURRENT RELEASE 1995 A very complex style, bursting with oaky and buttery malolactic characters. There are lovely honey notes in the nose and palate, plenty of oak albeit in balance, and the finish is soft and long. Goes well with crayfish.

Grosset Piccadilly

QUALITY ♛♛♛♛♕
VALUE ★★★½
GRAPES chardonnay
REGION Adelaide Hills, SA
CELLAR 🍾 5+
ALC./VOL. 13.5%
RRP $23.80

Grosset is in the Clare Valley but the emphasis for chardonnay fruit has switched in recent years to Piccadilly in the Adelaide Hills. Maker Jeffrey Grosset.

CURRENT RELEASE 1995 A typically fine, classy, understated Grosset white. The oak is lightly played and the dominant fruit flavours are tropical and cashew nut. The balance is very fine with a juicy middle and real elegance. Try it with a yabbie tail salad.

Grosset Polish Hill

QUALITY ♛♛♛♕
VALUE ★★★
GRAPES riesling
REGION Clare Valley, SA
CELLAR 🍾 10
ALC./VOL. 13.0%
RRP $18.00

Polish Hill River is a sub-region of the Clare Valley and produces lighter wines than Watervale. Grosset makes both and they are fascinating to compare.

Previous outstanding vintages: '84, '86, '87, '88, '90, '93, '94

CURRENT RELEASE 1995 A very delicate wine in its youth, showing yeasty, straw-like and faint citrus aromas. The palate is lean and somewhat austere, and cellaring is recommended. Try oysters with the young wine, or smoked trout mousse when it's older.

Hanging Rock Howqua River Riesling

When it comes to cool climate, there are few cooler than Hanging Rock. Instead of refrigeration they simply open the doors of the winery during vintage. Maker John Ellis.
CURRENT RELEASE 1994 The wine is starting to show some bottle-age. There is a hint of kero creeping into the citrus-dominated nose. The palate is dominated by lime flavour and the acid, thanks to the cool climate, remains crisp. There is a Leo Buring slant to the style (and that's very flattering). It can be served well chilled; try it with pasta and a smoked salmon/cream sauce.

QUALITY ♛♛♛♛
VALUE ★★★★
GRAPES riesling
REGION Macedon, Vic.
CELLAR 🍾 3
ALC./VOL. 12.0%
RRP $13.00

Hanging Rock The Jim Jim Sauvignon Blanc

This vineyard is at the cutting edge of cool-climate viticulture. In indifferent years they will have to hire sun lamps. Maker John Ellis.
CURRENT RELEASE 1995 The wine reflects the climatic nature of the vineyard. It is lean, crisp and refreshing. The colour is pale and the nose is grassy with a slight pea pod aroma. The palate is light and crisp with grassy herbs and a hint of gooseberry. There is plenty of acid on the finish. It can be served lightly chilled; try it with an antipasto.

QUALITY ♛♛♛♛
VALUE ★★★½
GRAPES sauvignon blanc
REGION Macedon, Vic.
CELLAR 🍾 2
ALC./VOL. 12.0%
RRP $18.00

Hardys Bankside Chardonnay

Bankside is an old winery in the family history which burnt down. Vats from Bankside are still resident at Hardys McLaren Vale and they bear the charcoal scars of the fire.
CURRENT RELEASE 1994 Woodwork, the oak calls the tune. There is a nutty vanillan oak aroma on the nose. The palate is quite creamy with subtle barrel ferment characters There are peach and melon flavours underneath but it is oak über alles right through to the finish. It should be served moderately chilled. Try it with smoked trout.

QUALITY ♛♛♛⚐
VALUE ★★★½
GRAPES chardonnay
REGION Padthaway, SA
CELLAR 🍾 5
ALC./VOL. 13.5%
RRP $15.00

Hardys Eileen Hardy Chardonnay

QUALITY ♀♀♀♀♀
VALUE ★★★★½
GRAPES chardonnay
REGION Padthaway, SA; Yarra Valley, Vic
CELLAR 🍷 5+
ALC./VOL. 13.5%
RRP $26.00 Ⓢ

BRL Hardy acquired a large vineyard in Hoddles Creek, near the Yarra Valley. It is an ultra cool climate. Up there they consider the valley floor as warm to hot. Makers Peter Dawson and Tom Newton.

Previous outstanding vintages: '86, '89, '90, '92

CURRENT RELEASE 1994 This wine was the best chardonnay in the last *Guide*. Development has been slow but positive. It is complex and structured with many facets. The nose is toasty with caramel and peach smells. The palate features all the chardonnay elements. There are peach, nectarine, grapefruit and quince flavours that are framed by cedar, toasty oak. The finish is dry and conducive to another sip. It can cope with a rich seafood crepe. Don't over chill.

Hardys Nottage Hill Chardonnay

QUALITY ♀♀♀
VALUE ★★★½
GRAPES chardonnay
REGION McLaren Vale, SA
CELLAR 🍷 2
ALC./VOL. 12.5%
RRP $9.90

This is an ever-reliable label that won't bring tears to the wallet.

CURRENT RELEASE 1995 A straightforward style that leaves you in no doubt about the grape variety. The nose is peachy with a hint of smoke. The palate is an essay in peach and there is a whisper of oak on the finish. It should be served with a medium chill. Try it with KFC.

Hardys Nottage Hill Rhine Riesling

QUALITY ♀♀♀♀
VALUE ★★★★
GRAPES riesling
REGION not stated
CELLAR 🍷 1
ALC./VOL. 13.0%
RRP $8.00

It's getting harder to find cheap everyday drinking. This label is a sure bet and riesling is one of the most attractive styles.

CURRENT RELEASE 1995 It is a straightforward style with a definitive varietal signature. The nose has floral qualities and citrus. The palate is medium-bodied with lime flavours and there is soft acid on a medium length finish. It can be served well chilled. Try it with fish and chips.

Hardys Padthaway Unwooded Chardonnay

The accountants in the large companies must be jumping for joy at the non-wooded chardonnay craze, because oak is expensive.
CURRENT RELEASE 1995 You could be fooled by the nose which smells toasty as if the wine has been wooded. The palate shows peach, citrus and tropical fruit flavours and there is plenty of clean acid on the finish. It drinks well with a medium to full chill and veal fagottini is a good accompaniment.

QUALITY ♛♛♛♛
VALUE ★★★★
GRAPES chardonnay
REGION Padthaway, SA
CELLAR 🍷 2
ALC./VOL. 13.5%
RRP $14.50

Hardys R R Classic Dry White

The competition for the low ground of affordable bottle white wine is no less fierce than the tilting at the top. Drinkable whites under $10 are becoming rare.
CURRENT RELEASE 1995 A humble wine that won't break the bank. The nose has a hint of muscat and floral notes. The palate is fruity and light and it ain't exactly dry. The finish is tidy and undemanding. Serve well chilled with Thai food.

QUALITY ♛♛♛
VALUE ★★★
GRAPES sauvignon blanc, semillon
REGION Clare Valley & Padthaway, SA
CELLAR 🍷
ALC./VOL. 12.0%
RRP $7.50 ⓢ

Hardys R R Medium Dry White

'Medium Dry' is a brave term in days when every Australian is quick to declare, 'I only drink dry wine.' In truth many love a little sugar and this is a popular style.
CURRENT RELEASE 1995 It's well made and they've upped the alcohol since last year but the earth won't even shiver. It has a floral nose and the palate is quite sweet with an oily texture. The finish is soft but not cloying. Chill the hell out of it and take it to a cheap and cheery Chinese restaurant.

QUALITY ♛♛♛
VALUE ★★★
GRAPES riesling, gewurztraminer
REGION McLaren Vale & Padthaway, SA
CELLAR 🍷
ALC./VOL. 12.5
RRP $7.50 ⓢ

Hardys Siegersdorf Chardonnay

QUALITY ♟♟♟♟
VALUE ★★★½
GRAPES chardonnay
REGION not stated
CELLAR 🍾 2
ALC./VOL. 13.5%
RRP $12.50 Ⓢ

The original Siegersdorf (Victor's village) was a region in the Barossa Valley. These days the grapes come from other regions.
CURRENT RELEASE 1995 A well-made style that has obvious varietal character. The nose has peach and melon aromas and a smoky oak background. The palate is a mix of peach and nectarine and the oak combines to bring on a well-integrated finish. Serve with a medium chill; try it with roast chicken.

Hardys Siegersdorf Rhine Riesling

QUALITY ♟♟♟♟
VALUE ★★★★
GRAPES riesling
REGION not stated
CELLAR 🍾 2
ALC./VOL. 12.5%
RRP $12.00 Ⓢ

This wine has an interesting history. The first Siegersdorf riesling was made by Jim Irvine and it has also been made by Brian Croser (Petaluma). Maker Tom Newton.
CURRENT RELEASE 1995 A well-made wine that captures the essence of the variety. The nose has aromatic elements of citrus and crushed flowers. The palate offers lemon and lime flavours which are matched by crisp acid on a fresh finish. It can be served well chilled; try it with a seafood curry.

Hawkes Bridge Chardonnay

QUALITY ♟♟♟♟
VALUE ★★★★
GRAPES chardonnay
REGION Marlborough, NZ
CELLAR 🍾 6
ALC./VOL. 13.5%
RRP $20.00

This wine comes from the Mendoza chardonnay clone planted at Marlbrough, New Zealand. The grapes are picked with an eye to optimum ripeness.
CURRENT RELEASE 1995 It is a pungent style and in spite of the ripeness the nose has a smoky, herbal quality and hints of flinty smoke. The palate is medium-bodied with melon, peach and grapefruit and the finish is dry with subtle oak. It should be served lightly chilled. Try it with pan-fried yellow belly.

Hawkes Bridge Sauvignon Blanc

This is another label from New Zealand from a vineyard owned and operated by Mike and Judy Veal.
CURRENT RELEASE 1995 Pretty stylish in the emphatic New Zealand way. The nose has strong tropical fruit aroma with pea and herb undertones. The palate is full-bodied and there are tropical fruit flavours and gooseberry. The finish is dry and lingering. It can be served well chilled; try it with mussels.

QUALITY ♛♛♛♛
VALUE ★★★½
GRAPES sauvignon blanc
REGION Marlborough, NZ
CELLAR 🍾 2
ALC./VOL. 10.0%
RRP $18.00

Hay Shed Hill Chardonnay

This winery was established in 1979 and it was formerly Sussex Vale vineyard and winery. Maker Peter Stanlake.
CURRENT RELEASE 1995 This says 'chardonnay' to us. It is a typical varietal nose with loads of peach and melon with a smattering of wood. The palate is broad with peach and melon flavours and the finish is dominated by French oak. The oak is a bit assertive at the moment but cellaring should get the house in order. It should be served lightly chilled with smoked cod.

QUALITY ♛♛♛♛
VALUE ★★★½
GRAPES chardonnay
REGION Margaret River, WA
CELLAR 🍾 5
ALC./VOL. 13.9%
RRP $15.00

Heggies Botrytis Riesling

This vineyard was planted when riesling was the premier white variety in Australia, and the quest continues today.
CURRENT RELEASE 1994 Riesling character remains dominant but botrytis puts in a significant contribution. The palate is a mix of lime and honey and the finish shows a marmalade pectin quality that leaves the mouth feeling dry and clean. Serve well chilled with a summer pud.

QUALITY ♛♛♛♛
VALUE ★★★★
GRAPES riesling
REGION Eden Valley, SA
CELLAR 🍾 4
ALC./VOL. 10.5%
RRP $12.00 (375 ml)

Heggies Chardonnay

QUALITY ▼▼▼▼
VALUE ★★★★
GRAPES chardonnay
REGION Eden Valley, SA
CELLAR 🍾 6
ALC./VOL. 13.5%
RRP $20.00 Ⓢ

Chardonnay and Eden Valley are not a well-known quantity. Judging by this wine it is worth further investigation. Maker Simon Adams.
CURRENT RELEASE 1995 The colour is pale straw and the nose has strong peach aromas plus a hint of wood. The palate offers a creamy texture with peach, melon and cashew flavours to the fore. The finish shows off some well-integrated oak. It can be served with a medium chill; try it with lightly smoked chicken.

Heggies Riesling

QUALITY ▼▼▼▼⸳
VALUE ★★★★½
GRAPES riesling
REGION Eden Valley, SA
CELLAR 🍾 3
ALC./VOL. 11.5%
RRP $19.50

This is a classic cool-climate wine that comes from Eden Valley at an altitude of 560 metres. It ages very well. Maker Simon Adams.
CURRENT RELEASE 1991 This is a re-release so the customers can catch up with the progress in the bottle. It retains a youthful colour but the nose has toast and kero aromas. The palate is mouth-filling with a strong lime flavour. The acid remains fresh and gives a crispness to the finish. It can be served well chilled and it is great with a lobster bisque.

Heggies Viognier

QUALITY ▼▼▼▼
VALUE ★★★
GRAPES viognier
REGION Eden Valley, SA
CELLAR 🍾 3
ALC./VOL. 12.8%
RRP $19.50

This is something of a crusade with the Hill Smith clan. The variety originates in the northern part of the Rhone Valley. This is the largest planting in Australia. There are small amounts to be found around Canberra.
CURRENT RELEASE 1995 Very perfumed with some exotic spices and blossom aromas. The palate shows loquat and other tropical fruits plus a hint of sweetness. French oak adds a dusty dry quality to the finish. It can be served with a medium chill and it goes well with Moreton Bay bugs in a light ginger sauce.

Helm's Non Oaked Chardonnay

One of the pioneers of the Canberra district this vineyard was established in 1974 and now produces around 2000 cases a year.
CURRENT RELEASE 1995 Yet another in the nude chardonnay brigade. The colour is bleached straw and the nose has strong melon and tropical fruit aromas. The palate is medium-bodied with soft melon flavours and there is plenty of acid on a long dry finish. It can be served well chilled; try it with yabbies.

QUALITY ▼▼▼▼
VALUE ★★★★
GRAPES chardonnay
REGION Canberra district, NSW
CELLAR 🍾 2
ALC./VOL. 12.0%
RRP $13.50

Helm's Rhine Riesling Classic Dry

Rhine should be fine in the cold Canberra district. In these parts there is snow during the winter and vintage is usually around May.
CURRENT RELEASE 1995 Although it purports to be a 'classic dry' there is a measure of fruit on the palate. The nose offers lime aromas and that is the main flavour on the palate. There is penetrating acid on the finish. It can be served well chilled; try it with whitebait fritters.

QUALITY ▼▼▼▼
VALUE ★★★½
GRAPES riesling
REGION Canberra district, NSW
CELLAR 🍾 4
ALC./VOL. 12.0%
RRP $12.50

Henschke Barossa Ranges Eden Valley Chardonnay

Confusing, isn't it? Valleys and hills, Eden Valley is more hill than valley and without a clear line of demarcation. This wine comes from vines on one of the original Henschke plantings.
CURRENT RELEASE 1995 The colour is a pale yellow and the nose is dominated by some smoky oak. There is a ghost of peach aroma out the back. The palate is rich with peach and melon flavours but oak quickly steals the scene. It is strong and ranges long on the finish. If you chill this too much you'll get splinters, so serve near room temperature. It goes well with smoked quail.

QUALITY ▼▼▼▼
VALUE ★★★★
GRAPES chardonnay
REGION Eden Valley, SA
CELLAR 🍾 5
ALC./VOL. 13.3%
RRP $19.00

Henschke Croft Chardonnay

QUALITY 🍷🍷🍷🍷🍷
VALUE ★★★★½
GRAPES chardonnay
REGION Adelaide Hills, SA
CELLAR 🍾 6
ALC./VOL. 14.0%
RRP $22.50

Along with pinot noir, chardonnay is the apple of this district's eye. It is developing a solid reputation for some of Australia's best examples. Previous outstanding vintages: '94

CURRENT RELEASE 1995 This is a very well-worked wine that shows a lot of winemaking/cellar characters. There are toast and butterscotch aromas on the nose. The palate is complex and chewy with obvious malolactic characters and a creamy texture. The main flavours are peach and grapefruit. There is well-integrated wood on a long finish. Just a little chill and trot out the pig's trotters.

Henschke Green's Hill Riesling

QUALITY 🍷🍷🍷🍷
VALUE ★★★★
GRAPES riesling
REGION Adelaide Hills, SA
CELLAR 🍾 4
ALC./VOL. 12.4%
RRP $14.50

This is one of the new guard from the Lenswood vineyard. It is on the 550 metre contour line.

CURRENT RELEASE 1995 This is a more delicate style with very fine aromatics on the nose. The palate is elegant with a complex blend of lemon, lime and grapefruit flavours and these are matched by some strong acid on the finish. It is a very fine wine that should be served with a medium chill. It goes well with clam chowder.

Henschke Joseph Hill Gewurztraminer

QUALITY 🍷🍷🍷🍷
VALUE ★★★★
GRAPES gewurztraminer
REGION Eden Valley, SA
CELLAR 🍾 2
ALC./VOL. 13.2%
RRP $14.50

This is a vineyard located on the higher regions of the Eden Valley. The altitude pays dividends with this delicate variety.

CURRENT RELEASE 1995 The nose is very strong with lychee, geranium and violet aromas. The palate continues the lychee flavours and there is also a suggestion of honey in the texture. The finish remains crisp and fresh. It can be served well chilled and should be drunk while it is young and fresh. Try it with quiche.

Henschke Julius Eden Valley Riesling

This is named after Julius Henschke, one of the famous ancestors of the Henschke clan who was a highly acclaimed artist and sculptor. Maker Stephen Henschke, viticulturist Prue Henschke.
CURRENT RELEASE 1995 This is big wine with a bright green-gold colour and a pungent nose with hints of lime and kero. The palate has very strong lime flavours which are balanced by some snappin' fresh acid on a very crisp finish. It can take a big chill and it should also age well. Try it with whitebait fritters.

QUALITY ♛♛♛♛
VALUE ★★★★
GRAPES riesling
REGION Eden Valley, SA
CELLAR 🍾 6
ALC./VOL. 13.5%
RRP $14.50

Henschke Louis Eden Valley Semillon

Eden Valley semillon is a smoky (unknown quantity) and there is evidence it has much promise as a table wine. The cool climate of Eden Valley probably precludes its use for sweet whites.
CURRENT RELEASE 1995 The colour is pale straw and the nose is an interesting mix of honeysuckle, gooseberry and lanolin. The palate is grapey with a strong citrus tang. The finish weighs in adding balance and a dry lingering sensation. It will probably develop into a chewy style but at the moment it can be served well chilled with deep-fried flounder.

QUALITY ♛♛♛♛
VALUE ★★★★
GRAPES semillon
REGION Eden Valley, SA
CELLAR 🍾 6
ALC./VOL. 12.5%
RRP $14.50

Henschke Tillys Vineyard

Keeping this in the family, the vineyard is named after great aunt Ottilie Henschke. The wine is meant to be a generic style.
CURRENT RELEASE 1995 In days of yore this might have been called a white Burgundy style. It has slightly smoky oak with underlying fruit. The palate is a fruit salad of flavours with a hint of honey that should develop with bottle-age. The finish is dominated by some acerbic oak. It needs time; serve with a medium chill, and try it with lightly curried chicken.

QUALITY ♛♛♛
VALUE ★★★
GRAPES not stated
REGION Eden Valley, SA
CELLAR 🍾 5
ALC./VOL. 12.8%
RRP $12.50

Heritage Chardonnay

QUALITY ♛♛♛♛
VALUE ★★★★
GRAPES chardonnay
REGION Barossa Valley, SA
CELLAR ☖ 2–6
ALC./VOL. 14.0%
RRP $14.50

Proprietor/winemaker Stephen Hoff is now one of the Barossa Valley's good ol'/new boys. Along with Charlie Melton, Rocky O'Callaghan and others he is in the vanguard of the revival.
CURRENT RELEASE 1995 Lots of wood here, Yankee Doodle oak marching ever forward. The nose is toasty with underlying peach. The palate has a mouth-filling texture with peach flavour but this is quickly replaced by vanilla/caramel oak. It needs time; don't overchill and try it with pâté.

Hill Smith Estate Chardonnay

QUALITY ♛♛♛♛♝
VALUE ★★★★
GRAPES chardonnay
REGION Eden Valley, SA
CELLAR ☖ 5
ALC./VOL. 13.5%
RRP $15.75

As the Hill Smith clan discovered cool climate they went further and further up the hill in Eden Valley. This vineyard is near the top of the hill. Maker Simon Adams.
CURRENT RELEASE 1994 A very civilised wine with great balance. The nose has peach and melon aromas with a background of nutty oak. There is a creamy texture on the palate and peach is the dominant flavour. The finish displays toasty oak and a drying quality. Not too cold and try it with pasta with an ocean trout and cream sauce.

Hillstowe Buxton Chardonnay

QUALITY ♛♛♛♝
VALUE ★★★
GRAPES chardonnay
REGION McLaren Vale, SA
CELLAR ☖ 4
ALC./VOL. 13.5%
RRP $17.00

Buxton was the handsome Christian name of Buxton Forbes Laurie who planted the first vineyard on the Fleurieu Peninsula (south-east coast of South Australia) in the 1950s. The family currently has a vineyard in McLaren Vale. Maker Chris Laurie.
CURRENT RELEASE 1994 This is a full-bodied style with plenty of flavour. At the moment it is ruled by smoky oak. The nose has a smoky character and there are peach aromas in the background. The palate is dominated by peach flavour and there are strong wood influences on a fairly aggressive finish. The more it is chilled, the more the oak asserts itself. It goes well with smoked eel.

Hillstowe Udy's Mill Chardonnay

This is a high altitude vineyard in the Adelaide Hills that belongs to the Laurie family. Plans are afoot for a restaurant at the tasting-room in Hahndorf.
CURRENT RELEASE 1994 It has developed considerably since last year's review. The nose is peachy with pear and nuts as part of the equation. The palate is complex; peach, melon and cashew are the major flavours. The wood is subtle yet supportive and the finish is long and dry. It should be served with a slight chill. It goes well with tandoori prawns.

QUALITY ♛♛♛♛♝
VALUE ★★★½
GRAPES chardonnay
REGION Adelaide Hills, SA
CELLAR 🍾 5
ALC./VOL. 13.5%
RRP $25.00

Hollick Terra White

This is an unlikely blend (in terms of varieties) and it works well. This is a by-the-glass style in a chic bistro.
CURRENT RELEASE 1995 There is a cute mix of lime and herbs on both the nose and palate. There is a hint of sweet fruit and plenty of lively zest in the flavour department. Crisp acid makes for a lively finish. It can be served well chilled; try it with a warm salad of scallops.

QUALITY ♛♛♛♛
VALUE ★★★★
GRAPES sauvignon blanc, riesling
REGION Coonawarra, SA
CELLAR 🍾 2
ALC./VOL. 11.5%
RRP $12.90

Houghton Chablis

It won't be long before the word chablis is outlawed from Australian labels. It will be interesting to see what this wine will be called – fruit salad white perhaps?
CURRENT RELEASE 1995 The nose is toasty with a hint of herbs and cut-grass smells. There are strong grape flavours with hints of stone fruits. The finish is dry with soft acid. It can be served well chilled. Try it with a seafood pizza.

QUALITY ♛♛♛
VALUE ★★★
GRAPES not stated
REGION various, WA
CELLAR 🍾
ALC./VOL. 12.0%
RRP $11.00 Ⓢ

Houghton Frankland River Rhine Riesling

QUALITY ♛♛♛♛
VALUE ★★★★½
GRAPES riesling
REGION Frankland River, SA
CELLAR 🍾 3
ALC./VOL. 12.5%
RRP $12.00 Ⓢ

The Great Southern region in WA prides itself on riesling. They see their district knocking Clare and Eden Valley off their lofty perch as the producers of great Australian riesling.
CURRENT RELEASE 1995 Very floral with loads of spice. The nose has lime and crushed violet aromas. The palate continues the lime and there is a slightly oily texture. Crisp acid makes for a tingling finish. It can be served well chilled. Try it with Singapore noodles.

Houghton Semillon Sauvignon Blanc

QUALITY ♛♛♛♛
VALUE ★★★½
GRAPES semillon, sauvignon blanc
REGION Great Southern, WA
CELLAR 🍾 3
ALC./VOL. 12.5%
RRP $12.00

These two varieties tend to be thrown together like Laurel and Hardy. (As an aside this writing duo has been described as 'the Abbott and Costello of wine writers'. Guess which one is which?)
CURRENT RELEASE 1995 There are tropical fruit/lychee aromas plus heavy herb smells. The palate has a hint of sweetness which is matched by spice. Crisp acid makes for a lively finish. It can be served well chilled. Try it with a spaghetti marinara.

Houghton Show Reserve Chardonnay

QUALITY ♛♛♛♛
VALUE ★★★★
GRAPES chardonnay
REGION various, WA
CELLAR 🍾 3
ALC./VOL. 12.8%
RRP $18.00

The Show Reserve series is a valuable window on the past. It shows how the wines from the West stand the test of time and bottle-age. Maker Peter Dawson.
CURRENT RELEASE 1985 After 10 years the oak is still very evident. The colour is a bright gold and there is a nutty oak character on the nose. The palate has peach flavours and a chewy texture. There is plenty of wood on the dry finish. It should not be served too cold. Try it with smoked trout.

Houghton White Burgundy

This is a famous style that dates back many decades. It was started by the legendary Jack Mann who used to crush the grapes in a meat mincer. Maker Paul Lapsley.
CURRENT RELEASE 1995 This is standard issue and thus ever reliable. There are hints of toast, esters and grape aromas. The middleweight palate has gooseberry flavours with herbal undertones. The finish has crisp acid and zesty tingle that refreshes. It can be served well chilled; try it with a warm chicken salad.

QUALITY ♙♙♙♙
VALUE ★★★½
GRAPES chenin blanc, verdelho, muscadelle, chardonnay and a cast of thousands.
REGION various, WA
CELLAR 2
ALC./VOL. 12.5%
RRP $11.50 $

Howard Park Chardonnay

John Wade is truly a master winemaker. With only three vintages on the board, this is already a benchmark chardonnay.
Previous outstanding vintages: '93, '94
CURRENT RELEASE 1995 This is a beautiful chardonnay. Mid-yellow in colour, it smells of butter, spices, peach, honey and toasty oak – all subtle and in fine harmony. The palate is very intense and lively, with tight structure, terrific length and obvious potential to unfold its mysteries further with age. Try it with a ripe double brie.

QUALITY ♙♙♙♙♙
VALUE ★★★★½
GRAPES chardonnay
REGION 'cool areas of WA'
CELLAR 1–5+
ALC./VOL. 13.5%
RRP $29.00

Hugh Hamilton Chardonnay

This is an unwooded style under the banner of an offspring of a famous wine making dynasty. Maker Hugh Hamilton.
CURRENT RELEASE 1995 Although there is no wood, the nose has a hint of toast as well as tropical fruit aromas. The palate has a passionfruit element plus grapefruit and peach and there is clean acid on the finish. It can be served well chilled and is a treat with pan-fried quail in five spices.

QUALITY ♙♙♙♙
VALUE ★★★½
GRAPES chardonnay
REGION McLaren Vale, SA
CELLAR 2
ALC./VOL. 13.0%
RRP $15.50

Hungerford Hill Cowra Chardonnay

QUALITY ♛♛♛♛
VALUE ★★★★
GRAPES chardonnay
REGION Cowra, NSW
CELLAR 🍾 4
ALC./VOL. 13.5%
RRP $13.00

Dadaism finds the Hungry Hill labels or vice versa. The new labelling is quite striking and it will strike a chord with older wine buffs who can remember *Epicurean* magazine circa 1975. Maker Ian Walsh.

CURRENT RELEASE 1995 A full-on style with a bright green-gold colour and toasty oak with a background of peach on the nose. The palate has a mouth-filling texture. Peach is the main flavour and there is a vanilla component contributed by the American oak. The finish has a nutty quality and plenty of persistence. It can be served with a medium chill and it goes well with pork fillet in a mango sauce.

Hungerford Hill Griffith Botrytis Semillon

QUALITY ♛♛♛♛
VALUE ★★★★
GRAPES semillon
REGION Riverina, NSW
CELLAR 🍾 5
ALC./VOL. 11.0%
RRP $11.50 (375 ml)

It seems it has become fashionable to have a sweet semillon from Griffith in the portfolio. And why not? They are very special wines.

CURRENT RELEASE 1993 The nose has honey, marmalade and hints of citrus. The palate continues the marmalade theme and there is the bonus of butterscotch and raisined fruit flavours. The finish is powder dry with a pectin quality indicative of noble rot. It should be served well chilled and it is bonza with smoked ocean trout.

Hungerford Hill Young Semillon

QUALITY ♛♛♛♛
VALUE ★★★★
GRAPES semillon
REGION Young, NSW
CELLAR 🍾 6
ALC./VOL. 11.5%
RRP $12.50

This label has experienced a yo-yo-like existence, changing ownership, location and management. These days it is part of the Southcorp group and draws fruit from several districts.

CURRENT RELEASE 1995 Young by district and by nature. The colour is pale straw and the nose offers green peas and herbs. The palate is a mix of citrus and pea-pod flavours and these are matched by crisp acid on a lengthy finish. It can be served with a medium chill; try it with yabbies.

Jamieson's Run Chardonnay

Coonawarra is blended with warmer-climate fruit here, because Coonawarra solo takes too long to 'come around' and hit peak drinkability. Maker Gavin Hogg.
CURRENT RELEASE 1995 Lots of buttery characters, plus peachy fruit and distinct coconut/toasty American oak showing out on the nose. The profile is broad with some tannin grip. Decent, if unexciting. Try it with pasta and clams.

QUALITY ♛♛♛♝
VALUE ★★★
GRAPES chardonnay
REGION Coonawarra, McLaren Vale & Barossa Valley, SA
CELLAR 🍾 2
ALC./VOL. 12.0%
RRP $15.60 Ⓢ

Jamieson's Run Sauvignon Blanc

There are four wines in the Jamieson's club: the shiraz-based red, the chardonnay, this, and – showing a major change of heart for Mildara – a pinot.
CURRENT RELEASE 1995 The nose shows green fruit aromas which suggest some of the grapes were picked early for the aromatics. Not an outrageous vegetal syle, but soft and smooth with a nice full middle palate. Fine balance and drinkability, especially with steamed asparagus.

QUALITY ♛♛♛♛
VALUE ★★★½
GRAPES sauvignon blanc
REGION McLaren Vale, SA
CELLAR 🍾 1
ALC./VOL. 12.5%
RRP $15.60 Ⓢ

Jane Brook Chardonnay

The estate was established in 1972 by David and Beverley Atkinson. It is situated 25 km north-east of Perth. The sample came with a short cork which might discourage cellaring. Maker Lyndon Crockett.
CURRENT RELEASE 1994 French oak opens the bidding. There are strong toast and caramel aromas on the nose. The palate is subtle with grapefruit flavours. Oak soon plays its trump card dominating the finish. It should be served lightly chilled. Try it with pâté.

QUALITY ♛♛♛♝
VALUE ★★★
GRAPES chardonnay
REGION Swan Valley, WA
CELLAR 🍾 4
ALC./VOL. 12.9%
RRP $16.65

Jane Brook Sauvignon Blanc

QUALITY 🍷🍷🍷
VALUE ★★★
GRAPES sauvignon blanc
REGION Swan Valley, WA
CELLAR 🍾 2
ALC./VOL. 12.0%
RRP $15.15

This winery makes around 7000 cases per annum. It is a very progressive company and one of the first in Australia to harness the Internet.
CURRENT RELEASE 1995 The colour is pale straw and the nose has a toasty herbal aroma. There are tropical fruit characters on the palate with pineapple and passionfruit being the main flavours. The finish has clean acid and length. It can be served well chilled; try it with lightly spiced scallops.

Jane Brook Wood Aged Chenin Blanc

QUALITY 🍷🍷🍷
VALUE ★★★
GRAPES chenin blanc
REGION Swan Valley, WA
CELLAR 🍾 1
ALC./VOL. 14.1%
RRP $14.70

David and Beverley Atkinson of Jane Brook are having success in the export side of business.
CURRENT RELEASE 1995 Gently played oak gives this wine an extra dimension, the nose is soft and fig-like and the oak firms and dries the finish. Decent weight and length and the dry acid finish suggests it would be best drunk with food. Try calamari.

Jim Barry Watervale Riesling

QUALITY 🍷🍷🍷🍷
VALUE ★★★★½
GRAPES riesling
REGION Clare Valley, SA
CELLAR 🍾 3
ALC./VOL. 12.5%
RRP $9.90

This is meant to be a fighting brand but it seems to be wandering around looking for a skirmish. It has yet to be recognised as great value for money. Maker Mark Barry.
CURRENT RELEASE 1994 Hovers between richness and delicacy but comes down hard on the side of value. The nose is floral with a citrus undertone. The palate continues the citrus theme with lemon and lime flavours. Plenty of acid keeps the finish lively. It can be served well chilled. Try it with an asparagus quiche.

Jimmy Watson's Chardonnay

For the full story/disaster/diatribe/debacle refer to the entry in the red section. (It's fun indeed, all the huffing and puffing comes from limited minds and vested interests.)
CURRENT RELEASE 1995 The colour is a bright yellow and the nose has solid peach aromas. The palate is medium-bodied with peach and melon the major flavour components. These are followed by some nutty elements on a French oak driven finish. Just a light chill will do; try it with deep-fried flounder.

QUALITY ♙♙♙♙
VALUE ★★★★
GRAPES chardonnay
REGION Barossa Valley, Padthaway, SA
CELLAR ♙ 3
ALC./VOL. 13.0%
RRP $12.00

Jingalla Rhine Riesling

In an area that is not noted for distinguished labels, this stands out as one of the better attempts. At least it stands out on retail shelves.
CURRENT RELEASE 1994 A floral aromatic style that plays the varietal card to the max. The nose has crushed flowers and citrus aromas. The palate is full-on lime flavour to the point of being keen. Fresh acid makes for a bracing finish. It can be served well chilled and it is a candidate for a plate of oysters natural.

QUALITY ♙♙♙♙
VALUE ★★★★
GRAPES riesling
REGION Great Southern, WA
CELLAR ♙ 4
ALC./VOL. 12.0%
RRP $13.50

Jingalla Semillon

This is a vineyard planted on the first place in recorded history to become dry land. The Porongurup Ranges were the first out of the primordial soup to see a harsh sun and a bunch of bewildered trilobites. Maker Brenden Smith (contract).
CURRENT RELEASE 1994 Interesting wine that shows another facet of the variety. The nose has a distinctive mix of lantana and lychee nut aromas. The palate has green pea and gooseberry flavours that are lifted on a raft of American oak. The finish is tinder dry and chalky. Medium chill to thrill, try it with pasta and pipis.

QUALITY ♙♙♙♙
VALUE ★★★★
GRAPES semillon
REGION Great Southern, WA
CELLAR ♙ 4
ALC./VOL. 12.0%
RRP $16.00

Karina Vineyard Chardonnay

QUALITY 🍷🍷🍷🍷
VALUE ★★★★½
GRAPES chardonnay
REGION Mornington Peninsula, Vic.
CELLAR 🍾 5+
ALC./VOL. 13.0%
RRP $19.90

Karina is one of the quiet achievers of the Mornington Peninsula, where the noise level raised by some makers attracts a goodly share of the spotlight. Maker Graeme Pinney.
CURRENT RELEASE 1995 Very stylish stuff indeed! The aromas are of flowers, butter, cashew, cedar and bread-dough, with the tell-tale regional twist of honey. The flavour is big and long, with softness and balance. Serious wine which could repay short-term cellaring. Then drink with lobster.

Karina Vineyard Sauvignon Blanc

QUALITY 🍷🍷🍷🍷
VALUE ★★★½
GRAPES sauvignon blanc
REGION Mornington Peninsula, Vic.
CELLAR 🍾 1
ALC./VOL. 12.0%
RRP $18.95

This is from the small Dromana vineyard of Graeme Pinney, next door to Dromana Estate.
CURRENT RELEASE 1995 Lots of vegetabley asparagus and cabbage aromas early, which clear to reveal an excellent sauvignon with tropical and gooseberry flavours which have intensity and length. Deep, soft and persistent, a very drinkable sauvignon to serve with asparagus and lemon juice vinaigrette.

Karrivale Rhine Riesling

QUALITY 🍷🍷🍷🍷
VALUE ★★★★½
GRAPES riesling
REGION Great Southern, WA
CELLAR 🍾 6+
ALC./VOL. 12.2%
RRP $13.50

Campbell McGready's small vineyard in the Porongurup Ranges regularly produces some of WA's finest riesling, made at nearby Plantagenet. Previous outstanding vintages: '91
CURRENT RELEASE 1994 A trophy-winner at the Mt Barker Show, this has tight, youthful, citrus and floral aromas, a touch of austerity in its fine structure and firm acid backbone. Classic riesling that should cellar well. Drink with scallops.

Katnook Estate Botrytised Chardonnay

It's hard to imagine that with chardonnay fetching up to $2000 a tonne in Coonawarra that it's worthwhile making this sort of wine from it; however nice it tastes. Maker Wayne Stehbens. Previous outstanding vintages: '89
CURRENT RELEASE 1992 A terrifically sweet, rich dessert wine that's at the far end of the sticky scale. Deep amber hue, developed and very complex toffee/caramel nose. Luscious and syrupy on the tongue, with plenty of acid to enliven it. Drink now with crème brûlée.

QUALITY 🍷🍷🍷🍷🍷
VALUE ★★★★
GRAPES chardonnay
REGION Coonawarra, SA
CELLAR 🍾 1
ALC./VOL. 11.0%
RRP $16.00 (375ml)

Katnook Estate Chardonnay

Katnook's is always one of the biggest chardonnays that come across our path. It's for power drinkers who don't mind a bit of alcohol. Maker Wayne Stehbens. Previous outstanding vintages: '90, '92
CURRENT RELEASE 1993 A tightly-structured, slow-developing chardonnay, perfumed with tropical fruit salad aromas and a liberal quota of oak. The alcohol gives some astringency and heat to the finish. Could come together with time. A big style to go with crayfish.

QUALITY 🍷🍷🍷🍷
VALUE ★★★
GRAPES chardonnay
REGION Coonawarra, SA
CELLAR 🍾 1–5+
ALC./VOL. 14.5%
RRP $28.30

Katnook Estate Sauvignon Blanc

Katnook was one of the very first to market a premium sauvignon blanc. This is their 16th vintage. While we prefer our sauvignon very young, most of the earlier vintages have kept well. Maker Wayne Stehbens.
CURRENT RELEASE 1995 Pungent green-grass and riper tropical fruit aromas, invitingly attractive and fresh. The taste is very intense, juicy, crisp and lively. A high-quality sauvignon with harmony and length.

QUALITY 🍷🍷🍷🍷
VALUE ★★★½
GRAPES sauvignon blanc
REGION Coonawarra, SA
CELLAR 🍾 2+
ALC./VOL. 13.5%
RRP $20.00

Kay's Amery Sauvignon Blanc

QUALITY 🍷🍷🍷?
VALUE ★★★
GRAPES sauvignon blanc
REGION McLaren Vale, SA
CELLAR 🍾 2
ALC./VOL. 12.5%
RRP $16.00

McLaren Vale is renowned for its red wines but sauvignon blanc is one of the two whites which do very well there.
CURRENT RELEASE 1995 Light yellow hue, green-stick and slightly woolly aromas. The taste is admirably crisp and clean with delicate flavour, the lively acid carrying the day. Goes well with fresh cooked mussels.

Killerby Chardonnay

QUALITY 🍷🍷🍷🍷
VALUE ★★★½
GRAPES chardonnay
REGION south-west coastal, WA
CELLAR 🍾 4
ALC./VOL. 13.4%
RRP $18.00

Killerby is a family affair, with founder Barry Killerby's widow Betty, son Ben, daughter Anna and Anna's husband Matt Aldridge all playing a part. Maker Matt Aldridge.
Previous outstanding vintages: '92, '93, '94
CURRENT RELEASE 1995 There's more than a hint of Burgundian character here, although the palate has a trace of sweetness and could use more zip. There are buttery and honeyed flavours aplenty with well-balanced oak and effective use of malolactic fermentation. Try it with chicken stir-fry.

Kingston Estate Chardonnay

QUALITY 🍷🍷🍷
VALUE ★★★½
GRAPES chardonnay
REGION Riverland, SA
CELLAR 🍾 1
ALC./VOL. 13.0%
RRP $10.00

This brand is named after Kingston-on-Murray (river) – not Kingston the crayfish capital on the SA south coast. Maker Bill Moularadellis.
CURRENT RELEASE 1995 The climate of the region shows up here: the wine is very developed and forward, with a deep yellow colour and a mellow aroma of fig jam and pineapples. The palate is full, very soft and a trifle soupy, with the alcohol and wood showing through the fruit. A generous style which goes well with chicken schnitzel.

Kingston Reserve Chardonnay

Fermented and aged for 12 months in oak, says the label. HH wonders if less wood mightn't suit this kind of fruit better.
CURRENT RELEASE 1993 A very developed style of chardonnay: deep golden colour, big toasty aged bouquet with honey and mellow herbal/peach fruit. The palate is very big and slightly cumbersome. It's filled out with quite a middle-aged spread. Still, a big lump of a wine and lots of bang for your buck. Try it with roast turkey.

QUALITY ♛♛♛♙
VALUE ★★★½
GRAPES chardonnay
REGION Riverland, SA
CELLAR ↓
ALC./VOL. 13.0%
RRP $17.00

Knight Granite Hills Chardonnay

Winemaker Lew Knight believes this is the best chardonnay he's made to date. Knight recently celebrated the 25th anniversary of Granite Hills, which was established in 1970.
CURRENT RELEASE 1994 An unusual chardonnay, showing peachy and vegetal fruit aromas and possibly some botrytis influence. It's very big, rich and oily in the mouth (from high glycerol) and while it tastes quite sweet, Lew Knight assures us the wine is dry. Try it with an asparagus quiche.

QUALITY ♛♛♛♙
VALUE ★★★
GRAPES chardonnay
REGION Macedon, Vic.
CELLAR ↓ 3+
ALC./VOL. 13.5%
RRP $18.00

Krondorf Chardonnay

The 1996 harvest produced almost a glut of chardonnay fruit and grape prices happily began to tail off. Mildara Blass's chardonnays have always been fairly priced.
CURRENT RELEASE 1995 A gentle wine with a subdued nose, melon/peach fruit and a whisper of wood. The flavour is mediumweight with softness and length. Excellent commercial chardonnay at a fair price. Serve with crab.

QUALITY ♛♛♛♙
VALUE ★★★½
GRAPES chardonnay
REGION Barossa & Eden Valleys, McLaren Vale, SA
CELLAR ↓ 2
ALC./VOL. 13.0%
RRP $11.00 Ⓢ

Krondorf Rhine Riesling

QUALITY ♀♀♀?
VALUE ★★★½
GRAPES riesling
REGION Eden Valley, SA
CELLAR 🍾 5
ALC./VOL. 11.5%
RRP $11.00 ⓢ

Krondorf means crown village and harks back to the Barossa's German-speaking early settlers.
CURRENT RELEASE 1995 Again, an inexpensive riesling made from premium grapes. Refined, subtle but true floral aroma, with a slate/mineral overtone. It's fruity on the palate and ends with a crisp dry finish. Serve with shellfish.

Krondorf Show Chardonnay

QUALITY ♀♀♀♀?
VALUE ★★★½
GRAPES chardonnay
REGION McLaren Vale, Barossa & Eden Valleys, SA
CELLAR 🍾 2
ALC./VOL. 13.0%
RRP $20.00 ⓢ

This winery has had many lives, but it became big news in the late '70s/early '80s when Grant Burge and Ian Wilson took it over, built it up, and sold it to Mildara. Maker Nick Walker.
Previous outstanding vintages: '90, '91, '92, '93
CURRENT RELEASE 1994 Showing quite developed character, this '94 is deep yellow coloured, and smells of honey, resin and toasty aged characters. It's rich and full-bodied in the mouth, big and gutsy and a real contrast to its stablemate, the Yarra Ridge Chardonnay. A good lobster style.

Lakes Folly Chardonnay

QUALITY ♀♀♀♀?
VALUE ★★★½
GRAPES chardonnay
REGION Hunter Valley, NSW
CELLAR 🍾 4
ALC./VOL. 12.0%
RRP $33.00

This is the tip of the boutique iceberg that was founded in 1963. Dr Max is now a senior citizen (sorry Max) but he was a big noise in the revival of the Australian wine industry. Maker Stephen Lake.
Previous outstanding vintages: '81, '83, '84, '86, '89, '91, '92
CURRENT RELEASE 1994 Developing impressively since the last review. It has a high-tone oak aromas and cashew characters on the nose. There are peach and tropical fruit flavours on the palate and the transition to the oaked finish is very smooth. It can be served with a medium chill. As we said last year, try it with a salad Nicoise.

Lark Hill Chardonnay

Science academics David and Sue Carpenter have devoted 20 years to this adventurous cool-climate vineyard, 860 metres high up on the Lake George escarpment, near Canberra. Maker Sue Carpenter.
CURRENT RELEASE 1995 This is a delicate, light-bodied, and probably slow-ageing chardonnay which promises better things in a year or two. The nose shows sawdusty oak and the palate is very soft, round and gentle with cool-grown reserve. Try it with prosciutto and figs.

QUALITY ♛♛♛♛
VALUE ★★★½
GRAPES chardonnay
REGION Canberra district, NSW
CELLAR 🍾 4+
ALC./VOL. 13.5%
RRP $22.70

Lawson's Dry Hills Gewurztraminer

The hills are alive with the sound of traminer! This winery is the endeavour of Ross Lawson and it was established in 1992. Maker Claire Allan.
CURRENT RELEASE 1995 Wham, bam, thank you ma'm. This is a wine with attitude. The nose reeks of lychee and crushed flowers. The palate is intense with a high impact of gooseberry fruit. This is balanced by some crisp acid on a protracted finish. It can be served well chilled; try it with ocean trout dumplings in a light Pernod sauce.

QUALITY ♛♛♛♛½
VALUE ★★★★
GRAPES gewurztraminer
REGION Marlborough, NZ
CELLAR 🍾 3
ALC./VOL. 12.5%
RRP $18.00

Lawson's Dry Hills Sauvignon Blanc

This is a small vineyard in the Blenheim/Marlborough district. The annual production is around 3300 cases. Maker Claire Allan.
CURRENT RELEASE 1995 New Zealand sauvignon blanc is on a revival curve after it palled in the marketplace. This is a good example of the second wave. The nose is concentrated with tomato leaf and green pea aromas. The palate offers tropical fruit like pineapple and mango as well as gooseberry. There is crisp refreshing acid on the finish. Serve well chilled with green lip mussels.

QUALITY ♛♛♛♛
VALUE ★★★★
GRAPES sauvignon blanc
REGION Marlborough, NZ
CELLAR 🍾 3
ALC./VOL. 11.5%
RRP $18.00

Leasingham Bin 37 Chardonnay

QUALITY ♟♟♟♟
VALUE ★★★½
GRAPES chardonnay
REGION Clare Valley, SA
CELLAR 🍷 5
ALC./VOL. 13.5%
RRP $15.50

Once were warriors – the Leasingham bin numbers that is... Bin 5 and Bin 7 were a hot item in the early '70s, now they mean little to the average consumer and Bin 37 doesn't count for a hill of beans in this crazy world.

CURRENT RELEASE 1994 Don't laugh but this wine smells like roast turkey. It has a strong oak-dominated nose with underlying peach. The palate has peach flavours and a strong bacon taint. The finish has lots of toast character. Don't over chill and serve with roast turkey – what else?

Leasingham Bin 7 Rhine Riesling

QUALITY ♟♟♟♟♟
VALUE ★★★★★
GRAPES riesling
REGION Clare Valley, SA
CELLAR 🍷 6
ALC./VOL. 12.5%
RRP $13.95 Ⓢ

Best Bargain White

This label launched careers (Tim Knappstein, Tim Adams) and the cause of riesling as the grape variety for the Clare Valley. Maker Richard Rowe.

Previous outstanding vintages: too numerous to mention

CURRENT RELEASE 1995 Right in the groove, this is a classic with plenty of cellar potential. The colour is pale and the nose has full-on aromatics and citrus. It sings a siren's song and the captivating palate delivers the coup de grâce to any reservations. It is intense with zesty lime flavours that are braced by some steely acid. The finish is very fresh with clean acid and good length. It is perfect with oysters natural and can be served well chilled.

Leasingham Classic Clare Rhine Riesling

This is a stand-aside label reserved for what the wine makers at BRL Hardy consider regional classics. It is a cellar proposition. Maker Richard Rowe.
CURRENT RELEASE 1994 There is already evidence of bottle development on the nose. Just a hint of kero and lime aromas but the colour remains a virginal pale straw. The palate has tingling lime flavours typical of Clare and the acid remains fresh. It will age for a long time. Chill well and try it with Tassie oysters natural.

QUALITY ♛♛♛♛♕
VALUE ★★★★½
GRAPES riesling
REGION Clare Valley, SA
CELLAR 🍾 6
ALC./VOL. 12.0%
RRP $21.00

Leconfield Chardonnay

This winery was the vision of the late Syd Hamilton from the famous winemaking family. In typical fashion he started the project in his early eighties and lived to see the first vintages. Maker Ralph Fowler.
CURRENT RELEASE 1995 Temperature is critical, serve it too cold and you get a rhapsody in oak. The colour is pale lemon-yellow and the nose smells of nutty/toasty oak. The palate is a complicated mix of grapefruit, peach and melon flavours with oak throwing in nutty characters. The finish bristles with oak. It has enough power to cope with a buttery dish like chicken liver pâté

QUALITY ♛♛♛♛
VALUE ★★★★
GRAPES chardonnay
REGION Coonawarra, SA
CELLAR 🍾 5
ALC./VOL. 13.0%
RRP $19.00

Leconfield Riesling

As a party game, name the number of wineries in Coonawarra that make and market a riesling. You'll find they are surprisingly few.'
CURRENT RELEASE 1995 A straightforward style that is a pleasant drink. The nose is dominated by citrus aromas and the palate has strong lime flavour with a hint of sugar. This is balanced by some crisp acid on an incisive finish. It can be served well chilled and it goes well with stir-fried chicken.

QUALITY ♛♛♛♛
VALUE ★★★★
GRAPES riesling
REGION Coonawarra, SA
CELLAR 🍾 3
ALC./VOL. 11.5%
RRP $12.50

Leeuwin Estate Art Series Chardonnay

QUALITY 🍷🍷🍷🍷
VALUE ★★★
GRAPES chardonnay
REGION Margaret River, WA
CELLAR 🍾 3–8
ALC./VOL. 14.0%
RRP $48.90

The Art Series is a bit like one of the famed first growth wineries in Bordeaux. It features a different work of art on the label each year. This year the painting is a ripper!
Previous outstanding vintages: '80, '81, '82, '83, '86, '87, '88, '89, '91, '92
CURRENT RELEASE 1993 A big, bold, ostentatious style as usual. The wine wears its oak on its sleeve, and you'll notice the superior quality. The nose is toasty and nutty with an underscore of varietal aromas. The palate is rich and chewy with a medley of peach, melon and apricot flavours with a cashew nut background. The wood adds a savoury component to the long dry finish. It needs more time in the bottle. Try it with a rich dish of pork and beans.

Leeuwin Estate Riesling

QUALITY 🍷🍷🍷
VALUE ★★★
GRAPES riesling
REGION Margaret River, WA
CELLAR 🍾 3
ALC./VOL. 12.5%
RRP $17.10

The frog on the label reminds us of an old Canned Heat track called 'Bullfrog Blues'. The owner of Leeuwin certainly has had the post-stockmarket crash blues but seems to be winning through. Maker Bob Cartwright.
CURRENT RELEASE 1995 There is nothing subtle about the rieslings from Leeuwin. This is a big wine with citrus aromas on the nose. The palate has plenty of impact with a mouth-filling lemon essence flavour. The finish is soft and a trifle short. Serve well chilled with frogs legs.

Leeuwin Prelude Chardonnay

As the musical connotation suggests, this is an opening or a preview of what is to come. It is a piece before the main body of music. Just for the record it is pronounced 'prel-ude'. Don't go for the Honda 'pre-lude'.
Previous outstanding vintages: '94
CURRENT RELEASE 1995 This is a point of departure: in a masked line up you could be forgiven for thinking this was a sav' blanc. It has a pea-pod nose with a charred oak background. The palate is a tad reluctant with subdued melon characters that are over-ridden by toasty oak. The finish is propelled by nutty oak flavours. Don't overchill and try it with a warm salad of quail.

QUALITY ♟♟♟
VALUE ★★
GRAPES chardonnay
REGION Margaret River, WA
CELLAR 🍾 3
ALC./VOL. 13.5%
RRP $22.00

Lenswood Chardonnay

When he's not flying his Boeing Stearman, not so youthful (age is catching us all) Tim Knappstein is doing the vinous equivalent of aerobatics with chardonnay and pinot noir.
Previous outstanding vintages: '93
CURRENT RELEASE 1994 Great stuff! This is the big Kahuna where chardonnay is concerned. There has been a lot of work done with things like barrel ferment on lees. It has a rich, full and nutty nose. The palate is highly seductive with a chewy texture and broad spectrum fruit flavours including melon, peach and grapefruit. The finish shows off some dexterous oak. It should be lovingly chilled to just below room temperature. Try it with chicken casserole.

QUALITY ♟♟♟♟♟
VALUE ★★★★★
GRAPES chardonnay
REGION Adelaide Hills, SA
CELLAR 🍾 6
ALC./VOL. 14.0%
RRP $28.50

Lenswood Sauvignon Blanc

QUALITY ♛♛♛♛
VALUE ★★★★
GRAPES sauvignon blanc
REGION Adelaide Hills, SA
CELLAR 🍾 4
ALC./VOL. 12.5%
RRP $19.00

Tim Knappstein has a sufficient dash of derring-do to own and aerobat a Boeing Stearman (that's a bi-plane to the uninitiated) and he tends to approach winemaking at a similar cutting edge. Maker Tim Knappstein.

CURRENT RELEASE 1995 Varietal flavour to the max. It is a pungent wine with a potent nose dominated by mango and pineapple aromas. These flavours are confirmed on the palate which also shows some herbal characters. The finish is snapping fresh with crisp acid. It can be served with a medium chill; try it with a warm salad of pesto chicken.

Lillydale Vineyards Chardonnay

QUALITY ♛♛♛♛
VALUE ★★★
GRAPES chardonnay
REGION Yarra Valley, Vic.
CELLAR 🍾 2
ALC./VOL. 11.5%
RRP $14.50 Ⓢ

The Lillydale Vineyards wines are among the lighter styles to come from the Yarra Valley. They are grown in the cooler country near Seville. Maker Alex White.

CURRENT RELEASE 1995 This has a pale colour and is very delicate and fruit-driven, with a herbaceous and slightly lollyish nose, hinting at nectarine and cashew nut. It's a good lighter style but would be better with more oomph. Try it with a delicate crab dish.

Lindemans Bin 65 Chardonnay

QUALITY ♛♛♛♛
VALUE ★★★½
GRAPES chardonnay
REGION not stated
CELLAR 🍾 2
ALC./VOL. 13.0%
RRP $9.50 Ⓢ

The Poms knew all about this wine years before it was ever released in Australia. It is also a big hit in the US and could be touted as one of our most successful exports. Makers Phillip John and a cast of thousands.

CURRENT RELEASE 1995 This is a sunny straightforward style that is easy to drink. The nose is peachy and there is a whiff of toast. The palate has peach and melon flavours and the finish is discreet and dry. Just the thing for a designer sanger at lunchtime.

Lindemans Nursery Vineyard Rhine Riesling Classic Release

Classic Coonawarra riesling is not really in the lexicon but here is one that has truly earned its badges of rank.
CURRENT RELEASE 1985 The colour is a bold green-gold and there are typical development hints on the nose. There is citrus and hints of kero. The palate is intense with mouth-filling lime flavour and the finish has retained plenty of fresh acid to add a crisp character. It can be served well chilled; put it alongside a smoked trout.

QUALITY ♛♛♛♛♛
VALUE ★★★★★
GRAPES riesling
REGION Coonawarra, SA
CELLAR 🍷 3
ALC./VOL. 11.5%
RRP $19.00

Lindemans Padthaway Chardonnay

Roll out the barrel. A decade ago this was a much vaunted addition to the Lindemans portfolio; these days it is a workhorse with wood.
CURRENT RELEASE 1995 Lindemans claim to have subdued the oak in recent years, but it's still a wine for lumber lovers. The nose is a miscellany of oak, butterscotch, and peach. The palate has a buttery texture and oak swamps the finish. It should be served near room temperature. Try it with smoked turkey.

QUALITY ♛♛♛♝
VALUE ★★★½
GRAPES chardonnay
REGION Padthaway, SA
CELLAR 🍷 2
ALC./VOL. 13.0%
RRP $13.00

Lindemans Padthaway Sauvignon Blanc

Padthaway was the great white hope (as well as red) for viticulture producing grapes at an affordable price. Salinity problems may cast doubts over the long-term viability of the project. Maker Phillip John.
CURRENT RELEASE 1995 A tone poem in varietal character. The chords all ring true. The nose is about tropical fruits and herbs. The palate has passionfruit and pineapple flavours and there is plenty of keen acid that makes for a zesty finish. It can be served well chilled and it is bonza with mussels poached in white wine.

QUALITY ♛♛♛♛
VALUE ★★★★
GRAPES sauvignon blanc
REGION Padthaway, SA
CELLAR 🍷 2
ALC./VOL. 11.5%
RRP $13.00

Madfish Bay Premium Dry White

QUALITY ♛♛♛♛
VALUE ★★★
GRAPES chardonnay 80%, semillon 15%, sauvignon blanc 5%
REGION Great Southern & Pemberton, WA
CELLAR 🍾 2
ALC./VOL. 13.5%
RRP $15.30

Madfish Bay is a real place, the label assures us. This is the lower-priced brand of Howard Park's John and Wendy Wade.
CURRENT RELEASE 1995 The nose is rich and intriguingly spicy, and the flavour is medium-weight: rich and smooth, ending dry with some phenolic thickness. A more than decent quaffing white. Try it with pumpkin risotto.

Massoni Red Hill Chardonnay

QUALITY ♛♛♛♛
VALUE ★★½
GRAPES chardonnay
REGION Mornington Peninsula, Vic.
CELLAR 🍾 2
ALC./VOL. 13.0%
RRP $29.00

Founders Leon and Vivienne Massoni retired last year, selling their shares in Massoni-Home to partner Ian Home (Yellowglen founder) and his wife Sue.
CURRENT RELEASE 1995 The nose is a riot of vanilla, honey and passionfruit and there's a suggestion of botrytis. The palate is lean and quite high in acid, with tangy honeyed flavours and the wine is probably best drunk fairly young. Try it with honey prawns.

Matua Valley Judd Estate Chardonnay

QUALITY ♛♛♛♛
VALUE ★★★½
GRAPES chardonnay
REGION Gisborne, NZ
CELLAR 🍾 2
ALC./VOL. 12.5%
RRP $18.00

The Judd Estate is a privileged site in the rather wet and high-vigour Gisborne region of New Zealand. Maker Ross Spence.
CURRENT RELEASE 1994 They've thrown the chardonnay-maker's textbook at this. It's crammed with buttery, honey and toasty developed complexities which make it a full-on Burgundian style. Retains elegance and length, but some may see it as too interventionist at the expense of fruit. Serve with crumbed lamb's brains.

Maxwell Chardonnay

Mark Maxwell is an accomplished winemaker, who took over from his father Ken's mead making venture at McLaren Vale.
CURRENT RELEASE 1995 A big and slightly heavy chardonnay which has sunny, fig-like aromas and a lot of warmth on the palate. Plenty of intensity and weight, and the strength of the fruit dominates the oak. A good mate for sweetbreads.

QUALITY ♇♇♇♇
VALUE ★★★★½
GRAPES chardonnay
REGION McLaren Vale, SA
CELLAR 🍾 2
ALC./VOL. 13.0%
RRP $13.95 (cellar door)

McWilliams Eden Valley Show Rhine Riesling

Every now and then McWilliams buy a few tonnes of something special from somewhere outside their stamping ground, and out it under a limited release label. They're usually excellent.
CURRENT RELEASE 1988 A deep golden colour heightens the anticipation, and the bouquet is everything you'd hoped for: fabulous buttered toast-aged complexities still with echoes of floral fruit. The palate is soft and smooth yet not lacking acid; full, rounded and leaves the mouth full of lingering after-aromas which are truly memorable. Try it with smoked trout.

QUALITY ♇♇♇♇♇
VALUE ★★★★½
GRAPES riesling
REGION Eden Valley, SA
CELLAR 🍾 2
ALC./VOL. 12.0%
RRP $15.30

McWilliams Hanwood Chardonnay

Each wine in the Hanwood range has a different Northern Territory Aboriginal painting on the label.
CURRENT RELEASE 1995 This little trimmer is a light-bodied, fruit-style chardonnay which offers excellent flavour for the price. Toast and cashew aromas lead into a smooth, flavoursome palate that has good weight and fruitiness without sweetness. Good value! Try it with vegetarian lasagna.

QUALITY ♇♇♇♇
VALUE ★★★★½
GRAPES chardonnay
REGION Riverina, NSW
CELLAR 🍾
ALC./VOL. 13.0%
RRP $9.40 Ⓢ

McWilliams J.J. McWilliam Botrytis Semillon

QUALITY 🍷🍷🍷🍷🍷
VALUE ★★★★½
GRAPES semillon
REGION Riverina, NSW
CELLAR 🍾 3+
ALC./VOL. 10.0%
RRP $20.00 (375 ml) ⓢ

J.J. McWilliam was the founder of the winemaking dynasty which spans five generations. The company is still wholly family owned. Maker Jim Brayne.

CURRENT RELEASE 1993 A rich, heady, unctuous wine with very intense vanilla, poached apricot, botrytised fruit flavours, luscious sweetness and a long follow-through. We doubt whether old J.J. would have understood this sort of thing, but that's of no matter. Sip with a rich fruit flan.

McWilliams Mount Pleasant Chardonnay

QUALITY 🍷🍷🍷🍷
VALUE ★★★★
GRAPES chardonnay
REGION Hunter Valley, NSW
CELLAR 🍾 2
ALC./VOL. 12.0%
RRP $12.90 ⓢ

The chardonnays at Mount Pleasant are the sprinters while the semillons are the stayers.

CURRENT RELEASE 1994 These wines develop massive yellow colour very quickly. This one has a toasty oaky bouquet showing some development, and the flavour is soft and mouth-filling. A lot of stuffing here and generous peachy flavour, albeit not terrifically complex. Could take a decent chill, then serve with poultry.

McWilliams Mount Pleasant Elizabeth

QUALITY 🍷🍷🍷🍷?
VALUE ★★★★½
GRAPES semillon
REGION Hunter Valley, NSW
CELLAR 🍾 5
ALC./VOL. 10.5%
RRP $12.90 ⓢ

McWilliams has the aged semillon market sewn up, but how they manage to put a five-year-old wine on sale at such a price is beyond comprehension. It retails for as little as $8.99. Maker Phil Ryan.

Previous outstanding vintages: '79, '82, '83, '86, '87, '89

CURRENT RELEASE 1991 This seems like a bigger style of Elizabeth, perhaps due to the drought year, and it may be ageing faster than usual, although the colour shows more age than the bouquet or flavour. Fresh lemony, herbal, lanolin scents and the taste is lean and dry, with a touch of austerity yet plenty of flavour. Goes well with roast chicken.

McWilliams Mount Pleasant Lovedale Semillon

Lovedale is an individual vineyard wine, formerly known as Anne Riesling. The area is a flat, undistinguished looking piece of poor sandy soil, but, boy, does it grow good semillon! Maker Phil Ryan.
Previous outstanding vintages: '84
CURRENT RELEASE 1986 At 10 years, the colour is deep golden and the nose shows burnt toast, lanolin, herbal and honey aromas which translate faithfully onto the palate. It's a top-year semillon of high class and should live for several years yet. Serve it with a good ripe brie.

QUALITY 🍷🍷🍷🍷🍷
VALUE ★★★★★
GRAPES semillon
REGION Hunter Valley, NSW
CELLAR 🍾 5
ALC./VOL. 11.0%
RRP $30.00

Mildara Church Hill Chardonnay

A lot of people insist on calling this wine Churchill, but we don't suppose it really matters . . .
CURRENT RELEASE 1995 Hard to get excited, but at $6.95 on discount, who's arguing? It's a soft, fruity, herb-flavoured basic white wine, with marginal chardonnay character and no obvious wood. Acceptable quaffing dry white. Try it with fish and chips.

QUALITY 🍷🍷🍷
VALUE ★★★
GRAPES chardonnay
REGION Sunraysia, Vic.
CELLAR 🍾
ALC./VOL. 12.0%
RRP $10.00 $

Miranda High Country Chardonnay

This is a new label minted for a range of wines sourced from King Valley growers, who used to be in league with Brown Brothers.
CURRENT RELEASE 1995 Interesting herbaceous and tropical fruit characters are developing along tea-leafy lines; the fruit-driven flavour is soft, round and easy on the gums. Drink soon, with scallops.

QUALITY 🍷🍷🍷
VALUE ★★★½
GRAPES chardonnay 89%, semillon 7%, riesling 4%
REGION King Valley, Vic.
CELLAR 🍾 2
ALC./VOL. 13.5%
RRP $12.00 $

Miranda Rovalley Ridge Show Reserve Chardonnay

QUALITY ♛♛♛♛
VALUE ★★★★
GRAPES chardonnay 90%, semillon 10%
REGION Eden Valley, SA 90%, King Valley, Vic.10%
CELLAR 🍾 3
ALC./VOL. 14.0%
RRP $16.95 ⓢ

Ex-Californian Shayne Cunningham has done wonders for the quality (and show success) of Miranda in recent years. This wine is made at the old Rovalley winery in the Barossa.
CURRENT RELEASE 1994 Unusual style with tea-leafy fruit and an oily viscosity. The peachy, cedary flavours are very attractive and the palate is soft and avoids bone-dry austerity. The fruit and wood are a perfect match and all that's needed to consummate the marriage is a rich yabbie bisque.

Mitchell Semillon

QUALITY ♛♛♛♛♛
VALUE ★★★★
GRAPES semillon
REGION Clare Valley, SA
CELLAR 🍾 3
ALC./VOL. 12.5%
RRP $13.85

A wine to give the Hunter a fright. Maker, Andrew Mitchell, has lightened off the wood and refined this wine in recent vintages, and it's better than ever.
CURRENT RELEASE 1995 The French oak and barrel-ferment characters make for a comely and alarmingly chardonnay-ish style, with aromas of cashew and melon in its youth. There's good flavour concentration, subtle wood and fine balance, tailing out to an extended finish. Teams well with lighter poultry dishes.

Mitchell Watervale Riesling

Value-minded readers will be well aware that the finest Aussie riesling can be had for half the price of the equivalent chardonnay, which is largely to do with fashion. Mitchell's is unbelievably cheap for the quality in the bottle.
Previous outstanding vintages: '86, '88, '91, '92, '93, '94
CURRENT RELEASE 1995 One of the best Mitchell rieslings HH can remember: fresh lime-citrus and flowery aromas with a hint of doughiness that will turn gently into toast. Crisp and lively yet rich and full in the mouth. A very intense, generous and long-finishing riesling that drinks well now with trout and almonds, but should age beautifully.

QUALITY ♛♛♛♛♛
VALUE ★★★★★
GRAPES riesling
REGION Clare Valley, SA
CELLAR 🍾 10
ALC./VOL. 13.0%
RRP $13.00

Best Riesling

Mitchelton Chinaman's Bridge Sauvignon Blanc

Chinese market gardeners abounded in the Seymour-Nagambie region last century, and the bridge over the Goulburn dates back to that bygone era. Maker Don Lewis.
CURRENT RELEASE 1995 Is there any limit to the talents of this man Lewis? A cracking sauvignon blanc, this has strikingly fresh tropical/herbaceous fruit scents and a certain cool-grown sweaty overtone that's not disagreeable. Crisply acid, lively and refreshing to drink while young, with Nicoise salad.

QUALITY ♛♛♛♛♛
VALUE ★★★★
GRAPES sauvignon blanc
REGION King Valley, Strathbogie Ranges & Yarra Valley, Vic.
CELLAR 🍾 1
ALC./VOL. 12.5%
RRP $16.00 ⓢ

Best Sauvignon Blanc

Mitchelton Victoria Reserve Chardonnay

QUALITY ♟♟♟♟♝
VALUE ★★★½
GRAPES chardonnay
REGION mainly Yarra Valley & Strathbogie Ranges, Vic.
CELLAR 🍾 1–5+
ALC./VOL. 13.5%
RRP $23.35 ⓢ

This wine gets the full treatment: barrel fermentation, malolactic, stirred lees, skin contact, and a multitude of different oaks, all in the name of complexity.
Previous outstanding vintages: '92, '93
CURRENT RELEASE 1994 A rather closed, slightly austere wine that should come out of its shell and delight after another year in the bottle. At time of tasting it was very dry and austere, with some oak astringency, while there was obvious power and depth on the palate and a lively tang. Put it away, then drink with crayfish.

Montana 'B' Sauvignon Blanc

QUALITY ♟♟♟♟♝
VALUE ★★★½
GRAPES sauvignon blanc
REGION Marlborough, NZ
CELLAR 🍾 1
ALC./VOL. 12.0%
RRP $20.00

From Montana's large Brancott Estate in Marlborough. Half was barrel-fermented in French oak, and some underwent a malolactic.
CURRENT RELEASE 1993 This is a serious attempt to build a long-term relationship from a variety that's usually treated a bit like a one-night stand! The palate is complex, structured and serious – once you get past that asparagus character on the nose. Interesting wine; try it with asparagus quiche.

Montana Church Road Chardonnay

QUALITY ♟♟♟♟♝
VALUE ★★★★
GRAPES chardonnay
REGION Hawkes Bay, NZ
CELLAR 🍾 3+
ALC./VOL. 13.5%
RRP $18.00 ⓢ

Counting the chardonnays in the Montana portfolio is a bit like trying to keep track of Southcorp's. There are about seven available in Australia under the Montana brand.
CURRENT RELEASE 1994 A very smart wine with a deep yellow hue and a lovely complex bouquet of rich, ripe, developing, chardonnay fruit sensitively harmonised with oak. There is a certain elegance to the palate and the aftertaste is all about balance. Goes well with rich seafood bisque.

Montana Church Road Reserve Chardonnay

These wines are made at the McDonald Winery, bought and re-developed by Montana in the late 1980s. It's in Church Road, Taradale, Hawkes Bay.
CURRENT RELEASE 1993 A humdinger of a chardonnay! Very New Zealand, very complex. It has a full yellow colour and a multi-faceted bouquet which reflects bottle-age as well as sophisticated winemaking. Smooth and round, with subtle French oak and high-quality fruit giving buttery, peachy and toasted-nut accents. Gaining honey as it ages. Serve with lobster.

QUALITY 🍷🍷🍷🍷🍷
VALUE ★★★★½
GRAPES chardonnay
REGION Hawkes Bay, NZ
CELLAR 🍾 3
ALC./VOL. 13.0%
RRP $20.00

Montana Marlborough Black Label Chardonnay

This is a big brother to the standard Marlborough chardonnay, and is all barrel-fermented. Maker Peter Hubscher and team.
CURRENT RELEASE 1994 Totally different style to the standard wine: complex oaky barrel-fermented bouquet showing toasty wood and malolactic characters. The palate is soft and complex, and the flavour lingers well. Maintains your interest to the last drop. Try it with roast chicken.

QUALITY 🍷🍷🍷🍷
VALUE ★★★★
GRAPES chardonnay
REGION Marlborough, NZ
CELLAR 🍾 2
ALC./VOL. 13.5%
RRP $15.00 $

Montana Marlborough Chardonnay

Ostensibly an unwooded chardonnay – 5 per cent saw some oak. Montana was making unwooded chardonnay long before it became fashionable.
CURRENT RELEASE 1995 Gentle, peachy chardonnay aromas; soft, fruity and very quaffable with roundness and some length. Try a bottle – and see why the Brits get through 80 000 cases of it a year! Goes well with prosciutto melone.

QUALITY 🍷🍷🍷
VALUE ★★★
GRAPES chardonnay
REGION Marlborough, NZ
CELLAR 🍾 1
ALC./VOL. 12.5%
RRP $12.00 $

Montana Marlborough Rhine Riesling

QUALITY	🍷🍷🍷🍷
VALUE	★★★½
GRAPES	riesling
REGION	Marlborough, NZ
CELLAR	🍾 2
ALC./VOL.	11.5%
RRP	$12.00 Ⓢ

The Kiwis make riesling in a style that's more German than Australian: aromatic and slightly sweet.

CURRENT RELEASE 1994 This is lightly floral with some toasty development, and the palate is fuller than expected, with balanced sweetness and fruit. It's developing some honeyed character and fills the mouth, lingering well. Try it with prawn and mango salad.

Montana Marlborough Sauvignon Blanc

QUALITY	🍷🍷🍷
VALUE	★★★
GRAPES	sauvignon blanc
REGION	Marlborough, NZ
CELLAR	🍾 1
ALC./VOL.	12.0%
RRP	$12.00 Ⓢ

Montana is by far the biggest winemaker in New Zealand, with over 50 per cent of the crush. It produces an ocean of this famous wine, and it all comes off their own vines.

CURRENT RELEASE 1995 The worst season in Marlborough's short viticultural history produced a decent but unexciting wine, which simply lacks fruit generosity. The nose is tangy, sharp-edged capsicum and lantana, the palate is lean and acid without a lot of fruit. Drink it up while it's young, with salads.

Montana 'O' Chardonnay

QUALITY	🍷🍷🍷🍷
VALUE	★★★
GRAPES	chardonnay
REGION	Gisborne, NZ
CELLAR	🍾 2
ALC./VOL.	13.5%
RRP	$20.00

The series with initials on their labels are Montana's top-of-the-tree, based on individual vineyards around the country. This one's from their Ormond Estate at Gisborne.

CURRENT RELEASE 1993 This is a quite oaky wine which comes across as a bit lean on the palate, although it's a nice contrast to Montana's Hawkes Bay styles. The palate is lemony, subtle and crisply acidic, with good structure and a dry aftertaste. Best with food: try scallops.

Montana Saints Gisborne Chardonnay

Gisborne is one of New Zealand's three main grape-growing areas, although perhaps not as famous as Marlborough and Hawkes Bay.
CURRENT RELEASE 1994 Touches of pineapple and resiny oak here. It's a full, round shape and has a firmer, more assertive finish than the Marlborough versions due to the overt American oak. Try it with a mild Thai chicken curry in coconut milk.

QUALITY 🍷🍷🍷🍷
VALUE ★★★
GRAPES chardonnay
REGION Gisborne, NZ
CELLAR 🍾 2+
ALC./VOL. 13.0%
RRP $15.00 ⓢ

Montrose Chardonnay

Montrose is the big-brother of the Mudgee district, where it towers above the cluster of very small boutique wineries. It's part of the Orlando Wyndham group. Maker Robert Paul.
CURRENT RELEASE 1995 This is an impressive wine and great value. It has some finesse and subtlety, with nicely restrained but apparent cedary oak, crisp acid finish, a degree of style and satisfying completeness. Head and shoulders above its sister wine, Craigmoor. Pasta with clams would suit.

QUALITY 🍷🍷🍷🍷
VALUE ★★★★
GRAPES chardonnay
REGION Mudgee, NSW
CELLAR 🍾 2
ALC./VOL. 13.0%
RRP $15.30 ⓢ

Montrose Poet's Corner Classic Dry White

There's a slim connection between the poet Henry Lawson and Mudgee, although the Orlando Wyndham group is a bit coy these days about where the fruit for this wine comes from. Maker Robert Paul.
CURRENT RELEASE 1995 This is a blindingly good wine at a giveaway price! The colour is light yellow-green. There are fresh green, grassy/lemony fruit scents and the wine is tangy and crisp with pristine varietal character. The palate has good presence and finish. Wine of this quality, at this price and made in this quantity, is a great winemaking achievement. Drink with yabbie salad.

QUALITY 🍷🍷🍷🍷
VALUE ★★★★★
GRAPES semillon, sauvignon blanc, chardonnay
REGION not stated
CELLAR 🍾 3
ALC./VOL. 12.0%
RRP $10.00 ⓢ

Moondah Brook Chardonnay

QUALITY ♆♆♆♆
VALUE ★★★★
GRAPES chardonnay
REGION various, WA
CELLAR 🍾 4
ALC./VOL. 13.5%
RRP $15.00 ⓢ

Over in the West, a creek is a brook, don't you know. Witness Jane Brook, Piesse Brook, Henley Brook, Smith Brook, Willyabrup Brook ...
CURRENT RELEASE 1995 Darn. Seduced by high-toast American oak again! But it is a pleasurable fall. The wine is admirably intense, the oak adding to its considerable richness and power, lengthening the finish and suggesting it will live for a few years. Try it with barbecued chicken.

Moondah Brook Chenin Blanc

QUALITY ♆♆♆♆
VALUE ★★★
GRAPES chenin blanc
REGION Gingin, WA
CELLAR 🍾 2
ALC./VOL. 12.5%
RRP $15.00 ⓢ

Clever use of oak transports this wine from the ordinary to a very pleasant quaffing white. Maker Paul Lapsley.
CURRENT RELEASE 1995 Toasty aromas show a little age development and a whisper of wood. There's good flavour and balance and the wood is nicely understated. A trace of sweetness does not unbalance it, and the flavours would go well with pasta with an eggplant sauce.

Morris Chardonnay

QUALITY ♆♆♆
VALUE ★★½
GRAPES chardonnay
REGION Barossa Valley & McLaren Vale, SA
CELLAR 🍾
ALC./VOL. 13.0%
RRP $12.90 ⓢ

Hot-climate regions such as Rutherglen, while best suited to fortifieds and gutsy reds, have a hard time making fine dry whites. So Orlando source grapes from other regions for this wine.
CURRENT RELEASE 1995 A heavy, slightly rough wine which at least offers a heap of flavour. The wood treatment is somewhat leaden and perhaps it's best teamed with a lightly spiced chicken curry.

Mount Avoca Chardonnay

The Pyrenees produces gutsy whites, so chardonnay should be better suited than most. Maker Rod Morrish.
CURRENT RELEASE 1995 This is full-bodied, the fruit playing the lead role, but one could wish for a little more excitement. Light yellow hue; fresh, undeveloped straw and cashew nut aromas; good balance, body and length. Serve with calamari.

QUALITY ♛♛♛♟
VALUE ★★★
GRAPES chardonnay
REGION Pyrenees, Vic.
CELLAR 🍾 3
ALC./VOL. 13.5%
RRP $20.00

Mount Avoca Pyrenees Dry White

Who needs generic handles like chablis and white Burgundy? Pyrenees Dry White says it all.
CURRENT RELEASE 1995 Another flavoursome white from Mount Avoca, smelling of nuts, vanilla and a hint of herbs. There's good intensity of fruit for an inexpensive wine, and it drinks well with a full chill. Serve with Caesar salad.

QUALITY ♛♛♛
VALUE ★★★
GRAPES trebbiano 43%, semillon 36%, sauvignon blanc 21%
REGION Pyrenees, Vic.
CELLAR 🍾 1
ALC./VOL. 12.0%
RRP $14.00

Mount Avoca Sauvignon Blanc

The Barrys of Mount Avoca like to avoid herbaceousness in their wines. They generally succeed and this is typical of the style. Maker Rodney Morrish.
CURRENT RELEASE 1995 Nice and ripe with a pale yellow hue, cashew nut and slightly stalky aromas, and a quite full-throttle palate. It's pungent, slightly aggressive and unsubtle, with some alcohol hotness on the finish. Chill well, and serve with prawns.

QUALITY ♛♛♛♟
VALUE ★★★
GRAPES sauvignon blanc
REGION Pyrenees, Vic.
CELLAR 🍾 2
ALC./VOL. 13.0%
RRP $17.00

Mount Horrocks Cordon Cut Riesling

QUALITY ♛♛♛♛♛
VALUE ★★★★
GRAPES riesling
REGION Clare Valley, SA
CELLAR 🍷 3
ALC./VOL. 11.0%
RRP $15.80

This style results from gentle vine surgery during the ripening period: you snip the canes leaving the grapes to shrivel slightly before picking. This increases the sugar concentration.

CURRENT RELEASE 1995 A lumducious sweetie! Full yellow hue, rich apricot-raisiny nose possibly with a hint of botrytis, very rich and sweet on the tongue. Beerenauslese style. Stunning to sip with fresh grapes or a ripe peach.

Mountadam Chardonnay

QUALITY ♛♛♛♛♛
VALUE ★★★★
GRAPES chardonnay
REGION Eden Valley, SA
CELLAR 🍷 8
ALC./VOL. 14.5%
RRP $29.00

Adam Wynn is to chardonnay as Chopin was to the prelude. He is simply masterful at building wines of great character and style.
Previous outstanding vintages: '90, '91, '92
CURRENT RELEASE 1994 Big stuff! This is rich Rubenesque-style flavour and structure. The colour is a pale green-gold and the nose is a medley of peach, nuts, figs and guava. The palate has a mouth-filling texture with peach, cashew, melon and fig flavours in layers. The oak has bonded to the fruit, it adds support and dimensions like length and grip. The wine should be served lightly chilled; try it with pipis in a black bean sauce.

Mountadam Riesling

QUALITY ♛♛♛♛
VALUE ★★★½
GRAPES riesling
REGION Eden Hills, SA
CELLAR 🍷 5
ALC./VOL. 11.5%
RRP $17.00

While this variety doesn't sit naturally with the maker's French training, Adam Wynn makes a fair fist of delivering a better than average riesling.

CURRENT RELEASE 1994 An obvious cool-climate style which also packs a power punch. The nose has the usual aromatic pyrotechnics. The high-impact palate has a shock of lime flavour with plenty of depth. The finish is crisp with a refreshing quality. It should be served well chilled with some salty freshly shucked oysters.

Murrindindi Chardonnay

Hey, nice new label! The Cuthbertson family have built this up from a weekend hobby into a professional vineyard, selling most of their grapes to Mildara.
CURRENT RELEASE 1995 The colour is pale and the nose is light with pineapple and other tropical scents. The oak is underplayed leaving refined fruit in full view. There are intense yet delicate flavours of melon and fruit salad, with a hint of oak richness, and a long, soft, agreeable finish. It will build more character with a year's age. A delicious wine – serve with scallop and leek gratin.

QUALITY 🍷🍷🍷🍷🍷
VALUE ★★★★½
GRAPES chardonnay
REGION Murrindindi, Vic.
CELLAR 🍾 5
ALC./VOL. 13.0%
RRP $19.00

Best Chardonnay

Ninth Island Straits Dry White

Using pinot noir as part of a white blend might sound radical but think of the majority of champagne bases and it doesn't sound out of court.
CURRENT RELEASE 1995 A complex wine with a complex nose and palate. There are grass, gooseberry and straw aromas on the nose. The palate has a meaty pinot quality plus rich gooseberry flavours. This is balanced by fresh acid on a crisp finish. It can be served well chilled. Try it with scallops in a light curry sauce.

QUALITY 🍷🍷🍷🍷
VALUE ★★★
GRAPES pinot noir, sauvignon blanc, semillon
REGION northern Tas.
CELLAR 🍾 1
ALC./VOL. 12.0%
RRP $15.75

Nobilo Sauvignon Blanc

This is a big winery from New Zealand with an annual production in the region of 200 000 cases. For golf buffs, Frank Nobilo is a cousin. Maker Greg Foster.
CURRENT RELEASE 1995 This is regulation New Zealand sauvignon blanc. It has a green pea aroma plus cut grass on the nose. Thankfully the palate is slightly restrained and manages some decorum. There are herb and grassy flavours and the finish remains crisp. It is just the thing for green lip mussels.

QUALITY 🍷🍷🍷🍷
VALUE ★★★
GRAPES sauvignon blanc
REGION Marlborough, NZ
CELLAR 🍾 3
ALC./VOL. 12.5%
RRP $16.95

Normans Lone Gum Chardonnay

QUALITY ♛♛♛♝
VALUE ★★★½
GRAPES chardonnay
REGION Murray Valley, SA
CELLAR 🍷 1
ALC./VOL. 13.0%
RRP $8.90

This is a new label from the Normans stable. The fruit comes from a Murray River vineyard where a lone gum stands in the middle.
CURRENT RELEASE 1996 This is a young, fresh style with just a hint of wood. The nose is dominated by citrus aromas and the palate is medium-bodied with grapefruit and nectarine flavours. There is a dusting of oak on the dry finish. It should not be served too cold; try it with veal in a lemon sauce.

Notley Gorge Chardonnay

QUALITY ♛♛♛♛
VALUE ★★★★
GRAPES chardonnay
REGION Tamar Valley, Tas.
CELLAR 🍷 1–5
ALC./VOL. 12.8%
RRP $21.00

This vineyard/winery has an annual production of 1800 cases. It was established in 1983 in what was known as 'apple country'.
CURRENT RELEASE 1995 The nose has a strong melon aroma and the palate offers the same flavours. There are also hints of peaches and apricot. The steely backbone is also very impressive, as is the lingering finish. It can be served well chilled; try it with veal in a light lemon sauce.

Notley Gorge Sauvignon Blanc

QUALITY ♛♛♛♛
VALUE ★★★★
GRAPES sauvignon blanc
REGION Tamar Valley, Tas.
CELLAR 🍷 2
ALC./VOL. 11.5%
RRP $14.50

The fact that N is next to M on the keyboard must hang heavy but there is nothing motley about the wines being produced by this small winery. Maker Doug Bowen (no relation to Coonawarra's Doug Bowen).
CURRENT RELEASE 1995 Zesty, charming style with a plenty of life. The colour is a pale lemon-yellow and the nose has pea-pod and tropical fruit aromas. The middleweight palate has passionfruit and gooseberry flavours which are bound to some bracing acid on a clean and lingering finish. It can be served well chilled; try it with steamed Chinese vegetables.

Oakridge Estate Chardonnay

An up-and-coming Yarra producer more notable for its lovely cabernet, Oakridge is located at Seville in the higher, cooler reaches of the valley. Maker Michael Zitzlaff.
CURRENT RELEASE 1995 A lean style as reflects the cool 1995 vintage, and the nose shows a touch of aldehyde. The flavour is light-bodied, pleasant and finishes smoothly. Suits antipasto.

QUALITY ♛♛♛
VALUE ★★½
GRAPES chardonnay
REGION Yarra Valley, Vic.
CELLAR 🍾 2
ALC./VOL. 12.5%
RRP $16.00

Olsen Sauvignon Blanc

This tiny-production brand emanates from Hawthorn Cellars, Melbourne, and is put together by Glenn Olsen in a most professional manner.
CURRENT RELEASE 1995 Pale hue, light fresh guava/passionfruit nose has distinct echoes of the tropics. The taste is delicate and bracing with lively acid. Try it with mud crab.

QUALITY ♛♛♛♛
VALUE ★★★
GRAPES sauvignon blanc
REGION King Valley, Vic.
CELLAR 🍾 1
ALC./VOL. 12.5%
RRP $14.95

Olsen Semillon Sauvignon Blanc

This one's a blend of fruit from King Valley and Welshmans Creek, wherever that may be! Maker Glenn Olsen.
CURRENT RELEASE 1995 Delicate doughy and cashew nut aromas, some gooseberry and lantana as well. The palate is a trifle flimsy but it's a pleasant glugger with steamed dim sum.

QUALITY ♛♛♛
VALUE ★★★
GRAPES semillon, sauvignon blanc
REGION King Valley, Welshmans Creek, Vic.
CELLAR 🍾
ALC./VOL. 12.0%
RRP $14.95

Orlando Jacob's Creek Chablis

QUALITY ♛♛♛
VALUE ★★★
GRAPES semillon, sauvignon blanc
REGION various
CELLAR 🍷 1
ALC./VOL. 12.0%
RRP $9.00 ⓢ

The days of this label are numbered: it will probably revert to 'semillon sauvignon blanc' when generic names like chablis are canned. While the full price is $9, the JC range is usually found for $6.99.

CURRENT RELEASE 1995 This is a light, basic wine which will offend no one. The aromas remind of straw and hay – reflecting the semillon grape – while in the mouth it's fairly neutral and somewhat short. A decent glugger with no faults. It will please many. Goes with mussels.

Orlando Jacob's Creek Chardonnay

QUALITY ♛♛♛♛
VALUE ★★★★½
GRAPES chardonnay
REGION various
CELLAR 🍷 1
ALC./VOL. 12.5%
RRP $9.00 ⓢ

This is the big mover in the Jacob's Creek range, and the '95 shows more quality than expected for the humble price. Maker: Phil Laffer and team.

CURRENT RELEASE 1995 Very clean, fresh, fruity aromas of peach and cashew nut are reflected on the light-bodied but satisfying palate. There's a trace of sweetness but it's finer and has better length of flavour than the '94. Could be the best Jacob's Chardonnay yet made.

Orlando Jacob's Creek Riesling

QUALITY ♛♛♛
VALUE ★★★½
GRAPES riesling
REGION various 'dryland' areas
CELLAR 🍷
ALC./VOL. 12.0%
RRP $9.00 ⓢ

With the 1995, Orlando has eliminated hot-area irrigated fruit to try to improve the quality. It's a finer wine than the '94.

CURRENT RELEASE 1995 A lively, fresh style that carries a bath-powder fragrance. The palate is quite tight and racy with acid to balance the fruity softness. Drink it as young as possible while it's fresh, with spring rolls.

Orlando St Helga Riesling

This is Orlando's main commercial riesling, made from the same mature Eden Valley vineyard since 1973. It is always keen value for money. Maker Bernard Hickin.
Previous outstanding vintages: '86, '90, '91, '92, '93
CURRENT RELEASE 1995 A peak vintage for St Helga: lovely floral, stone-fruit and tropical, sweet aromatic bouquet, already showing good complexity. The palate is fine with crisp yet ripe flavours, avoiding the slight greenness of the '94. Perfect with pan-fried whiting.

QUALITY ♥♥♥♥♥
VALUE ★★★★½
GRAPES riesling
REGION Eden Valley, SA
CELLAR ▮ 5+
ALC./VOL. 12.0%
RRP $13.85 ⓢ

Orlando St Hilary Chardonnay

St Hilary lagged behind in the chardonnay stakes for years, but a concerted effort to lift its quality has borne fruit. Maker Phil Laffer and team.
CURRENT RELEASE 1995 The best St Hilary to date, full in the mouth yet not overdone, with well-harmonised barrel fermented oak character, and soft round complex mouth flavours. There's a degree of finesse that's been a long time coming. Drink with scampi.

QUALITY ♥♥♥♥
VALUE ★★★★
GRAPES chardonnay
REGION Padthaway, SA
CELLAR ▮ 1
ALC./VOL. 13.0%
RRP $15.30 ⓢ

Orlando Steingarten Riesling

This was originally made from grapes from the vineyard of the same name, an experimental but ultimately impractical vineyard high in the stony Barossa hills. Now it's a selection of the best grapes from the company's Eden Valley vineyards.
Previous outstanding vintages: '92, '94
CURRENT RELEASE 1995 An outstanding Australian riesling, the essence of Eden Valley, with pristine slatey/mineral and stone-fruit aromas; ripe, fine, pure and very very stylish. Drink it with scallops.

QUALITY ♥♥♥♥♥
VALUE ★★★★★
GRAPES riesling
REGION Eden Valley, SA
CELLAR ▮ 10
ALC./VOL. 12.0%
RRP $17.70 ⓢ

Osborne's Chardonnay

QUALITY 🍷🍷🍷🍷
VALUE ★★★★
GRAPES chardonnay
REGION Mornington Peninsula, Vic.
CELLAR 🍾 4
ALC./VOL. 13.0%
RRP $20.00

This is a new label from the Merricks area. The wine has a harmless deposit of tartaric crystals which in the trade are known as wine diamonds.
CURRENT RELEASE 1994 A slightly off-the-wall style which has some froggy character. The nose is a mix of vegetables and peach aromas. The palate is chewy with peach and melon and a mouth-filling texture. The finish shows some well integrated oak and impressive length. Don't overchill, and try it with lobster bisque.

Paradise Enough Chardonnay

QUALITY 🍷🍷🍷🍷🍷
VALUE ★★★★★
GRAPES chardonnay
REGION Gippsland, Vic.
CELLAR 🍾 5
ALC./VOL. 13.1%
RRP $21.00

Founded in 1987 this is a 4-ha. vineyard that takes no prisoners when it comes to style. It shows an uncompromising attitude to winemaking. Maker John Bell.
CURRENT RELEASE 1994 A year in the bottle and the full winemaking treatment have rendered a very complex style. The nose is rich with lees aromas, almonds, grapefruit and peach. The palate is chewy and complex with peach and grapefruit flavours plus well integrated oak. The finish is dry and lingering. It is an exuberant style that should be served only lightly chilled. Try it with scallops coated in almonds.

Paringa Estate Chardonnay

QUALITY 🍷🍷🍷🍷
VALUE ★★★½
GRAPES chardonnay
REGION Mornington Peninsula, Vic.
CELLAR ⊸ 2–6
ALC./VOL. 12.5%
RRP $25.00

This winery was established in 1985 and it boasts a limited production (up to 1500 cases) of sought-after wines. Maker Lindsay McCall. Previous outstanding vintages: '91, '92, '93, '94
CURRENT RELEASE 1995 The nose gets off to a very nutty start thanks to the obvious oak. There are also peach and melon aromas. The palate is complex with some peach, melon and grapefruit. It is a little leaner than other years but no less attractive. The finish has complex oak with hints of toast and smoke. Don't overchill, and serve with veal sausages.

Pendarves Chardonnay

When he is not fighting the wine and health fight or curing the sick, Doctor Philip Norrie is a wine historian with several books to his credit.
CURRENT RELEASE 1995 This is a bright young wine with lots of potential. The nose is a mixture of nutty oak aromas plus varietal peach smells. The palate is forthright in its expression of peach flavours and the oak makes for a dry and satisfying finish. It should be served with a modest chill; it goes well with chicken dumplings in a rich broth.

QUALITY ♀♀♀♀
VALUE ★★★½
GRAPES chardonnay
REGION Hunter Valley, NSW
CELLAR 🍾 5
ALC./VOL. 13.0%
RRP $17.60

Penfolds Koonunga Hill Chardonnay

Koonunga Hill is climbing up the Penfolds ladder in terms of status and price.
CURRENT RELEASE 1995 Both label and style have been refined. The nose is toasty with hints of peach. The palate is full-on peach with a mouth-filling texture and this is married to a subtle wood finish. It can be served moderately chilled; try it with kassler.

QUALITY ♀♀♀♀
VALUE ★★★★
GRAPES chardonnay
REGION various, SA
CELLAR 🍾 2
ALC./VOL. 13.0%
RRP $9.90 Ⓢ

Penfolds The Valleys Chardonnay

If only Penfolds could make white wine like they can make red wine! This is yet another new label in the quest for the great Penfolds white. It is so called because the fruit comes from two valleys.
CURRENT RELEASE 1995 As usual there is plenty of evidence of wood. There is savoury oak on the nose. Peach and melon flavours dominate the palate and there is also the texture bestowed by barrel fermentation. There is plenty of charred oak on the finish. It is a very dry style that should not be overchilled. It goes well with smoked chicken.

QUALITY ♀♀♀?
VALUE ★★★½
GRAPES chardonnay
REGION Clare Valley, Eden Valley, SA
CELLAR 🍾 3
ALC./VOL. 12.5%
RRP $15.00 Ⓢ

Pepper Tree Wines Chardonnay

QUALITY 🍷🍷🍷🍷
VALUE ★★★½
GRAPES chardonnay
REGION Hunter Valley, NSW; Coonawarra, SA
CELLAR 🍾 5
ALC./VOL. 12.8%
RRP $17.00

This is a complex in the Hunter Valley that combines a guesthouse and restaurant. It was founded in 1993. Maker Chris Cameron.

CURRENT RELEASE 1995 An interesting wine with a slightly funky nose. There are earthy characters and wood smells. The palate has strong peach flavours and these are combating some stern oak on the finish. It needs a bit more time in the bottle and should not be served too cold. Try it with smoked chicken.

Petaluma Chardonnay

QUALITY 🍷🍷🍷🍷🍷
VALUE ★★★★
GRAPES chardonnay
REGION Adelaide Hills, SA
CELLAR ⇨ 2–10
ALC./VOL. 13.5%
RRP $32.00

This is a pulse-quickening label, they are always shooting for the stars. The objective is to make long-term cellaring wines. Maker Brian Croser. Previous outstanding vintages: '89, '90, '91, '92, '93

CURRENT RELEASE 1994 This is a complex wine with plenty of potential. The nose offers peach and melon aromas with a hint of wood. The palate is creamy but quite light, the fruit restrained and somewhat tight. Peach and melon are the dominant flavours and there is also a nutty character. The finish shows an impressive integration of oak which imparts a slight aniseed character. It should be served slightly chilled and it goes well with pan-fried veal in a lemon cream sauce.

Petaluma Riesling

This is one of the benchmarks in the land of riesling. It usually expresses both the region and the variety.
Previous outstanding vintages: '80, '84, '87, '90, '92, '93, '94
CURRENT RELEASE 1995 As ever it is an immaculately turned out style that clings resolutely to its price point. It has a floral aromatic nose and the palate is full of lime and a background of tropical fruit. The acid zing on the finish will put spring in your step. It can be served well chilled. How about a mud crab in a light ginger sauce?

QUALITY ♛♛♛♛½
VALUE ★★★★
GRAPES riesling
REGION Clare Valley, SA
CELLAR 🍷 5
ALC./VOL. 12.5%
RRP $19.00

Peter Lehmann Chardonnay

Chardonnay is a Johnny-come-lately in the Barossa. Fashion trends drove the growers to invest in the variety. Grown on the valley floor, it makes worthy rather than sensational wines.
CURRENT RELEASE 1995 There is a strong talcum powder aroma on the nose as well as peach characters. The palate is big, buxom and buttery with straightforward peach flavour. This is followed by a soft, lightly wooded finish. It can take a medium chill; try it with an egg and bacon pie.

QUALITY ♛♛♛½
VALUE ★★★½
GRAPES chardonnay
REGION Barossa Valley, SA
CELLAR 🍷 3
ALC./VOL. 12.5%
RRP $13.40 Ⓢ

Peter Lehmann Eden Valley Riesling

I'm confused, has Lehmann annexed Eden Valley? I remember his solemn declaration, after many long lunches, that he would have no truck with any fruit outside his beloved Barossa.
CURRENT RELEASE 1995 The nose has a strong biscuit and toast aroma as well as underlying citrus. The palate is soft and round with lemon being the major flavour. There is clean acid on a long finish. It needs the big chill to thrill. It goes well as a pre-dinner drink.

QUALITY ♛♛♛♛
VALUE ★★★★½
GRAPES riesling
REGION Eden Valley, SA
CELLAR 🍷 2
ALC./VOL. 11.0%
RRP $10.25 Ⓢ

Peter Lehmann Semillon

QUALITY ♀♀♀♀
VALUE ★★★★
GRAPES semillon
REGION Barossa Valley, SA
CELLAR 🍾 2
ALC./VOL. 12.0%
RRP $10.25 Ⓢ

There is new livery for the Peter Lehmann label and to comment on the concept is like reviewing a book or film and giving away the plot. Make up your mind, taste is not a matter for argument.
CURRENT RELEASE 1995 This wine needs a course at Jenny Craig. It is a full-blown mouth-filling style. The nose is toasty with cooked biscuit aromas. The palate has a fat buttery texture and soft gooseberry fruit. There is plenty of oak on the finish. This rather rotund style needs a medium chill. It can be tried with chicken and mushroom risotto.

Peter Lehmann Semillon Chardonnay

QUALITY ♀♀♀♀
VALUE ★★★★
GRAPES semillon, chardonnay
REGION Barossa Valley, SA
CELLAR 🍾 2
ALC./VOL. 12.5%
RRP $10.25 Ⓢ

Still they come, this is a shotgun marriage of varieties not exactly made in heaven but forged in the marketplace by consumer demand.
CURRENT RELEASE 1995 The nose has a strong toasty aroma with a hint of gun powder and wood. The palate has strong grape flavours including gooseberry and peach flavours. There are some dry wood effects on the finish. It can be served with a medium chill. Try it with fried rice.

Pewsey Vale Autumn Botrytis Rhine Resling

QUALITY ♀♀♀♀
VALUE ★★★★
GRAPES riesling
REGION Eden Hills, SA
CELLAR 🍾 4
ALC./VOL. 14.0%
RRP $13.00

In 1961 the Hill Smiths led the tribes from the Barossa floor in an attempt to find a new cool-climate location. They were ahead of their time and although correct their efforts have never been properly recognised.
CURRENT RELEASE 1992 A big style that is showing the benefit of accelerated bottle-age due to being marketed in a 375 ml bottle. The nose has a strong lime aroma plus hints of honey. The palate is a mix of lemon, lime and marmalade and this is followed by crisp acid plus a warmth of alcohol on the finish. Serve well chilled with a rich fruit cake.

Pewsey Vale Riesling

Pewsey Valey was first planted by Joseph Gilbert in 1847. It was re-established by the Hill Smiths in the 1960s.
CURRENT RELEASE 1995 This is a cross between a regional and cellar style. The nose has toasty elements (cellar) plus plenty of lively citrus (region). The palate offers abundant keen lime flavour and this is followed by crisp acid on a long lingering finish. It can be served well chilled and it is grand with oysters natural.

QUALITY ????
VALUE ★★★★½
GRAPES riesling
REGION Eden Valley, SA
CELLAR 6
ALC./VOL. 12.5%
RRP $ 11.00 $

Pewsey Vale Sauvignon Blanc

The cool climate of the vineyard does well for this variety. The object is to capture as much flavour intensity as possible and retain freshness.
CURRENT RELEASE 1995 The nose has a mix of canned pea, herbs and cut grass. The palate is round and soft with tropical fruit characters, gooseberry and herbs. The finish displays clean, crisp acid and refreshing qualities. It is best served with a decent chill. Try it with oysters Czarina.

QUALITY ????
VALUE ★★★★
GRAPES sauvignon blanc
REGION Eden Valley, SA
CELLAR 2
ALC./VOL. 12.5%
RRP $13.25

Pibbin White Pinot Noir

Sometimes you have to suspend disbelief and go with the flow. This is basically a sparkling wine base looking for a bubble.
CURRENT RELEASE 1995 The colour is a bright onion skin and the nose has a meaty aroma on a strawberry background. The palate is quite rich with developed fruit flavours and truffle undertones. There is firm acid on the finish. It is an off-the-wall style that would go well with a heap of chill and a hill of duck liver pâté.

QUALITY ????
VALUE ★★★
GRAPES pinot noir
REGION Southern Vales, SA
CELLAR 2
ALC./VOL. 12.5%
RRP $16.00

Pierro Chardonnay

QUALITY ♛♛♛♛♙
VALUE ★★★
GRAPES chardonnay
REGION Margaret River, WA
CELLAR 🍾 2–6
ALC./VOL. 13.5%
RRP $39.15

Nearly every wine writer has to mention that the proprietor is married to a Cullen – done it again. Pierro produces 5000 cases a year.
Previous outstanding vintages: '90, '91, '92, '93
CURRENT RELEASE 1994 Lots of decadent oak and opulent fruit here. This is the full quid: barrel fermented, unfiltered, lees special. Savoury is the key word. It has a barrel aroma on the nose and there are peaches and melons lurking in the background. The palate has a creamy mouth-filling texture with loads of peach and melon flavour. The finish is welded by integrated oak. It is an almost seamless transition between oak and fruit. It should be served slightly chilled perhaps with a contrasting goat's cheese.

Pierro Semillon Sauvignon Blanc

QUALITY ♛♛♛♛
VALUE ★★★
GRAPES semillon, sauvignon blanc
REGION Margaret River, WA
CELLAR 🍾 3
ALC./VOL. 13.0%
RRP $19.90

This wine is the labour of love and more than a hobby for Dr Mike Peterkin who is one of the arbiters of style in the Margaret River district.
CURRENT RELEASE 1995 It is a very approachable wine with a sweet accent on the nose. There are flowers and cut grass aromas. The medium-bodied palate has some tropical fruit elements and a hint of sweetness. This is balanced by a crisp dry finish. It should be served well chilled. Try it with Caesar salad.

Pikes Chardonnay

How can you have a 'Hill River?' Sure water runs downhill, but the district of Polish Hill River still sounds a tad Irish which isn't so far fetched in Clare. (Polish Hill River is a sub-district to the east of the main valley.) Maker Neil Pike.
CURRENT RELEASE 1994 A slow developer that should deliver the goods. At the moment the oak is starting to make out with the fruit. The nose has some vanilla plus peach, melon and cashew aromas. The fruit is complex with barrel-ferment characters. The main flavours are peach, melon, fig and cashew and there is a strong oak element on the finish. Don't overchill and serve with a smoked salmon linguini with a cream sauce.

QUALITY ♛♛♛♛
VALUE ★★★★
GRAPES chardonnay
REGION Polish Hill River, SA
CELLAR 🍾 5
ALC./VOL. 13.0%
RRP $16.00

Pipers Brook Chardonnay

This model vineyard was established in 1974. These days it produces around 25 000 cases per annum and much of the production is exported. Maker Andrew Pirie and team.
Previous outstanding vintages: '84, '86, '90, '91, '92, '93, '94
CURRENT RELEASE 1995 A very subtle wine that should be served very lightly chilled. The nose has peach and barrel ferment aromas. The palate is complex with a creamy texture from the wood and layers of flavour from the fruit. The main flavours are peach and melon and these make a subtle transition to a wood-dominated finish. It has remarkable balance; try it with a crayfish salad.

QUALITY ♛♛♛♛♛
VALUE ★★★½
GRAPES chardonnay
REGION northern Tas.
CELLAR 🍾 3
ALC./VOL. 13.4%
RRP $28.00

Pipers Brook Gewurztraminer

QUALITY ♛♛♛♛
VALUE ★★★★
GRAPES gewurztraminer
REGION northern Tas.
CELLAR 🍾 4
ALC./VOL. 13.4%
RRP $19.00

If there is one winery that has a handle on the variety, this is it! It is easy to say this is the best in the land.
CURRENT RELEASE 1995 A poised style that can combine power, alcohol and finesse. The nose has a strong lychee aroma plus crushed flowers. The palate is a complex mix of lychee, tropical fruit and gooseberry. There is plenty of crisp acid on the finish. It can be served well chilled; try it with a creamy asparagus quiche.

Pipers Brook Riesling

QUALITY ♛♛♛♛
VALUE ★★★★
GRAPES riesling
REGION northern Tas.
CELLAR 🍾 6
ALC./VOL. 12.1%
RRP $19.00

This is part of the 'Alsace Trio' which includes pinot gris and gewurztraminer. Proprietor Andrew Pirie is a big fan of the wines from that region and it shows in his winemaking.
CURRENT RELEASE 1995 Close your eyes and you can be fooled into thinking this is gewurz'. It is extremely aromatic on the nose and there is loads of spice. The light to mediumweight palate has a honeyed quality as well as vital citrus flavours and there is crisp acid on the finish. It can be served well chilled; try it with Tom Yum soup.

Pipers Brook Summit Chardonnay

QUALITY ♛♛♛♛♛
VALUE ★★★★
GRAPES chardonnay
REGION northern Tas.
CELLAR 🍾 6
ALC./VOL. 14.5%
RRP $54.00

Recent releases of this wine have been hill tops rather than peaks. But this vintage is the veritable peak of Everest.
CURRENT RELEASE 1994 A wonderful wine from a year where the grapes obviously ripened properly. The colour is a bright green-gold and the nose has ripe mango, paw paw and peach aromas. The palate is equally complex and very rich. It is intense with strong peach and tropical fruit flavours. The wood has been deftly handled and it contributes to the overall exotica that the wine engenders. It is a very exciting wine that needs grilled Atlantic salmon to set it off.

Pirramimma Chardonnay

The Johnson Family have a large planting of chardonnay in the Southern Vales and much of it is contracted to the Mildara Blass Group. A small part finds itself in the family label. Maker Geoff Johnson.
CURRENT RELEASE 1994 The nose is a tad scarce with soft oak and peach and melon aromas. Peach and melon dominate the palate and there is a slight hint of vanillan oak on the finish. It can be served with a medium chill. Try it with a mild chicken curry.

QUALITY 🍷🍷🍷🍷
VALUE ★★★½
GRAPES chardonnay
REGION McLaren Vale, SA
CELLAR 🍾 3
ALC./VOL. 13.5%
RRP $17.00

Pirramimma Stock's Hill

Named after a vineyard commemorating a pioneering family in the district. Not casting aspersions on this wine in particular but the blend is very difficult to eulogise.
CURRENT RELEASE 1995 The nose has citrus and muted toast aromas. The palate is a mix of lemon and peach flavours and the finish is dry leaving a chalky character on the palate. It can be served well chilled; try it with fish and chips.

QUALITY 🍷🍷🍷
VALUE ★★★
GRAPES semillon 50%, chardonnay 50%
REGION McLaren Vale, SA
CELLAR 🍾 1
ALC./VOL. 13.0%
RRP $12.50

Plunkett Blackwood Ridge Sauvignon Blanc Semillon

This is a small vineyard high in the Strathbogie Ranges, Vic. It produces around 5000 cases a year. Maker Sam Plunkett.
CURRENT RELEASE 1995 This is a shotgun marriage between two star-crossed varieties and it works after a fashion. The palate offers gooseberry flavours and the nose has plenty of straw and cut-grass aroma. Crisp acid adds zest to the finish; serve well chilled with a leafy green salad.

QUALITY 🍷🍷🍷🍷
VALUE ★★★½
GRAPES sauvignon blanc 63%, semillon 37%
REGION Strathbogie Ranges, Vic.
CELLAR 🍾 2
ALC./VOL. 12.5%
RRP $14.50

Plunkett Blackwood Ridge Unwooded Chardonnay

QUALITY ♛♛♛
VALUE ★★★
GRAPES chardonnay
REGION Strathbogie Ranges, Vic.
CELLAR 🍷 1
ALC./VOL. 13.1%
RRP $12.50

The unwooded chardonnay genre is burgeoning and potentially boring. It makes for another facet of the variety that could be equated with no frills plain wrap.
CURRENT RELEASE 1995 The colour is pale lemon yellow and the nose offers soft citrus aromas plus peach and toast. The palate has a hint of sweetness and ripe peach flavour. Gentle acid completes the picture. Serve well chilled with yabbies.

Plunkett Strathbogie Ranges Chardonnay

QUALITY ♛♛♛⸮
VALUE ★★★½
GRAPES chardonnay
REGION Strathbogie Ranges. Vic.
CELLAR 🍷 4
ALC./VOL. 13.6%
RRP $17.00

The Plunkett family have a cellar door on the Hume Highway. The problem is most cars are doing 120 clicks when the sign flashes up and don't stop. It's well worth the wear and tear on the brake pads.
CURRENT RELEASE 1994 Toast seems to be a common Plunkett theme. There is toast, peach and melon on the nose. The palate shows sweet peach flavours and the toast makes another appearance on the finish which is dry and woody. It needs a light chill and it goes well with pâté.

Plunkett Strathbogie Ranges Riesling

QUALITY ♛♛♛⸮
VALUE ★★★½
GRAPES riesling
REGION Strathbogie Ranges, Vic.
CELLAR 🍷 5
ALC./VOL. 12.2%
RRP $14.50

The vineyard is 500 metres above sea level in a phylloxera-free area. The cool nights promote high acid levels.
CURRENT RELEASE 1995 The colour is very pale and there are soft lemon aromas plus hints of peel on the nose. The middleweight palate has lime as the dominant flavour and the elegant finish is graced by crisp acid. It can be served well chilled; try it with spaghetti pesto.

Preece Chardonnay

Mitchelton's Preece wines set new trends for label design when first released. They are aimed at the bistro-on-premises market. Maker Don Lewis.
CURRENT RELEASE 1995 A finer, better wine than the '94, this has a fresh, vibrant, lightly wooded flavour and is delicious to drink young. The nose has fresh doughy and creamy aromas with a hint of barrel fermentation, and it goes well with crab salad.

QUALITY ♟♟♟♟
VALUE ★★★★
GRAPES chardonnay
REGION mainly Goulburn & King Valleys, Vic.
CELLAR 2
ALC./VOL. 13.5%
RRP $14.65 Ⓢ

Preston Peak Semillon Chardonnay

Welcome to a new area and a new label. As a bit of inside information, wine writer, broker and Master of Wine Peter Scudamore-Smith keeps a fatherly eye on the enterprise.
CURRENT RELEASE 1995 Interesting style with a distinct biscuit character on the nose (probably an oak component). The palate has strong citrus flavour and this is followed by an interesting caramel oak character on the finish. It can be served with a medium chill; try it with a chicken pie.

QUALITY ♟♟♟♟
VALUE ★★★★
GRAPES semillon, chardonnay
REGION Toowoomba, Qld
CELLAR 3
ALC./VOL. 12.0%
RRP $14.95

Primo Estate Botrytis Riesling

The maker at this Adelaide Plains winery is a dab hand with this style. He studied noble rot at Roseworthy College and has been making it for over a decade. Maker Joe Grilli.
Previous outstanding vintages: '91, '93, '94
CURRENT RELEASE 1995 The colour is a handsome green gold and there are strong honey, apricot and citrus aromas on the nose. The palate has excellent mouthfeel and sweetness, and there are a mixture of flavours including dried apricot, marmalade and honey. The finish has a pectin character and strong acid. It can be served well chilled; try it with smoked salmon and caviar.

QUALITY ♟♟♟♟½
VALUE ★★★★½
GRAPES riesling
REGION Eden Valley, SA
CELLAR 6
ALC./VOL. 11.0%
RRP $17.70 (375 ml)

Red Hill Estate Chardonnay

QUALITY ♀♀♀♀
VALUE ★★★★
GRAPES chardonnay
REGION Mornington Peninsula, Vic.
CELLAR 🍾 4
ALC./VOL. 12.5%
RRP $18.00 (cellar door)

Red Hill is just as it sounds: the red volcanic soil ices the hilltops like a cake. This vineyard is the retirement project of Sir Peter Derham. Maker Jenny Bright.

CURRENT RELEASE 1995 Another very lightly wooded chardonnay from this region, where the delicacy of the fruit makes a distinctively finessy style. Shy, undeveloped fruit aroma with traces of herbaceousness and passionfruit. Zesty, juicy, sleek and lovely on the palate. A real crowd-pleaser. Serve with crudités.

Redgate Chardonnay

QUALITY ♀♀♀♀
VALUE ★★★★
GRAPES chardonnay
REGION Margaret River, WA
CELLAR 🍾 4
ALC./VOL. 13.9%
RRP $18.00

This wine was made from grapes grown in near-drought conditions which caused a crop reduction which increased the concentration in flavour.

CURRENT RELEASE 1995 The wine has peach and toasty oak aromas and the palate is broad, giving evidence of lees contact and barrel fermentation. The main flavours on the palate are lemon and grapefruit and the oak offers a dry and satisfying finish. It should be served lightly chilled and it goes well with pasta and a creamy sauce with smoked trout.

Redgate Classic Dry White

QUALITY ♀♀♀
VALUE ★★★
GRAPES semillon 85%, sauvignon blanc 15%
REGION Margaret River, WA
CELLAR 🍾 2
ALC./VOL. 12.5%
RRP $16.00

Here's another 'classic' and who knows what that means? This is described in the publicity blurb as 'mouth watering'.

CURRENT RELEASE 1995 The colour is pale straw and the nose has strong tinned pea and herb aromas. The palate gives the impression of sweetness and there are passionfruit, gooseberry and herbal flavours. The finish shows a trace of vanillan oak and plenty of acid. It can be served well chilled; try it with marron.

Redgate Sauvignon Blanc Reserve

This is no simple sauvignon blanc, it has been subjected to the wine-making goodies like barrel fermentation and lees contact. Maker Andrew Forsell.
CURRENT RELEASE 1995 The nose is pungent with lees, earth and herb aromas. It is close to sweaty armpit and there is no denying it has character. The palate is creamy with some tropical fruit and gooseberry which are balanced by some nutty/toasty oak. It should be served with a medium chill; try it with a mussel chowder. It won't win medals but it does win points for being interesting.

QUALITY 🍷🍷🍷🍷
VALUE ★★★½
GRAPES sauvignon blanc
REGION Margaret River, WA
CELLAR 🍾 5
ALC./VOL. 14.3%
RRP $19.00

Renmano Chairman's Selection Chardonnay

Part of the BRL Hardy group and the engine-room for mass production, Renmano also produces some well-made table wines under this label.
CURRENT RELEASE 1994 This style has been toned down a bit with bottle-age. It used to be a can-can dancer and now it's into tap dancing. If that sounds confusing, it's all about oak which is now a little more subtle. The nose has strong peach aromas. The palate is rich with peach and buttery oak. There is still nutty oak on the finish but it is more integrated. Serve with a medium chill and try it with tuna.

QUALITY 🍷🍷🍷🍷
VALUE ★★★½
GRAPES chardonnay
REGION McLaren Vale, SA
CELLAR 🍾 3
ALC./VOL. 13.0%
RRP $11.70

Reynolds Yarraman Semillon

QUALITY ♀♀♀♀♀
VALUE ★★★★
GRAPES semillon
REGION Hunter Valley, NSW
CELLAR 🍷 2
ALC./VOL. 11.7%
RRP $25.00 (cellar door)

Jon Reynolds made a name for himself at Houghton and Wyndham Estate before taking over the old Horderns winery near Wybong in the Upper Hunter to do his own thing.

CURRENT RELEASE 1992 This re-release is a lovely toasty aged wine showing forward development in its full yellow colour and mellow flavours. A classic aged Hunter: full, dry and soft with plenty of buttered toast and honey. Try it with chicken.

QUALITY ♀♀♀♀♀
VALUE ★★★★
GRAPES semillon
REGION Hunter Valley, NSW
CELLAR 🍷 6+
ALC./VOL. 11.5%
RRP $16.90

CURRENT RELEASE 1995 This is an impeccable young semillon that you can drink glass after glass and not tire of. It's a fresh-fruit style with restrained yet up-front, approachable flavour and softness – avoiding the austerity of more traditional wines. Great to drink now with seafood, and will cellar well.

Ribbon Vale Sauvignon Blanc

QUALITY ♀♀♀♀
VALUE ★★★★
GRAPES sauvignon blanc
REGION Margaret River, WA
CELLAR 🍷 3
ALC./VOL. 13.0%
RRP $17.15

This is a small winery/vineyard that was founded in 1977 and produces around 3500 cases per annum. Maker Michael Davies.

CURRENT RELEASE 1995 A typical sav blanc with all the trimmings. The nose has strong lychee and herbal smells. There is passionfruit, gooseberry and pineapple which are liberally sprinkled with herbs. The finish has crisp acid with agreeable length. It can be served well chilled; try it with a leafy garden salad.

Ribbon Vale Semillon

This is a barrel-fermented style from one of the early vineyards in Margaret River that was established in 1977. Maker Mike Davies.

CURRENT RELEASE 1995 The wood has made a profound impression on the wine. It invades the wine in a polite way. There is a creamy oak aroma and gooseberry smells on the nose. The palate is creamy in texture with hints of butter. The main flavour is gooseberry and there is a touch of herbs. Oak broadens the finish adding a smoky touch and a nutty character. Don't over chill; try it with smoked chicken.

QUALITY ♥♥♥♥
VALUE ★★★½
GRAPES semillon
REGION Margaret River, WA
CELLAR ▮ 5
ALC./VOL. 13.0%
RRP $17.20

Richmond Grove Barossa Rhine Riesling

Orlando/Wyndham (of which Richmond Grove is a part) belongs to the giant Pernod Ricard corporation in France. This utility label draws fruit from various regions.

CURRENT RELEASE 1994 A year in bottle has provided some developed characters. The nose offers a hint of kero plus toast and strong citrus aromas. The palate is full of simple lemon flavours which are supported by some soft acid on a relatively gentle finish. It can be served well chilled; try it with scallops in a light Pernod sauce.

QUALITY ♥♥♥♥
VALUE ★★★½
GRAPES riesling
REGION Barossa Valley, SA
CELLAR ▮ 2
ALC./VOL. 12.5%
RRP $9.95

Richmond Grove Watervale Rhine Riesling

Richmond Grove now has its HQ in the Barossa Valley and it has the services of one of the winemaking greats in the country. Maker John Vickery.

CURRENT RELEASE 1995 Very young and fresh at the moment. The colour is bleached straw and the nose is power-packed with citrus aromas. The palate offers keen lime flavour plus hints of other citrus. There is plenty of zesty acid on the fresh finish. It can be served well chilled and it goes nicely with sweetbreads in a light mustard sauce.

QUALITY ♥♥♥♥
VALUE ★★★★½
GRAPES riesling
REGION Clare Valley, SA
CELLAR ▮ 5
ALC./VOL. 12.0%
RRP $9.95

Ridgeview Sauvignon Blanc

QUALITY 🍷🍷🍷🍷
VALUE ★★★★
GRAPES sauvignon blanc
REGION Margaret River, WA
CELLAR 🍾 2
ALC./VOL. 13.5%
RRP $14.50

This Margaret River establishment continues to deliver very attractive wines at affordable prices.
CURRENT RELEASE 1995 This wine takes evasive action where the pitfalls of the variety are concerned – very civilised indeed. There are gooseberry and herb aromas on the nose and the gooseberry flavour is abundant on the palate. The finish is dry and provides balance. It can be served with a medium chill; try it with a cold salad of marron.

Robertson's Well Chardonnay

QUALITY 🍷🍷🍷🍷
VALUE ★★★½
GRAPES chardonnay
REGION Yarra Valley & Strathbogie Ranges, Vic., Adelaide Hills, SA
CELLAR 🍾 5
ALC./VOL. 13.0%
RRP $17.00 $

Jamieson's Run, Robertson's Well, Annie's Lane ... will we see a Cuthbertson's Creek next? (Hugh Cuthbertson is Mildara Blass's marketing manager.)
CURRENT RELEASE 1995 This is an alter-ego for Robertson's red: it's all about the subtlety of cool-climate fruit, while the red is full-frontal oaky. The chardonnay has a refined bouquet and palate, perhaps needing a little more time to build distinctive personality. The flavour is smooth and rich in a subtle, gently-wooded framework, and the finish lingers well. Try crab cakes.

Rochford Chardonnay

QUALITY 🍷🍷🍷🍷🍷
VALUE ★★★★
GRAPES chardonnay
REGION Macedon, Vic.
CELLAR ⇒ 2–6
ALC./VOL. 13.0%
RRP $28.00

This is a 7-ha. vineyard in the Macedon region that was established by Bruce Dowding in 1983. It has always been firmly oriented to quality.
CURRENT RELEASE 1995 Flash wine with flash packaging. The nose promises richness and the palate delivers. There are distinct almond and peach aromas on the nose. The palate has a chewy quality with peach, nectarine and fig flavours. Wood plays a major role on the finish adding nutty qualities. It should be served with a medium chill. Try it with smoked chicken.

Romsey Park Chardonnay

This is the second label for Rochford which is a small vineyard in the Macedon Region. Rochford has always had a certain style and the price of the 'second label' is an interesting indicator of where the sights are set. Maker Bruce Dowding.

CURRENT RELEASE 1995 This is a big soft wine with a mix of citrus and caramel oak. The colour is a bright lemon yellow and the nose has citrus and peach aromas. The palate is soft and almost buttery. There is a distinct grapefruit flavour and strong wood flavours of toast and caramel. It should be served lightly chilled; try it with scallops mornay.

QUALITY ▼▼▼▼
VALUE ★★★
GRAPES chardonnay
REGION Macedon, Vic.
CELLAR 🍾 5
ALC./VOL. 12.9%
RRP $20.00

Rosabrook Semillon Sauvignon Blanc

Nice middle-of-the-road packaging but the name is hardly inspiring. It is taken from the road that runs past the vineyard. The labelling is incorrect because sauvignon blanc is in ascendancy.

CURRENT RELEASE 1995 The nose is grassy with herbal notes and the palate offers some tropical fruit flavour plus citrus. It has a slightly coarse quality on the finish. The acid comes to the rescue adding balance. The wine can be served well chilled. Try it with tandoori chicken.

QUALITY ▼▼▼
VALUE ★★★
GRAPES sauvignon blanc 60%, semillon 40%
REGION Margaret River, WA
CELLAR 🍾 2
ALC./VOL. 11.5%
RRP $14.95

Rosemount Rose Label Orange Vineyard Chardonnay

The stylised label is very attractive albeit reminiscent of an LP record album cover for Carmen Jones circa 1955. Never mind, it looks as fine as the wine. Maker Phil Shaw.

CURRENT RELEASE 1994 An exciting style that has the muscles and leanness of an aerobics instructor. Pale straw colour and citrus and toast aromas on the nose. The flinty palate has strong grapefruit flavour plus hints of lemon rind. The finish is bracing with a subtle wood influence. It can be served well chilled with Italian style trippa.

QUALITY ▼▼▼▼▼
VALUE ★★★★★
GRAPES chardonnay
REGION Orange, NSW
CELLAR 🍾 6
ALC./VOL. 13.5%
RRP $22.00

Rosemount Roxborough Chardonnay

QUALITY ★★★★★
VALUE ★★★★½
GRAPES chardonnay
REGION Upper Hunter Valley, NSW
CELLAR 🍾 2–8
ALC./VOL. 13.5%
RRP $42.00

Roxborough rocked the socks off the Yanks in the 1980s because it is a massive, no holds barred style. Subtle it aint, but the best thing about the wine is it dares to be different and sticks doggedly to its style which is chardonnay to the max! Maker Phil Shaw.

Previous outstanding vintages: '85, '86, '87, '89, '90, '91, '92, '93

CURRENT RELEASE 1994 Like a Thelonious Monk tune – 'Straight No Chaser'. It's all here but a tad subdued. The nose has the usual buttery complexity but this time grapefruit aroma and flavour. The palate is thick and chewy with obvious barrel-ferment characters and the oak shows a wonderful concord with the fruit. A little less assertive perhaps, but still a full-blood Roxborough.

Rosemount Sauvignon Blanc

QUALITY ★★★★
VALUE ★★★½
GRAPES sauvignon blanc
REGION Upper Hunter Valley, NSW
CELLAR 🍾 2
ALC./VOL. 12.0%
RRP $12.00 ⓢ

Always quick off the mark, Rosemount are the wine sponsors of the Olympics. Not only that – they have minted their own bottle. Maker Phil Shaw.

CURRENT RELEASE 1995 A very drinkable style that won't break the bank. The colour is a pale lemon yellow and the nose has tropical fruit and herb aromas. The palate is medium-bodied and gooseberry makes the most impact. Crisp acid on the finish adds balance. Serve it well chilled with scallops.

Rosemount Show Reserve Chardonnay

Rosemount are masters of the art where chardonnay is concerned. The Show Reserve range is bred for the national show circuit. The use of oak is exemplary both in terms of time and type.
CURRENT RELEASE 1995 Barrel-fermented in French and American oak and matured for 11 months and the oak simply idles like a well-tuned engine. The nose has peach and creamy wood aromas. The palate is complex with a mouth-filling texture. Peach and melon are the major flavours and the oak forms a raft of support. It should be served lightly chilled; try it with pasta and a carbonara sauce.

QUALITY ★★★★★
VALUE ★★★★
GRAPES chardonnay
REGION Upper Hunter Valley, NSW
CELLAR 🍾 5
ALC./VOL. 13.0%
RRP $22.00

Rosemount Show Reserve Semillon

It's good to see a company that puts its money where its wine is . . . This wine is cellared until it is deemed ready for release, which is an expensive but rewarding process.
CURRENT RELEASE 1991 Except for the colour, time has been suspended. The green-gold hues give away the age but the nose and palate remain fresh. There is a strong citrus element on the nose as well as some grassy characters. The palate has a distinct lemon grass flavour which is coupled with gooseberry and citrus. There is evidence of barrel fermentation in the texture of the palate and the finish is impeccably turned out, showing perfect integration. It can be served with a medium chill; try it with snapper.

QUALITY ★★★★★
VALUE ★★★★½
GRAPES semillon
REGION Hunter Valley, NSW
CELLAR 🍾 7+
ALC./VOL. 13.0%
RRP $22.00

Rothbury Barrel Fermented Chardonnay

QUALITY 🍷🍷🍷🍷🍷
VALUE ★★★★★
GRAPES chardonnay
REGION Hunter Valley, NSW
CELLAR 🍾 2
ALC./VOL. 12.5%
RRP $19.30

Best White Wine

This is the top chardonnay of several from Rothbury. Just as we went to press, the Rothbury group (including Saltram, St Huberts and Baileys) was sold to Fosters Brewing where it joins the Mildara Blass pile. Makers Peter Hall and Keith Tulloch.

CURRENT RELEASE 1994 A crackerjack chardonnay that's had the full winemaker's manual thrown at it. Liberal oak, malolactic, lees, etc., etc., and a tremendously complex glass of wine results. Rich and powerful with an endless finish, it has smoky toast and nut characters over ripe melon/peach fruit and some butter and honey notes starting to creep in. A captivating mouthful. Serve with barbecued chicken.

Rothbury Cowra Chardonnay

QUALITY 🍷🍷🍷🍷
VALUE ★★★½
GRAPES chardonnay
REGION Cowra, NSW
CELLAR 🍾 2
ALC./VOL. 12.8%
RRP $13.90 ⓢ

Rothbury was the first major company to recognise the potential of Cowra, now a burgeoning grape-growing district.

CURRENT RELEASE 1995 This is a soft, easy-drinking, lightly-wooded, pleasant chardonnay at the right price. It's what Cowra does best. Shy cashew-nutty nose, subtle wood, a degree of style and shows good fruit quality. It's gentle on the tongue with a soft, clean finish. Drink now, with prawns or scampi.

Rothbury Trident

QUALITY 🍷🍷🍷🍷
VALUE ★★★★
GRAPES chardonnay, semillon, sauvignon blanc
REGION various
CELLAR 🍾 2
ALC./VOL. 12.0%
RRP $13.50 ⓢ

Neptune blundered out of the sea brandishing a trident, so this goes with seafood. It is also a three-pronged attack by three grape varieties. Maker Peter Hall.

CURRENT RELEASE 1994 The emphasis is on fruit. The nose is quite grassy with an underscore of peach. The palate is zesty with tangy tropical fruit characters. The finish shows off some fresh acid. It can be served well chilled; try it with crayfish.

Rouge Homme Richardson's White Block Chardonnay

First came the Red Block and as the day follows night, along comes the white. This is a value-for-money style at a competitive price. Maker Paul Gordon.
CURRENT RELEASE 1995 This is very good value for money and shows plenty of winemaking style. The nose has obvious toasty oak overtones plus some varietal aromas. The medium-bodied palate has a buttery texture and the main flavour is peach on a nutty background. The French oak on the finish is dry and dusty. It should be served with a medium chill. Try it with a goat's cheese and oyster pizza.

QUALITY ♛♛♛♛
VALUE ★★★★
GRAPES chardonnay
REGION Coonawarra, SA
CELLAR 3
ALC./VOL. 12.5%
RRP $13.00 Ⓢ

Rymill Chardonnay

The colourful new Rymill winery is at the northern end of Coonawarra's main strip. There are plans to treble its size and when the plane trees mature, it will truly be a showpiece. The chardonnay is a 'fruit style' barrel fermented but only 30 per cent aged in oak; no malolactic.
CURRENT RELEASE 1995 As a final tank sample, this was a most attractive, restrained, fruit-driven style with cashew/straw aromas. It was fairly straightforward, with a dry savoury finish and good length. Try it with crumbed lambs' brains.

QUALITY ♛♛♛♛
VALUE ★★★★
GRAPES chardonnay
REGION Coonawarra, SA
CELLAR 4
ALC./VOL. 12.5%
RRP $14.50

Rymill Sauvignon Blanc

1995 was a good year for Coonawarra whites, as the grapes were picked before the rain that disrupted reds, especially shiraz. Maker John Innes.
CURRENT RELEASE 1995 A soft, flavoursome sauvignon with estery and tropical fruit aromas rather than leafy greenness. The palate is full and round and has plenty of middle, while the finish carries quite an acid kick. Try it with mussel soup.

QUALITY ♛♛♛½
VALUE ★★★½
GRAPES sauvignon blanc
REGION Coonawarra, SA
CELLAR 2
ALC./VOL. 12.3%
RRP $14.50

Salisbury Estate Chardonnay

QUALITY ♀♀♀
VALUE ★★★
GRAPES chardonnay
REGION north-western Vic.
CELLAR ♦
ALC./VOL. 13.0%
RRP $10.00 Ⓢ

The Murray River irrigation areas are rich in sun, water and soil. They produce some of Australia's best-value, inexpensive chardonnays.
CURRENT RELEASE 1995 A straightforward fruit style with subtle – if any – oak. The profile is round and very soft, apparently with quite low acidity. It finishes fairly short but the fruit flavour is more than adequate at this oft-discounted price. Try it with whitebait fritters.

Salisbury Estate Riesling Dry

QUALITY ♀♀♀
VALUE ★★★
GRAPES riesling
REGION north-western Vic.
CELLAR ♦
ALC./VOL. 11.5%
RRP $10.00 Ⓢ

Riesling gives of its best in cool climates but it's remarkable how smart viticulture and high-tech winemaking can produce an attractive young wine.
CURRENT RELEASE 1995 A rich nose already showing development at six months of age, with vanilla and toast elements joining light floral notes. The light-bodied palate shows tart lemony acid and will fill out quickly with age. Drink young, with fish.

Salisbury Estate Sauvignon Blanc

QUALITY ♀♀♀⸱
VALUE ★★★★
GRAPES sauvignon blanc
REGION north-western Vic.
CELLAR ♦
ALC./VOL. 13.0%
RRP $10.00 Ⓢ

Seldom does this variety produce a decent wine in the Murray River irrigation areas, but the Alambie Wine Co. has once again managed to achieve the seemingly unachievable. Maker Bob Shields.
CURRENT RELEASE 1995 Fruity nectarine aromas laced with delicate herbaceousness. The taste is soft, fruity and up-front, and broadens on the mid-palate, with a little richness and good satisfying flavour. Age will only coarsen it, so drink as soon as possible, while it's fresh. Goes well with Thai ma-ho.

Salitage Chardonnay

John Horgan, brother of Denis (Leeuwin Estate) has signalled that he means business at his new Pemberton winery, with serious chardonnay and pinot. Maker Patrick Coutts.
Previous outstanding vintages: '93, '94
CURRENT RELEASE 1995 This is just a babe in arms, and has yet to develop its full bouquet. The texture is oily in the glass and the aromas are of fresh straw hay, with less obvious oak than the earlier vintages. There's a trace of sweetness and rich fruit to match. While it doesn't look in the same class as the crackerjack '94 at this stage, have another look in nine months or so.

QUALITY 🍷🍷🍷🍷
VALUE ★★★
GRAPES chardonnay
REGION Pemberton, WA
CELLAR ➔ 1–3+
ALC./VOL. 14.3%
RRP $26.50

Saltram Classic Chardonnay

This is always a good bet in the fighting varietal category. It had just been bottled when we tasted it, and needs time to settle down.
CURRENT RELEASE 1996 Slightly coarse nose with estery fruit and green oak accents which should be in harmony by the time you read this. There are estery, herbal flavours, a touch of sweetness and the palate is slightly unsettled. It does have good depth of fruit and will drink well until around 1998, with prawns.

QUALITY 🍷🍷🍷🍷
VALUE ★★★½
GRAPES chardonnay
REGION south-eastern Aust.
CELLAR 🍾 2
ALC./VOL. 12.5%
RRP $10.60 $

Saltram Classic Rhine Riesling

Saltram was part of the Rothbury Wines group, which has just been sold to Fosters Brewing.
CURRENT RELEASE 1994 Open floral, lightly toasty, up-front riesling style with gentle, mildly sweet entry and juicy fruity middle which dries towards the finish with clean acid. A handy drink with seafood and salad.

QUALITY 🍷🍷🍷🍷
VALUE ★★★½
GRAPES riesling
REGION Barossa & Eden Valleys, SA
CELLAR 🍾 3
ALC./VOL. 11.5%
RRP $10.60 $

Saltram Classic Semillon

QUALITY ♛♛♛♛
VALUE ★★★★½
GRAPES semillon
REGION Barossa Valley, SA
CELLAR 🍾 3
ALC./VOL. 12.0%
RRP $10.60 ⓢ

They tend to wood-age their semillon in the Barossa, and more often than not the wine tastes of little but oak. This is a happy exception.
CURRENT RELEASE 1995 Forward, full yellow colour, but the wine is subtle and harmonious to drink. The nose has nutty, toasty and lemony fruit characters, the oak barely discernible. There are no green flavours and the palate is light yet rich with a smooth dry finish, and sensitively balanced oak. Good value. Serve with escabeche.

Saltram Mamre Brook Chardonnay

QUALITY ♛♛♛♛
VALUE ★★★½
GRAPES chardonnay
REGION Barossa Valley & McLaren Vale, SA & King Valley, Vic.
CELLAR 🍾 3
ALC./VOL. 13.2%
RRP $17.70 ⓢ

Mamre Brook is a biblical name and the founder William Salter was a religious man. The stately house near the winery also bears the name Mamre Brook House.
CURRENT RELEASE 1995 The nose is all creamy barrel-ferment character and the overall oak impact is less than it used to be. The toasted nut characters flow through to the mouth, where it is full-bodied, rich and smooth with plenty of well-married fruit and oak-derived characters. Serve with poultry.

Saltram Pinnacle Chardonnay

QUALITY ♛♛♛♛½
VALUE ★★★½
GRAPES chardonnay
REGION Barossa Valley, SA
CELLAR 🍾 4+
ALC./VOL. 13.7%
RRP $24.00 ⓢ

Saltram has established a name over many years for big, buxom chardonnays. They are still thus, but not as woody as in the past. Maker Nigel Dolan.
CURRENT RELEASE 1994 This has a full yellow colour and a richly complex, mature bouquet of buttery, toasted nut smells and plenty of wood-derived and bottle-aged characters. The palate is smooth, round and very long. Ideal to team with crayfish.

Saltram Pinnacle Riesling

The Pinnacle range is just what you'd expect, Saltram's top of the pile. Winemaker is Nigel Dolan.
CURRENT RELEASE 1995 A fine, mineral style that is developing slowly, as befits a top-rank Eden Valley riesling. It still has youthful doughy/bready notes, and the palate is refined, delicate yet intense, with a soft but dry finish. There's a hint of tropical fruit in the long after-taste. Try with whiting.

QUALITY 🍷🍷🍷🍷
VALUE ★★★
GRAPES riesling
REGION Eden Valley, SA
CELLAR 🍾 7+
ALC./VOL. 12.0%
RRP $17.00 $

Sandalford 1840 Collection Chardonnay

The 1840 Collection pays homage to the year Sandalford was founded. The label shows a montage of images from that era: money, a map, a surveyor's mark and a legal blueprint.
CURRENT RELEASE 1995 A very light, rather shy wine with doughy yeast esters showing on the nose and rather neutral flavour, finishing with some phenolic thickness. Could benefit from a few months in the cellar to fill it out. Then try it with whitebait.

QUALITY 🍷🍷🍷
VALUE ★★½
GRAPES chardonnay
REGION mainly Mt Barker, WA
CELLAR 🍾 2
ALC./VOL. 13.0%
RRP $14.00 $

Sandalford 1840 Collection Semillon Sauvignon Blanc

Yet another delicious youngster from this formerly proud-but-faded Swan Valley identity. New owners, new lease of life.
CURRENT RELEASE 1995 Fragrant gooseberry and tropical fruit aromas prepare the tastebuds for a treat. It's lively in the mouth with plenty of typical grassy Margaret River semillon flavour. Excellent flavour, balance and immediate drinking appeal. Try it with avocado salad.

QUALITY 🍷🍷🍷🍷
VALUE ★★★★
GRAPES semillon, sauvignon blanc
REGION Margaret River & Swan Valley, WA
CELLAR 🍾 2
ALC./VOL. 12.0%
RRP $14.15 $

Sandalford Caversham Chenin Verdelho

QUALITY ♟♟♟♟
VALUE ★★★½
GRAPES chenin blanc, verdelho
REGION Swan Valley, WA
CELLAR 🍾 1
ALC./VOL. 13.0%
RRP $12.00 ⓢ

Sandalford has seen a few ownership changes in recent years. Caversham Estate is the name of its Swan Valley vineyard.

CURRENT RELEASE 1995 A fresh, clean, lightly spiced, unwooded style with straightforward, youthful tropical fruit flavour and good balance. An unusual but successful blend. Good with steamed dim sum.

Sandalford Margaret River Verdelho

QUALITY ♟♟♟
VALUE ★★★
GRAPES verdelho
REGION Margaret River, WA
CELLAR 🍾 1
ALC./VOL. 13.0%
RRP $17.00 ⓢ

Verdelho is a traditional WA specialty and adds an extra degree of interest to the white wine repertoire of many a Sandgroper winery. Maker Bill Crappsley.

CURRENT RELEASE 1995 Pale hue and fresh, aromatic, slightly tropical fruitiness is lifted by the trace of sweetness on the finish. A cleverly put together wine for drinking young, it is soft and lightweight and just a tad cosmetic, but very quaffable. Try a prawn and mango salad.

Sandalford Mt Barker Margaret River Chardonnay

QUALITY ♟♟♟♟♟
VALUE ★★★★
GRAPES chardonnay
REGION Mount Barker & Margaret River, WA
CELLAR 🍾 5+
ALC./VOL. 13.0%
RRP $18.50

Sandalford is now the property of Peter and Debra Prendiville. Sandalford's Margaret River vineyard is the largest single planting in the region. Maker Bill Crappsley.

CURRENT RELEASE 1995 A very classy wine, strongly scented with new oak at this stage but with more than enough fruit to match. Grilled nut, toast and vanilla are among the aromas, and the taste is savoury, complex, oak-driven and promises to develop into a captivating drop with another 6 to 12 months. Then drink with char-grilled crayfish.

Sandstone Semillon

Mike and Jan Davies have a business in mobile bottling lines, as well as consulting to wineries and making their own Sandstone wines on the side.
Previous outstanding vintages: '93, '94
CURRENT RELEASE 1995 Barrel fermentation has cleverly augmented the rich fruit in this wine and the result is a complex, powerful dry white which could wipe a lot of chardonnays off the table. Our sample needed a lot of breathing to reveal its true worth. It's a serious 'white Bordeaux' style that should repay cellaring. Enjoy it with Nicoise salad.

QUALITY ♀♀♀♀?
VALUE ★★★½
GRAPES semillon
REGION Margaret River, WA
CELLAR ⊸ 1–5+
ALC./VOL. 13.0%
RRP $21.90

Scarpantoni Sauvignon Blanc

Makers Michael and Fil Scarpantoni are proud to grow, make and bottle every one of their 10,000-case output on the property.
CURRENT RELEASE 1996 This is sauvignon blanc writ large! Pungent tropical fruit and gooseberry aromas with some feline overtones, and the palate holds rich, tangy citrusy fruit flavours and seems to retain a fair degree of sweetness. Should be a very popular style; serve with pimento salad or fresh goat's cheese.

QUALITY ♀♀♀♀
VALUE ★★★½
GRAPES sauvignon blanc
REGION McLaren Vale, SA
CELLAR ▯ 2
ALC./VOL. 13.0%
RRP $13.00

Schinus Chenin Blanc

Chenin is something of a chameleon grape, it does different things in the hands of different winemakers. Maker Garry Crittenden.
CURRENT RELEASE 1995 A style to offend nobody, which will probably sell up a storm at cellar door sales. Pale hue, lollyshop aromas of fresh, simple, unwooded young chenin fruit. The palate is lightweight and slightly short with a touch of sweetness. Try it with cold apple strudel.

QUALITY ♀♀♀
VALUE ★★★
GRAPES chenin blanc
REGION King Valley & Lake Boga, Vic. & McLaren Vale, SA
CELLAR ▯ 1
ALC./VOL. 13.0%
RRP $14.00

Schinus Sauvignon Blanc

QUALITY 🍷🍷🍷🍷
VALUE ★★★★½
GRAPES sauvignon blanc
REGION King Valley & Yarra Valley, Vic.; McLaren Vale, SA
CELLAR 🍾 1
ALC./VOL. 12.5%
RRP $12.00 (cellar door)

'How do they get the cat to sit on the bottle?' HH was once asked about sauvignon blanc. Some of them can be feline, but this one's not. Maker Garry Crittenden.

CURRENT RELEASE 1995 This frisky little number has a distinctive sauvignon blanc aroma of fresh gooseberry. The taste is intense but delicate, the palate is deliciously fruity and there's a good acid balance, finishing with some drying phenolics. Hi-fi varietal fruit with length. Try it with mussels marinière.

Scotchmans Hill Chardonnay

QUALITY 🍷🍷🍷🍷🍷
VALUE ★★★★
GRAPES chardonnay
REGION Geelong, Vic.
CELLAR 🍾 5+
ALC./VOL. 13.0%
RRP $21.00

The winery is located on Scotchman's Road, near Drysdale, on the Bellarine Peninsula, south-east of Geelong. There are stunning views across the bay to Melbourne. Maker Robin Brockett.

CURRENT RELEASE 1995 This up-and-coming Geelong maker has turned out a very restrained, fruit-driven chardonnay tasting of melon and cashew. Its delicacy is typical of the year in southern Victoria. Its youthful freshness and subtlety will give way to richness and complexity with a couple of years' bottle-age. Good with cold chicken and salads.

Scotchmans Hill Sauvignon Blanc

QUALITY 🍷🍷🍷
VALUE ★★½
GRAPES sauvignon blanc
REGION Geelong, Vic.
CELLAR 🍾 1
ALC./VOL. 12.8%
RRP $20.00

It's academic to review this: the '95 is sold out and there probably won't be a '96 on account of the source vineyard near Bannockburn having a very wet season.

CURRENT RELEASE 1995 The nose is very intense, honeyed and apricotty, suggesting some botrytis influence. Doesn't show the varietal lift of the '94, and the palate is lean and acid, lacking fruit in the middle. Try it with a vegetable terrine.

Seaview Edwards & Chaffey Unfiltered Chardonnay

This is a new arrow in the Seaview quiver. Unfiltered wines are not necessarily better than filtered, so we hope this isn't going to start a new fad. Maker Mike Farmilo.
CURRENT RELEASE 1994 Attractive peachy/guava style fruit with complexity from oak and malolactic giving smoky-bacon and buttery hints. The palate is full-bodied and rich with a firm, dry finish and plenty of alcohol warmth. A roast chicken style.

QUALITY ♟♟♟♟
VALUE ★★★
GRAPES chardonnay
REGION McLaren Vale, SA
CELLAR 🍾 2
ALC./VOL. 13.5%
RRP $21.70 Ⓢ

Seaview Verdelho

Another newie for Seaview, made in the slightly sweet style that nowadays typifies verdelho. Sugar obscures fruit quality, and we'd like to see this with a drier finish.
CURRENT RELEASE 1995 A shy, herbal aroma heralds an unwooded verdelho with a soft, agreeable, commercial palate that finishes with a juicy touch of sweetness. Try it with vegetarian foods.

QUALITY ♟♟♟
VALUE ★★★
GRAPES verdelho
REGION McLaren Vale, SA
CELLAR 🍾 1
ALC./VOL. 12.0%
RRP $10.80 Ⓢ

Seppelt Partalunga Chardonnay

Partalunga is one of those vineyards which might be Adelaide Hills, might be Eden Valley, depending on the outcome of present argument. This is a triple-trophy winner. Maker Ian McKenzie and team.
CURRENT RELEASE 1993 A rich, developed wine showing a lot of colour, oak and bottle-aged character, with fruit now taking a back seat. Needs to be drunk up. Try it with turkey.

QUALITY ♟♟♟♟
VALUE ★★★½
GRAPES chardonnay
REGION Eden Valley, SA
CELLAR 🍾 1
ALC./VOL. 13.0%
RRP $17.00 Ⓢ

Seppelt Rhymney Sauvignon Blanc

QUALITY ♀♀♀♀?
VALUE ★★★★½
GRAPES sauvignon blanc
REGION 'mainly cool Victorian vineyards'
CELLAR 🍾 4
ALC./VOL. 12.0%
RRP $14.50 Ⓢ

Rhymney was the name of a gold reef in the Great Western region during the gold mining era of last century. Seppelt has used it as a wine brand on and off. Maker Ian McKenzie and team.
CURRENT RELEASE 1995 The colour is pale – typical of young sauvignon blanc – and the nose has appropriate green-leaf and herbal aromas with hints of gooseberry. There's intense flavour in the mouth with searing acidity that some may find excessive, but it certainly helps give the wine length. A fine and tangy style to serve with Pacific oysters.

Sharefarmers Vineyard White

QUALITY ♀♀♀?
VALUE ★★★
GRAPES chardonnay 86%, sauvignon blanc 14%
REGION Coonawarra, SA
CELLAR 🍾 2
ALC./VOL. 13.5%
RRP $16.00

This is Petaluma's bistro dry white. The label says Coonawarra, but unless the tide can be turned, the vineyard will fall in the Naracoorte Ranges region in future.
CURRENT RELEASE 1995 An attractive everyday drinking dry white, which has some melon and cashew unwooded chardonnay aromas and a little richness in the mouth. The palate is soft, round and dry and very agreeable. Could be served with cold cuts.

Shaw & Smith Sauvignon Blanc

QUALITY ♀♀♀♀?
VALUE ★★★★
GRAPES sauvignon blanc
REGION Adelaide Hills, SA
CELLAR 🍾 1
ALC./VOL. 12.5%
RRP $18.50

Cousins Martin Shaw and Michael Hill Smith have a winning combination of winemaking and marketing expertise. Maker Martin Shaw.
CURRENT RELEASE 1995 Perhaps a shade less aromatic than previous releases, this is also lean and dry and very refined. Aromas of tobacco leaf and lime/lemon citrus translate perfectly into a crisp, tangy palate. Terrific with crab cakes.

Shaw & Smith Unoaked Chardonnay

Michael Hill Smith says fresh, lively unwooded chardonnays from cool-grown fruit offer an alternative to big, oaky, high-alcohol, blousy styles. But they must have fruit that is good enough to stand alone without a veneer of oak.
CURRENT RELEASE 1995 Although much simpler than their wooded chardonnay, this has charming fresh tropical-fruit and melon aromas and a light, soft, uncomplicated taste. A touch of herbaceousness gives it a slight resemblance to sauvignon blanc. Good with cold chicken and salad.

QUALITY ♛♛♛♕
VALUE ★★★
GRAPES chardonnay
REGION Adelaide Hills, SA
CELLAR 🍾 3
ALC./VOL. 12.5%
RRP $17.60

Sorrenberg Sauvignon Blanc

Established by Barry Morey in 1986, this is the essence of a boutique winery. It produces around 1000 cases per annum and the label pays homage to France. Maker Barry Morey.
CURRENT RELEASE 1995 An interesting point of departure because of the barrel fermentation. The nose has nutty aromas as well as herb and grape aromas. The palate has a distinct buttery texture. It is mouth-filling and rich with gooseberry as the primary flavour. The finish is dry and driven by wood. Don't over chill, and try it with pan-fried quail.

QUALITY ♛♛♛♕
VALUE ★★★½
GRAPES sauvignon blanc 85%, semillon 15%
REGION Beechworth, Vic.
CELLAR 🍾 2
ALC./VOL. 12.5%
RRP $17.00

St Hallett Chardonnay

When Bob McLean took control of St Hallett in the late '80s he and winemaker Stuart Blackwell turned it into a success story. They started making more contract wine for other companies; now they sell more of their own than they make for others.
CURRENT RELEASE 1995 A lovely smooth chardonnay that caresses the tongue. Abundant barrel-fermented character is well combined with cashew chardonnay fruit. Loads of immediate appeal. Drink with seafood.

QUALITY ♛♛♛♛
VALUE ★★★★
GRAPES chardonnay
REGION Eden & Barossa Valleys, SA
CELLAR 🍾 2
ALC./VOL. 13.5%
RRP $16.00

St Hallett Semillon Select

QUALITY ♛♛♛♛
VALUE ★★★★
GRAPES semillon
REGION Barossa Valley, SA
CELLAR 🍾 2
ALC./VOL. 12.5%
RRP $16.00

A tiny first effort of 300 cases, which will only be found in restaurants. Expect to see this grow into bigger and better things.
CURRENT RELEASE 1994 Very big fruit carries this generous barrel-fermented wine. Full-bodied, round and opulent, it has subtle oak, with impressive depth of lemony and creamy/lanolin varietal fruit characters. Goes with smoked salmon blinis.

St Huberts Roussanne

QUALITY ♛♛♛♛
VALUE ★★★½
GRAPES roussanne
REGION Yarra Valley, Vic.
CELLAR 🍾 3
ALC./VOL. 12.4%
RRP $17.80

Roussanne plays second fiddle to marsanne in the Rhone Valley's Hermitage Blanc. It is a rare creature indeed in Australia.
CURRENT RELEASE 1996 A most impressive wine, tasted soon after it was bottled. Fine spicy aromas with hints of cashew nut and these flavours reappear in the mouth, where it has a soft, rounded, elegant structure with a lot of flavour. Very easy to drink young and should team well with perch.

Stonier's Reserve Chardonnay

QUALITY ♛♛♛♛♛
VALUE ★★★★
GRAPES chardonnay
REGION Mornington Peninsula, Vic.
CELLAR 🍾 4+
ALC./VOL. 14.0%
RRP $30.00

For years we've been told that cool climates produce the finest flavours and best quality, but only recently are we seeing proof. Put it down to the learning curve, almost as notorious as Keating's J curve. Maker Tod Dexter.
Previous outstanding vintages: '91, '93
CURRENT RELEASE 1995 A glorious, seamless wine to thrill the most jaded buds. Subtle, smoky bouquet hinting at barrel fermentation and complicated Burgundy-style winemaking. The palate is tremendously deep and multi-faceted, with generous tropical and peachy fruit, subtle oak, and finishing soft and rich. The right wine for lobster thermidor.

Taltarni Fumé Blanc Reserve Sauvignon Blanc

Sauvignon blanc and French oak are the apple of the eye of proprietor Dominique Portet. The region seems suited to the variety (albeit with low yields) and French oak maintains his connection with his native land.
CURRENT RELEASE 1995 Never say Nevers again – the oak has a big influence over this wine. You'll detect it on the nose which also has strong herbal aromas. The palate is mainly gooseberry with a hint of apricot. Oak makes the finish dry and dusty. It should be served with a medium chill. It is bon with a spaghetti pesto.

QUALITY ♟♟♟♟♞
VALUE ★★★★½
GRAPES sauvignon blanc
REGION Pyrenees, Vic.
CELLAR 🍾 3
ALC./VOL. 13.5%
RRP $19.00

Taltarni Sauvignon Blanc

The sauvignon blanc and the fumé blanc from this marque are distinguished from each other by the use of wood. This wine is sans oak. Maker Greg Gallagher.
CURRENT RELEASE 1995 Pea-green boats and owls and pussy cats. Never mind the whimsy, the nose has a pungent pea-green character. The pungent nature of the nose is not matched by the palate which is refined with gooseberry, citrus and passionfruit flavours. Fresh acid makes for an incisive finish. Try it well chilled with yabbies.

QUALITY ♟♟♟♟
VALUE ★★★★
GRAPES sauvignon blanc
REGION Pyrenees, Vic.
CELLAR 🍾 2
ALC./VOL. 13.5%
RRP $17.00

Tamburlaine Chardonnay Reserve

This is the premium white wine from this small maker in the Hunter. The annual production is 12 000 cases. Makers Greg Silkman and Mark Davidson.
CURRENT RELEASE 1995 All the bells and whistles here, barrel and malolactic fermentation and loads of flavour. The nose is nutty with yeast and peach aromas. The palate is quite rich with peach flavour on a nutty background and there is plenty of oak on the finish. It shouldn't be served too cold. Try it with kassler and sauerkraut.

QUALITY ♟♟♟♟♞
VALUE ★★★★
GRAPES chardonnay
REGION Hunter Valley, NSW
CELLAR 🍾 5
ALC./VOL. 13.4%
RRP $20.00

Tarrawarra Chardonnay

QUALITY 🍷🍷🍷🍷̷
VALUE ★★★★
GRAPES chardonnay
REGION Yarra Valley, Vic.
CELLAR 🍾 4
ALC./VOL. 13.7%
RRP $28.00

Big reputation from a standing start in 1983 when rag-trade mogul (this goes with that) Marc Besen put his love of wine into action with a state of the art vineyard/winery with high hopes for great wines. The hopes have been realised many times over. Maker Martin Williams.

Previous outstanding vintages: '88, '90, '91, '92

CURRENT RELEASE 1993 Bottle-age before release is the key. The colour is a bright green-yellow and the nose has strong peach aromas. Complex palate like a revolving mirrored ball, it reflects peach, melon, fig and cashew flavours. These are wedded to a sophisticated oak treatment that offers some nutty goodies. Good stuff that should have a medium chill and can strut along with turkey and cranberry sauce.

Tatachilla Keystone

QUALITY 🍷🍷🍷̷
VALUE ★★★½
GRAPES semillon, chardonnay
REGION McLaren Vale, SA
CELLAR 🍾 2
ALC./VOL. 13.5%
RRP $14.50

This label was struck to resurrect the era when Tatachilla was one of the most exported wines. That was circa 1960.

CURRENT RELEASE 1995 This is an entertaining style that balances herbs and fruit. The nose has peach aromas plus a sprinkling of mixed herbs. The palate is an amalgam of chardonnay peach and grassy semillon flavours. The finish is crisp and clean. It can be served well chilled; try it with a chicken and mushroom casserole.

Tatachilla Riesling

In the late '50s and early '60s the name Tatachilla used to burn bright. It all but guttered out and after several false starts it is now back in business in what used to be known as the Southern Vales Co-op.
CURRENT RELEASE 1995 The colour is pale lemon yellow and the nose has strong fresh citrus aromas. There are fresh lime flavours on the intense palate and it is matched with crisp acid on a clean dry finish. It can be served well chilled; try it with oysters natural.

QUALITY 🍷🍷🍷🍷
VALUE ★★★½
GRAPES riesling
REGION Adelaide Hills, SA
CELLAR 🍾 4
ALC./VOL. 11.0%
RRP $12.00

Tatachilla Sauvignon Blanc

There are strong rumours some of the old (circa 1959) wines from the original Tatachilla are in the cellars of Buckingham Palace. Lucky Liz.
CURRENT RELEASE 1995 The colour is pale and the nose has plenty of herbs and tropical fruit aromas. The palate is a mix of sweet tropical fruit flavours like pineapple, passionfruit and gooseberry. These are supported by some crisp acid on a firm dry finish. Serve well chilled with white asparagus.

QUALITY 🍷🍷🍷🍷
VALUE ★★★½
GRAPES sauvignon blanc
REGION Adelaide Hills, McLaren Vale, SA
CELLAR 🍾 2
ALC./VOL. 12.0%
RRP $14.00

T'Gallant Holy Stone

The packaging deserves special mention, it breaks new ground by being see-through. Holy stone was used to scrub the decks of the couta boats on the Mornington Peninsula, hence the regional reference.
CURRENT RELEASE 1995 The colour is a delicate pink and the nose is powerful with strawberry and honey aromas. The texture on the palate is also honeyed and sweet berry fruit supplies the flavour. Crisp acid on the finish offers persistence and allows the wine to be served medium to well-chilled. It is a great tiffin drink.

QUALITY 🍷🍷🍷🍷
VALUE ★★★½
GRAPES pinot noir, chardonnay
REGION Mornington Peninsula, Vic.
CELLAR 🍾 2
ALC./VOL. 13.3%
RRP $16.50

T'Gallant Lot 2 Chardonnay

QUALITY ♟♟♟♪
VALUE ★★
GRAPES chardonnay
REGION Mornington Peninsula, Vic.
CELLAR 🍾 2
ALC./VOL. 13.9%
RRP $21.00

The name refers to the fact that the grapes were grown on two vineyards on 'poorer soils' and the publicity blurb says it 'will silence the critics who clutch to [sic] the belief that wooden wines are better.' MS: In this case hear me roar, 'no wood, no good!' Makers Kathleen Quealy and Kevin McCarthy.

CURRENT RELEASE 1994 The texture is almost off-putting and a little extra freshness would add to the score. The nose has strong citrus elements with a hint of honey. The palate is thick and the honeyed character gives the impression of sweetness and the main flavour is grapefruit. There is clean acid on the finish. Serve well chilled with a mild chicken curry.

T'Gallant Tribute Pinot Gris

QUALITY ♟♟♟♟
VALUE ★★★★
GRAPES pinot gris
REGION Mornington Peninsula, Vic.
CELLAR 🍾 4
ALC./VOL. 14.5%
RRP $22.00

The 'tribute' is aimed at the early settlers of Red Hill and Main Ridge who learned to use the 'good red soils' of the district. Given that logic every winery with red soil could have a tribute release. Makers Kathleen Quealy and Kevin McCarthy.

CURRENT RELEASE 1995 A thumper of a white wine that red lovers will like because it is almost over the top. The nose has a toasty suggestion of wood (there was none used) and the palate is a mixture of fruit flavours with tropical, stone fruit and gooseberry in equal measure. The finish is dry and assertive. It can be served with a medium chill. Try it with a rich seafood soup.

T'Gallant White Pinot Noir

Give them an A for innovation, the folks at T'Gallant are always ready to make and market something different. Some attempts are better than others.
CURRENT RELEASE 1995 Big wine made from whole-bunch pressed pinot noir. The colour is pale pink and the nose has a slight meaty quality. The palate tastes like an overblown sparkling wine base with strawberry flavours but the overall impression is of flatness. The finish is soft. It can be served well chilled. It goes well with smoked chicken.

QUALITY ♛♛♛
VALUE ★★★
GRAPES pinot noir
REGION Mornington Peninsula, Vic.
CELLAR ◊
ALC./VOL. 14.1%
RRP $16.00

Thistle Hill Chardonnay

This winery was established in 1976 and it is the pride and joy of David and Leslie Robertson The vineyard covers 11 ha. and produces around 3500 cases. Maker David Robertson.
CURRENT RELEASE 1993 A medium-bodied wine with a pale yellow colour and the nose is dominated by citrus. The palate is full of grapefruit and lemon flavours and there is some evidence of barrel fermentation. The finish is harmonious with a creamy oak treatment. It can be served with a medium chill; try it with a serve of smoked chicken.

QUALITY ♛♛♛♛
VALUE ★★★★
GRAPES chardonnay
REGION Mudgee, NSW
CELLAR ◊ 5
ALC./VOL. 12.5%
RRP $13.50

Thistle Hill Semillon

Mudgee means 'a nest in the hills' and it should not be confused with the Murrumbidgee Irrigation Area which is well to the south. Mudgee is a cool location high in the hills.
CURRENT RELEASE 1995 The colour is pale straw and the nose has a distinct yeast aroma with a whisper of damp straw. The palate has some citrus flavours with a touch of gooseberry and there is an influence of American oak which adds a dry character to the finish. It should not be over chilled; try it with grilled mullet.

QUALITY ♛♛♛♛
VALUE ★★★½
GRAPES semillon
REGION Mudgee, NSW
CELLAR ◊ 4
ALC./VOL. 12.0%
RRP $12.00

Tim Knappstein Chardonnay CHRISTMAS '96

QUALITY 🍷🍷🍷🍷
VALUE ★★★
GRAPES chardonnay
REGION Clare Valley 78%, Adelaide Hills 22%, SA
CELLAR 🍾 5
ALC./VOL. 13.5%
RRP $21.00

This is an interesting mix of fruit from two districts but the winemaking techniques and the wood treatment get in the way of the fruit.
CURRENT RELEASE 1994 The wood steals the show – it dominates the nose with nutty butterscotch aromas. The palate has peach and melon flavours but wood tap dances its way into the picture with toasty characters. There is also a chewy texture and the finish is very dry. Just a little chill and try it with gypsy ham on rye.

Tim Knappstein Fumé Blanc

QUALITY 🍷🍷🍷🍷
VALUE ★★★½
GRAPES sauvignon blanc, semillon
REGION Clare Valley, Adelaide Hills, SA
CELLAR 🍾 3
ALC./VOL. 12.5%
RRP $18.00

Tim Knappstein is out of here, he is no longer connected with the label or Clare Valley winery. He is concentrating his efforts on Lenswood.
CURRENT RELEASE 1995 The wine is pale in colour and the nose has herbs and tropical fruit aromas. The palate is a mix of sweetness, fruit and wood and there is a barrel ferment influence which almost lifts the wine out of the boring category. It can be served well chilled; try it with a spaghetti marinara.

Tim Knappstein Gewurztraminer

QUALITY 🍷🍷🍷🍷🍷
VALUE ★★★★½
GRAPES gewurztraminer
REGION Clare Valley, SA
CELLAR 🍾 3
ALC./VOL. 12.5%
RRP $15.00

This variety has a pact with the devil. It is very difficult to handle, one false move and it turns coarse and oily. This one is an example of how it should be done.
CURRENT RELEASE 1995 The nose has plenty of spicy aromatics and the colour is very pale and clean. The palate is very fresh with lychee and gooseberry flavours and then there is superb acid on a crisp finish. It can be served well chilled. Try it with a Cajun fish.

Tisdall Mount Helen Chardonnay

The vineyard was the result of the vision of Dr Peter Tisdall of Echuca. The grand scheme didn't pan out and he had to sell the winery and vineyards to the Mildara Blass group. Maker Toni Stockhausen.

CURRENT RELEASE 1995 Very stylish wine with loads of flavour. The nose gives a hint of things to come with the peach and wood aromas. The palate is complex with peach, melon and apricot flavours that are wedded to the wood which dominates the finish. It adds a fresh vanilla flavour and increases the length. It should be given a gentle chilling and then be trotted out beside a chicken and mushroom casserole.

QUALITY 🍷🍷🍷🍷🍷
VALUE ★★★★½
GRAPES chardonnay
REGION Strathbogie Ranges, Vic.
CELLAR 🍾 5
ALC./VOL. 13.0%
RRP $19.00

Trentham Estate Sauvignon Blanc

Sauvignon blanc from the rather hot climate near Mildura requires careful handling to get good results. Here's a good example. Maker Tony Murphy.

CURRENT RELEASE 1995 The nose is a pleasant mix of tropical fruit and cut-grass aromas. The medium-bodied palate offers passionfruit, pineapple and gooseberry flavours. Crisp acid makes for a refreshing finish. Try it well chilled with a warm salad of yabbies.

QUALITY 🍷🍷🍷🍷
VALUE ★★★★½
GRAPES sauvignon blanc
REGION Mildura, Vic.
CELLAR 🍾 3
ALC./VOL. 11.0%
RRP $10.10

Tuck's Ridge Chardonnay

Tuck's Ridge has 25 ha. under vine and most of the fruit is sold to larger producers. The first plantings were in 1987.

CURRENT RELEASE 1995 Very refined style which has an edge of complexity. The nose has a nutty element and there is also a large peach component. The palate offers a mixture of melon, fig and quince flavours and there is toasty, nutty oak on a firm finish. Serve with a little chill and try it with a mushroom risotto.

QUALITY 🍷🍷🍷🍷🍷
VALUE ★★★★
GRAPES chardonnay
REGION Mornington Peninsula, Vic.
CELLAR 🍾 6
ALC./VOL. 13.4%
RRP $20.30

Tuck's Ridge Riesling

QUALITY ♟♟♟♟
VALUE ★★★★
GRAPES riesling
REGION Mornington Peninsula, Vic.
CELLAR 🍾 4
ALC./VOL. 12.3%
RRP $13.85

This is one of the Mornington Peninsula's largest producers and as a consequence the prices reflect the scale of production. Maker Daniel Greene.
CURRENT RELEASE 1995 An interesting nose with a strong lychee element. There are also grace notes of lime and lemon. The palate has a strong citrus flavour and there is abundant acid on a crisp dry finish. It can be served well chilled and it would go a bomb with whiting fillets in beer batter.

Twin Islands Chardonnay

QUALITY ♟♟♟
VALUE ★★★
GRAPES chardonnay
REGION Marlborough, NZ
CELLAR 🍾 1
ALC./VOL. 11.0%
RRP $13.20

Low alcohol chardonnay is an interesting diversion. At low levels you can be forgiven for confusing it with a sauvignon blanc.
CURRENT RELEASE 1995 This is a very aromatic style with a grassy nose and hints of citrus. The palate is lightweight with soft peach flavours. The finish is dry and crisp. It can be served well chilled. Try it on a picnic with chicken sandwiches.

Twin Islands Sauvignon Blanc

QUALITY ♟♟♟⸮
VALUE ★★★½
GRAPES sauvignon blanc
REGION Marlborough, NZ
CELLAR 🍾 1
ALC./VOL. 12.0%
RRP $13.20

This is the second label to Nautilus which is an Australian-made New Zealand wine belonging to the Hill Smith group of companies.
CURRENT RELEASE 1995 It's all about tinned pea and green leaves. These are the flavours encountered on the nose and the pea theme mixes with gooseberry on the palate. The finish has clean acid and lingers for a decent amount of time. It can be served well chilled; try it with an asparagus quiche.

Tyrrell's Lost Block Semillon

How do you lose a block? We do ours frequently. Never mind, Tyrrell is a long-standing name with a well-deserved reputation for great wines. They get a heart-felt gold medal for continually delivering the goods.
CURRENT RELEASE 1995 A charmer with all the much-vaunted austerity that accompanies Hunter chardonnay. There is a strong citrus nose with a cut-grass background. On the palate the main feature is gooseberry flavour which is braced by crisp acid finish with impressive length. It should be served well chilled and fried sardines are a good match.

QUALITY ?????
VALUE ★★★★½
GRAPES semillon
REGION Hunter Valley, NSW
CELLAR ➽ 2–6
ALC./VOL. 11.7%
RRP $16.00

Tyrrell's Shee-oak Chardonnay

It's a bit like one-day cricket versus a Test match. For those with a short attention span unoaked chardonnay is the go.
CURRENT RELEASE 1995 This is a drinkable wine with a strong melon and citrus nose. The palate is rich with melon and grapefruit flavours and there is substantial acid on a crisp finish. The lack of wood means it can be served well chilled. It goes well with pipis in a black bean sauce.

QUALITY ????
VALUE ★★★½
GRAPES chardonnay
REGION Hunter Valley, NSW
CELLAR ↓ 2
ALC./VOL. 13.0%
RRP $16.50

Tyrrell's Vat 1 Semillon

This is a blast from the past that shows the way things can develop with bottle age. This is 10 years young. The sash on the label intones: WINE OF THE VINTAGE.
Previous outstanding vintages: '75, '76, '77, '84, '86, '89, '90, '91, '92, '93
CURRENT RELEASE 1986 Fully developed and ready to rip. The colour is a bright green-gold and the nose has pungent honeysuckle aromas plus developed fruit aromas. The palate has built up plenty of intensity with lychee and gooseberry flavours. Acid remains strong and vibrant, making for a fresh finish. It could be served lightly chilled; try it with tripe in a parsley sauce.

QUALITY ?????
VALUE ★★★★★
GRAPES semillon
REGION Hunter Valley, NSW
CELLAR ↓ 4
ALC./VOL. 12.0%
RRP $25.00

Tyrrell's Vat 47 Pinot Chardonnay

QUALITY ♛♛♛♛♝
VALUE ★★★★
GRAPES chardonnay
REGION Hunter Valley, NSW
CELLAR 🍷 5+
ALC./VOL. 12.5%
RRP $28.00

Murray Tyrrell was the pioneer of chardonnay in the Hunter Valley. Right from the start he made outstanding wines. The 1995 is the 25th vintage. Previous outstanding vintages: '73, '77, '79, '80, '84, '86, '89, '91, '93, '94

CURRENT RELEASE 1994 Still available and starting to show the benefit of bottle-age. It remains a very smart young wine that is doing well in the show circuit. The nose is toasty with some obvious peach aroma. The palate is concentrated with plenty of varietal flavour. Oak still dominates the finish. Don't overchill and serve with char-grilled quail.

QUALITY ♛♛♛♛♛
VALUE ★★★★
GRAPES chardonnay
REGION Hunter Valley, NSW
CELLAR ➡ 3–10+
ALC./VOL. 13.0%
RRP $28.00

CURRENT RELEASE 1995 This is a healthy bawling infant. The colour is pale straw and the nose is a mix of peach, citrus and almond aromas. The palate is equally complex with grapefruit, melon and peach flavours and the oak treatment weaves a harmonious coda. It needs time in the cellar but it can be served now with pork dumplings. Don't overchill.

QUALITY ♛♛♛♛♝
VALUE ★★★★
GRAPES chardonnay
REGION Hunter Valley, NSW
CELLAR ➡ 3–10+
ALC./VOL. 13.4%
RRP $28.00

CURRENT RELEASE 1995 This is the 'Old Vine' version of the 25th commemorative vintage. It is made from grapes grown at the original Penfolds HDV vineyard that was planted in 1968. It was fermented in new Nevers oak. This shows on the nose and the palate. There are smoky aromas on the nose and the palate has peach and grapefruit flavours. The finish is tight with strong oak flavour. It needs time in the bottle. Don't overchill and serve with smoked trout.

Vasse Felix Chardonnay

No beg pardons when it comes to this variety made at this winery. They aren't afraid to get the grapes ripe and let the wood rip.
CURRENT RELEASE 1995 Full frontal chardonnay with a robust nose. There is toasty wood, apricot and peach aromas on the nose and big mouthfeel on the palate which is chocked full of peach and melon flavours. The finish shows some rather brazen oak that grabs the attention of the mouth. It is a white wine that will suit red wine drinkers. Don't over chill, and try it with duck liver pâté.

QUALITY ♆♆♆♆
CELLAR 🍾 3.5
GRAPES chardonnay
REGION Margaret River, WA
CELLAR ⬬ 2–7
ALC./VOL. 14.5%
RRP $20.50

Vasse Felix Classic Dry White

Classic Dry White is a term coined by Wolf Blass to cover a multitude of sins. Usually there is nothing at all classic about the shotgun marriage of mismatched varieties.
CURRENT RELEASE 1995 This is a medium-bodied wine with a strong toasty nose. The mouthfeel is the strong point of the palate which also offers peach and green pea flavours. The finish is dry and lingering. It can be served well chilled and it goes well with frittata.

QUALITY ♆♆♆♆
VALUE ★★★
GRAPES semillon, sauvignon blanc, chardonnay
REGION Margaret River, WA
CELLAR 🍾 2
ALC./VOL. 13.0%
RRP $17.00

Vasse Felix Noble Riesling

Botrytis-affected white wines are not usually associated with Margaret River. The climate and winds must make it difficult for noble rot to prosper.
CURRENT RELEASE 1994 A positive frenzy of fruit in this powerful wine. The colour is a bold green-gold and the nose is a medley of apricot, mango, peach and citrus. The palate fills the mouth and there is marmalade, butterscotch, citrus and dried apricots. The finish is dry and lingering. It can be served well chilled; try it with gravlax Atlantic salmon.

QUALITY ♆♆♆♆♆
VALUE ★★★★
GRAPES riesling
REGION Margaret River, WA
CELLAR 🍾 6
ALC./VOL. 10.5%
RRP $19.75 (375 ml)

White Wines

Vasse Felix Semillon

QUALITY ♛♛♛♛
VALUE ★★★★
GRAPES semillon
REGION Margaret River, WA
CELLAR 🍷 4
ALC./VOL. 12.5%
RRP $17.00

This is the first tilt at the variety for Vasse Felix. Margaret River semillon is something of a sleeper where the region is concerned and this is a promising debut.

CURRENT RELEASE 1995 The nose offers an overture of toasty oak on a gooseberry background. The palate continues the gooseberry theme and there is a reasonable depth of flavour. The finish bristles with toasty oak and there is a slightly resinous quality. Don't overchill because it will emphasise the oak. Try it with a seafood crepe and capsicum salsa.

Voyager Estate Chenin Blanc

QUALITY ♛♛♛♛
VALUE ★★★★
GRAPES chenin blanc
REGION Margaret River, WA
CELLAR 🍷 2
ALC./VOL. 12.8%
RRP $14.90

Achtung, trivia buffs, who did the voice-over to the movie *Zulu*? What's it got to do with wine? You've just got to see the Cape Dutch architecture at this winery, straight out of Africa. The answer is Richard Burton. Maker Stuart Pym.

CURRENT RELEASE 1995 This is a pungent style with a strong apple and pear nose. The medium-bodied palate has a touch of sweetness which is balanced by a tart green apple character. The finish is fresh and clean. It could be served well chilled; try it with marron in a light cream sauce.

Wa-de-Lock Chameleon White Pinot

QUALITY ♛♛♛
VALUE ★★★
GRAPES pinot noir
REGION Gippsland, Vic.
CELLAR 🍷 1
ALC./VOL. 12.0%
RRP $13.70

While some of these styles are made from a saigner performed on dry red pinot material, this was whole-bunch pressed with the intention of making a white or slightly taché pink wine with minimal skin contact.

CURRENT RELEASE 1995 A very subtle shade of pink, this ostensibly dry white wine has a caramel/vanilla aspect to its smoky pinoid nose. There are hints of spice and honey as well. The palate has plenty of weight and pinot fullness, and a soft round finish with a trace of marzipan. Unusual, but a nice drop. Try it with smoked chicken.

Wa-de-Lock Sauvignon Blanc

According to the label, the parish name of Wa-de-Lock is thought to derive from old Scottish, meaning a wall of water: it's bounded by the McAlister and Avon rivers. Maker Graeme Little.
CURRENT RELEASE 1995 Here's an attractive sauvignon enhanced on the nose by a little discreet oak, with light-bodied grapey taste that finishes very soft, yet dry. Straightforward but enjoyable drinking with tomato, basil and bocconcini salad.

QUALITY 🍷🍷🍷🍸
VALUE ★★★
GRAPES sauvignon blanc
REGION Gippsland, Vic.
CELLAR 🍾 1
ALC./VOL. 12.5%
RRP $15.65

Wairau River Chardonnay

Herbaceous flavours, abetted by skin-contact, malolactic fermentation (to drop the high acidities) and occasional botrytis coincide to give Marlborough chardonnay a most individual style.
CURRENT RELEASE 1994 Developed yellow colour and a voluminous bouquet of rich honey, mealy, vegetably characters, now showing definite bottle-age. Very typical of the region, the palate gives an enormous mouthful of opulent, full-frontal flavour. Drink up soon, with vegetarian foods.

QUALITY 🍷🍷🍷🍷🍸
VALUE ★★★
GRAPES chardonnay
REGION Marlborough, NZ
CELLAR 🍾 1
ALC./VOL. 13.5%
RRP $25.00

Wairau River Sauvignon Blanc

Owners Phil and Chris Rose are substantial grape growers in Marlborough. Contract winemaker John Belsham makes the wines, which have all been impressive, although few in number.
CURRENT RELEASE 1994 Starting to show the cabbagey vegetable characters that Marlborough sauvignon can build with age. It is getting a little clumsy in the mouth and may tend towards blowsy with more age. Plenty of acid and squashy, vegetal flavours. Chill well and serve with asparagus.

QUALITY 🍷🍷🍷🍸
VALUE ★★★
GRAPES sauvignon blanc
REGION Marlborough, NZ
CELLAR 🍾
ALC./VOL. 13.5%
RRP $18.85

Wandin Valley Estate Reserve Chardonnay

QUALITY ♛♛♛♝
VALUE ★★★
GRAPES chardonnay
REGION Hunter Valley, NSW
CELLAR 🍾 2
ALC./VOL. 12.3%
RRP $18.00 (cellar door)

James Davern, producer of TV soap *A Country Practice*, gets a little weekend pruning practice in the country at his Lower Hunter Valley vineyard. Maker Geoff Broadfield.

CURRENT RELEASE 1995 Rich and somewhat oak-dominant, this wine has lots of American oak vanilla and some honey, together with dried apricot aromas. A decent wine but it's hard to see the oak-flavour diminishing with time. Drink now, with smoked chicken.

Wandin Valley Pavilion Dry White

QUALITY ♛♛♝
VALUE ★★★
GRAPES semillon, chardonnay, sauvignon blanc
REGION Hunter Valley, NSW
CELLAR 🍾 2
ALC./VOL. 11.0%
RRP $12.50 (cellar door)

Wandin Valley has a traditional English pavilion and cricket ground at the winery in Wilderness Rd, Rothbury, which can be booked for corporate entertainment. Maker Geoff Broadfield.

CURRENT RELEASE 1995 This tastes like a traditional Hunter semillon, with a touch of sulphur, a slatey straw-like nose and a lean, lemony acid palate. A soft, simple quaffing dry white that goes well with shellfish.

Warramate Riesling

QUALITY ♛♛♛♛
VALUE ★★★½
GRAPES riesling
REGION Yarra Valley, Vic.
CELLAR 🍾 3
ALC./VOL. 12.0%
RRP $15.00

This is a small vineyard in the Yarra Valley that was established in 1970 by Jack Church. Production is around 1000 cases per annum.

CURRENT RELEASE 1995 This is a fragrant style that has plenty of concentrated power. The nose is full of aromatic citrus and spice smells. The palate is firm and intense with strong lime flavours that are backed by crisp acid on a lingering finish. Serve well chilled with flathead in beer batter.

Water Wheel Sauvignon Blanc

Maker Peter Cumming says the riper fruit in this wine 'generates obtuse fruit flavours...' which sounds both obtuse and abstruse to us. No matter: Water Wheel wines across the board offer some of the best value in the country.
CURRENT RELEASE 1995 A pale colour with a slight CO_2 gas fizz in the glass. The aromas are many: peppermint, crushed green leaves, herbs and citrus. The flavour has delicacy and finesse, a certain leanness and a juicy freshness. Good balance and a worthy partner for Greek salad.

QUALITY ♛♛♛♛
VALUE ★★★★
GRAPES sauvignon blanc
REGION Bendigo, Vic.
CELLAR 1
ALC./VOL. 13.0%
RRP $14.50

Wellington Chardonnay

Ex-Riverina College wine science lecturer Andrew Hood has a thriving contract winemaking business in southern Tassie. Wellington is his own label, from various Tasmanian vineyards. Previous outstanding vintages: '93, '94
CURRENT RELEASE 1995 A lightly oaked style, this has subtle, slowly developing cool-climate fruit, which has a faintly herbaceous note and subtle supporting wood. A stylish wine, fresh and clean with tropical flavours on the palate. Well worth tracking down. Drink with Tassie scallops.

QUALITY ♛♛♛♛♛
VALUE ★★★★
GRAPES chardonnay
REGION northern Tas.
CELLAR 5+
ALC./VOL. 12.8%
RRP $17.50

Wellington Sweet Riesling

Andrew Hood made this not with botrytised grapes but by freeze-concentrating the juice, like a high-tech ice wine.
CURRENT RELEASE 1995 Light yellow hue, and an oily viscosity. The sweet aroma recalls honey and fresh bread-dough, with a tea-leafy aspect. The acid is searingly high, and despite quite a lot of sweetness it has a rather astringent finish. This could do exciting things with a year or two in the cellar. Try it with fruit salad and double cream.

QUALITY ♛♛♛♛
VALUE ★★★
GRAPES riesling
REGION Tasmania
CELLAR 4+
ALC./VOL. 11.5%
RRP $15.00 (cellar door) (375ml)

Wetherall Chardonnay

QUALITY ♛♛♛♛
VALUE ★★★★
GRAPES chardonnay
REGION Coonawarra, SA
CELLAR 🍷 1
ALC./VOL. 13.0%
RRP $15.00 (cellar door)

The Wetheralls sell most of their grapes but with young Michael Wetherall keen to make and market their own label, we'll see more of this brand in future. Only 450 cases made.
CURRENT RELEASE 1994 Very lightly wooded, this soft, up-front wine has a touch of asparagus in its bouquet, with gentle structure, pleasant flavour and good length. Just right with yabbies.

Willow Creek Unwooded Chardonnay

QUALITY ♛♛♛♛
VALUE ★★★
GRAPES chardonnay
REGION Mornington Peninsula, Vic.
CELLAR 🍷 2
ALC./VOL. 13.1%
RRP $17.40

Every day another unwooded chardonnay springs up, as if it's something new and revolutionary. Never mind that most chardonnay in France has always been unwooded.
CURRENT RELEASE 1995 This has oodles of sex appeal, busting out with riotous pineapple and passionfruit aromas and deep tropical fruit flavours in the mouth. Very clean and well made, with uncommonly good length and finish for an unwooded chardonnay. Good with cold white meats and salad.

Willows (The) Semillon

QUALITY ♛♛♛♛
VALUE ★★★★
GRAPES semillon
REGION Barossa Valley, SA
CELLAR 🍷 3
ALC./VOL. 12.0%
RRP $13.50

The grapes for this wine came from 58-year-old vines. It's been wood-aged in typical Barossa semillon style. Maker Peter Scholz.
Previous outstanding vintages: '92, '93
CURRENT RELEASE 1994 Five months in barrel have given a definite oaky bouquet that dominates the fruit and gives an aggressive resiny overtone. It's much better in the mouth, where the tart lemony semillon fruit reasserts itself, and the lasting impression is of finesse and tight structure. It has typical semillon leanness and dry finish, and could be cellared. Serve with lemon chicken.

CURRENT RELEASE 1995 A Rubenesque-style that makes a virtue out of being well-endowed in the flesh department. The nose has scented straw and lemon aromas. The palate is opulent with a mouth-filling texture. The main flavour is lemon and there are also gooseberry undertones. Soft acid fills out the finish. It is a wine that can be served well chilled. Try it with chicken and mushroom pie.

QUALITY ????
VALUE ★★★★
GRAPES semillon
REGION Barossa Valley, SA
CELLAR 🍾 2
ALC./VOL. 12.0%
RRP $14.50

Wirra Wirra Chardonnay

The Wirra style is decidedly individual; some would say eccentric. Woodhenge, ferret-legging, old church bells, etc. But we've noticed a disturbing trend towards normality recently. Maker Ben Riggs.
Previous outstanding vintages: '91, '93
CURRENT RELEASE 1994 Very much the house style – deep yellow hue, oaky but also rich and long. Starting to show some bottle-age, and the oak shows signs of coming into balance. There is a trace of austerity from the oak on the back palate. Serve with char-grilled chicken.

QUALITY ????
VALUE ★★★
GRAPES chardonnay
REGION McLaren Vale, Adelaide Hills, SA
CELLAR 🍾 3+
ALC./VOL. 14.0%
RRP $20.00

Wirra Wirra Hand Picked Riesling

There are two ways to pick grapes: by hand or machine. The former is becoming a rarity in this country, but in most cases you couldn't tell the difference in the wine.
CURRENT RELEASE 1995 This is a big, rich, fairly broad riesling in the typical McLaren Vale style. The nose has powder-puff florals, a trace of volatility, and the palate is soft and rich. Serve with macaroni cheese.

QUALITY ????
VALUE ★★★
GRAPES riesling
REGION McLaren Vale 80%, Clare Valley 20%, SA
CELLAR 🍾 5
ALC./VOL. 13.0%
RRP $13.50

Wirra Wirra Late Picked Riesling

QUALITY ♥♥♥♥♀
VALUE ★★★★½
GRAPES riesling
REGION McLaren Vale, SA
CELLAR 🍷 4
ALC./VOL. 11.5%
RRP $13.50 (375ml)

This little sweetie joins the Wirra Sweet Semillon at the sticky end of the Trott portfolio. Maker Ben Riggs.
CURRENT RELEASE 1995 A very attractive auslese style, smelling of doughy yeastiness and ripe floral riesling fruit that's very fresh and vibrant. There are traces of apricot and honey in the palate which suggest a fair degree of botrytis. Overall impression is of lightness and elegance rather than lusciousness. The fresh acid finish should help it age. Serve with fruit salad.

Wirra Wirra Semillon Sauvignon Blanc

QUALITY ♥♥♥♥
VALUE ★★★½
GRAPES semillon 65%, sauvignon blanc 35%
REGION McLaren Vale, SA
CELLAR 🍷 5+
ALC./VOL. 12.7%
RRP $17.00

This style has a good history as an each-way style – you can enjoy it young, or cellar and watch it grow into a rich, complex, full-bodied white. Maker Ben Riggs.
Previous outstanding vintages: '83, '90, '92, '93, '94
CURRENT RELEASE 1995 Stylish smoky, cedary French oak and cut-grass fruit greet the nose. The palate is savoury, oak-driven at present and rich with a steely backbone of acid to help it age. Good length. Could be served with Thai fish cakes.

Wolf Blass Chardonnay

QUALITY ♥♥♥♥
VALUE ★★★★½
GRAPES chardonnay
REGION McLaren Vale, Barossa Valley, SA
CELLAR 🍷 2
ALC./VOL. 12.5%
RRP $12.60 ⓢ

Wolf Blass was probably the smartest acquisition Mildara's Ray King made. It has passed down the food chain somewhat now – the Mildara Blass big fish, having eaten many minnows, has itself been swallowed by the Foster's shark.
CURRENT RELEASE 1995 A delicious drop. Full yellow colour thanks to wood maturation, the oak also obvious in the rich toast, honey and butterscotch bouquet. Generous flavour for the money and very attractive. More style than expected from a wine that sells as low as $9.95. Drink with seafood chowder.

Wolf Blass Classic Dry White

We can remember when such unfashionable grapes as muscadelle and crouchen (remember crouchen!) made an appearance in this blend. Mr Blass was never one to worry about convention. Today, it's all very PC.
CURRENT RELEASE 1995 Quite an advanced, deep yellow colour here. The nose reveals lots of oak, in a smoky, toasty bouquet. Wood is less obvious in the mouth flavour, which is soft, round and slightly oily, with good balance and drinkability. Try it with roast chicken.

QUALITY ♛♛♛♛
VALUE ★★★½
GRAPES chardonnay, semillon, colombard
REGION mainly McLaren Vale, SA
CELLAR 🍾 2
ALC./VOL. 12.5%
RRP $14.70 Ⓢ

Wolf Blass Gold Label Riesling

This is one of Australia's great unsung riesling heroes. It comes off the top of the hill at Quelltaler, where the best red loam soils over limestone are found. Maker Chris Hatcher.
CURRENT RELEASE 1995 Restrained limey, slatey, mineral nose, fresh and undeveloped. The palate is very fine and intense, beautifully balanced and while it's a glorious drink now, it will richly repay cellaring. Serve with King George whiting.

QUALITY ♛♛♛♛♛
VALUE ★★★★½
GRAPES riesling
REGION Clare Valley, SA
CELLAR 🍾 8+
ALC./VOL. 11.5%
RRP $14.70 Ⓢ

Wolf Blass Green Label Traminer Riesling

Could this wine have been inspired by Deinhard's Green Label, a semi-sweet fruity German white?
CURRENT RELEASE 1995 Lightly aromatic muscaty frontignac aromas are ethereal and spicy. The palate is all fragrant lychee and spatlese-level sweetness. A real crowd-pleaser. Serve chilled with fresh fruit.

QUALITY ♛♛♛♛
VALUE ★★★½
GRAPES gewurztraminer, frontignac
REGION Barossa Valley, SA
CELLAR 🍾
ALC./VOL. 11.0%
RRP $12.60 Ⓢ

Wolf Blass Spatlese Rhine Riesling

QUALITY	♟♟♟♟?
VALUE	★★★★
GRAPES	riesling
REGION	Eden Valley & Coonawarra, SA
CELLAR	🍾 7+
ALC./VOL.	12.5%
RRP	$14.70 Ⓢ

This is a bit of a joke in the Blass bunker: it wins heaps of medals, it ages into a stunning wine, the winemakers drink heaps of it, but no one else seems to be awake to it.

CURRENT RELEASE 1995 Wow! A lovely rich, botrytis-affected riesling filled with honey, tea-leafy, orange peel and apricot scents. The colour is brilliant mid-yellow, the palate rich and full with long flavour and sweetness that dries somewhat on the finish. Try it with liver pâté.

Wolf Blass Yellow Label Rhine Riesling

QUALITY	♟♟♟?
VALUE	★★★★
GRAPES	riesling
REGION	Clare & Eden Valley, SA
CELLAR	🍾 2
ALC./VOL.	11.0%
RRP	$12.60 Ⓢ

Riesling sales have weakened so much that what was once largely Riverland fruit is now 100 per cent quality grapes from Clare and Eden Valley. Maker Chris Hatcher.

CURRENT RELEASE 1995 This wine shows why riesling drinkers are the smart ones, 'cause that's where the value is. Clean floral typical riesling aromas; soft fruity taste with subliminal sweetness and a herbal edge. Remarkable value for money – you can get it for $9.95!

Woodstock Riesling

QUALITY	♟♟♟
VALUE	★★★½
GRAPES	riesling
REGION	McLaren Vale, SA
CELLAR	🍾 4
ALC./VOL.	12.0%
RRP	$11.10

Woodstock's Scott and Ann Collett are great contributors to the atmosphere of the Vales. They recently hired John Weeks, one of the Flying Winemakers who put Aussie-made French wine on the map.

CURRENT RELEASE 1994 A pleasant straightforward appley style of riesling, pale-hued and straw-like to sniff. A decent wine with no faults, and goes well with lemon sole.

Wyanga Sauvignon Blanc

This winery used to be called Lulgra then Wyanga Park but the new title is 'Wyanga Winemakers of Gippsland'. It was established in 1970. Maker Andrew Smith.
CURRENT RELEASE 1995 A very pungent style. The nose is a real punch in the hooter with strong pea-pod and herbal smells. The palate has a hint of sweetness as well as varietal flavours. There is a little coarseness and the finish is quite dry. It can be served with a medium to full chill. Try it with a leafy green salad.

QUALITY ♥♥♥
VALUE ★★★
GRAPES sauvignon blanc
REGION Lakes Entrance, Vic.
CELLAR 2
ALC./VOL. 13.5%
RRP $16.50

Wynns Chardonnay

Wynns' winemaker Peter Douglas has been making the Wynns whites at Coonawarra for the past three years. Before that, the juice was tankered to the Barossa for fermentation and ageing.
CURRENT RELEASE 1995 The white grapes were picked well before the rain came, and quality is very fine. This has peachy, tropical fruit aromas with toast and vanilla oak scents in support. A good, lighter style chardonnay which shouldn't be over chilled. Try it with yabbies.

QUALITY ♥♥♥♥
VALUE ★★★★
GRAPES chardonnay
REGION Coonawarra, SA
CELLAR 4
ALC./VOL. 13.0%
RRP $13.00 ⓢ

Wynns Riesling

In keeping with EC agreements and the change from hermitage to shiraz, this becomes riesling instead of rhine riesling. Bravo! Maker Peter Douglas.
CURRENT RELEASE 1995 A fine, delicate style of riesling, with pale hue and slightly confectionery aromatics, coupled with a tart acid palate that's fresh and clean, and rich in stone-fruit flavour. Needs time to fill out a bit, then drink with scampi.

QUALITY ♥♥♥⸮
VALUE ★★★★
GRAPES riesling
REGION Coonawarra, SA
CELLAR 5
ALC./VOL. 11.5%
RRP $11.00 ⓢ

Yalumba Christobel's Dry White

QUALITY 🍷🍷🍷
VALUE ★★★
GRAPES semillon, sauvignon blanc, marsanne
REGION Barossa & Eden Valleys, SA
CELLAR 🍾 1
ALC./VOL. 11.9%
RRP $10.50 ⓢ

Christobel Hill Smith was a member of the founding family, whose 'vitality bewitched those around her', according to the label.
CURRENT RELEASE 1995 A very light-bodied, rather simple wine that won't make any enemies. The shy nose is vaguely herbal and the taste is slightly weak, but also soft, dry-finishing and very quaffable. Try it with summer salads.

Yalumba Family Reserve Botrytis Semillon

QUALITY 🍷🍷🍷🍷𐦂
VALUE ★★★★★
GRAPES semillon
REGION Eden Valley, SA
CELLAR 🍾 6+
ALC./VOL. 12.5%
RRP $13.00 (375ml) ⓢ

The family in this case is the Hill Smiths, who own S. Smith & Son/Yalumba. These days the head honcho is manging director Robert Hill Smith.
CURRENT RELEASE 1995 Deep yellow hue; rich apricot, honey and citrus peel complexity with vanilla joining in on the palate. It's a delicious sticky, perhaps not as oaky as previous vintages, and the palate is very tight and long with wonderful lusciousness and harmony. Could repay another year or two in bottle and should be sensational when mature. Drink with crème brûlée.

Yalumba Family Reserve Chardonnay

QUALITY 🍷🍷🍷𐦂
VALUE ★★★½
GRAPES chardonnay
REGION not stated
CELLAR 🍾 1
ALC./VOL. 13.5%
RRP $13.00 ⓢ

Yalumba's white winemaker Alan Hoey has lightened the oak impact of this wine in recent times.
CURRENT RELEASE 1995 The nose is subdued and there's minimal oak character, with a shy nose of herbal fruit. The taste is light to mediumweight with a smooth, round structure and warm finish. Not a wine of great character, but very fair value at $12–$13. Try with chicken schnitzel.

Yalumba Family Reserve Rhine Riesling

The Barossa is a place of complex surnames: the grapes for this wine were grown by the Bartholomaeus and Saegenschnitter families!
CURRENT RELEASE 1994 A fine style smelling of vanilla, straw and candy, with the beginnings of toasty development. The palate is dry and finishes cleanly with a nice but subtle grip. Fully ready to drink. Try it with pumpkin ravioli.

QUALITY 🍷🍷🍷
VALUE ★★★
GRAPES riesling
REGION Eden Valley, SA
CELLAR 🍾 3
ALC./VOL. 11.5%
RRP $13.30 Ⓢ

Yalumba Oxford Landing Chardonnay

Wyndham Hill Smith purchased the Oxford Landing property for Yalumba in 1958. He correctly figured that the liberal amounts of sun, soil and water wouldn't do the vines any harm.
CURRENT RELEASE 1995 This is simply one of the best chardonnays of its price to be found anywhere in the world. But it needs to be drunk within a year or two of release as it ages quickly. Full, peachy, 'in-your-face' chardonnay fruit, now picking up some bottle development. Soft, fruity, easy on the gums and hard to fault at the price. Good stuff with chicken.

QUALITY 🍷🍷🍷
VALUE ★★★★½
GRAPES chardonnay
REGION Riverland & Barossa Valley, SA; Sunraysia, Vic.
CELLAR 🍾
ALC./VOL. 12.5%
RRP $8.00 Ⓢ

Yalumba Oxford Landing Rhine Riesling

Oxford Landing is Yalumba's vast Riverland vineyard at Qualco, where they grow inexpensive grapes for cheaper wines.
CURRENT RELEASE 1994 A light and fairly straightforward wine which is well priced and offers a softly toasty/straw bouquet and a lean, slightly short but attractively flavoured palate. Serve with fish.

QUALITY 🍷🍷🍷
VALUE ★★★½
GRAPES riesling
REGION Eden Valley & Riverland, SA
CELLAR 🍾
ALC./VOL. 11.0%
RRP $8.00 Ⓢ

Yalumba Reserve Chardonnay

QUALITY 🍷🍷🍷🍷
VALUE ★★★½
GRAPES chardonnay
REGION Eden Valley, SA
CELLAR 🍾 2
ALC./VOL. 13.5%
RRP $19.00 ⓢ

There are now enough reserves in Australian wine to start an A team. Some of them aren't true reserve wines, but this is. Maker Alan Hoey.
CURRENT RELEASE 1994 They've thrown the chardonnay-makers handbook at this one: toasted oak and smoky, buttery malolactic and lees characters give a full bouquet. The flavour is rich and smooth with fruit sweetness and fine balance. A graceful and complex wine. Try it with chicken kebabs.

Yalumba Reserve Viognier

QUALITY 🍷🍷🍷🍷
VALUE ★★★
GRAPES viognier
REGION Barossa Valley, SA
CELLAR 🍾 2
ALC./VOL. 12.0%
RRP $18.00 ⓢ

Yalumba has made a pet vocation of promulgating viognier, that obscure grape from the northern Rhone Valley. This one was grown by the Vaughan family of Angaston.
CURRENT RELEASE 1995 Attractive nutty aromas with faint traces of spice and musk. There is some typical viognier richness on palate and, while it's not quite up to the '95 Heggies, it's a very appealing wine and a real alternative. Try it with spring rolls.

Yalumba Reserve Watervale Riesling

QUALITY 🍷🍷🍷🍷?
VALUE ★★★★
GRAPES riesling
REGION Clare Valley, SA
CELLAR 🍾 5+
ALC./VOL. 12.0%
RRP $15.00 ⓢ

This new label is for exceptional parcels of wine that aren't necessarily repeated every year. Maker Brian Walsh and team.
CURRENT RELEASE 1994 Green tints in the colour are the first good sign, and the bouquet is smoothly floral and slightly bready with some development. The taste is seamless – beautifully balanced with rich stone-fruit flavours on a soft, dry finish. Very good length. Drink with grilled whiting.

Yarra Burn Chardonnay

This is another small Yarra Valley winery which has succumbed to the brand-buying spree of the major companies. It was sold to BRL Hardy in 1995. Maker David Fyffe.
CURRENT RELEASE 1995 This is a delicate and lightly-wooded chardonnay. It's lean and lively, perhaps a little meagre on the palate as many Yarra whites are for '95. The acid is frisky and the finish dry, with some barrel-ferment complexity. Good with eggplant dip.

QUALITY ♛♛♛♛
VALUE ★★★½
GRAPES chardonnay
REGION Yarra Valley, Vic.
CELLAR 🍾 3
ALC./VOL. 12.5%
RRP $19.30 ⓢ

Yarra Burn Sauvignon Blanc Semillon

BRL Hardy has plans to increase the grape intake at Yarra Burn and use it as a processing centre for the region.
CURRENT RELEASE 1995 Pale yellow colour and fresh grassy, gooseberry aromas introduce a delicate, refreshing dry white. Crisp, zippy and fruity, it has good harmony and smooth drinkability. Suits asparagus salad.

QUALITY ♛♛♛♛
VALUE ★★★½
GRAPES sauvignon blanc 60%, semillon 40%
REGION Yarra & King Valleys, Vic.
CELLAR 🍾 2
ALC./VOL. 11.9%
RRP $15.45

Yarra Ridge Chardonnay

Chardonnay is probably the one variety that impresses most consistently in the Yarra. Maker Rob Dolan does it well at Yarra Ridge.
CURRENT RELEASE 1995 This is a classy chardonnay, showing some herbaceousness which is typical for Yarras from the cool '95 season. The colour has a green tint and the nose holds spicy, buttery and honeyed characters with well-adjusted oak. The palate floods with flavour, the fruit having delicious texture, weight and nuances. Try it with barbecued king prawns.

QUALITY ♛♛♛♛♛
VALUE ★★★★
GRAPES chardonnay
REGION Yarra Valley, Vic.
CELLAR 🍾 5+
ALC./VOL. 12.7%
RRP $20.00 ⓢ

Yarra Ridge Reserve Chardonnay

QUALITY ♥♥♥♥⁒
VALUE ★★★½
GRAPES chardonnay
REGION Yarra Valley, Vic.
CELLAR 🍶 6+
ALC./VOL. 13.0%
RRP $25.00 ⓢ

This is the first time Yarra Ridge has seen fit to release a reserve chardonnay, following the gathering trend in this country. Maker Rob Dolan.

CURRENT RELEASE 1995 Although it had been bottled just one week when we tried it, the wine showed enormous promise and surprising harmony. Full yellow in hue, it smelled of creamy and buttery barrel-ferment aromas, smoky and fruit-driven despite evidence of classy oak. The palate had delicious smooth fruit, a little richness and fine balance. Try it with crab risotto.

Yarra Ridge Sauvignon Blanc

QUALITY ♥♥♥♥
VALUE ★★★
GRAPES sauvignon blanc
REGION Yarra Valley and Strathbogie Ranges, Vic.
CELLAR 🍶 1
ALC./VOL. 13.0%
RRP $20.00 ⓢ

This has always been the pacesetter for sauvignon blanc in the Yarra Valley. Maker Rob Dolan.

CURRENT RELEASE 1995 Crushed vine leaves and green-stick aromas, along with citrusy aspects. There's stylish cool-grown fruit here, not the skeletal kind but smooth and gentle, fruity and eminently drinkable. Try it with mussel soup.

Yarra Valley Hills Kiah Yallambee Chardonnay

QUALITY ♥♥♥♥♥
VALUE ★★★★½
GRAPES chardonnay
REGION Yarra Valley, Vic.
CELLAR 🍶 6+
ALC./VOL. 13.0%
RRP $18.50 (cellar door)

This small vineyard owned by Terry Hill has made a lot of heads turn in a short space of time with its classy, fruit-driven dry whites. Maker Steve Webber.

Previous outstanding vintages: '93

CURRENT RELEASE 1995 Stylish wine indeed. Fine cedar, toast and spices on the nose and the oak impact is subtle. In the mouth it shows delicious peach/nectarine fruitiness, finesse and harmony. Barrel-ferment character adds complexity. Would team well with scallops.

Yarraman Road Chardonnay

The Blom family bought this property from Rosemount in 1994. It was formerly Penfolds' Wybong Park. Maker David Lowe.

CURRENT RELEASE 1995 The colour is quite deep, signalling a forward, warm-area style. The nose is soft and open, with rich buttery/honeyed malolactic complexities and the palate has good weight of soft, peachy flavour ending with a little sweetness. Try it with chicken supreme.

QUALITY ♛♛♛♛
VALUE ★★★
GRAPES chardonnay
REGION Hunter Valley, NSW
CELLAR 🍾 2
ALC./VOL. 13.0%
RRP $24.00

Sparkling Wines

All Saints St Leonards Cabernet Sauvignon

Saints alive! This is an All Saints wine made from grapes grown at neighbouring St Leonards, both properties being owned by the Brown brethren of Milawa.
CURRENT RELEASE *non-vintage* Rich, ripe, plum/licorice nose, very ripe for a bubbly and reflects high alcohol. The entry is sweet, swells to fill the mouth with ripe fruit flavour and a big dollop of tannin, moving into a dry, firm finish that lingers well. Roast turkey and rich gravy here.

QUALITY ♀♀♀♀
VALUE ★★★★
GRAPES cabernet sauvignon
REGION Rutherglen, Vic.
CELLAR 🍾 3+
ALC./VOL. 14.0%
RRP $18.50

All Saints St Leonards Méthode Traditionelle

Wahgunyah is a very holy place, what with all those saints jostling for a place on the label. Maker Neil Jericho (retired).
CURRENT RELEASE 1993 This is normally a chenin blanc blend but the '93 is all chardonnay. Pale yellow; fresh, light, undeveloped aromas of melon and straw. While the palate has flavour it's somewhat heavy-handed and seems to need more acid. Chill well, and serve with mixed nuts.

QUALITY ♀♀♀
VALUE ★★½
GRAPES chardonnay
REGION Rutherglen, Vic.
CELLAR 🍾 1
ALC./VOL. 12.2%
RRP $15.50

Andrew Garrett Pinot Chardonnay NV

QUALITY ♛♛♛
VALUE ★★★½
GRAPES pinot noir, chardonnay
REGION Padthaway, SA & Cowra, NSW
CELLAR 🍶
ALC./VOL. 12.0%
RRP $12.60

There used to be a chardonnay NV and a pinot noir NV, but new owner Mildara Blass has rolled them together into one wine.

CURRENT RELEASE *non-vintage* The colour is a developed pink, turned to light amber with age. The nose is smoky, bready and very pinoid, with good complexity, but the palate is contrastingly light and while it's soft, it doesn't have a lot of finesse. Fair value, though, and would go with smoked salmon.

Andrew Garrett Sparkling Burgundy

QUALITY ♛♛♛
VALUE ★★★
GRAPES shiraz
REGION McLaren Vale, SA
CELLAR 🍶
ALC./VOL. 12.5%
RRP $12.60

This style was instigated by former Garrett winemaker and spurgler, Warren Randall, who has since left the fold. It's had 12 months on lees. Maker Phil Reschke.

CURRENT RELEASE *non-vintage* With a medium purple-red colour and a nose of cherry and plum-skin, this is a young, fruity, straightforward style which has a lot of sweetness on entry and leaves you wanting a slightly drier finish and more complexity. Try it with the Sunday barbie.

Blue Pyrenees Midnight Cuvée

QUALITY ♛♛♛♛
VALUE ★★★★
GRAPES not stated
REGION Pyrenees, Vic.
CELLAR 🍶 5
ALC./VOL. 12.3%
RRP $30.00

Nothing to do with bushrangers, the grapes are actually harvested by hand under lights when the grapes are coolest. It looks like picking at a day-night cricket match.

CURRENT RELEASE *non-vintage* It is a fine style with a lively nose that has a soda-bread aroma and yeast autolysis smells. The palate is dominated by citrus flavours and lively bubbles tickle the palate. The finish shows strong firm acid and it cleanses the mouth. It is a great pre-dinner drink and should be served well chilled.

Blue Pyrenees Reserve Brut

There is a lot of high-powered winemaking that goes into this style. After all there are direct links to Krug in this French-owned company, so you'd expect some influence.
CURRENT RELEASE 1991 There is a strong bread aroma and a hint of cheese on the nose. The bubbles are very fine and they enliven the palate. The major flavour is citrus and there are some green apple characters. There is abundant acid on the finish and it can be served well chilled as a pre-dinner drink or with chicken at a picnic race meeting.

QUALITY ♛♛♛♛♝
VALUE ★★★★
GRAPES chardonnay 55%, pinot noir 35%, pinot meunier 10%
REGION Pyrenees, Vic.
CELLAR 🍾 3
ALC./VOL. 12.5%
RRP $24.00

Bowen Estate Sanderson

Doug and Joy Bowen always made a few cases of sparkling wine for home consumption. In 1990 they got a little carried away and now there is more than they can drink.
CURRENT RELEASE 1990 This blanc-de-blanc style has recently been disgorged. The time in the bottle has developed a nutty character and there is obvious yeast autolysis. The palate is rich and chewy with lemon and nutty flavours plus some lively bubbles. The finish is dry and clean. It should be served well chilled as a pre-dinner drink.

QUALITY ♛♛♛♛
VALUE ★★★★
GRAPES chardonnay
REGION Coonawarra, SA
CELLAR 🍾 4
ALC./VOL. 11.5%
RRP $25.00

Brown Brothers Pinot Chardonnay Brut

QUALITY ♥♥♥♥?
VALUE ★★★★½
GRAPES pinot noir, chardonnay
REGION Whitlands, Vic.
CELLAR 🍾 4
ALC./VOL. 12.5%
RRP $21.00

The Brown brothers were not really renowned for froth and bubble. Ernest table wines and sultry fortifieds were more their ilk. But recently their sparkling wines have been wowing the show circuit, and rightly so!

CURRENT RELEASE 1992 This is a full style with plenty of weight. The fruit was grown in the high altitude Whitlands region and the wine has strong grape aromas on the nose. There are also hints of Vegemite and meaty qualities. The palate is substantial with richly developed fruit flavours. Lively bubbles provide a counterpoint and the finish has impressive length. It is a dry style that can be served well chilled; try it with smoked salmon.

Charles Melton Sparkling Burgundy

QUALITY ♥♥♥?
VALUE ★★★½
GRAPES not stated
REGION Barossa Valley, SA
CELLAR 🍾 4+
ALC./VOL. 14.0%
RRP $16.00 (cellar door)

Graeme 'Charlie' Melton is one of the characters among the small winemakers of the Barossa. He's also a staunch defender of the sparkling burgundy style.

CURRENT RELEASE *non-vintage* (1995 disgorgement) Vivid youthful purple-red colour reflects the youth of this wine. The shy nose offers grassy and earthy notes; the palate has a sweet entry with herbal plum and licorice flavours, moving into a soft but dry vanilla finish. It's a wine of guts rather than subtlety. Try it with duck.

Cloudy Bay Pelorus

Have dolphin will travel. The symbol of this wine is a dolphin called Pelorus Jack, but now the entire Cape Mentelle and Cloudy Bay range has sprouted a dolphin crest. Makers Kevin Judd and Harold Osborne.
Previous outstanding vintages: '90
CURRENT RELEASE 1991 Typical Pelorus style: forward full-yellow colour; complex bready developed bouquet with buttery malolactic and slightly feral aspects. The palate is rich and gutsy but retains some grace and the dry finish lingers on and on. When in NZ, try Bluff oysters. Otherwise, big Pacifics.

QUALITY ♛♛♛♛♛
VALUE ★★★★
GRAPES pinot noir, chardonnay
REGION Marlborough, NZ
CELLAR 🍾 3
ALC./VOL. 13.0%
RRP $32.00

Clover Hill

This is the third release from Taltarni's substantial Clover Hill vineyard in Tasmania's chilly Pipers River region. Makers Chris Markell, Dominique Portet and Greg Gallagher.
Previous outstanding vintages: '92
CURRENT RELEASE 1993 This has a very complex, bready, champagne-like bouquet with a hint of burnt-toast. The palate is leaner than the nose leads you to expect, with a zesty, zippy lemon/citrus acid tang. The finishing impression is of fine balance and great length. Taltarni is developing a most interesting style, a bubbly with lots of character. Try it with shellfish canapes.

QUALITY ♛♛♛♛♛
VALUE ★★★★½
GRAPES chardonnay 95%, pinot noir 5%
REGION Pipers River, Tas.
CELLAR 🍾 4
ALC./VOL. 11.6%
RRP $28.00

Croser

QUALITY ★★★★★
VALUE ★★★★
GRAPES pinot noir 75%, chardonnay 25%
REGION Adelaide Hills, SA
CELLAR 3+
ALC./VOL. 12.5%
RRP $31.00

'I could drink a case of you, and still be on my feet ...' sang Joni Mitchell in the '70s. Is this what Brian Croser had in mind when he named this bubbly after himself?
Previous outstanding vintages: '86, '88, '90, '92
CURRENT RELEASE 1993 With more pinot noir than usual, the '93 Croser has a rich, smoky, pinoty bouquet with hints of strawberry. This is arguably the most Champagne-like Croser to date, yet it's still distinctively Australian. The fruit is delicate, tight, yet soft and it finishes with pronounced acid on a long dry finish. Goes well with chat potatoes slathered with chive-cream and caviar.

Deakin Estate Brut

QUALITY ★★★½
VALUE ★★★★½
GRAPES chardonnay, colombard, chenin blanc
REGION Murray Valley, Vic.
CELLAR 1
ALC./VOL. 13.%
RRP $10.00 $

Best Bargain Sparkling

Deakin Estate is part of the Yunghanns-owned Wingara Wine Group. It replaces their former Riverland label, Sunnycliff. The brandname celebrates former PM Alfred Deakin, who had a role in the Murray irrigation scheme. Maker Mark Zeppel.
CURRENT RELEASE 1995 This is great value in a light, fruit-driven, straightforward bubbly, which is the style the Riverland does best. The colour is light yellow, the nose is fresh and lifted with floral fruit and the taste is soft and again fruity with cashew and melon flavours and a pleasingly dry finish.

Domaine Chandon Blanc de Blancs Chardonnay

DCA celebrated its 10th vintage anniversary in 1996. What an amazing success story it's been. As in Champagne, the straight chardonnay is given extra time on lees because it's the slowest-ageing cuvée. Only 2000 cases released.
CURRENT RELEASE 1991 The colour is quite pale and the wine remarkably fresh for its age. The nose has toasted bread aromas of complexity and richness. The palate is smooth, creamy and soft yet tight and long, with great flavour and finesse. This should continue to age slowly, retaining its delicacy. Serve with crab won tons.

QUALITY ♕♕♕♕♕
VALUE ★★★★★
GRAPES chardonnay 100%
REGION various
CELLAR 🍾 5+
ALC./VOL. 12.5%
RRP $30.00 Ⓢ

Domaine Chandon Brut Rosé

Since our labelling laws changed to fit in with Europe's, these wines are given a vintage instead of a blend number. This is because the new law allows a single-vintage wine to be up to 15 per cent of other vintages. It used to be 5 per cent. DC uses more than 5 per cent reserve wine.
CURRENT RELEASE 1993 Fresh pink hue with a faint shade of purple. The nose has a touch of strawberry which follows onto the palate where there are hints of cherry and candy; soft and fruity. Smooth drinkability is helped along by the liqueur. A lovely drink and a fascinating contrast to the Blanc de Blancs. Serve with smoked salmon.

QUALITY ♕♕♕♕⟨
VALUE ★★★★
GRAPES pinot noir 58%, chardonnay 42%
REGION various
CELLAR 🍾 4+
ALC./VOL. 12.5%
RRP $30.00 Ⓢ

Domaine Chandon Vintage Brut

QUALITY ♛♛♛♛♛
VALUE ★★★★½
GRAPES chardonnay 47%, pinot noir 51%, pinot meunier 2%
REGION various, Vic., SA & Tas.
CELLAR 🍷 4
ALC./VOL. 12.5%
RRP $30.00 Ⓢ

The '93 Brut has a handsome new label, with more white, less dark green, and the name Chandon is played up. Maker Wayne Donaldson and team.
CURRENT RELEASE 1993 Yet another stunner: DCA has not put a foot wrong in 10 years. The latest release shows the benefit of reserve wine. The colour is mid-brassy yellow, the nose has complex bready, strawberry and candy aromas with a trace of coconut and some Vegemite developed pinot/yeast character. The taste is full in the mouth, complex for an Australian bubbly and long. The finish achieves softness without obvious sweetness. Good aperitif style, with gravlax.

Garden Gully Sparkling Burgundy

QUALITY ♛♛♛♛♛
VALUE ★★★★★
GRAPES shiraz
REGION Great Western, Vic.
CELLAR 🍷 8
ALC./VOL. 13.0%
RRP $18.00

The label on this wine is so bad it's good! The winery is co-owned by Warren Randall and Brian Fletcher and the vineyard was planted in 1952. It is a great cellar door location on the Western Highway.
Previous outstanding vintages: '93
CURRENT RELEASE 1994 Big peppery shiraz style that doesn't want for flavour. The colour is black purple and the nose is loaded with pepper. It is richer than last year's example with a hint of sweetness on the palate. There is also lovely plum and blackberry fruit flavour on the palate and the finish is tinder dry. The bubbles also make a convincing contribution to this outstanding drink. Serve well chilled with roast turkey.

Glenara Pinot Noir Méthode Champenoise

Sparkling wine is a high-tech business and these days it's hard for a boutique winery to be in the race. Here's an exception to the rule.

CURRENT RELEASE 1994 Very faint pink colour, which is echoed by decidedly pinoid strawberry, grapey aromas. There is good palate weight and the flavour is more than simple fruit. The finish has a little tannin grip which helps dry the aftertaste. Serve with smoked salmon and capers.

QUALITY ♉♉♉⸮
VALUE ★★★
GRAPES pinot noir (organic)
REGION Adelaide Hills, SA
CELLAR 🍾 2
ALC./VOL. 12.4%
RRP $20.00 ☻

Grant Burge Pinot Noir Chardonnay Méthode Traditionelle

That man Burge manages to transcend the usual small-winery limitations and field excellent wines in a number of styles. This is exhibit A.

CURRENT RELEASE *non-vintage* Very fine, yet complex, bouquet of candied fruit, with a hint of dried pineapple. The palate really sparkles, with fine mousse and vibrant fruit lifted by refreshing acidity. The finish is the high-point – it is very long, dry and harmonious with an aftertaste of apples. Serve with oysters.

QUALITY ♉♉♉♉♉
VALUE ★★★★★
GRAPES pinot noir, chardonnay
REGION not stated
CELLAR 🍾 2
ALC./VOL. 11.5%
RRP $18.00

Best Sparkling Wine

Hanging Rock Macedon

This was the sparkler of the year in the last edition of the *Guide*. It produced an interesting reaction from several quarters. We love it because it simply can't be ignored. Maker John Ellis.

CURRENT RELEASE *non-vintage* Absolutely fabulous! It is rich, meaty, quirky and packed with flavour. The nose is candied with toffee and aldehyde aromas. The palate is chewy with a honeyed texture. There is plenty of weight and candied character. The finish is soft and dry and the bubbles add interest. It pays homage to Bollinger RD, or does Bollinger pay homage to it? Serve well chilled with a rich chicken dish.

QUALITY ♉♉♉♉♉
VALUE ★★★★
GRAPES pinot noir, chardonnay
REGION Macedon, Vic.
CELLAR 🍾 2
ALC./VOL. 12.5%
RRP $36.00

Hardys Grand Reserve Champagne

QUALITY ♆♆♆
VALUE ★★★
GRAPES not stated
REGION not stated
CELLAR 🍷
ALC./VOL. 12.0%
RRP $9.00 ⓢ

Any insomniac will tell you that at 4 a.m. on the TV re-re-reruns of *Cop Shop* they are always drinking Hardys Grand Reserve. Like the flared trousers, the label has changed.

CURRENT RELEASE *non-vintage* This is a semi-dry sparkling wine that is meant as a party propellant. It has a neutral nose, soft body with distinct grape flavours and a clean finish. Serve well chilled and use as a base to a punch.

Hardys Sir James Brut de Brut

QUALITY ♆♆♆
VALUE ★★★
GRAPES pinot noir, chardonnay
REGION various, SA
CELLAR 🍷
ALC./VOL. 12.0%
RRP $14.50

This is meant to be a step up the quality ladder and a step down in sugar level. It shows signs of becoming serious.

CURRENT RELEASE *non-vintage* The wine is a tad tormented by a slightly swampy nose. There are some pinot smells in the background and the palate is dry with some fine bubbles. The finish is also dry. It can be served well chilled at a picnic race meeting.

Hardys Sir James Cuvée

QUALITY ♆♆♆
VALUE ★★★
GRAPES mainly pinot noir and chardonnay
REGION various, SA
CELLAR 🍷
ALC./VOL. 12.5%
RRP $14.50 ⓢ

Sir James 'call me Jim' Hardy is a very likeable and distinguished Australian. He is rightly one of Australia's living wine icons.

CURRENT RELEASE *non-vintage.* Turn up the CD and let the party roar! It's plain but it is fun. There is a slight smoky character plus hints of yeast on the nose. The palate is neutral save of a hint of sweetness and the finish is dry. It can be served well chilled.

Hardys Sir James Vintage

This is the big Kahuna in the Hardys sparkling wine stable. It is big in body as well as alcohol and the grapes come from a very expensive BRL Hardy investment at Hoddles Creek, Vic.
CURRENT RELEASE 1992 Little change since the last review. It has a rich meaty pinot-dominated nose with hints of gunsmoke and burnt toast. The palate is chewy with a creamy mouthfeel. The bubbles are energetic and the finish is dry. It is a substantial wine that would go well with pressed chicken.

QUALITY ████
VALUE ★★★½
GRAPES chardonnay, pinot noir
REGION Yarra Valley, Vic.
CELLAR 1
ALC./VOL. 13.0%
RRP $19.90 Ⓢ

Hugh Hamilton Sparkling Shiraz

This is another recruit to the swelling ranks of the sparkling red clan. It is made in the traditional manner. Maker Hugh Hamilton.
CURRENT RELEASE 1994 This is a rich ripe style with all the old-fashioned values. Sweet fruit is paramount and there is also lots of berry character and the nose is a mix of iron tonic and mushroom smells. The bubbles stop the sweetness being oppressive and the finish is clean and dry. It would be great with turkey and cranberry sauce.

QUALITY ████
VALUE ★★★★
GRAPES shiraz
REGION McLaren Vale, SA
CELLAR 4
ALC./VOL. 11.5%
RRP $18.75

Jane Brook B. D. R. Cabernet Merlot

To be honest we don't know what B. D. R. means. But it is nice to have a little mystery in life.
CURRENT RELEASE non-vintage Open with caution, the pressure is almost lethal. The colour is a mid ruby and the nose has a meaty/yeasty character. This is enlivened by the bubbles and there are some sweet raspberry flavours. The finish is chalky and very dry. It can be served well chilled; try it with char-grilled tuna.

QUALITY ███▌
VALUE ★★★½
GRAPES cabernet sauvignon, merlot
REGION Swan Valley, WA
CELLAR 🍾
ALC./VOL. 11.0%
RRP $19.50

Jane Brook Elizabeth Jane Chardonnay

QUALITY 🍷🍷🍷🍷
VALUE ★★★½
GRAPES chardonnay
REGION Swan Valley, WA
CELLAR 🍾 1
ALC./VOL. 12.8%
RRP $19.50

Scanting on the edge, labelling wise. The wine comes from Western Australia and the winery was one of the first in Australia to be on the Internet.
CURRENT RELEASE 1994 The nose has apple, yeast and citrus aromas. The palate is a mix of sweet and sour plus chardonnay flavours and there is plenty of acid on a crisp finish. It should be served well chilled as a pre-dinner drink.

Jansz Brut Cuvée

QUALITY 🍷🍷🍷🍷
VALUE ★★★
GRAPES pinot noir, chardonnay
REGION Pipers River, Tas.
CELLAR 🍾 3+
ALC./VOL. 12.0%
RRP $29.80

Heemskerk is now part of the JAC group, which includes the Rochecombe and Buchanan vineyards. Maker Steve Goodwin.
Previous outstanding vintages: '91, '92
CURRENT RELEASE 1993 This was slightly disjointed at time of tasting, with the sweetness from the liqueur sitting slightly apart and the acidity also being quite pronounced. The aromas are of dry grass/straw and the fruit is undeniably refined. Should be better balanced in a few months. Try it with crab salad.

Killawarra Brut Crémant

QUALITY 🍷🍷🍷
VALUE ★★★
GRAPES various
REGION not stated
CELLAR ⊂ 1–2
ALC./VOL. 11.0%
RRP $10.00 $

Yet another new label on the crowded bubbly shelves. Crémant, in the rare case it's taken literally, means half-sparkling – with lower gas pressure in the bottle.
CURRENT RELEASE *non-vintage* This wine may need a few months 'on cork', as they say, as it was tasting very shy and closed-up. The nose had a whiff of sulphur and the palate was wispy with some sweetness but not a lot of flavour. Add orange juice for a Buck's Fizz.

Killawarra Premier Brut

This is arguably the sparkling wine of the year. After winning the sparkling trophy at the '96 Sydney Wine Show it made the Sydney International Top 100, where it was one of the bargains of the show. Maker Ian Shepherd.

CURRENT RELEASE 1993 This is the bubbly to serve the brood on Christmas Day – it will bridge the gap between the beer drinkers and the most exacting fizzicists. It is a complex wine with stacks of smoky, bready yeast-derived characters and has plenty of body with a fair degree of liqueuring. Frothy creamy mousse and lovely mouthfeel. Amazing value, discounting as low as $10.99. Serve with salmon roe on blinis.

QUALITY ♛♛♛♛♝
VALUE ★★★★★
GRAPES pinot noir 78%, chardonnay 22%
REGION mainly Coonawarra & Padthaway, SA
CELLAR 🍷 1
ALC./VOL. 11.0%
RRP $13.50 Ⓢ

Killawarra Premier Sparkling Pinot Noir

Killawarra's winemaker Ian Shepherd is looking to produce wines in an original style. There's nothing new under the sun, but this one does have a few unusual points.

CURRENT RELEASE *non-vintage* This has an enticing hot pink hue, echoing the high red grape content. There are creamy, smoky characters in the bouquet from yeast and pinot interaction, and a nice fluffy mousse. The palate has high acidity and a little phenolic thickness on the finish. Serve with smoked salmon blinis.

QUALITY ♛♛♛♝
VALUE ★★★
GRAPES pinot noir
REGION south-eastern Australia 90%, New Zealand 10%
CELLAR 🍷 3
ALC./VOL. 12.0%
RRP $13.50

Kingston Estate Cuvée Premier

Winemaker Bill Moularadellis says the style he's after is crisp, delicate and refreshing. This is his first attempt at bubbly.

CURRENT RELEASE 1995 Faintly pink colour reflecting the pinot grapes. The nose is restrained and candy-like from the pinot, and the taste is light and slightly short but it's a clean, well-made sparkler that certainly is pleasantly refreshing. Chill well and serve with gravlax.

QUALITY ♛♛♛
VALUE ★★★½
GRAPES pinot noir 80%, chardonnay 20%
REGION Riverland, SA
CELLAR 🍷 1
ALC./VOL. 12.0%
RRP $11.00

Lark Hill The Canberra Fizz

QUALITY ▼▼▼▼
VALUE ★★★½
GRAPES pinot noir, chardonnay
REGION Canberra district, NSW
CELLAR 🍾 1–3
ALC./VOL. 12.5%
RRP $22.00

David and Sue Carpenter's first bubbly was 'champanised' for them by Rodney Hooper at Charles Sturt University winery. It spent 24 months on lees.

CURRENT RELEASE 1993 The colour is pale and the nose shows simple peachy, herbal fruit. The palate is light and lacks a little character, tasting mainly of tart green apple. It is a well-made, slightly austere wine that seems to need a little more time. Good with oysters.

Lectus Cuvée

QUALITY ▼▼▼▼
VALUE ★★★★
GRAPES chardonnay 40%, pinot noir 40%, pinot meunier 20%
REGION 'cool areas of Vic.'
CELLAR 🍾 5
ALC./VOL. 12.0%
RRP $29.00

Not a car but a new bubbly from the Mornington Peninsula. Lectus in Latin means 'the very best, first choice, excellent'. High aspirations and maybe high anxiety.

CURRENT RELEASE Cuvée 1/92 An uncompromising style with a yeasty nose and a lively bead. The palate is austere yet complex with a mix of citrus flavours dominated by chardonnay. The finish is dry with an impressive mouth-cleansing quality. It should be served well chilled as a pre-dinner drink.

McWilliams Kanandah Chardonnay Pinot Noir Vintage

QUALITY ▼▼▼▼
VALUE ★★★½
GRAPES chardonnay 68%, pinot noir 32%
REGION Yarra Valley, Vic.
CELLAR 🍾 2
ALC./VOL. 11.5%
RRP $15.30

J.J. McWilliam's dad had a vineyard at Corowa until phylloxera arrived. J.J. then upped sticks and moved to Junee, and eventually Hanwood. Some of his fifth-generation descendants now work for the family firm.

CURRENT RELEASE 1990 This has more cooked-bread yeast development than the NV version, with hints of Vegemite, sweet pinot fruit and some complexity. The flavour is quite rich, dry and full, with lively acid. It could take a decent chill.

McWilliams Kanandah Pinot Noir Chardonnay Brut

Kanandah is Aboriginal for 'land where the sun sets'. This is Macs' cheap and cheerful bottle-fermented fizz.

CURRENT RELEASE *non-vintage* The colour is pale and faintly brassy from the red grape content. The nose is vaguely bready with straw/hay aromas and the taste is pleasingly dry, light-bodied, soft and easy to drink. It would go well with freshly shelled nuts.

QUALITY ♛♛♛
VALUE ★★★½
GRAPES pinot noir, chardonnay
REGION not stated
CELLAR 🍾
ALC./VOL. 11.5%
RRP $9.70 $

Milburn Park Pinot Noir Chardonnay Brut

The Alambie Wine Co., which makes this, was the brainchild of Sunraysia citrus grower Peter McLaren. Milburn Park is the top-priced of several Alambie brands.

CURRENT RELEASE 1994 The nose is shy and elusive, the mouth flavour is all on the fore-palate and falls away towards the finish, but what's there is pleasant enough. While it's fresh, delicate and straightforward, others might see it as bland. Don't overchill. Serve with smoked oysters.

QUALITY ♛♛♛
VALUE ★★★
GRAPES pinot noir, chardonnay
REGION Sunraysia, Vic.
CELLAR 🍾
ALC./VOL. 12.0%
RRP $13.70

Montana Deutz Blanc de Blancs

Although Deutz was taken over by Louis Roederer recently, long-time Deutz boss André Lallier is still involved with Montana.

CURRENT RELEASE 1990 This is remarkably delicate and undeveloped for a six-year-old! The nose is very fine with traces of toastiness and the taste is light-bodied, crisp and appley with fine bubbles. The finish strikes a good balance between dryness and drinkability. Ideal as an aperitif.

QUALITY ♛♛♛♛
VALUE ★★★
GRAPES chardonnay
REGION Marlborough, NZ
CELLAR 🍾 2+
ALC./VOL. 12.0%
RRP $23.00

Montana Deutz Marlborough Cuvée

QUALITY ♥♥♥♥?
VALUE ★★★★
GRAPES pinot noir 60%, chardonnay 40%
REGION Marlborough, NZ
CELLAR ↓ 2
ALC./VOL. 12.0%
RRP $26.50

Montana entered into a joint venture with Champagne Deutz back in 1987, with a view to making better bubbly. The relationship has borne rich fruit. Maker Peter Hubscher and team.

CURRENT RELEASE *non-vintage* Finesse is the key word here. The bouquet is complex with rich, smoky, bready nuances and everything about the wine is subtle and polished. It is very clean and high-tech, and poles apart from anything Deutz produces in Champagne. A stylish sparkling wine to serve with oysters.

Montana Fricanté Méthode Traditionelle

QUALITY ♥♥♥?
VALUE ★★★½
GRAPES not stated
REGION not stated
CELLAR ↓
ALC./VOL. 11.0%
RRP $11.00

Montana is New Zealand's biggest wine producer by far, with over 50 per cent of the total crush. Unusual for a big company, it chooses not to enter its wines in shows.

CURRENT RELEASE *non-vintage* This is made in typical Asti style – a light, simple, fresh, ultra-fruity muscat-flavoured semi-sweet bubbly. It's a real crowd pleaser – good for casual sipping with fresh fruit.

Montana Lindauer Brut

QUALITY ♥♥♥?
VALUE ★★★½
GRAPES pinot noir 60%, chardonnay 20%, chenin blanc 20%
REGION various, NZ
CELLAR ↓
ALC./VOL. 11.5%
RRP $11.75

Montana produces 250 000 cases of this enormously successful bottle-fermented bubbly a year, 75 000 of which find their way to the UK.

CURRENT RELEASE *non-vintage* The nose is fruit-driven, fresh and creamy; the taste light-bodied, delicate and clean. Eighteen months on lees has resulted in the merest hint of autolysis. A technically excellent, well-balanced, very drinkable bubbly. Serve with canapés.

Montana Lindauer Special Reserve

This cuvée differs from the standard Lindauer by being all pinot and chardonnay, some hand-picked and whole-bunch pressed, and having 24 to 30 months on yeast, compared with 18.
CURRENT RELEASE *non-vintage* Pinot noir shows out strongly here – the colour is slightly pink and the bouquet is smoky and very pinoid. It has more weight and character than the standard brew. The palate is creamy and enlivened by crisp acid. Good summer sipping with cucumber sandwiches.

QUALITY 🍷🍷🍷🍷
VALUE ★★★
GRAPES pinot noir 70%, chardonnay 30%
REGION Hawkes Bay & Marlborough, NZ
CELLAR 🍾
ALC./VOL. 11.5%
RRP $16.00

Orlando Carrington Vintage Brut

The latest addition to the Carrington fizz family, which is pretty good value, budget bubbly.
CURRENT RELEASE 1994 A jump up in quality from the standard Carrington non-vintage wines, with a more complex bouquet of light breadiness and a broad, pleasing, if slightly short-finishing, palate.

QUALITY 🍷🍷🍷
VALUE ★★★★
GRAPES various
REGION various
CELLAR 🍾
ALC./VOL. 11.5%
RRP $8.50

Orlando Trilogy

Nice name for a bubbly, reflecting the use of all three classic champagne varieties – the vinous holy trinity. It's Orlando's flagship sparkler, made, like the Carringtons, by the transfer method.
CURRENT RELEASE *non-vintage* A soft, creamy sparkling wine with attractive bready yeast complexity on the bouquet. Soft rather than bone-dry, the palate offers unusually good depth of flavour and interest for the price. Drink with canapés.

QUALITY 🍷🍷🍷🍷
VALUE ★★★★
GRAPES pinot noir 80%, chardonnay 12%, pinot meunier 8%
REGION various, including King Valley, Vic.
CELLAR 🍾
ALC./VOL. 11.5%
RRP $13.50

Red Hill Estate Brut

QUALITY ♛♛♛♛♙
VALUE ★★★★
GRAPES chardonnay 60%, pinot noir 40%
REGION Mornington Peninsula, Vic.
CELLAR 🍾 5
ALC./VOL. 12.6%
RRP $22.00

This is the labour of love of Sir Peter Derham who has semi-retired to the property on the Mornington Peninsula. Maker Jenny Bright.

CURRENT RELEASE 1994 A complex style that shows plenty of winemaking skill. The bubbles are manic and the nose is a mix of apple and cooked bread smells. The palate is complex with citrus, apple and apricot kernel flavours. The finish shows plenty of dry acid and lots of refreshing qualities. It should be served well chilled; try it with smoked chicken.

Schinus The Longest Lunch

QUALITY ♛♛♛♙
VALUE ★★★
GRAPES pinot noir, chardonnay
REGION Coal River Valley, Tas.
CELLAR 🍾 2
ALC./VOL. 11.5%
RRP $20.00 (cellar door)

Garry Crittenden is part-owner of the Tolpuddle vineyard in southern Tasmania, which grows the grapes for this bubbly, as well as supplying Domaine Chandon.

CURRENT RELEASE 1993 A vegetal style with a pale pink colour and an emphasis on sappy, herbaceous pinot noir character. There is yeast character too and the palate opens with a fair degree of sweetness from the liqueuring. Underneath is plenty of full, broad flavour. Chill it well and serve with barbecued mussels.

Seaview Brut de Brut Champagne

QUALITY ♛♛♛
VALUE ★★★½
GRAPES mainly pinot noir, muscadelle, chenin blanc & semillon
REGION various
CELLAR 🍾
ALC./VOL. 11.0%
RRP $8.90

A new addition to the Seaview portfolio, made drier than the standard Brut. Seaview is the only mass-produced bubbly that's fermented in the same bottle in which you buy it.

CURRENT RELEASE *non-vintage* At the cheaper end of the fizz market, winemakers have become expert at producing very soft, low-acid wines that manage to retain freshness. This has plenty of flavour but seems to lack acid, rendering the palate rather dull and flat. But it does have character and some evidence of age on lees, which is good news at the price.

Seaview Edwards & Chaffey Pinot Noir Chardonnay

This is the Edmond Mazure repackaged – Seaview's top-line sparkler. It gets three years on lees. Edwards & Chaffey were not the founders of Seaview, but they made it famous.
Previous outstanding vintages: '89, '90, '91
CURRENT RELEASE 1992 Marked bottle-age shows here, with a toasted bread bouquet and a big, rich, developed flavour that really fills the mouth. It's getting slightly broad and perhaps a little too soft, but there's no denying it is a lovely drink. Try it with canapés.

QUALITY ♛♛♛♛⸺
VALUE ★★★★
GRAPES pinot noir 83%, chardonnay 17%
REGION Strathbogie Ranges, Vic. & Adelaide Hills, SA
CELLAR 🍾 1
ALC./VOL. 12.0%
RRP $24.00

Seaview Pinot Noir Chardonnay

This is the second successive release of this wine to be named Australia Day Wine of the Year, by virtue of the Sydney International Top 100 judging. It gets at least 20 months age on lees.
Previous outstanding vintages: '90, '91, '92
CURRENT RELEASE 1993 For the past four years this has arguably been the best value for money in Oz fizz, often trumping wines double its price in shows. Complex bready bouquet is attractively creamy; a soft and slightly sweet entry followed by plenty of fresh, clean flavour where the quality and delicacy of the fruit really shines. Good balance and dry finish.

QUALITY ♛♛♛♛
VALUE ★★★★½
GRAPES pinot noir, chardonnay
REGION Adelaide Hills, Coonawarra, Padthaway, Eden Valley and Clare, SA; Yarra Valley & Pyrenees, Vic.
CELLAR 🍾 2
ALC./VOL. 11.5%
RRP $15.85

Seppelt Fleur de Lys Pinot Noir Chardonnay

Seppelt makes two Fleurs, a vintage and cheaper non-vintage. They are reliable, quality bubblies at a fair price.
CURRENT RELEASE *non-vintage* Bright medium-yellow colour; the nose shows toasty aged base-wine and the palate is soft and broad and starting to lose its freshness and vibrancy. There is plenty of soft developing flavour and it's fair value for money, especially when discounted.

QUALITY ♛♛♛
VALUE ★★★
GRAPES pinot noir, chardonnay
REGION various
CELLAR 🍾
ALC./VOL. 11.5%
RRP $11.00

Seppelt Fleur de Lys Vintage Brut

QUALITY ♛♛♛♛⌕
VALUE ★★★★
GRAPES pinot noir, chardonnay, pinot meunier
REGION various
CELLAR 🍾 2
ALC./VOL. 11.5%
RRP $15.00

While this also comes from a range of vineyards, they tend to be cooler climatically, producing finer fruit than the non-vintage version. Maker Pamela Geddes.

CURRENT RELEASE 1991 This is serious stuff, the nose showing glacé fruits and strawberry/smoky pinot-like characters. The taste is rich and deep yet very dry on the finish with candy-apple flavour. There's creamy mousse and a well-judged hint of firmness. A serious style of bubbly to serve with caviar.

Seppelt Harpers Range Pinot Noir Chardonnay

QUALITY ♛♛♛♛
VALUE ★★★½
GRAPES pinot noir, chardonnay, pinot meunier
REGION Tumbarumba, Tooma & Barooga, NSW; Drumborg, Vic.
CELLAR 🍾 3
ALC./VOL. 11.0%
RRP $18.00

This is the first release of bubbly with the brandname Harpers Range. It surfs on the fame of the red wine of the same name, which won a Jimmy Watson Trophy. This spent three years on its lees.

CURRENT RELEASE 1991 This is a crisper, friskier, more acidic wine than the Sunday Creek, with a drier finish. The colour is pale and the nose reveals smoky pinot noir fruit and some cracked yeast complexities. A good wine to serve with salmon roe or caviar.

Seppelt Harpers Range Sparkling Burgundy Shiraz

QUALITY ♛♛♛♛
VALUE ★★★
GRAPES shiraz
REGION Clare & Barossa Valleys, SA; Great Western, Geelong & Strathbogie Ranges, Vic.
CELLAR 🍾 5+
ALC./VOL. 13.5%
RRP $18.00

Seppelt created a stir when it scrapped its old splurgundy label for a trendy coloured one. The name reflects a gradual phasing out of the burgundy name.

CURRENT RELEASE 1992 More alcohol, more ripeness, and a higher price. This is a change in style towards a slightly jammy licorice, chocolate, almost porty fruit style, with big rich concentrated palate flavour. There's plenty of tannin and alcohol on the finish. Very long finish and not too sweet. Drink it with Peking duck.

Seppelt Salinger

This is the top of the Seppelt ziggurat, and reflects the very personal style preference of chief winemaker Ian McKenzie for fruit-driven bubblies.
Previous outstanding vintages: '90
CURRENT RELEASE 1991 With a light yellow colour and delicate fruit characters, the emphasis throughout this wine is on freshness. Very much an Australian sparkling wine, it makes no attempt to ape Champagne and while some will think it lacks complexity, it's a delicious drink. The bubbles are fluffy, the balance is superb and the fruit quality shines through like a ray of sunshine. Drink it with oysters.

QUALITY ♛♛♛♛♝
VALUE ★★★★
GRAPES chardonnay, pinot noir
REGION Tumbarumba & Tooma, NSW, Adelaide Hills, SA; Drumborg & Great Western, Vic.
CELLAR 🍾 5
ALC./VOL. 11.0%
RRP $27.80

Seppelt Sunday Creek Pinot Noir Chardonnay

Another new label from Seppelt whose cup runneth over with bubbles. Maker Ian McKenzie.
CURRENT RELEASE *non-vintage* This opens with a lemonade-like lollyish nose, no doubt an expression of the chameleon-like pinot noir, and becomes more bready as it warms in the glass. The taste is full, rich and herbal with accent on fruit in typical house style. Crisp acid balances the liqueur on the finish. A general-purpose aperitif.

QUALITY ♛♛♛♝
VALUE ★★★½
GRAPES pinot noir, chardonnay
REGION Coonawarra & Padthaway, SA; Barooga, NSW; Great Western & Drumborg, Vic.
CELLAR 🍾 2
ALC./VOL. 12.0%
RRP $11.25

Taltarni Blanc de Blanc Tête De Cuvée

QUALITY ♛♛♛♛
VALUE ★★★★
GRAPES chardonnay
REGION Pyrenees, Vic.
CELLAR 🍾
ALC./VOL. 12.0%
RRP $22.00

Forgive the French but the boss is a Frenchman who can't get out of the habit. The translation is this is a chardonnay-based bubbly from the first crush. Maker Greg Gallagher.

CURRENT RELEASE *non-vintage* Very lively mousse and lots of citrus character make this an attractive style. There are some cooked-bread and citrus aromas on the nose. The major flavour is citrus with a leaning to the grapefruit end of the spectrum. The finish has strong acid and a refreshing zing. It should be served well chilled as a pre-dinner drink.

Taltarni Brut Cuvée

QUALITY ♛♛♛♛
VALUE ★★★★★
GRAPES chardonnay, pinot noir, pinot meunier
REGION Pyrenees, Vic.
CELLAR 🍾 1
ALC./VOL. 12.0%
RRP $19.00

This was the first style that started the line of sparkling wine for Taltarni. It was greeted with great enthusiasm when it was marketed in the early 1980s.

CURRENT RELEASE *non-vintage* A straightforward and pleasant style that drinks well. The nose has strong yeast aromas and the palate is grapey with plenty of bubbles. The finish shows plenty of acid and refreshing qualities. It should be served well chilled as a pre-dinner drink.

Taltarni Brut Taché

QUALITY ♛♛♛♛
VALUE ★★★
GRAPES chardonnay, pinot noir
REGION Pyrenees, Vic.
CELLAR 🍾 1
ALC./VOL. 12.5%
RRP $19.00

Taché means stained and in this case that means a dash of red wine to bring up the colour to a delicate pink.

CURRENT RELEASE *non-vintage* The colour is a delicate salmon pink and the nose has plenty of fruit. The palate is quite sweet to start with but this is balanced by a pleasant tart flavour. There is plenty of acid on the finish. Serve it well chilled as a pre-dinner drink.

Tatachilla Sparkling Malbec

A bit of lateral thinking with this Cinderella variety doesn't go astray. The fruity characters are well-suited to this style.
CURRENT RELEASE *non-vintage* The fruit was obviously ripe because it has developed that sweet berry flavour and slightly buttery texture. The nose is full of ripe fruit smells and the bubbles balance the sweetness on the palate. The plum flavours are offset by a trace of tannin on the dry finish. It should be served well chilled; try it with a rhubarb tart.

QUALITY ♟♟♟♟♟
VALUE ★★★★½
GRAPES malbec
REGION Padthaway, SA
CELLAR ∎
ALC./VOL. 14.2%
RRP $16.80

Vasse Felix Extra Brut

This company is very versatile and seems set (with the exception of fortified wines) to have every style in the portfolio. Sparkling wine from this district is very rare.
CURRENT RELEASE *non-vintage* This is a big style and the only criticism is directed at the bead which is a tad coarse. The nose has candied fruit aromas and plenty of yeast influence. The palate is big, soft and round with meaty pinot characters and the citrus influence of chardonnay. The finish is dry and long. It has a Bollinger facet in its make-up. Serve it well chilled with pressed chicken.

QUALITY ♟♟♟♟
VALUE ★★★½
GRAPES pinot noir, pinot meunier, chardonnay
REGION Margaret River, WA
CELLAR ∎ 3
ALC./VOL. 12.0%
RRP $28.35

Wilson's Pinot Chardonnay

Remember the ad campaign: 'Ian Wilson has the frogs on the hop'? It was a valiant attempt by one man with limited resources to break into the premium fizz biz. Sadly, Wilson died an untimely death. The wine continues to be produced at Bridgewater Mill.
CURRENT RELEASE 1993 Great package; pretty good wine, too. The nose has an unusual minty, aromatic pinot fruitiness and the taste is light, attractive and slightly candied – again from pinot noir grapes. There is good intensity and persistence, although not a lot to show for its 18 months on yeast. Try it with crudités.

QUALITY ♟♟♟♟
VALUE ★★★
GRAPES pinot noir 57%, chardonnay 43%
REGION not stated
CELLAR ∎
ALC./VOL. 12.0%
RRP $23.00

Wolf Blass Vintage Brut

QUALITY ♆♆♆♆
VALUE ★★★
GRAPES pinot noir, chardonnay
REGION Eden & Barossa Valleys, SA
CELLAR 🍷
ALC./VOL. 11.0%
RRP $17.20

Méthode champenoise, brut, cuvée ... all these French words. How come Herr Blass never laid a Sekt on us?
CURRENT RELEASE 1994 Refined, fruit-driven fizz that's very much in the Yellowglen mould. It's good, too. Pale young colour, sweet candied pinot noir and herbal chardonnay aromas, and the palate is soft and fruity with good quality grapes apparent. Fairly mono, but a clean refreshing drink.

Yalumba Angas Brut

QUALITY ♆♆♆
VALUE ★★★½
GRAPES various
REGION not stated
CELLAR 🍷
ALC./VOL. 11.5%
RRP $8.70 ⓢ

You have to be a pioneer to have a town named after you, and such was George Fife Angas, squire of Angaston – Yalumba's stamping ground.
CURRENT RELEASE *non-vintage* Candy, lolly, spicy aromas reflect some malolactic fermentation, employed to give the base wine more complexity. Crisp and lightly flavoured, without the obvious sweetness that mars many in its price range. Easy to drink, with a soft finish. Good value, everyday bubbly.

Yalumba Angas Brut Rosé

QUALITY ♆♆♆♆
VALUE ★★★½
GRAPES cabernet sauvignon 50%, others including shiraz, carignan, cinsault, grenache 50%
REGION Murray River, SA
CELLAR 🍷
ALC./VOL. 11.5%
RRP $8.70 ⓢ

A fruit-salad blend which has generally been the quality leader at its price point. Maker Louisa Rose and team.
CURRENT RELEASE *non-vintage* Good freshness here. Light salmon-pink hue; green leafy early harvested cabernet aroma. Opens up with some sweetness from the liqueur, then crisp tangy acid cuts in and also some confectionery/berry red-grape flavour. A commendable rosé to serve with salmon pâté on toast.

Yalumba Cuvée One Prestige Pinot Noir Chardonnay

Long-winded name but this wine delivers where it counts. Sparkling winemaker Louisa Rose recently took over from Geoff Linton, who did much to develop Yalumba's bubbly range.

CURRENT RELEASE *non-vintage* As a non-vintage blend, this shows the benefit of older wine as well as yeast-age, with good bready, biscuity champagne characters. The colour is light and brassy, reflecting the red pinot content. The palate is smooth, smoky and complex, showing secondary characters as well as fruit. A pleasant lighter style to drink with canapés.

QUALITY ▼▼▼▼
VALUE ★★★★
GRAPES pinot noir, chardonnay
REGION 'finest cool-climate sites'
CELLAR 1
ALC./VOL. 12.0%
RRP $16.00

Yalumba Cuvée Two Prestige Cabernet Sauvignon

'Sparkling burgundy' is enjoying a revival, and while the style itself is eccentric enough, Yalumba's cabernet version is even more so. Most of them are made from shiraz.

CURRENT RELEASE *non-vintage* This is a pleasant wine which offers smooth, developed red-wine flavours without being too sweet. Once you've come to terms with the green-leafy cabernet bouquet, it has a savoury palate filled with chocolate and vanilla flavours. A good alternative style that's great to sip around the barbie while you're waiting for the snags to cook.

QUALITY ▼▼▼▼
VALUE ★★★½
GRAPES cabernet sauvignon
REGION Coonawarra, McLaren Vale, Barossa Valley, SA
CELLAR 6
ALC./VOL. 13.0%
RRP $16.00

Yalumba D

QUALITY 🍷🍷🍷🍷⸴
VALUE ★★★½
GRAPES pinot noir, chardonnay
REGION various, including Eden Valley, SA
CELLAR 🍾 3
ALC./VOL. 12.0%
RRP $25.75

A fine wine deserves fine packaging, and the D label and bottle do full justice to what's inside. Maker Geoff Linton has now been kicked upstairs.
Previous outstanding vintages: '90, '91, '92
CURRENT RELEASE 1993 This is an ultra-serious wine with a stiff upper lip. Brilliant light yellow in colour, it has a fine, restrained nose with mild yeastiness and straw/dry grass notes. The palate is restrained and tightly structured with lively acid and a lemony citric tang, very dry on the finish. It seems to reflect chardonnay more than pinot noir. Cries out for oysters.

Yellowglen Brut Crémant

QUALITY 🍷🍷🍷🍷
VALUE ★★★★
GRAPES pinot noir, chardonnay
REGION not stated
CELLAR 🍾
ALC./VOL. 11.5%
RRP $16.00

Although they're the same price and much the same base wine, this often shows up better than the regular Pinot Noir Chardonnay NV Brut in blind tastings. Crémant is supposed to denote a sparkler with half the usual pressure.
CURRENT RELEASE *non-vintage* Candied nose reflecting pinot noir grapes, soft, fruity and with a little toasty yeast development. The palate is generous, soft and fairly dry with liveliness and style. Good with salted pistachios.

Yellowglen Brut Rosé

QUALITY 🍷🍷🍷
VALUE ★★★
GRAPES not stated
REGION not stated
CELLAR 🍾
ALC./VOL. 11.5%
RRP $16.00

Dollar for dollar, the sparkling offerings from Mildara Blass are well behind those of the Southcorp group, but Yellowglen is a hit nonetheless.
CURRENT RELEASE *non-vintage* Mild pink colour goes hand-in-hand with definite red grape aromas. There are herbaceous green cabernet smells with a lolly, sherbety aspect. A basic rosé style, soft, fresh and fruity with a slightly short finish. Fine with smoked salmon blinis.

Yellowglen Cuvée Victoria

These days Yellowglen's sparklers are blended from all over the place, although its roots are at Ballarat. So what this Adelaide Hills/ Eden Valley cuvée has to do with Victoria is a moot point. Previous outstanding vintages: '90, '91
CURRENT RELEASE 1992 A delicate, refined style which has lovely fruit-driven flavour, some complexity of character and good length. The nose shows subtle smoky, bready pinot noir and yeast interaction. The mousse is fluffy and the bubbles frisky. A seamless wine which has delicacy without sacrificing flavour. Try it with shellfish.

QUALITY ♛♛♛♛♝
VALUE ★★★½
GRAPES pinot noir 55%, chardonnay 45%
REGION Adelaide Hills & Eden Valley, SA
CELLAR 🍾 1
ALC./VOL. 11.0%
RRP $28.00

Yellowglen 'Y' Premium

Mildara has a liberal attitude to pinching other wineries' label ideas, and this is a direct borrow from the Californian winery Jordan, which markets a bubbly called 'J'.
CURRENT RELEASE 1990–91 Very much in Yellowglen style: lightly coloured, fresh, young and vibrantly fruity, with little yeastiness but attractive green-apple fruit, a sherbety zesty acid finish and lively bubbles. Not a hugely complex wine but a lovely drink with prawns.

QUALITY ♛♛♛♛♝
VALUE ★★★½
GRAPES chardonnay 55%, pinot noir 45%
REGION Coonawarra & Eden Valley, SA; Yarra Valley & Ballarat, Vic.
CELLAR 🍾 1
ALC./VOL. 11.1%
RRP $21.00

Fortified Wines

All Saints Australian Formula 1 Grand Prix Port

A gift-boxed port which was produced as a memento of Melbourne's first Formula One Grand Prix. Expect to see collectors drag them out, tired and oxidised in 20 years to flog around the auctions.

CURRENT RELEASE *non-vintage* A fairly youthful, grapey, slightly muscaty, very sweet commercial tawny which will interest car freaks more than tawny port true believers. It has plenty of fruit and crowd-pleasing sugar. Can't help imagining Damon Hill shaking a big bottle of this and spraying the vanquished with sticky stuff.

QUALITY ♛♛♛
VALUE ★★½
GRAPES not stated
REGION north-east Vic.
CELLAR 🍾
ALC./VOL. 18.5%
RRP $29.95

All Saints Classic Release Muscat

Under the expert guidance of new owners Brown Brothers, All Saints has emerged from decline to be the showpiece of the Rutherglen district.

CURRENT RELEASE *non-vintage* Medium-deep amber-tawny colour; lovely smoky muscaty fruit nose; quite viscous, oily and sweet on the tongue. A good muscat and typical of the region. Serve with a slice of fruit cake.

QUALITY ♛♛♛♛
VALUE ★★★½
GRAPES red frontignac
REGION Rutherglen, Vic.
CELLAR 🍾
ALC./VOL. 18.0%
RRP $16.50

All Saints Classic Release Tokay

QUALITY ♛♛♛♛♚
VALUE ★★★★
GRAPES muscadelle
REGION Rutherglen, Vic.
CELLAR 🍷
ALC./VOL. 17.0%
RRP $16.50

Best Bargain Fortified

This has an average age of eight years. Tokay is made from white grapes which don't achieve the baumés of the muscats, so it's a less sweet, less alcoholic and marginally lighter style.

CURRENT RELEASE *non-vintage* Essence of tokay! Full amber colour; wonderfully aromatic bouquet of molasses, vanilla and tea-leaf. It's lush, sweet and youthful in the mouth with a trace of spirit astringency on the finish. Lovely balance and length. Sip with blue cheeses.

All Saints Show Reserve Amontillado

QUALITY ♛♛♛♛♚
VALUE ★★★★
GRAPES not stated
REGION Rutherglen, Vic.
CELLAR 🍷
ALC./VOL. 19.0%
RRP $29.00

Sherry is an under-appreciated wine style these days, but amontillado is the one beginners should start on. It's just the thing with soup on a cold winter night.

CURRENT RELEASE *non-vintage* A lovely dry-finishing fino/amontillado atyle, showing lots of flor yeast character and a pale amber colour. Some wood evident and a little richness towards the finish, which lingers well. Serve with quail consommé.

All Saints Show Reserve Old Liqueur Muscat

QUALITY ♛♛♛♛♛
VALUE ★★★★
GRAPES red frontignac
REGION Rutherglen, Vic.
CELLAR 🍷
ALC./VOL. 18.5%
RRP $45.00

A new attraction at All Saints is the Hall of Fame, where you can soak up the history of all 20 local wineries. This muscat made the Sydney International Top 100 in 1996.

CURRENT RELEASE *non-vintage* Explosive stuff! Amazingly concentrated, powerful old muscat with layers of rancio, dried fruit and vanilla flavours that go on and on after the swallow. The nose is more a matter of aged complexity than muscat aromatics. A superior muscat that goes well with Stilton cheese.

All Saints Show Reserve Old Liqueur Tokay

The reborn All Saints has an excellent restaurant called The Terrace, and you can dine outside in fine weather. It's well worth a detour.
CURRENT RELEASE *non-vintage* The age of this wine shows in its excitingly dark, green-edged amber colour. Tremendous complexity of tea leaf, nutty, vanilla and caramel aromas. The palate flavour is smooth, viscous and luscious, with an elegant, balanced and not-too-sweet finish. Great with Mungabareena cheese.

QUALITY ★★★★★
VALUE ★★★★★
GRAPES muscadelle
REGION Rutherglen, Vic.
CELLAR ▪
ALC./VOL. 17.0%
RRP $45.00

All Saints Show Reserve Old Tawny

A working cooper's shop, a museum of old winery and vineyard equipment, and a kids' playground are among the amenities at this renovated old winery.
CURRENT RELEASE *non-vintage* This is a top-rank tawny, with an average age of at least 20 years. The nose is rich and loaded with complex rancio. The palate has richness and power, lots of weight and length of aftertaste, drying with acid and wood tannin the longer it persists, rendering the mouth clean and ready for another sip. Try it with Milawa Gold cheese.

QUALITY ★★★★★
VALUE ★★★★
GRAPES not stated
REGION Rutherglen, Vic.
CELLAR ▪
ALC./VOL. 18.5%
RRP $38.00

Angove's Fino Dry Flor Sherry

Angove's is an old family company that's full of surprises. It has a strong market for this wine, as it does for its Stone's Green Ginger Wine.
CURRENT RELEASE *non-vintage* There's a soft, slightly developed character here and the nutty flor yeast nose has a touch of cheesiness. It is broad and soft in the mouth with a salty flor yeast tang. Could use a little more freshness and life, but a very handy fino at the price, to be served well chilled.

QUALITY ★★★
VALUE ★★★½
GRAPES not stated
REGION Riverland, SA
CELLAR ▪
ALC./VOL. 17.4%
RRP $12.25

Bazzani Vintage Port

QUALITY ♟♟♟♟
VALUE ★★★
GRAPES shiraz
REGION Pyrenees, Vic.
CELLAR 🍾 5
ALC./VOL. 17.5%
RRP $13.00 (375 ml)

It's great to see another example of this style on the market. This one comes in half bottles which is very sensible because it speeds up the maturation.

CURRENT RELEASE 1993 The colour is a relatively young brick-red. The nose is dominated by the heads and tails of the spirit. The palate is ripe with lush blackberry fruit flavours and these are balanced by a very dry finish. It's quite Portuguese in style and is already starting to throw a crust. Try it with Stilton.

Bethany Old Quarry Port

QUALITY ♟♟♟♟
VALUE ★★★½
GRAPES shiraz, grenache
REGION Barossa Valley, SA
CELLAR 🍾 1
ALC./VOL. 18%
RRP $13.50

No, it's not rock hard, the winery is located in an abandoned quarry above the hamlet of Bethany.

CURRENT RELEASE *non-vintage* This is a middleweight with a red colour and hints of tawny brown. The palate tends to be elegant with sweet berry characters that are matched by some mellow spirit on a gentle finish. It is an after-dinner style.

Bethany White Port

QUALITY ♟♟♟
VALUE ★★★
GRAPES muscadelle, frontignac, riesling
REGION Barossa Valley, SA
CELLAR 🍾 1
ALC./VOL. 18%
RRP $13.50

You don't see the term 'white port' on many labels these days. It was once quite popular but it was replaced by cream sherry.

CURRENT RELEASE *non-vintage* The colour is a pale orange and the nose has a strong lactic character. The palate has hints of honey plus some sweet dried-fruit flavours. The finish has gentle spirit. It could be served chilled.

Bleasdale Pioneer Port

This is a long-standing line from one of the pioneers of the Langhorne Creek district.

CURRENT RELEASE *non-vintage* This is an interesting style that uses a white grape variety in the mix. The nose has rancio and dried-fruit aromas. The palate is complex with vanilla, dried fruit and a mouth-filling texture. The finish balances the sweetness on the palate with some clean spirit. Try it with coffee and petit fours.

QUALITY ♕♕♕♕
VALUE ★★★★
GRAPES shiraz, grenache, verdelho
REGION Langhorne Creek, SA
CELLAR ╽
ALC./VOL. 18.0%
RRP $18.00

Brown Brothers Late Bottled Vintage Port

If vintage port is a misunderstood style, the 'late bottled' version simply does not compute these days. Space doesn't permit a full explanation but sit back, sip and enjoy. Maker Neil Jericho.

CURRENT RELEASE 1986 The colour vacillates between deep brick-red and tawny brown. The nose has sweet developed fruit flavours and clean spirit. The palate is medium to full-bodied with sweet shiraz-berry flavours. The finish has attractive length with well-rounded wood characters and a hint of tannin. It is just the thing for a cheese platter and mixed nuts.

QUALITY ♕♕♕♕
VALUE ★★★★
GRAPES shiraz
REGION north-east Vic.
CELLAR ╽
ALC./VOL. 18.0%
RRP $17.60

Brown Brothers Liqueur Muscat

A long-enduring style that is running against the odds. While sales of fortified wines decline, this wine seems to be attracting more attention.

CURRENT RELEASE *non-vintage* The modified solera system employed in production adds a homogeneous quality to the wine. It is a blend of several years with intense raisin characters on the nose. On the palate you'll find dried fruit, sweet berries and a touch of rancio. The texture is syrupy yet this is freshened by some dusty oak and cleansing acid. Good after dinner with coffee, chocolate and good chat.

QUALITY ♕♕♕♕♕
VALUE ★★★★½
GRAPES red frontignac
REGION north-east Vic.
CELLAR ╽
ALC./VOL. 18.0%
RRP $24.00

Brown Brothers Reserve Muscat

QUALITY ♀♀♀♀
VALUE ★★★★
GRAPES red frontignac
REGION north-east Vic.
CELLAR 🍷
ALC./VOL. 18.0%
RRP $15.25

Are the Brothers Brown republicans? Where's the 'Royal' in front of the Reserve? In this case reserve means the economy model.

CURRENT RELEASE *non-vintage* A real sweetie for a reasonable price. The colour is a mid-amber and there are dried-fruit aromas on the nose. The palate is rich and sweet with straightforward muscat fruit flavour and a syrup-like texture. The finish is dry and there is also a hint of dusty oak. It is great with fruit cake.

Brown Brothers Reserve Port

QUALITY ♀♀♀
VALUE ★★★
GRAPES shiraz, grenache, mataro, carignan, cabernet sauvignon
REGION north-east Vic.
CELLAR 🍷
ALC./VOL. 18.0%
RRP $12.20

This wine is in a market niche all by itself. It is priced to go but also has more complexity than could be expected for the reasonable price.

CURRENT RELEASE *non-vintage* A young fruity style with hints of older material. The nose is fruity and the colour is mid-amber. The palate is plummy with some nutty characters, and vanilla is thrown in for good measure. The finish has clean spirit and good balance. Good to sip while watching *X Files*.

Brown Brothers Very Old Port

QUALITY ♀♀♀♀
VALUE ★★★★
GRAPES shiraz
REGION north-east Vic.
CELLAR 🍷
ALC./VOL. 18.5%
RRP $23.70

Old-time drinkers can recall when this was a very limited release that was bottled in a clear Baitz liqueur bottle. Since then the bottle and style have changed.

CURRENT RELEASE *non-vintage* The beat goes on, this wine is almost a constant. It is a middleweight tawny with a mid-brown colour and the nose has rancio and raisin characters as well as some earthy wood. There are dried-fruit flavours on the palate plus a touch of rancio and a whisper of chocolate. The finish shows off cleansing acid and clean spirit. Great with a politically incorrect cigar after dinner.

Brown Brothers Very Old Tokay

This style has been described as 'liquid Christmas pudding'. It is an apt description for the wines that result.

CURRENT RELEASE *non-vintage* The nose is strident with mixed fruit and mature wine aromas. There are also distinct malt extract and caramel aromas. The palate is concentrated with toffee and treacle flavours and there is a marked rancio character. The finish has fresh acid and a cleansing quality. It is great with sticky date pudding.

QUALITY ♛♛♛♛♛
VALUE ★★★★½
GRAPES muscadelle
REGION north-east Vic.
CELLAR ╬
ALC./VOL. 18.5%
RRP $28.50

Buller & Son (R. L.) Aged Madeira

Misnamed to be sure, this wine hangs out in the sherry fringe. It could be described as a medium dry amontillado. Maker Dick Buller.

CURRENT RELEASE *non-vintage* The colour is a light, lustrous amber and the nose has rancio and lactic aromas. The palate is medium sweet with a background of nutty rancio. It is balanced by some warming spirit and clean acid. It's great mid-afternoon with tea cake.

QUALITY ♛♛♛♛♛
VALUE ★★★★½
GRAPES not stated
REGION Rutherglen, Vic.
CELLAR ╬ 1
ALC./VOL. 17.8%
RRP $19.50

Buller & Son (R. L.) Liqueur Port

Traditionally liqueur port is made by storing the barrels as close as possible to the tin roof of the winery to promote evaporation.

CURRENT RELEASE *non-vintage* The colour is a deep ruby and the nose has cheese and berry characters. The palate has a rich texture with sweet shiraz fruit flavours. There is warming alcohol on a dry finish. It is meant for after-dinner drinking.

QUALITY ♛♛♛♛
VALUE ★★★★
GRAPES shiraz
REGION Rutherglen, Vic.
CELLAR ╬ 1
ALC./VOL. 17.8%
RRP $19.50

Buller & Son (R. L.) Muscat

QUALITY ♠♠♠♠½
VALUE ★★★★½
GRAPES red frontignac
REGION Rutherglen, Vic.
CELLAR 🍾 1
ALC./VOL. 17.8%
RRP $19.50

This is the region's motherlode and Buller has always been one of the names to watch for when it comes to quality. This wine is made in a solera system.
CURRENT RELEASE *non-vintage* The colour is a deep tawny brown and there is dried-fruit and rich rancio characters on the nose. The palate is deep and rich with raisins and prune flavours. The sweetness is mouth-filling. There is a persistent raisin flavour on the finish which is marked by acid and spirit. It is great with soft cheese and nuts.

Buller & Son (R. L.) Tawny Port

QUALITY ♠♠♠♠
VALUE ★★★★
GRAPES shiraz
REGION Rutherglen, Vic.
CELLAR 🍾 1
ALC./VOL. 17.8%
RRP $19.50

Buller's winery at Rutherglen offers a rustic cellar door and a substantial bird park to entertain children and adults alike.
CURRENT RELEASE *non-vintage* This is a well-balanced style poised between age and freshness. The colour is a medium brick-red and the nose is a mix of dusty oak and dried-fruit aromas. The medium-bodied palate has intense raisin characters plus a rancio background. There is also an element of freshness and some lively spirit on the finish. Serve after dinner.

Campbells Liquid Gold Tokay

A sexy new concept in packaging to celebrate Campbells' 125th anniversary. This is a partner to the same maker's Rutherglen Muscat, in the same tall, heavy, elegant half-litre bottle. Maker Colin Campbell.

CURRENT RELEASE *non-vintage* A charming, seductive wine, without particular aged rancio but incredible clarity and intensity of tokay fruit and lusciousness. The colour is lightish amber and the nose has wonderfully intense honey, tea-leafy, vanilla nuances. The palate is very sweet and powerful, with lots of toffee on the finish. Positively addictive. Have it with caramels and coffee.

QUALITY ?????
VALUE ★★★★
GRAPES muscadelle
REGION Rutherglen, Vic.
CELLAR ♦
ALC./VOL. 17.5%
RRP $35.00 (500ml)

Campbells Rutherglen Muscat

This is the first wine to be labelled with the new 'Muscat of Rutherglen' regional logo. The logo was the brainchild of a clubbing together of the district's muscat makers in 1995 to dream up ways to promote muscat.

CURRENT RELEASE *non-vintage* This is truly delicious muscat, very rich, sweet and luscious yet fresh and fruity. It has a full tawny-amber colour and there is some wood-aged rancio, but it is more about lusciousness and intense muscat flavour. Raisin and rose-petal characters, plenty of body and an emphatic finish with terrific length. Great with brandied figs and mascarpone.

QUALITY ?????
VALUE ★★★★
GRAPES red frontignac
REGION Rutherglen, Vic.
CELLAR ♦
ALC./VOL. 17.5%
RRP $35.00 (500ml)

Campbells Vintage Port

QUALITY ♛♛♛
VALUE ★★½
GRAPES touriga
REGION Rutherglen, Vic.
CELLAR 🍾 4
ALC./VOL. 18.0%
RRP $21.30

Touriga is one of the superior grapes used in Portuguese ports, but rarely seen in Australia. Maker Colin Campbell.

CURRENT RELEASE 1988 A mature VP but, alas, one which doesn't scale the heights. A somewhat dry reddish style which lacks spirit complexity. The bouquet hints at black olives, cherry skin and leather, and the taste is smooth, mild and easy to drink. Try it with a mild blue cheese like True Blue.

Cassegrain Cassaé

QUALITY ♛♛♛♛♝
VALUE ★★★½
GRAPES not stated
REGION Hastings Valley, NSW
CELLAR 🍾
ALC./VOL. 18.0%
RRP $18.95 (375ml)

This is a fortified, wood-aged grape juice in a style reminiscent of the Cognac district's Pineau des Charentes. The latest blend is the best yet; age has improved it. Maker John Cassegrain.

CURRENT RELEASE *non-vintage* The colour has a brown tint: medium orange/amber, reflecting oxidation in the barrel. The nose has caramel and vanilla, citrus peel and traces of wood-aged rancio. A very unusual, yet complex, sweet aperitif style with balanced oak and a hot spirity finish that lingers impressively long. Chill as an aperitif or serve with cheese and fruit after dinner.

Chambers Rosewood Amontillado Sherry

QUALITY ♛♛♛♛
VALUE ★★★½
GRAPES not stated
REGION Rutherglen, Vic.
CELLAR 🍾
ALC./VOL. 19.1%
RRP $24.00

This wine is classically dry: Bill Chambers prefers the traditional Spanish style of amontillado to the more usual, sweetened Australian styles.

CURRENT RELEASE *non-vintage* The colour is light-medium amber; the nose shows lots of flor yeast character and a touch of vanilla. In the mouth it's very dry and there are fine vanilla, dried-peel, flor and wood characters. An austere but lovely style that will not appeal to everyone. Serve with tapas.

Chateau Reynella Vintage Port

Reynella is arguably the most famous name in Australian vintage port. Although made side by side with Hardys today, they are contrasting styles.
Previous outstanding vintages: '67, '71, '75, '77, '79, '81, '82, '87
CURRENT RELEASE 1993 A classic of its style: very dense vivid purple, and the nose dominated by floral aromatic spirit. Together with the rich plummy, blackberry fruit this gives a licorice-like aroma and flavour. It's an immensely rich, warming port with powerful fruit and tannin that dries the finish and leaves the mouth with a pronounced grip to counter the early sweetness. Needs five years cellaring minimum. Then serve with Stilton.

QUALITY 🍷🍷🍷🍷🍷
VALUE ★★★★★
GRAPES shiraz
REGION McLaren Vale, SA
CELLAR 🍾 5–15+
ALC./VOL. 20.0%
RRP $18.00

Best Fortified Wine

Currency Creek Old Barrel White Port

There are not too many white ports floating about. But Phil Tonkin's is definitely a wine for heroes. It was made from botrytis-affected riesling, aged for 10 years in old Jim Beam barrels.
CURRENT RELEASE *non-vintage* Very rich and complex with plenty of wood-aged character, mild sweetness and a powerful, dry, lingering finish that satisfies thoroughly. A fascinating style and well worth hunting down.

QUALITY 🍷🍷🍷🍷
VALUE ★★★½
GRAPES riesling
REGION Currency Creek, SA
CELLAR 🍾
ALC./VOL. 19.5%
RRP $18.70 (375ml)

d'Arenberg Nostalgia

QUALITY ♛♛♛♛
VALUE ★★★★½
GRAPES grenache, shiraz
REGION McLaren Vale, SA
CELLAR 🍾
ALC./VOL. 13.5%
RRP $16.00

Port has always been an item on the d'Arenberg list. If nothing else it was something to take on fishing trips in the '50s by maker D'Arry Osborn. This means there is plenty of aged material to use as a base for blending.

CURRENT RELEASE *non-vintage* This is a very sweet liqueur style backed up by some fresh acid on a bracing finish. The colour is amber with hints of orange. The nose is quite complex with vanilla, peel, caramel and rancio characters. The palate is medium-bodied and complex with dried-fruit characters and rancio flavours and the finish lingers long with fresh acidity.

d'Arenberg Vintage Port

QUALITY ♛♛♛♛
VALUE ★★★★
GRAPES shiraz
REGION McLaren Vale, SA
CELLAR 🍾 6
ALC./VOL. 17.0%
RRP $17.90

Blessed be the vintage port makers because verily we say unto thee – this is an endangered style that is too good to be lost. Maker Chester Osborn.

CURRENT RELEASE 1993 Made from grapes from old shiraz vines. The nose has spirit and ripe fruit aromas. The chewy palate has blackberry flavours with a hint of iron tonic. There is tannin and spirit on a clean dry finish. It drinks well but cellaring will enhance the style. Try it with walnuts and Stilton.

De Bortoli Liqueur Muscat 10 Year Old

QUALITY ♛♛♛♛♛
VALUE ★★★★★
GRAPES red frontignac
REGION Riverina, SA; Rutherglen, Vic.
CELLAR 🍾
ALC./VOL. 19.0%
RRP $13.00

Just between us, and don't tell anyone else, this is one of the best grabs from the bottle shop. There is a tad of Rutherglen injected into the blend.

CURRENT RELEASE *non-vintage* Like biting into a bunch of fresh red frontignac berries. It explodes in the mouth. The nose is fragrant with spirit and dried fruit aromas. The palate is a mix of treacle and dried fruit but there are also some fresh elements. The finish shows some high-toned spirit. Great with coffee and a box of chocolates.

Fairfield Liqueur Tokay

Fairfield is an historic site in the Rutherglen district that would make a perfect wine museum. It makes a small quantity of fine wine.

CURRENT RELEASE *non-vintage* This is a lovely spicy fortified that shows poise and great balance. The colour is honey gold and the nose offers honey, apricot and a hint of almond aromas. The medium-bodied palate is flavoured with apricots and spice. There is some warming spirit on a satisfying finish. It is great over vanilla ice cream.

QUALITY 🍷🍷🍷🍷⁄
VALUE ★★★★½
GRAPES muscadelle
REGION Rutherglen, Vic.
CELLAR 🍾 1
ALC./VOL. 18.0%
RRP $18.00

Hardys Show Port

There is a long history to this wine. Before the laws changed it used to bear a vintage year. The last was 1954 and these became collectors' items. The quality of the wine has never flagged.

CURRENT RELEASE *non-vintage* Is this a port? It is dry enough to be a sherry style. The nose shows full-blown rancio characters with peel, nuts, vanilla and malt. The palate is similar, complex with mixed flavours and a dry finish à la sherry. The complexity is a big bonus and the finish has grand length. Sip after dinner with a Cuban cigar.

QUALITY 🍷🍷🍷🍷🍷
VALUE ★★★★½
GRAPES shiraz, grenache
REGION various SA
CELLAR 🍾
ALC./VOL. 19.5%
RRP $35.00

Hardys Tall Ships Tawny Port

What looked like a once-off to commemorate 1988 and the square riggers entering Sydney harbour continues. Either they made too much or Sir Jim wants a nautical theme in the portfolio.

CURRENT RELEASE *non-vintage* Great value for money, it got the gong in last year's *Guide*. It remains a textbook tawny with a red-brown colour. The nose smells of raisins and dried peels. The palate is quite fruity with sweet raisined fruit plus prunes and a hint of rancio. The finish shows mellow brandy spirit. Sip after dinner.

QUALITY 🍷🍷🍷🍷
VALUE ★★★★
GRAPES not stated
REGION McLaren Vale, SA
CELLAR 🍾
ALC./VOL. 17.5%
RRP $10.00 $

Hardys Vintage Port

QUALITY ♟♟♟♟
VALUE ★★★½
GRAPES shiraz
REGION McLaren Vale, SA
CELLAR 🍾 9
ALC./VOL. 19.0%
RRP $22.00

A distinguished line-up of older back numbers is a great way to find out what vintage port is all about. These days they are almost a quirky style that brings a tear to the eye of nostalgia buffs. Hardys take the trouble to age theirs before release.
Previous outstanding vintages: '47, '55, '69, '70, '71, '72, '75, '76, '78, '81
CURRENT RELEASE 1983 Little change since the last review (things happen slowly with VP). The nose is about diesel and dust. It has a petroleum character and underlying blackberry fruit and brandy. It's still a big style with a rousing palate of blackberry flavours from extractive fruit. The domineering tannin on the finish has a trace of bitterness. It's a bruiser; serve it with ripe, crusty Stilton.

Hardys Whiskers Blake Tawny Port

QUALITY ♟♟♟
VALUE ★★★
GRAPES not stated
REGION McLaren Vale, Riverland, Barossa Valley, SA
CELLAR 🍾 9
ALC./VOL. 18.0%
RRP $11.50 ⓢ

Profoundly deaf and heavily whiskered, Blake was an old duffer in the service of the Hardy family. His claim to fame was scaring birds with a shotgun. These days he would have retired with a big fat Work Cover claim for industrial deafness.
CURRENT RELEASE *non-vintage* A lighter style with a medium amber/tawny colour. There are dried fruit and spirit aromas on the nose. The palate is medium-bodied with sweet fruit flavours and hints of dried apricot. The finish shows some firm spirit on a lingering finish. After dinner.

Jim Barry Old Walnut Tawny Port

Here's a wine with an identity crisis: is it a tawny or is it an old sweet white? What's in a name? It's what is in the glass that counts.

CURRENT RELEASE *non-vintage* It is a lovely old fortified wine of some kind. The colour is light amber and the nose offers abundant nutty aroma like an oloroso sherry. The palate is sweet and mellow with vanilla and caramel flavours and there is cleansing acid on the finish. Try it with Anzac biscuits.

QUALITY ♛♛♛♛
VALUE ★★★
GRAPES not stated
REGION Clare Valley, SA
CELLAR 🍾
ALC./VOL. 18.5%
RRP $55.00

Jim Barry Sentimental Bloke Port

When this wine was first released in the mid-'70s, Clare was claiming C. J. Dennis as a local hero. These days the packaging looks a tad corny.

CURRENT RELEASE *non-vintage* There is a good balance between the young material and the aged rancio portion. The nose is nutty with caramel and vanilla aromas. The palate is quite fruity and sweet with hints of raisins and there is clean acid on the finish. An after-dinner tipple.

QUALITY ♛♛♛¿
VALUE ★★★
GRAPES not stated
REGION Clare Valley, SA
CELLAR 🍾
ALC./VOL. 18.5%
RRP $24.00

Kay Brothers Centenary Very Old Tawny Port

Brothers Frederick and Herbert Kay founded this winery in 1890. Their descendants bottled this port to commemorate the centenary.

CURRENT RELEASE *non-vintage* Here's a port that shows lots of age as well as real red grape richness. With a tawny-brown colour, it smells very complex with stacks of rancio and some old woodsy smells. It is very rich and powerful in the mouth with tremendous length and power. It goes on and on with a warm harmonious aftertaste. Goes well with Stilton cheese.

QUALITY ♛♛♛♛¿
VALUE ★★★★
GRAPES not stated
REGION McLaren Vale, SA
CELLAR 🍾
ALC./VOL. 19.0%
RRP $25.00 (375ml)

Kay Brothers Tawny Port

QUALITY ♟♟♟
VALUE ★★★
GRAPES not stated
REGION McLaren Vale, SA
CELLAR ♦
ALC./VOL. 18.0%
RRP $15.00

Port sales have lifted recently, which gives hope to the beleaguered port-makers of the wine industry.

CURRENT RELEASE *non-vintage* This is a decent middle-rank port with some genuine wood-aged character adding interest to the dominant younger, fruity material. The colour is correct medium tawny-amber; the nose has hints of walnut and the palate is smooth and sweet. Good after-dinner sipping.

Kay's Amery Liqueur Muscat

QUALITY ♟♟♟
VALUE ★★★
GRAPES red frontignac
REGION McLaren Vale, SA
CELLAR ♦
ALC./VOL. 18.0%
RRP $15.00

McLaren Vale is not as famous for muscat as it is for port, but there are some credit-worthy efforts. Maker Colin Kay.

CURRENT RELEASE *non-vintage* This might lack the well-defined muscat fruit of the best Rutherglennies, but it's a pleasant drink. The colour is medium amber, the nose a matter of caramel and vanilla, and the taste is sweet and plain and lacks a little in luscious muscat fruit. Makes a decent ice cream topping.

Lauriston Show Muscat

QUALITY ♟♟♟♟♟
VALUE ★★★★★
GRAPES red frontignac
REGION not stated
CELLAR ♦
ALC./VOL. 19.5%
RRP $21.00

The other side of the Lauriston show coin and equally well decorated and very highly regarded. Although the origin of the fruit is not stated the style is different from that at Rutherglen.

CURRENT RELEASE *non-vintage* The blend for this wine goes back over 20 years. The nose is very complex with powerful muscat and dried-fruit aromas. The palate is complex with crushed berries, mixed peel and muscat flavours. The finish has dusty, dry characters and a lingering wood rancio and warming spirit. It is great with a very moist brandy laden fruit cake.

Lauriston Show Port

This is a part of the BRL Hardy group. The winery started life as Angle Vale in the early '70s. The material for this wine was obviously drawn from Berri, Renmano and Hardy stocks.

CURRENT RELEASE *non-vintage* A very complex style that could be classed as a liqueur style. The colour is an orange tawny and the nose leaps out of the glass with rancio and spirit aromas. The palate is an enjoyable mix of dried fruit, orange peel, mandarin, rancio and toffee flavours. These are enhanced by clean acid and warming spirit. It is great after dinner.

QUALITY ♥♥♥♥♥
VALUE ★★★★★
GRAPES not stated
REGION not stated
CELLAR 🍶
ALC./VOL. 18.5%
RRP $21.00

Lindemans CP 74 Reserve Oloroso Sherry

Another guessing game with the bin number. The CP stands for Chris Pfeiffer who worked for Lindemans as a fortified winemaker from 1974 to 1985. The minimum age of the blend is 15 years old.

CURRENT RELEASE *non-vintage* Lovely old fortified that can't be trifled with, it needs serious consideration. There is a deep amber colour and much rancio rousing the nose. The palate has impressive depth and there is mellow sweetness and fruit cake flavours which are balanced by clean acid on an incisive finish. Just the thing for tiffin with some tea cake and Aunt Agatha.

QUALITY ♥♥♥♥♥
VALUE ★★★★★
GRAPES pedro ximinez, palomino, trebbiano
REGION Corowa, NSW
CELLAR 🍶
ALC./VOL. 18.0%
RRP $23.00

Lindemans Macquarie Tawny Port

QUALITY 🍷🍷🍷🍷
VALUE ★★★★
GRAPES grenache, shiraz
REGION Barossa Valley, SA
CELLAR 🍾
ALC./VOL. 18.5%
RRP $14.50

New livery for this long enduring wine. The new label probably means there is a new brand manager on the block. Changing labels is a bit like a dog marking out its territory.
CURRENT RELEASE *non-vintage* The colour is light amber and the nose has a hint of rancio plus raisined fruit. The palate is medium-bodied and on the dry side. While it avoids sweetness it is quite rich and there is refreshing acid and clean spirit on the finish. Great after dinner with a cigar.

Lindemans Reserve Amontillado Sherry Z898A

QUALITY 🍷🍷🍷🍷🍷
VALUE ★★★★★
GRAPES pedro ximinez, palomino
REGION Corowa, NSW; Barossa Valley, SA
CELLAR 🍾
ALC./VOL. 19.0%
RRP $23.00

Don't ask about the bin number, we don't know. The wine in this blend starts as RP 10 fino sherry and selected barrels are put aside for further cellar-age. The average age of the blend is 15 years old.
CURRENT RELEASE *non-vintage* This isn't the frowzy, full-blown style; there is a whisper of sweetness and freshness that keeps the wine alive. The nose is nutty with well-defined rancio character. The palate is smooth and mouth-filling with that tad of sweetness adding weight. The finish is beautifully dry. It is brilliant with a gamey soup. How about a squab consommé?

Lindemans Reserve Madeira 1940 Solera

Worth bribing your wine merchant to get you a bottle, this is a very limited release and as the label suggests the solera was started in 1940 and the youngest wine in the blend is 15 years old. It's not really like a madeira but it is in a category all of its own.

CURRENT RELEASE *non-vintage* A classic with great complexity and style. Rancio character dominates the nose and as a salute to Madeira there is also a hint of burnt rope. The palate is soft with delicate fruit flavours. The mellow character is juxtaposed by clean acid on a lengthy finish. It is spectacular with a game or beef consommé

QUALITY ♛♛♛♛♛
VALUE ★★★★★
GRAPES palomino, trebbiano, semillon, verdelho
REGION Corowa, Hunter Valley, NSW; Rutherglen, Vic.
CELLAR 🍾 1
ALC./VOL. 18.0%
RRP $23.00

Lindemans Reserve Rutherglen Liqueur Tokay WH2

The bin number gives an oblique clue to the origin of the solera. The base material was purchased from W. H. Chambers in Rutherglen. The average age of the material in the blend is 12 years.

CURRENT RELEASE *non-vintage* The apotheosis of a Rutherglen tokay, the wine has a deep amber-green colour and a powerful bouquet of malt extract and cold black tea. There is a velvety smoothness on the palate which offers a sensuous mix of sweet fruit and wood age. The finish is like a smooth follow-through on a grooved golf swing. It is brilliant with genuinely homemade vanilla ice cream.

QUALITY ♛♛♛♛♛
VALUE ★★★★★
GRAPES muscadelle
REGION Corowa, NSW; Rutherglen, Vic.
CELLAR 🍾
ALC./VOL. 18.0%
RRP $23.00

Lindemans Reserve Tawny Port RF1

QUALITY ♦♦♦♦♦
VALUE ★★★★★
GRAPES shiraz, grenache
REGION Barossa Valley, SA; Corowa, NSW
CELLAR 🍷
ALC./VOL. 19.0%
RRP $23.00

'Benchmark, beacon, definitive, brilliant,' call it what you will, all the adjectives apply. The solera was based on wine bought from Gramp's at Rowland Flat in the early '50s. That explains the bin number.

CURRENT RELEASE *non-vintage* This is like balancing a full wine glass on the point of a sabre. It is so fine, complex and mellow. The nose has nutty rancio characters and the palate is complex with vanilla, chocolate and developed fruit flavours. The finish is masterful with hints of new oak, young wine and fine spirit. A great wine for coffee, cigars and a game of poker.

Lindemans RP10 Fino Sherry

QUALITY ♦♦♦♦♦
VALUE ★★★★★
GRAPES palomino, pedro ximinez, monbadon
REGION Barossa valley, SA; Corowa, NSW
CELLAR 🍷
ALC./VOL. 18.0%
RRP $23.00

Will we hear the last post for sherry-making in Australia? With stuff like this around we hope not. The solera started in Corowa, NSW, and these days it is matured in the Barossa Valley.

CURRENT RELEASE *non-vintage* This is a fine example of a fino style. It is bleached straw in colour with a star bright lustre. The nose has nutty rancio aromas, yeast and spirit. The palate is suitably dry and austere. It is mouth-cleansing with outstanding length and freshness. It makes a great pre-dinner drink and could be served chilled.

McWilliams Show Series Amontillado

QUALITY ♦♦♦♦♦
VALUE ★★★★½
GRAPES palomino, pedro ximinez
REGION Riverina, NSW
CELLAR 🍷
ALC./VOL. 18.5%
RRP $27.40

If you want to be controversial at dinner parties, just declare that the Riverina makes some of the greatest wines in Australia. Then produce a bottle of this.

CURRENT RELEASE *non-vintage* A great Australian sherry, pale amber in hue, smelling powerfully of the rancio that comes with extreme wood-age, and as complex as all-get-out to taste. This is a little sweeter than some show amontillados, but to most palates it's dry. Goes beautifully with consommé.

McWilliams Show Series MCW 11 Liqueur Muscat

This is an ancient show blend that Macs have been tinkering with over the years. Perhaps it's not as muscaty as Rutherglen's best, but it's a great fortified.
CURRENT RELEASE *non-vintage* This is a dark, treacley coloured, sump-oily thing that will blow your brains apart. The concentration is awesome, the flavour intensity, power and length of aftertaste will make the hair stand up on the back of your neck. Wonderful with chocolates and coffee.

QUALITY 🍷🍷🍷🍷🍷
VALUE ★★★★½
GRAPES red frontignac
REGION Riverina, NSW
CELLAR 🍾
ALC./VOL. 18.5%
RRP $46.00

McWilliams Show Series Oloroso Sherry

Macs are one of the few wine companies with extensive stocks of old sherry, perhaps because they're a family company and don't have to make every drop pay its rent.
CURRENT RELEASE *non-vintage* This is one of the great wine styles, a winter warmer to serve with a bowl of hearty soup. The colour is medium-amber, the nose is complex with flor yeast among the nutty, rancio aged characters and the palate has classic intensity and length, finishing quite dry with spirit and wood. Simply sublime.

QUALITY 🍷🍷🍷🍷🍷
VALUE ★★★★½
GRAPES palomino, pedro ximinez
REGION Riverina, NSW
CELLAR 🍾
ALC./VOL. 19.5%
RRP $27.40

Morris Black Label Liqueur Muscat

Morris's have repackaged their fortifieds and these replace the cheaper Mick Morris series, which has been deleted now that Mick has retired. His son David now makes the wine.
CURRENT RELEASE *non-vintage* A fresh, young, grapey muscat with straightforward fruity style and just a hint of wood-aged character. The palate is very sweet, slightly syrupy, clean and up-front. Good as an ice-cream topping.

QUALITY 🍷🍷🍷
VALUE ★★★
GRAPES red frontignac
REGION Rutherglen, Vic.
CELLAR 🍾
ALC./VOL. 17.5%
RRP $10.30

Morris Black Label Old Tawny Port

QUALITY	♀♀♀
VALUE	★★★
GRAPES	not stated
REGION	Rutherglen, Vic.
CELLAR	🍾
ALC./VOL.	17.5%
RRP	$10.30

This is the youngest of the Morris tawnies. What constitutes an old tawny? Good question; there's no requirement.

CURRENT RELEASE *non-vintage* Straightforward commercial port with raisiny, grapey fruit aroma, and a gentle touch of wood-aged character. It's quite sweet and lively on the palate and finishes much shorter than the dearer ports, although it offers fair value for money.

Mountadam Ratafia Pinot Noir

QUALITY	♀♀♀♀½
VALUE	★★★★
GRAPES	pinot noir
REGION	Eden Valley, SA
CELLAR	🍾
ALC./VOL.	18.5%
RRP	$20.00 (375 ml)

Here's an interesting point of departure, ratafia is a fortified table wine that should be drunk cold. One theory goes it was the wine used to toast the ratification of a peace treaty, hence the name ratafia.

CURRENT RELEASE *non-vintage* The colour is a pretty party-frock pink and the nose is loaded with ripe strawberry aromas. The palate is intense with strong, sweet strawberry flavours. The finish is clean and fresh with a hint of warming alcohol. It makes a very entertaining pre-dinner drink. Serve very well chilled.

Mountadam Ratafia Riesling

QUALITY	♀♀♀♀
VALUE	★★★★½
GRAPES	riesling
REGION	Eden Valley, SA
CELLAR	🍾
ALC./VOL.	18.0%
RRP	$20.00 (375 ml)

The wine is aged in old (i.e. almost neutral in terms of flavour input) casks. It is fortified and the essential element is the preservation of varietal flavour. Full marks for the high camp art-deco label!

CURRENT RELEASE *non-vintage* The colour is a bright green-gold and the nose has strong aromatics plus a waft of spirit. It is riesling to the core on the palate. There are lemon and lime flavours with plenty of depth. The finish is clean with a zing of fresh acid. Serve well chilled as a pre-dinner drink to startle your guests who were expecting champagne or sherry.

Normans King William Tawny Port

Why King Bill? The Norman Conquests of course when poor old King Harry copped an arrow in the eye. Maker Brian Light.
CURRENT RELEASE *non-vintage* A medium to light style with a mid-amber colour and rancio and old wood aromas on the nose. The palate is complex with raisin, chocolate and vanilla flavours and clean acid saves the finish from cloying. It is a good coffee and chocolates style.

QUALITY 🍷🍷🍷🍷🍷
VALUE ★★★★½
GRAPES shiraz, grenache
REGION McLaren Vale, SA
CELLAR 🍾
ALC./VOL. 17.5%
RRP $17.00 $

Penfolds Club Port

It doesn't take much money to join this club. You don't need a nominee, just the cash at the drive-in bottle shop.
CURRENT RELEASE *non-vintage* It is a very drinkable sweet red style with a hint of rancio. The nose has some dried-fruit aspects plus a nutty character. The medium-bodied palate is full of sweet dried-fruit flavours and gentle but warming spirit can be found on the finish. Just the thing for après business lunch.

QUALITY 🍷🍷🍷🍷
VALUE ★★★½
GRAPES shiraz, grenache
REGION various SA
CELLAR 🍾 1
ALC./VOL. 18.0%
RRP $12.00 $

Penfolds Grandfather Port

If you stretch your mind you can believe there are a few molecules of 1915 material in this honourable blend. It is a great and rare fortified. Blender Dean Kraehenbuhl.
CURRENT RELEASE *non-vintage* The average age is over 20 years and it shows a brilliant rancio character. It has a bronze olive colour and the nose smells of many elements including toffee, coffee and marzipan. The rich palate has dried-fruit, peel and caramel flavours. These are followed by warming brandy spirit on a nutty finish. Great after dinner and one of the best.

QUALITY 🍷🍷🍷🍷🍷
VALUE ★★★★
GRAPES shiraz, mataro
REGION Barossa Valley, SA
CELLAR 🍾 1
ALC./VOL. 19.0%
RRP $80.00

Penfolds Great Grandfather Port

QUALITY ♆♆♆♆♆
VALUE ★★★★
GRAPES not stated
REGION Barossa Valley, SA
CELLAR 🍾 1
ALC./VOL. 19.0%
RRP $POA

Flushed with the success of Grange, the marketers set the maker a quest for another 'bound for glory' wine. Here is the result.

CURRENT RELEASE *non-vintage* This is an antique style and the sort of drink you should experience once in a lifetime (if you can afford it). The nose is nutty with a strong rancio character. There are many components including, coffee, caramel, toffee and wood. The palate has mouth-filling texture with peel, dried fruit, marzipan and coffee. The finish is warming and satisfying. It is a reflective, sipping style.

Penfolds Ten Year Old Port

QUALITY ♆♆♆♆
VALUE ★★★½
GRAPES shiraz, grenache
REGION various, SA
CELLAR 🍾
ALC./VOL. 19.0%
RRP $19.50 ⓢ

For a port to carry an age (i.e. 10 year old) the majority of the material must be at least the age stated or more.

CURRENT RELEASE *non-vintage* For a 10-year-old this is a bit of a sprinter. The nose is fresh with toffee and dried-fruit characters. The palate has prune and raisin flavours and there is spirit on the finish. It drinks well and is perfect for the few remaining long-lunching business drunks.

Peter Lehmann Reserve Fino Sherry

QUALITY ♆♆♆♆♆
VALUE ★★★★★
GRAPES palomino
REGION Barossa Valley, SA
CELLAR 🍾
ALC./VOL. 17.5%
RRP $10.00 (cellar door only)

This is a family tipple usually served at the Lehmann household. Obviously they are not drinking fast enough because there is some available at cellar door. Maker Andrew Wigan.

CURRENT RELEASE *non-vintage* This is a bone-dry style that is very fresh and lively. The colour is pale yellow green. The nose is nutty with typical flor yeast smells. The palate is quite smooth and balanced with muted grape flavours and there is plenty of acid on the finish. It is a very clean pre-dinner drink.

Redgate White Port

Once upon a time white port was a very popular tipple in this country, the style was also labelled as cream sherry. This is an unusual example.
CURRENT RELEASE *non-vintage* The colour is pale and the nose is a mix of aromatic floral characters and citrus aromas. The palate is quite sweet with some dried-fruit flavours with a touch of spice. The finish shows some warming brandy. It could be served chilled with a white chocolate dessert.

QUALITY ♕♕♕♕
VALUE ★★★½
GRAPES riesling, sauvignon blanc
REGION Margaret River, WA
CELLAR ↓
ALC./VOL. 18.2%
RRP $14.50

Renmano Cromwell Tawny Port

Did you know Oliver Cromwell died from malaria? Now you do your life will hardly take a change of direction, but you can bore your friends.
CURRENT RELEASE *non-vintage* The colour is tawny brownish red and there is a hint of muscat fruit on the nose. The palate is quite sweet and rich with raisined flavours. There is also evidence of some older material in the blend. The finish is long and clean. A good value after-dinner drink.

QUALITY ♕♕♕
VALUE ★★★★
GRAPES grenache, gordo, shiraz
REGION Riverland, SA
CELLAR ↓
ALC./VOL. 18.0%
RRP $8.00

Renmano Rumpole Tawny Port

What the younger generation of wine drinkers will make of Rumpole is a moot point. He drank claret at Pommeroy's Wine Bar anyway.
CURRENT RELEASE *non-vintage* This is a light-hearted and lightweight tawny. The colour is a light amber and the nose offers sweet fruit aromas. The palate is sweet and rather like an oloroso sherry and the finish shows a trace of continuing sweetness. After dinner.

QUALITY ♕♕♕
VALUE ★★★
GRAPES shiraz, grenache
REGION Riverland, SA
CELLAR ↓
ALC./VOL. 18.0%
RRP $12.50 $

Rockford P. S. Marion Tawny Port

QUALITY 🍷🍷🍷🍷🍷
VALUE ★★★★★
GRAPES shiraz
REGION Barossa Valley, SA
CELLAR 🍷
ALC./VOL. 19.0%
RRP $15.50 (cellar door)

Proprietor Rocky O'Callaghan's second passion after wine is river boats on the Murray. This explains the name which belongs to a steam-driven paddleboat. Money from the sale of the port will be donated to the restoration of the boat. Maker Robert O'Callaghan.

CURRENT RELEASE *non-vintage* A typical Barossa tawny. The colour is a mid tawny amber and the nose is nutty with a mix of spirit and fruit. The palate is nutty with dried-fruit, rancio and chocolate/vanilla flavours. The finish is very long and quite dry. This is a wine to show off.

Rovalley Cobweb Port

QUALITY 🍷🍷🍷🍷
VALUE ★★★★
GRAPES not stated
REGION Barossa Valley, SA
CELLAR 🍷
ALC./VOL. 18.0%
RRP $12.50 ⓢ

Rovalley has a long history in fortified wine. The Miranda takeover has introduced a range of table wines.

CURRENT RELEASE *non-vintage* The colour is quite dark and the nose has hints of muscats and dried fruits. The palate is soft and mouth-filling with sweet dried-fruit flavours. The sweetness continues through to the finish. It is an after-dinner style.

Seppelt DP 57 Rutherglen Show Tokay

QUALITY 🍷🍷🍷🍷🍷
VALUE ★★★★★
GRAPES muscadelle
REGION Rutherglen, Vic.
CELLAR 🍷
ALC./VOL. 19.0%
RRP $21.00 (375ml)

It must seem to the novice that the wine industry sets out to confuse us all. Tokay is a misnomer for the muscadelle grape, which itself is somewhat misnamed as it is not a member of the muscat family and doesn't smell muscaty!

CURRENT RELEASE *non-vintage* Yet another great fortified from Seppelt. The bouquet overflows with tea-leafy, toffee and malty aromas and the palate is lusciously smooth and mellow with rancio. The finish riccochets around the mouth for ages. Drink with caramels or chocolates.

Seppelt DP 63 Rutherglen Show Muscat

Rutherglen muscat is one of the great styles of Australia. It would be bringing showers of fame and glory on the heads of Seppelt if fortified wines were not the pariahs of the wine world today.

CURRENT RELEASE *non-vintage* Enormously complex, powerful and long flavoured, this classic muscat has perfumes of raisins, muscat fruit and the mellow complexities derived from extended wood maturation. Its luscious fruit and sweetness make it a great partner for blue cheese and bikkies.

QUALITY ♜♜♜♜♜
VALUE ★★★★★
GRAPES red frontignac
REGION Rutherglen, Vic.
CELLAR ╽
ALC./VOL. 18.0%
RRP $21.00 (375ml)

Seppelt Viva 1 Liqueur Shiraz

Traditional fortified winery runs head-on into the 21st century, and the resultant packaging looks like the Pope on acid.

CURRENT RELEASE 1995 This is a sweet fortified, like a young ruby port. There's plenty of floral aromatic spirit character but little oak. Smooth, rich, lively and fruity on the palate. A very appealing young sweet red to serve chilled as an aperitif.

QUALITY ♜♜♜♜
VALUE ★★★
GRAPES shiraz
REGION Barossa Valley, SA
CELLAR ╽
ALC./VOL. 18.0%
RRP $16.50

Seppelt Viva 2 Liqueur Chardonnay

Fred Nile meets Annie Sprinkle! This is what happens when someone gets the bright idea to create a new style of wine to re-awaken public interest in fortifieds. Creator James Godfrey.

CURRENT RELEASE 1995 You've seen chardonnay in every kind of guise; now here's a fortified version. Glowing deep yellow colour, floral brandy spirit dominates the nose, the taste is sweet, honeyed, spicy, non-varietal but appealing. The soft, rich palate has length and easy drinkability. Chill as an aperitif.

QUALITY ♜♜♜♜
VALUE ★★★
GRAPES chardonnay
REGION Riverland, SA
CELLAR ╽
ALC./VOL. 17.0%
RRP $16.50

Seppeltsfield DP 38 Show Oloroso

QUALITY	🍷🍷🍷🍷🍷
VALUE	★★★★★
GRAPES	palomino
REGION	Barossa Valley, SA
CELLAR	🍾
ALC./VOL.	22.0%
RRP	$18.50 (375ml)

Seppelt, hitherto one of our most conservative wine companies, suddenly went completely ballistic in 1995 and re-launched all its show fortifieds in sexy half-bottles with abstract arty labels. Hopefully, this will boost sales.

CURRENT RELEASE *non-vintage* Never mind any preconceptions about sherry, this is a great aged sweet fortified. It is medium-deep amber in colour and looks like an old tokay, but the complex walnut, vanilla and fruit cake smells are all its own. Terrifically rich in the mouth with a long, long tail. Serve it with a rich soup.

Seppeltsfield DP 116 Show Amontillado

QUALITY	🍷🍷🍷🍷🍷
VALUE	★★★★★
GRAPES	palomino
REGION	Barossa Valley, SA
CELLAR	🍾
ALC./VOL.	22.0%
RRP	$18.50 (375ml)

This was our Penguin award-winner for best fortified wine two years ago, and the wine is still as good as ever. Maker James Godfrey and team.

CURRENT RELEASE *non-vintage* A beautiful wine, loaded with citrus peel, vanilla and rancio complexities that dazzle the senses. With an average age of 16 years, it has plenty of mellow wood-aged character and just a hint of the flor character of a fino. Perfect with quail consommé.

Seppeltsfield DP 117 Show Fino

QUALITY	🍷🍷🍷🍷🍷
VALUE	★★★★★
GRAPES	palomino
REGION	Barossa Valley, SA
CELLAR	🍾
ALC./VOL.	17.0%
RRP	$18.50 (375ml)

Seppelt's have dropped the naughty word 'sherry' off their labels with the repackaging of their erstwhile sherries. Maker James Godfrey.

CURRENT RELEASE *non-vintage* Tasted fresh off the bottling line, this was looking at its very best. Very fresh, appley, with clean nutty aldehyde aromas and a whisper of wood, it tastes crisp and lively, tangy and appetite-stimulating. Serve it chilled before dinner. (Check that you buy the new half-bottle with the groovy label: anything in the old dumpy bottle is likely to be stale.)

Tatachilla Fine Old Tawny Port

McLaren Vale is often overlooked as a region that can produce fine fortified wines. In this case three varieties are employed to produce the goods.
CURRENT RELEASE *non-vintage* The colour is a mid to light amber and the nose has rancio characters with a hint of raisin. The palate is medium sherry-like and not overly sweet. There are dried-fruit flavours plus nuts and spice. The finish shows some clean fortifying spirit. It drinks well after dinner.

QUALITY 🍷🍷🍷🍷
VALUE ★★★★
GRAPES grenache, shiraz, frontignac
REGION McLaren Vale, SA
CELLAR 🍾
ALC./VOL. 17.5%
RRP $17.60

Wirra Wirra Fine Old Tawny

The base of this blend is 18-year-old shiraz, with a little grenache and touriga thrown in for good measure.
CURRENT RELEASE *non-vintage* The colour is medium amber/tawny and the bouquet is all fruit cake, walnuts and rancio giving a smooth, mellow, aged style. There's plenty of sweetness and mellowness to taste. A port that slips down very agreeably with Stilton.

QUALITY 🍷🍷🍷🍷🍷
VALUE ★★★★½
GRAPES shiraz, grenache, touriga
REGION McLaren Vale, SA
CELLAR 🍾
ALC./VOL. 18.0%
RRP $17.70

Yalumba Clocktower Tawny Port

How many times have the hands on the Yalumba clock rotated while this port has been sitting ageing in the vats? It's a sobering thought.
CURRENT RELEASE *non-vintage* This is more like a ruby port with a lot of spirit character than a conventional tawny. It's quite sweet and has ample fruit flavour and a dominant licorice note. Good for sipping with rich fruit cake.

QUALITY 🍷🍷🍷
VALUE ★★★★
GRAPES not stated
REGION not stated
CELLAR 🍾
ALC./VOL. 17.5%
RRP $9.00

Yalumba Director's Special Old Tawny Port

QUALITY ♥♥♥♥
VALUE ★★★★
GRAPES not stated
REGION Barossa Valley, SA
CELLAR ▯
ALC./VOL. 17.5%
RRP $12.00

The name conjures images of fusty old men's clubs full of leather armchairs and cigar smoke. It's a stereotype port needs to overcome.
CURRENT RELEASE *non-vintage* Textbook tawny-red colour; the bouquet boasts good depth of wood-aged character and some rancio. The palate holds abundant sweet, mellow, raisin and prune fruit and good aged complexity, leading into a long and well-balanced finish. Just the ticket for aged cheddar.

Yalumba Galway Pipe Port

QUALITY ♥♥♥♥♥
VALUE ★★★★½
GRAPES not stated
REGION Barossa Valley, SA
CELLAR ▯
ALC./VOL. 18.7%
RRP $28.00

Good old Sir Henry Galway must indeed have been a great mate of the Hill Smiths back in the 1920s – they named two wines after him (Galway Hermitage is t'other).
CURRENT RELEASE *non-vintage* Still the market leader in its price category, and it's easy to see why. This is a very rich, mellow, smooth old tawny which boasts a lot of rancio and also some fruit from younger blending material. It floods the mouth with toffee, raisin, prune and vanilla flavours which resonate long on the aftertaste. Superior tawny to sip with good coffee and cigars.

Yalumba Ten-Year-Old Premium Port

QUALITY ♥♥♥♥
VALUE ★★★½
GRAPES not stated
REGION Barossa Valley, SA
CELLAR ▯
ALC./VOL. 18.5%
RRP $18.80

This is what happens when the marketing department are let loose with a budget and a mission: an unusual bottle and quirky orange label meant to evoke Portugal.
CURRENT RELEASE *non-vintage* A true tawny port colour: medium amber/tawny red, and the slightly subdued bouquet shows some oak vanilla and mellow aged characters. It is very smooth in the mouth with sweetness that dries towards the finish. Try it with a creamy blue cheese.

The Overflow

This section is an at-a-glance assessment of the wines that simply wouldn't fit in the main body of the text. The wines are in no way diminished in status because they appear in this section. The blunt fact is there were far too many good Australian wines submitted for inclusion in this *Guide*.

REDS	QUALITY	VALUE	RRP
All Saints Heritage Red 1995	▌▌▌	★★★★	$9.50
Arrowfield Cabernet Merlot 1994	▌▌▌	★★★½	$12.00
Arrowfield Cowra Cabernet 1993	▌▌▌	★★★	$14.00
Arrowfield Shiraz 1994	▌▌▌	★★★½	$12.00
Arrowfield Show Reserve Cabernet Sauvignon 1993	▌▌▌▌	★★½	$20.00
Arthurs Creek Estate Cabernet Sauvignon 1992	▌▌▌▌	★★★	$27.00
Bremerton Blend 1994	▌▌▌▌	★★★★	$13.50
Bremerton Shiraz 1994	▌▌▌▌	★★★½	$13.50
Brookland Valley Cabernet Merlot 1993	▌▌▌▌	★★★½	$21.00
Brown Brothers Dolcetto 1995	▌▌▌	★★★	$13.50
Brown Brothers Nebbiolo 1993	▌▌▌▌	★★★½	$13.50
Buller & Sons (R.L.) Calliope Shiraz 1994	▌▌▌▌	★★★★	$14.50
Campbells Bobbie Burns Shiraz 1994	▌▌▌▌	★★★	$16.00
Chain of Ponds Pinot Noir 1993	▌▌▌▌	★★★	$22.00
Chateau Leamon Cabernet Sauvignon 1993	▌▌▌	★★½	$20.50
Chateau Leamon Shiraz 1994	▌▌▌▌	★★★	$17.50
Coriole Redstone 1994	▌▌▌	★★★	$14.50
Coriole Sangiovese 1994	▌▌▌	★★★	$14.50
d'Arenberg High Trellis Cabernet Sauvignon 1994	▌▌▌▌	★★★½	$19.00
d'Arenberg Old Vine Shiraz	▌▌▌▌	★★★★	$19.00
d'Arenberg The Ironstone Pressings	▌▌▌▌▌	★★★★½	$19.00

David Traeger Cabernet 1993	🍷🍷🍷	★★★	$14.50
De Bortoli Cabernet Shiraz Merlot 1994	🍷🍷🍷🍷	★★★½	$19.90
Delatite Cabernet Sauvignon 1994	🍷🍷🍷	★★½	$18.50
Delatite Merlot 1994	🍷🍷🍷🍷	★★★½	$18.50
Delatite Shiraz 1994	🍷🍷🍷🍷	★★★½	$18.50
E & E Black Pepper Shiraz 1993	🍷🍷🍷	★★½	$29.00
Elderton Cabernet Shiraz Merlot 1994	🍷🍷🍷🍷	★★★½	$25.00
Evans & Tate Margaret River Cabernet Sauvignon 1994	🍷🍷🍷🍷	★★★★	$22.00
Evans & Tate Margaret River Merlot 1994	🍷🍷🍷🍷	★★★★	$22.00
Frankland Estate Isolation Ridge Shiraz 1994	🍷🍷🍷🍷🍷	★★★★	$19.00
Galah Wine Clare Valley Cabernet Sauvignon 1994	🍷🍷🍷🍷	★★★★	$15.00 (mail order)
Geoff Merrill Cabernet Sauvignon 1991	🍷🍷🍷🍷	★★★	$22.00
Geoff Merrill Mount Hurtle Grenache 1995	🍷🍷🍷🍷	★★★½	$12.00
Gilberts Mt Barker Shiraz 1994	🍷🍷🍷🍷	★★★★	$16.00
Grant Burge Cameron Vale Cabernet Sauvignon 1994	🍷🍷🍷🍷	★★★	$19.00
Grant Burge Hillcot Merlot 1994	🍷🍷🍷	★★★	$13.00
Hanson Cabernet Sauvignon 1993	🍷🍷🍷🍷🍷	★★★★	$26.00
Hanson Pinot Noir 1995	🍷🍷🍷🍷	★★★½	$26.00
Hugh Hamilton Cabernet Shiraz 1994	🍷🍷🍷🍷	★★★½	$17.00
Hugh Hamilton Shiraz 1994	🍷🍷🍷🍷	★★★½	$17.00
Hugo Cabernet Sauvignon 1994	🍷🍷🍷🍷🍷	★★★★½	$12.50 (cellar door)
Kay's Amery Grenache 1995	🍷🍷🍷🍷	★★★	$15.00
Killerby April Classic Red 1996	🍷🍷🍷	★★★	$13.00
Kominos Wines Cabernet Sauvignon 1993	🍷🍷🍷🍷	★★★★	$14.00
Kominos Wines Shiraz 1994	🍷🍷🍷🍷	★★★★	$14.00
Main Ridge Estate Half Acre Pinot Noir 1994	🍷🍷🍷🍷	★★★½	$26.00
Manning Park Native Cabernet 1993	🍷🍷🍷🍷	★★★½	$26.00
Martinborough Vineyard Pinot Noir 1994	🍷🍷🍷🍷🍷	★★★½	$39.00
Mitchell Cabernet Sauvignon 1994	🍷🍷🍷🍷	★★★★	$17.90
Moorooduc Estate Cabernet 1993	🍷🍷🍷🍷	★★★	$27.00

Wine	Glasses	Stars	Price
Orlando Russet Ridge 1994	▼▼▼▼	★★★½	$19.90
Paringa Estate Pinot Noir 1994	▼▼▼▼▼	★★★★½	$28.00
Pattersons Mount Barker Shiraz 1992	▼▼▼	★★½	$21.00
Pendarves Chambourcin 1995	▼▼▼	★★★	$16.00
Pendarves Pinot Noir 1995	▼▼▼▼	★★★½	$19.00
Pendarves Shiraz 1994	▼▼▼▼	★★★★	$16.00
Pepper Tree Wines cabernet sauvignon, cabernet franc, merlot 1995	▼▼▼▼	★★★★	$22.00
Pepper Tree Wines Classics 1995	▼▼▼▼▼	★★★½	$18.00
Peter Lehmann Shiraz 1991	▼▼▼▼▼	★★★★½	$19.00
Peter Lehmann Stonewell Barossa Shiraz 1991	▼▼▼▼▼	★★★★½	$19.00
Plantagenet Cabernet Sauvignon 1993	▼▼▼▼	★★★	$22.00
Redgate Bin 588 Cabernet 1993	▼▼▼▼	★★★½	$20.00
Redgate Cabernet Franc 1992	▼▼▼▼	★★★½	$16.00
Ribbon Vale Merlot 1993	▼▼▼▼	★★★½	$18.00
Riddoch Cabernet Shiraz 1994	▼▼▼▼	★★★★	$13.00
Sandalford 1840 Collection Cabernet Shiraz Malbec 1994	▼▼▼	★★★½	$14.00
Scarpantoni Cabernet Sauvignon 1994	▼▼▼▼	★★★★	$12.50
Stanley Brothers John Hancock Shiraz 1994	▼▼▼▼	★★★★	$17.00
Stanley Brothers Thoroughbred Cabernet 1993	▼▼▼▼▼	★★★★	$17.00
Stonier's Pinot Noir 1995	▼▼▼▼	★★★	$18.00
Strathbogie Vineyards Pinot Noir 1994	▼▼▼▼	★★★½	$18.00
Summerfield Cabernet Sauvignon 1994	▼▼▼▼	★★★½	$20.00
Summerfield Shiraz 1994	▼▼▼▼▼	★★★½	$20.00
Taltarni Merlot Cabernet 1994	▼▼▼▼	★★★★	$19.00
Tatachilla Keystone Grenache Shiraz 1995	▼▼▼▼	★★★★	$14.50
Tatachilla Partners Cabernet Sauvignon Shiraz 1995	▼▼▼▼	★★★★	$20.00
Thistle Hill Pinot Noir 1993	▼▼▼	★★★	$18.00
Virgin Hills 1995	▼▼▼▼	★★★	$28.00
Wandin Valley Reserve Cabernet Sauvignon 1994	▼▼▼▼	★★★½	$18.00
Waninga Cabernet Sauvignon 1993	▼▼▼▼	★★★½	$18.50
Warramate Shiraz Cabernet 1993	▼▼▼▼	★★★	$20.00
Wendouree Cabernet Malbec 1994	▼▼▼▼▼	★★★★	$19.00
Wendouree Cabernet Sauvignon 1994	▼▼▼▼	★★★½	$20.00
Wildwood Cabernets 1994	▼▼▼▼▼	★★★★	$20.00
Wildwood Merlot Cabernet Franc 1994	▼▼▼▼	★★★½	$25.00

Willespie Cabernet Sauvignon 1993	🍷🍷🍷🍷	★★★½	$18.50
Willow Creek Pinot Noir 1994	🍷🍷🍷🍷🍷	★★★★	$20.00
Wilson Vineyard Cabernet Sauvignon 1994	🍷🍷🍷🍷🍷	★★★★	$15.50
Wilton Estate Cabernet Merlot 1995	🍷🍷🍷🍷	★★★½	$12.00
Wilton Stock Route Shiraz Cabernet Merlot 1995	🍷🍷🍷	★★★	$9.00
Woodstock Shiraz 1994	🍷🍷🍷🍷	★★★½	$15.00
Woodstock The Stocks Shiraz 1994	🍷🍷🍷🍷🍷	★★★★½	$22.00
Wyanga Cabernet Sauvignon 1992	🍷🍷🍷	★★★	$19.90

WHITES

Abbey Vale Sauvignon Blanc 1995	🍷🍷🍷🍷🍷	★★★★½	$18.50
Alkoomi Frankland Riesling 1995	🍷🍷🍷	★★½	$15.50
Arrowfield Cowra Chardonnay 1996	🍷🍷🍷	★★½	$14.00
Arrowfield Show Reserve Chardonnay 1995	🍷🍷🍷	★★½	$20.00
Botobolar Chardonnay 1995	🍷🍷🍷🍷	★★★★	$15.95
Botobolar Marsanne 1995	🍷🍷🍷🍷	★★★½	$16.50
Bremerton Watervale Riesling 1995	🍷🍷🍷🍷	★★★★	$14.00
Brown Brothers Chenin Blanc 1995	🍷🍷🍷🍷	★★★½	$12.75
Brown Brothers Pinot Grigio 1995	🍷🍷🍷🍷🍷	★★★★½	$14.00
Brown Brothers Spatlese Lexia 1995	🍷🍷🍷🍷	★★★★	$9.90
Brown Brothers Verdelho 1995	🍷🍷🍷🍷	★★★½	$14.00
Campbells Bobbie Burns Chardonnay 1995	🍷🍷🍷🍷	★★★	$16.00
d'Arenberg Olive Grove Chardonnay 1995	🍷🍷🍷🍷	★★★½	$19.00
De Bortoli Windy Peak Rhine Riesling 1995	🍷🍷🍷🍷🍷	★★★★½	$13.50
De Bortoli Yarra Valley Semillon 1994	🍷🍷🍷🍷	★★★★	$14.50
Delatite Late Picked Riesling 1994	🍷🍷🍷🍷	★★★½	$13.50
Delatite Limited Release Sauvignon Blanc 1995	🍷🍷🍷🍷	★★★★	$16.00
Doonkuna Estate Chardonnay 1995	🍷🍷🍷🍷🍷	★★★★½	$16.00 (cellar door)
Driftwood Chardonnay 1995	🍷🍷🍷🍷🍷	★★★★	$19.00
Evans & Tate Classic Dry White 1996	🍷🍷🍷🍷	★★★★	$17.00

Wine	Glasses	Stars	Price
Evans & Tate Margaret River Chardonnay 1995	4	★★★★	$20.00
Evans & Tate Margaret River Sauvignon Blanc 1996	4½	★★★★½	$18.00
Fiddlers Creek Chardonnay 1995	3	★★★	$9.00
Glenara Adelaide Hills Riesling 1995	3½	★★★½	$14.00
Goona Warra Chardonnay 1995	3½	★★★½	$17.50
Henschke Sauvignon Blanc Semillon 1995	4	★★★★	$12.50
Hugo Chardonnay 1995	4	★★★★	$17.50
Karl Seppelt Chardonnay 1995	3½	★★★½	$14.65
Karrivale Riesling 1995	4	★★★★½	$13.50
Katnook Estate Riesling 1994	4	★★★½	$16.00
Martinborough Vineyard Chardonnay 1994	4½	★★★½	$39.00
Pattersons Mount Barker Chardonnay 1994	4	★★★	$17.00
Pendarves Mudgee Semillon 1994	4	★★★★	$15.00
Pendarves Sauvignon Blanc Semillon 1995	3½	★★★½	$15.00
Pendarves Verdelho 1995	3½	★★★½	$15.00
Plantagenet Chardonnay 1995	4	★★★★	$22.00
Plantagenet Mt Barker Riesling 1995	3	★★★	$14.50
Scarpantoni Chardonnay 1993	3	★★★	$12.50
Smithbrook Chardonnay 1995	3½	★★½	$27.50
Stonier's Chardonnay 1995	4	★★★★	$17.00
Strathbogie Chardonnay 1994	3	★★★	$17.00
Strathbogie Riesling 1995	3½	★★★½	$13.50
Sutherland Chardonnay 1993	4	★★★★	$15.00 (cellar door)
Sutherland Chenin Blanc 1993	3	★★★	$13.50 (cellar door)
Tamburlaine Semillon 1996	3½	★★★★½	$16.00
Tamburlaine Verdelho 1996	4	★★★★	$16.00
Tatachilla Chardonnay 1995	4	★★★★	$17.90
Tatachilla Growers Chenin Blanc, Semillon, Sauvignon Blanc 1995	3	★★★	$12.50
Thistle Hill Riesling 1993	3	★★★	$14.50
Tim Knappstein Fumé Blanc 1995	3	★★★	$13.50
Tim Knappstein Riesling 1995	4½	★★★★½	$12.50

Wellington Riesling 1995	🍷🍷🍷🍷	★★★★	$15.00 (mail order)
Wilton Estate Chardonnay 1993	🍷🍷🍷🍷	★★★½	$12.00
Woodstock Chardonnay 1995	🍷🍷🍷🍷	★★★	$14.00
Wyanga Unwooded Chardonnay 1995	🍷🍷🍷	★★★	$15.00

SPARKLING

De Bortoli Sacred Hill Brut NV	🍷🍷🍷	★★★	$8.90
Domaine Chandon Blanc de Noirs 1991	🍷🍷🍷🍷🍷	★★★★	$30.00
Domaine Chandon Cuvée Riche NV	🍷🍷🍷🍷🍷	★★★½	$30.00
Domaine Chandon Late Disgorged 1990	🍷🍷🍷🍷🍷	★★★★	$30.00

FORTIFIED

Campbells Allen's	🍷🍷🍷🍷🍷	★★★★	$80.00
d'Arenberg Vintage Fortified 1995	🍷🍷🍷🍷	★★★★	$19.90

Food/Wine Combinations – Reds

BEEF *(carpaccio, dried, hamburgers, kebabs, meatballs, pan-fried, pot-roast, raw, roast, steak, rissoles, steak and kidney pie)*

Andrew Garrett Shiraz
Angove's Sarnia Farm Cabernet Sauvignon
Balgownie Estate Shiraz
Balgownie Shiraz Cabernet
Balnaves Cabernet Sauvignon
Black Jack Shiraz
Bleasdale Bremerview Shiraz
Bowen Estate Shiraz
Bremerton Lodge Cabernet Sauvignon
Campbells Silverburn Red
Capel Vale Merlot
Chambers Cabernet Sauvignon 1993
Charles Sturt University Limited Release Cabernet Shiraz
Chateau Tahbilk Shiraz
Cullen Cabernet Sauvignon Merlot
Evans & Tate Margaret River Shiraz
Giaconda Pinot Noir
Hardys Thomas Hardy Cabernet Sauvignon
Ingoldby Shiraz
Kay Brothers Amery Block 6 Shiraz
Krondorf Shiraz Cabernet
Leasingham Classic Clare Cabernet Sauvignon
Lillydale Vineyards Pinot Noir
Lindemans Limestone Ridge
Moss Wood Cabernet Sauvignon
Mount Avoca Cabernet
Orlando Jacaranda Ridge Cabernet Sauvignon
Penfolds Bin 389 Cabernet Shiraz

Penley Estate Hyland Shiraz
Petaluma Coonawarra
Peter Lehmann Cabernet Sauvignon
Renmano Chairman's Selection Cabernet Sauvignon
Riddoch Run Shiraz
Sandalford Cabernet Sauvignon
Scotchmans Hill Pinot Noir
Seaview Shiraz 1993
Stonier's Reserve Cabernet
Tamburlaine The Chapel
Tarrawarra Pinot Noir
Wetherall Shiraz
Wynns Coonawarra Estate Cabernet Sauvignon
Wynns Shiraz
Yarra Yering Dry Red Wine No.2

BUFFALO (fillet)

Kangaroo Island Trading Company Cabernet Merlot
St Mary's Shiraz
Wild Duck Creek Duck Muck

CASSEROLES (beef, cassoulet, goulash, Irish stew, kid, osso bucco, lamb, savoury mince, shepherd's pie, veal)

Balgownie Estate Cabernet Sauvignon
Boston Bay Cabernet Sauvignon
Chapel Hill Shiraz
Chatsfield Shiraz
David Wynn Patriarch Shiraz
Garry Crittenden Nebbiolo
Glenara Shiraz
Goundrey Reserve Shiraz
Hollick Terra Red
Jane Brook Cabernet Merlot
Jim Barry McCrea Wood Cabernet Malbec
Jim Barry McCrea Wood Shiraz 1993
Jimmy Watson Cabernet Shiraz

Leeuwin Estate Prelude Cabernet Sauvignon
Lengs & Cooter Grenache
Lindemans Hunter River Reserve Shiraz Bin 8200
Lindemans Nyrang Shiraz
Penfolds Bin 128 Coonawarra
Penfolds Old Vine Shiraz Grenache Mourvedre
Peter Lehmann Mentor 1991
Pewsey Vale Cabernet Sauvignon
Pirramimma Cabernet Savignon
Riddoch Run (The) Cabernet Sauvignon
Taltarni Merlot
Taltarni Shiraz
Valley of Vines
Water Wheel Cabernet Sauvignon
Wendouree Shiraz Malbec
Wolf Blass Brown Label Classic Shiraz
Yalumba Family Reserve Shiraz
Zema Estate Cabernet Sauvignon

CHEESE

Balnaves Cabernet Sauvignon 1993
Brands Original Vineyard Shiraz
Gramp's Grenache
Hanging Rock Victoria Shiraz
Parker Estate Terra Rossa First Growth
Rosemount Balmoral Syrah
St Hallett Old Block Shiraz
Tyrrell's Show Reserve Shiraz Cabernet
Wolf Blass Black Label Cabernet Shiraz
Wynns John Riddoch Cabernet Sauvignon
Yalumba Octavius (The) Shiraz

CURRY

Elderton Command Shiraz

DUCK (confit, Peking, roast, warm salad, Westlake, wild)

Ashton Hills Pinot Noir
Cassegrain Chambourcin
Coldstream Hills Reserve Pinot Noir
Craiglee Shiraz 1993
Delatite Pinot Noir
Leasingham Bin 56 Cabernet Malbec
Majella Shiraz
Mitchelton Victoria Reserve Shiraz

FISH (salmon, soup, tuna)

Barralt Pinot Noir
Chateau Xanadu Featherwhite
Coldstream Hills Pinot Noir
Lark Hill Pinot Noir

GAME (hare, Guinea fowl, goose, mutton bird, pheasant, pigeon, quail, rabbit, squab, venison, wild boar)

Bannockburn Serré Pinot Noir
Barwang Cabernet Sauvignon
Blue Pyrenees Estate
Bowen Estate Cabernet Sauvignon
Bridgewater Mill Millstone Shiraz
Buller & Son Beverford Cabernet Sauvignon 1992
Campbells Rutherglen Durif
Cassegrain Shiraz
Chateau Reynella Basket Pressed Cabernet Sauvignon
Chateau Reynella Basket Pressed Shiraz
Dalwhinnie Pyrenees Shiraz
De Bortoli Yarra Valley Cabernet Sauvignon
Dromana Estate Cabernet Merlot
Dromana Estate Pinot Noir
Grant Burge Hillcot Merlot
Green Point Pinot Noir
Happs Merlot

Hardys Bankside Grenache
Hardys Bankside Shiraz
Hardys Eileen Hardy
Hay Shed Hill Cabernet Sauvignon
Heggies Merlot
Heggies Pinot Noir
Hollick Coonawarra 1994
Ingoldby Cabernet Sauvignon
Ingoldby Grenache
Lengs & Cooter Shiraz
Lindemans St George Cabernet Sauvignon
Maxwell Ellen Street Shiraz
Mitchell Growers (The) Grenache
Mount Avoca Shiraz
Mount Helen Cabernet Sauvignon Merlot
Mount Langi Ghiran Shiraz
Mountadam Pinot Noir
Peter Lehmann Shiraz
Pibbin Wines Pinot Noir
Pierro Pinot Noir
Prentice Le Roy's Blend
Red Hill Estate Pinot Noir
Saltram Barossa Reserve Grenache
Seppelt Great Western Shiraz
St Hallett Gamekeeper's Reserve
St Huberts Cabernet Merlot
Te Mata Coleraine Cabernet Merlot
Vasse Felix Shiraz
Wellington Pinot Noir
Wignalls Pinot Noir
Wirra Wirra RSW Shiraz
Yarra Ridge Pinot Noir
Zema Estate Shiraz

KANGAROO (char-grilled, pan-fried, stewed)

Cassegrain Five Mile Hollow Red
Craiglee Shiraz 1994
Heggies Merlot
Seaview Cabernet Sauvignon

Tim Knappstein Cabernet Sauvignon
Yarra Ridge Cabernet Sauvignon

KID *(casserole, roast)*

Bleasdale Frank Polts Cabernet Merlot Malbec
Garry Crittenden Barbera
Richmond Grove Barossa Shiraz

LAMB *(barbecue, kebabs, mutton, pink, pumped, rack of, sausages, satays, shanks, smoked, straps)*

Baileys Touriga
Banrock Station Shiraz Cabernet
Buller & Son Victoria Classic
Dalfarras Shiraz
Darling Park Cabernet Merlot
De Bortoli Yarra Valley Pinot Noir
Freycinet Cabernet Sauvignon
Hardys Padthaway Cabernet Sauvignon
Heritage Estate Shiraz
Hickinbotham Mornington Peninsula Merlot
Hill Smith Estate Cabernet Sauvignon Shiraz
Hollick Coonawarra 1993
Hollick Ravenswood
Katnook Estate Cabernet Sauvignon
Leasingham Bin 61 Shiraz
Leasingham Classic Clare Shiraz
Lindemans Padthaway Cabernet Merlot
Lindemans Pyrus Classic Release 1985
Mildara Coonawarra Cabernet Sauvignon
Orlando St Hugo Cabernet Sauvignon
Osborne's Pinot Noir
Pauletts Shiraz
Penfolds Clare Estate
Preece Cabernet Sauvignon
Primo Estate Adelaide Shiraz
Rosemount Estate Shiraz Cabernet

Taltarni Cabernet Sauvignon 1992
Tatachilla Foundation Shiraz
Tatachilla Merlot
Tisdall Shiraz Cabernet
Tuck's Ridge Cabernet Sauvignon
Tyrrell's Old Winery Pinot Noir
Vasse Felix Cabernet Sauvignon
Wandin Valley Estate Ruby Cabernet
Yarra Yering Dry Red Wine No.1

OFFAL *(kidneys, liver, oxtail, pate, sweetbreads, tripe)*

Balnaves Shiraz
Bannockburn Shiraz
Brown Brothers Tarrango
Cape Mentelle Shiraz
Jim Barry McCrea Wood Shiraz 1994
Mount Ida Shiraz
Orlando Russet Ridge Cabernet Sauvignon
Trinity Ridge Merlot Noir
Vasse Felix Classic Dry Red

PASTA *(meat, game, tomato sauce)*

Baldivis Estate Blue Rock
Basedows Oscar's Heritage
Castle Crossing Chambourcin
Cowra Estate Shiraz Cabernet
Garry Crittenden Granaccia
Notley Gorge Pinot Noir
Penfolds Magill Estate Shiraz
Peter Lehmann Clancy's Gold Preference
Redman Coonawarra Shiraz
Tuck's Ridge Pinot Noir

PIZZA

Brown Brothers Everton
Kingston Estate Merlot

PORK *(barbecue, kassler, pig's trotters, roast, spare ribs)*

All Saints Estate Selection Shiraz
All Saints Maturation Reserve Cabernet Sauvignon
Allandale Matthew Shiraz
David Wynn Cabernet Sauvignon
Fox Creek Shiraz
Mildara Alexanders

RISOTTO

Fire Gully Cabernet Merlot
Geoff Merrill Mount Hurtle Shiraz
Paringa Estate Pinot Noir
Prince Albert Pinot Noir
Tyrrell's Brokenback Shiraz

SAUSAGES

Annie Lane Cabernet Merlot
Eaglehawk Shiraz Merlot Cabernet
Hardys RR Traditional Dry Red
Leeuwin Art Series Cabernet Sauvignon
Madfish Bay Premium Dry Red
Meadowbank Vineyard Cabernet
Mitchell Peppertree Vineyard Shiraz
Pauletts Cabernet Merlot
Pikes Clare Valley Shiraz
Redbank Sally's Paddock
Yalumba Galway Hermitage

VEAL (chops, pan-fried, roast, schnitzel)

Andrew Garrett Cabernet Merlot
Forest Hill Cabernet Sauvignon
Hillstowe Buxton Cabernet Merlot
Hillstowe Carey Gully Pinot Noir
Kay's Amery Shiraz
Moondah Brook Cabernet Sauvignon
Mountadam The Red
Richmond Grove Coonawarra Cabernet Sauvignon
Schinus Cabernet
St Hallett Faith Shiraz

VEGETABLES

Mount Trio Pinot Noir
Plantagenet Pinot Noir

Food/Wine Combinations – Whites

ANTIPASTO

Coriole Chenin Blanc
Hanging Rock The Jim Jim Sauvignon Blanc
Oakridge Estate Chardonnay

ASIAN FOOD (Chinese, Thai, Vietnamese)

Brookfields Sauvignon Blanc
Brown Brothers Gewurztraminer
Brown Brothers Semillon
Dalfarras Marsanne
Dalfarras Rhine Riesling
Hardys RR Classic Dry White
Hardys RR Medium Dry White
Orlando Jacob's Creek Riesling
Peter Lehmann Semillon Chardonnay
Pipers Brook Riesling
Yalumba Reserve Viognier

CAKE (fruit)

Pewsey Vale Autumn Botrytis Rhine Riesling

CHEESE

Brands Laira Family Reserve Chardonnay
Brown Brothers Noble Riesling

Cape Jaffa Sauvignon Blanc
Cloudy Bay Sauvignon Blanc
Goundrey Chardonnay
Pierro Chardonnay

CHICKEN (curry, fried, roast, smoked, stir fry)

Balnaves Chardonnay
Bethany Chardonnay
Cassegrain Fromenteau Reserve Chardonnay
Dalfarras Chardonnay
Evans & Tate 'Tate White'
Evans & Tate Two Vineyards Chardonnay
Hardys Siegersdorf Chardonnay
Heggies Chardonnay
Killerby Chardonnay
Leconfield Coonawarra Riesling
McWilliams Mount Pleasant Chardonnay
Morris Chardonnay
Penfolds The Valleys Chardonnay
Preston Peak Semillon Chardonnay
Ribbon Vale Semillon
Rochford Chardonnay
Rosabrook Semillon Sauvignon Blanc
Scotchmans Hill Chardonnay
Seaview Edwards & Chaffey Unfiltered Chardonnay
Tatachilla Keystone
T'Gallant Lot 2 Chardonnay
T'Gallant White Pinot Noir
Thistle Hill Chardonnay
Tisdall Mount Helen Chardonnay
Wolf Blass Classic Dry White
Yarraman Road Chardonnay

CRAYFISH (bugs, crab, marron, prawns, lobster, scampi, yabbies)

Allandale Semillon Sauvignon Blanc

Angove's Butterfly Ridge Colombard Chardonnay
Bridgewater Mill Chardonnay
Chateau Xanadu Secession
Coldstream Hills Reserve Chardonnay
Gilberts Riesling
Goundrey Reserve Riesling
Green Point Chardonnay
Grosset Piccadilly
Katnook Estate Chardonnay
Krondorf Show Chardonnay
Lillydale Vineyards Chardonnay
Massoni Red Hill Chardonnay
Miranda Rovalley Ridge Show Reserve Chardonnay
Mitchelton Victoria Reserve Chardonnay
Montana Church Road Reserve Chardonnay
Montrose Poet's Corner Classic Dry White
Orlando St Hilary Chardonnay
Preece Chardonnay
Saltram Classic Chardonnay
Sandalford Mt Barker Margaret River Chardonnay
Shaw & Smith Sauvignon Blanc
Stonier's Reserve Chardonnay
Wynns Chardonnay
Wynns Riesling

CRÈME BRÛLÉE

Chateau Xanadu Noble Semillon
Katnook Estate Botrytised Chardonnay
Yalumba Family Reserve Botrytis Semillon

DIM SUM

Chimera Sauvignon Blanc Semillon
Sandalford Caversham Chenin Verdelho

FOOD/WINE COMBINATIONS – WHITES

FAST FOOD (fish and chips, Hungry Jack's, KFC)

Fiddlers Creek Semillon
Gramps Chardonnay
Hardys Nottage Hill Chardonnay
Hardys Nottage Hill Rhine Riesling
Mildara Church Hill Chardonnay
Pirramimma Stock's Hill

FISH (all varieties, including whitebait)

Alkoomi Mount Frankland Early White
Allandale Semillon
Bowen Estate Chardonnay
Boyntons of Bright Semillon
Brands Laira Riesling
Brown Brothers Dry Muscat Blanc
Brown Brothers Family Reserve Chardonnay
Browns of Padthaway Chardonnay
Canobolas-Smith Chardonnay
Castle Rock Riesling
Cockfighter's Ghost Semillon
Darling Park Chardonnay
De Bortoli Noble One
Fiddlers Creek Sauvignon Blanc
Freycinet Chardonnay
Hardys Bankside Chardonnay
Hardys Eileen Hardy Chardonnay
Hawkes Bridge Chardonnay
Hay Shed Hill Chardonnay
Helm's Rhine Riesling Classic Dry
Henschke Louis Eden Valley Semillon
Hillstowe Buxton Chardonnay
Hungerford Hill Griffith Botrytis Semillon
Jimmy Watson's Chardonnay
Lawson's Dry Hills Gewurztraminer
Lindemans Nursery Vineyard Rhine Riesling Classic Release
Mitchell Watervale Riesling
Orlando St Helga Riesling

Pipers Brook Summit Chardonnay
Primo Estate Botrytis Riesling
Redgate Chardonnay
Renmano Chairman's Selection Chardonnay
Rosemount Show Reserve Semillon
Salisbury Estate Chardonnay
Saltram Classic Semillon
Saltram Pinnacle Riesling
Sandalford 1840 Collection Chardonnay
St Hallett Semillon Select
Thistle Hill Semillon
Tuck's Ridge Riesling
Tyrrell's Lost Block Semillon
Wirra Wirra Semillon Sauvignon Blanc
Woodstock Riesling
Wolf Blass Gold Label Riesling
Yalumba Reserve Watervale Riesling

FRUIT (including prosciutto melone)

All Saints Late Harvest Semillon
Coldstream Hills Chardonnay
Lark Hill Chardonnay
McWilliams J.J. McWilliam Botrytis Semillon
Montana Marlborough Chardonnay
Mount Horrocks Cordon Cut Riesling
Wellington Sweet Riesling
Wirra Wirra Late Picked Riesling
Wolf Blass Green Label Traminer Riesling

FROG'S LEGS

Leeuwin Estate Riesling

GAME (pheasant, squab)

All Saints Chardonnay
Mountadam Chardonnay

MUSSELS

Hawkes Bridge Sauvignon Blanc
Kay's Amery Sauvignon Blanc
Lawson's Dry Hills Sauvignon Blanc
Lindemans Padthaway Sauvignon Blanc
Nobilo Sauvignon Blanc
Orlando Jacob's Creek Chablis
Rymill Sauvignon Blanc

NOODLES (Singapore)

Bleasdale Sandhill Verdelho
Houghton Frankland River Rhine Riesling

OCTOPUS/CALAMARI

Chateau Xanadu Semillon
Forest Glen Chardonnay
Mount Avoca Chardonnay

OFFAL (lamb's brains, sweetbreads, pâté, tripe)

Barrett Chardonnay
Capel Vale Chardonnay
Glenara Unwooded Chardonnay
Matua Valley Judd Estate Chardonnay
Maxwell Chardonnay
Richmond Grove Watervale Rhine Riesling
Rymill Chardonnay

Tyrrell's Vat 1 Semillon
Wolf Blass Spatlese Rhine Riesling

OYSTERS

Andrew Garrett Sauvignon Blanc
Delatite Sauvignon Blanc
Forest Hill Riesling
Four Sisters
Jingalla Rhine Riesling
Leasingham Classic Clare Rhine Riesling
Mountadam Riesling
Pewsey Vale Riesling
Pewsey Vale Sauvignon Blanc
Seppelt Rhymney Sauvignon Blanc
Tatachilla Riesling

PASTA

Blue Pyrenees Chardonnay
Chateau Xanadu Chardonnay
Hanging Rock Howqua River Riesling
Hardys Padthaway Unwooded Chardonnay
Hill Smith Estate Chardonnay
Houghton Semillon Sauvignon Blanc
Jamieson's Run Chardonnay
Jingalla Semillon
Moondah Brook Chenin Blanc
Montrose Chardonnay
Pikes Chardonnay
Plunkett Strathbogie Ranges Riesling
Rosemount Show Reserve Chardonnay
Taltarni Fumé Reserve Sauvignon Blanc
Tim Knappstein Fumé Blanc
Wirra Wirra Hand Picked Riesling

QUICHE

Jim Barry Watervale Riesling
Knight Granite Hills Chardonnay
Montana 'B' Sauvignon Blanc
Pipers Brook Gewurztraminer
Twin Islands Sauvignon Blanc

RISOTTO/PAELLA/PIZZA

Barwang Chardonnay
Castle Rock Chardonnay
David Wynn Unwooded Chardonnay
Goundrey Unwooded Chardonnay 1995
Houghton Chablis
Peter Lehmann Semillon
Rouge Homme Richardons's White Block Chardonnay
Tuck's Ridge Chardonnay
Yarra Ridge Reserve Chardonnay

SALADS

Antipodean
Capel Vale Special Reserve Sauvignon Blanc
Chain of Ponds Semillon 1994
Chapel Hill Unwooded Chardonnay
Geoff Merrill Who Cares? The Whites
Leeuwin Prelude Chardonnay
Mitchelton Chinaman's Bridge Sauvignon Blanc
Mount Avoca Pyrenees Dry White
Pierro Semillon Sauvignon Blanc
Plunkett Blackwood Ridge Sauvignon Blanc Semillon
Ribbon Vale Sauvignon Blanc
Sandstone Semillon
Water Wheel Sauvignon Blanc
Wyanga Sauvignon Blanc
Yalumba Christobel's Dry White
Yarra Burn Sauvignon Blanc Semillon

SCALLOPS

All Saints Marsanne
Boston Bay Riesling
Chain of Ponds Chardonnay 1994
Hollick Terra White
Jane Brook Sauvignon Blanc
Karrivale Rhine Riesling
Miranda High Country Chardonnay
Murrindindi Chardonnay
Ninth Island Straits Dry White
Orlando Steingarten Riesling
Paradise Enough Chardonnay
Richmond Grove Barossa Rhine Riesling
Rosemount Sauvignon Blanc

SAUSAGES (curried, smoked)

Brokenwood Semillon 1994
Delatite Deadman's Hill Gerwurztraminer

TURKEY (roast)

Kingston Reserve Chardonnay

VEGETABLES

Andrew Garrett Chardonnay
Andrew Garrett Semillon
Ashbrook Semillon
Colonnade Chardonnay
David Wynn Sauvignon Blanc
Dulcinea Vineyard Sauvignon Blanc
Goundrey Classic White
Jamieson's Run Sauvignon Blanc
Karina Vineyard Sauvignon Blanc

McWilliams Hanwood Chardonnay
Scotchmans Hill Sauvignon Blanc
Seaview Verdelho
Tatachilla Sauvignon Blanc
Wairau River Chardonnay
Wairau River Sauvignon Blanc

Index of Common Names

(F) = Fortified; (R) = Reds; (S) = Sparkling; (W) = Whites

ABBOTT'S PRAYER, *see* Henschke (R)
ALCHEMY, *see* Canobolas-Smith (R)
ALEXANDERS, *see* Mildara (R)
ANGELUS (THE), *see* Wirra Wirra (R)
BALMORAL, *see* Rosemount (R)
BANKSIDE, *see* Hardys (R)
BARKLEY (THE), *see* Campbells (R)
BUXTON, *see* Hillstowe (R&W)
CAREY GULLY, *see* Hillstowe (R&W)
CHAIRMAN'S SELECTION, *see* Renmano (R&W)
CHINAMAN'S BRIDGE, *see* Mitchelton (R&W)
CHURCH HILL, *see* Mildara (R&W)
CHURCH ROAD, *see* Montana (W)
CLOCKTOWER, *see* Yalumba (F)
COLERAINE, *see* Te Mata (R)
CROMWELL, *see* Renmano (F)
DEAD MAN'S HILL, *see* Delatite (W)
DEVIL'S RIVER, *see* Delatite (R)
DORRIEN, *see* Seppelt (R)
DUNGEON GULLY, *see* Delatite (R)
EDWARDS AND CHAFFEY, *see* Seaview (R&S)
ELLEN STREET, *see* Maxwell (R)
FERGUS (THE), *see* Tim Adams (R)
FIVE MILE HOLLOW, *see* Cassegrain (R&W)
GAIA, *see* Grosset (R)
GALWAY PIPE, *see* Yalumba (F)
GRANGE, *see* Penfolds (R)
GREEN'S HILL, *see* Henschke (W)
HANWOOD, *see* McWilliams (R)
HARPERS RANGE, *see* Seppelt (S)
HIPPOCRENE, *see* Wilson Vineyard (S)
HUT BLOCK, *see* Richard Hamilton (R)
JACOB'S CREEK, *see* Orlando (W)
JUD'S HILL, *see* Brian Barry (W)
KANANDAH, *see* McWilliams (S)
KING WILLIAM, *see* Normans (F)
LAIRA, *see* Brands (R&W)
LAWSON'S, *see* Orlando (R)
LIMESTONE RIDGE, *see* Lindemans (R)
LINDAUER, *see* Montana (S)
LONE GUM, *see* Normans (R&W)
LOST BLOCK, *see* Tyrrell's (W)
MAMRE BROOK, *see* Saltram (W)
MARLBOROUGH, *see* Montana (W)
MESHACH, *see* Grant Burge (R)
METALA, *see* Stonyfell (R)
MOUNT PLEASANT, *see* McWilliam's (W)
NOSTALGIA, *see* d'Arenberg (F)
NOTTAGE HILL, *see* Hardys (R&W)
OLD QUARRY, *see* Bethany (F)
OLD WALNUT, *see* Jim Barry (F)
OSCAR'S HERITAGE, *see* Basedow (R)
OXFORD LANDING, *see* Yalumba (R&W)
PATRIARCH, *see* David Wynn (R)
PELORUS, *see* Cloudy Bay (W)
PINNACLE, *see* Saltram (W)
POET'S CORNER, *see* Montrose (W)
PYRUS, *see* Lindemans (R)
RED (THE), *see* Mountadam (R)
ROSE OF VIRGINIA, *see* Charles Melton (R)
RUMPOLE, *see* Renmano (F)

INDEX OF COMMON NAMES 429

SALLY'S PADDOCK, *see* Redbank (R)
SARNIA FARM, *see* Angoves (R&W)
SENTIMENTAL BLOKE, *see* Jim Barry (F)
SHEE-OAK, *see* Tyrrell's (W)
SHOW RESERVE, *see* All Saints (F)
SIEGERSDORF, *see* Hardys (W)
SIR JAMES, *see* Hardys (S)
ST GEORGE, *see* Lindemans (R)

STOCKS (THE), *see* Woodstock (R)
TALL SHIPS, *see* Hardys (F)
TILLY'S VINEYARD, *see* Henschke (W)
TR, *see* Tollana (R)
UDY'S MILL, *see* Hillstowe (W)
WHISKERS BLAKE, *see* Hardys (F)
WHO CARES?, *see* Geoff Merrill (R&W)
YARRA VALLEY, *see* De Bortoli (R)

Wine Terms

The following are commonly used winemaking terms.

ACID There are many acids that occur naturally in grapes and it is in the winemaker's interest to retain the favourable ones because these promote freshness and longevity.
AGRAFE A metal clip used to secure champagne corks during secondary bottle fermentation.
ALCOHOL Ethyl alcohol (C_2H_5OH) is a by-product of fermentation of sugars. It is the stuff that makes people happy and it adds warmth and texture to wine.
ALCOHOL BY VOLUME (A/V) The measurement of the amount of alcohol in a wine. It is expressed as a percentage, eg. 13.0% A/V means there is 13.0% pure alcohol as a percentage of the total volume.
ALDEHYDE An unwanted and unpleasant organic compound formed between acid and alcohol by oxidation. It is removed by sulphur dioxide.
ALLIER A type of oak harvested in the French forest of the same name.
APERITIF A wine that stimulates the appetite.
AROMATIC A family of grape varieties that have a high terpene content. Riesling and gewürztraminer are examples, and terpenes produce their floral qualities.
AUTOLYSIS A Vegemite or fresh-baked bread taste and smell imparted by spent yeast cells in sparkling wines.
BACK BLEND To add unfermented grape juice to wine; or to add young wine to old wine in fortifieds.
BARREL FERMENTATION The process of fermenting a red or white wine in a small barrel, thereby adding a creamy texture and toasty or nutty characters, and better integrating the wood and fruit flavours.
BARRIQUE A 225-litre barrel.

BAUMÉ The measure of sugar in grape juice used to estimate potential alcohol content. It is usually expressed as a degree, eg. 12 degrees baumé juice will produce approximately 12.0% A/V if it is fermented to dryness. The alternative brix scale is approximately double baumé and must be divided by 1.8 to estimate potential alcohol.

BENTONITE A fine clay (drillers mud) used as a clarifying (fining) agent.

BLEND A combination of two or more grape varieties and/or vintages. *see* Cuveé

BOTRYTIS CINEREA A fungus that thrives on grape vines in humid conditions and sucks out the water of the grapes thereby concentrating the flavour. Good in white wine but not so good in red. (There is also a loss in quantity.)

BREATHING Uncorking a wine and allowing it to stand for a couple of hours before serving; this introduces oxygen and dissipates bottle odours. Decanting aids breathing.

BRIX *see* Baumé

BRUT The second lowest level of sweetness in sparkling wine; it does not mean there is no added sugar.

BUSH VINE Although pruned the vine is self-supporting in a low-to-the-ground bush; still common in the Barossa Valley.

CARBONIC MACERATION Fermentation in whole (uncrushed) bunches. This is a popular technique in Beaujolais. It produces bright colour and softer tannins.

CHARMAT PROCESS A process for making sparkling wine where the wine is fermented in a tank rather than a bottle.

CLONE (CLONAL) A recognisable sub-species of vine within a varietal family, eg. there are numerous clones of pinot noir and these all have subtle character differences.

COLD FERMENTATION (Also Controlled Temperature Fermentation) Usually applied to white wines where the ferment is kept at a low temperature (10-12 degrees Centigrade)

CORDON The arms of the trained grape vine that bear the fruit.

CORDON CUT A technique of cutting the fruit-bearing arms and allowing the berries to dehydrate to concentrate the flavour.

CRUSH Crushing the berries to liberate the free-run juice (qv). Also used as an expression of a wine company's output: 'This winery has a 1000-tonne crush.'

CUVÉE A Champagne term meaning a selected blend or batch.

DISGORGE The process of removing the yeast lees from a sparkling wine. It involves freezing the neck of the bottle and firing out a plug of ice and yeast. The bottle is then topped up and recorked.
DOWNY MILDEW A disease that attacks vine leaves and fruit. It is associated with humidity and lack of air circulation.
DRIP IRRIGATION An accurate way of watering a vineyard. Each vine has its own dripper and a controlled amount of water is applied.
DRYLAND VINEYARD A vineyard that has no irrigation.
ESTERS Volatile compounds that can occur during fermentation or maturation. They impart a distinctive chemical taste.
FERMENTATION The process by which yeast converts sugar to alcohol with a by-product of carbon dioxide.
FINING The process of removing solids from wine to make it clear. There are several methods used.
FORTIFY The addition of spirit to increase the amount of alcohol in a wine.
FREE-RUN JUICE The first juice to come out of the press or drainer (as opposed to pressings).
GENERIC Wines labelled after their district of origin rather than their grape variety. eg. Burgundy, Chablis, Champagne etc. These terms can no longer legally be used on Australian labels. (cf. *Varietal*.)
GRAFT Changing the nature/variety of a vine by grafting a different variety on to a root stock.
IMPERIAL A 6-litre bottle (ie. contains eight 750 ml bottles).
JEROBOAM A 4.5-litre champagne bottle.
LACCASE A milky condition on the surface of red wine caused by noble rot (see botrytis cinerea). The wine is usually pasteurised.
LACTIC ACID One of the acids found in grape juice; as the name suggests it is milky and soft.
LACTOBACILLUS A micro-organism that ferments carbohydrates (glucose) or malic acid to produce lactic acid.
LEES The sediment left after fermentation. It consists mainly of dead yeast cells.
MALIC ACID One of the acids found in grape juice. It has a hard/sharp taste like a Granny Smith apple.
MALOLACTIC FERMENTATION A secondary fermentation process that converts malic acid into lactic acid. It is encouraged in red

wines when they are in barrel. If it occurs after bottling, the wine will be fizzy and cloudy.

MERCAPTAN   Ethyl mercaptan is a sulphur compound with a smell like garlic, burnt rubber or asparagus water.

MÉTHODE CHAMPENOISE   The French method for producing effervescence in the bottle; a secondary fermentation process where the carbon dioxide produced is dissolved into the wine.

METHOXYPYRAZINES   Substances that give sauvignon blanc and cabernet sauvignon that added herbaceousness when the grapes aren't fully ripe.

MOUSSE   The froth or head on sparkling wine.

MUST   *see* Free-run juice

NOBLE ROT   *see* Botrytis cinerea

NON-VINTAGE   A wine that is a blend of two or more years.

OAK   The least porous wood, genus *Quercus*, and used for wine storage containers

OENOLOGY   The science of winemaking.

ORGANIC VITICULTURE   Growing grapes without the use of pesticides, fungicides or chemical fertilizers. Certain chemicals (eg. copper sulphate) are permitted.

ORGANIC WINES   Wines made from organically grown fruit without the addition of chemicals.

OXIDATION   Browning caused by excessive exposure to air.

pH   The measure of the strength of acidity. The higher the pH the higher the alkalinity and the lower the acidity. Wines with high pH values should not be cellared.

PHENOLICS   A group of chemical compounds which includes the tannins and colour pigments of grapes. A white wine described as 'phenolic' has an excess of tannin, making it taste coarse.

PHYLLOXERA   A louse that attacks the roots of a vine, eventually killing the plant.

PIGEAGE   To foot-press the grapes.

PRESSINGS   The juice extracted by applying pressure to the skins after the free-run juice has been drained.

PUNCHEON   A 500-litre barrel.

PRICKED   A wine that is spoilt and smells of vinegar, due to excessive volatile acidity. (cf. Volatile.)

RACKING   Draining off wine from the lees or other sediment to clarify it.

SAIGNÉE   French for bleeding: the winemaker has run off part of the juice of a red fermentation to concentrate what's left.

SKIN CONTACT Allowing the free-run juice to remain in contact with the skins; in the case of white wines usually for a very short time.

SOLERO SYSTEM Usually a stack of barrels used for blending maturing wines. The oldest material is at the bottom and is topped up with younger material from the top barrels.

SOLIDS Minute particles suspended in a wine.

SULPHUR DIOXIDE SO_2 (Code 220) A chemical added to a wine as a preservative and a bactericide.

SUR LIE Wine that has been kept on lees and not racked or filtered before bottling.

TACHÉ A French term that means to stain, usually by the addition of a small amount of red wine to sparkling wine to turn it pink.

TANNIN A complex substance derived from skins, pips and stalks of grapes as well as the oak casks. It has a preservative function and imparts dryness and grip to the finish.

TERROIR Arcane French expression which describes the complete growing environment of the vine, including climate, aspect, soil, etc., and the direct effect this has on the character of its wine.

VARIETAL An industry-coined term used to refer to a wine by its grape variety, eg. 'a shiraz'. (cf. *Generic*.)

VÉRAISON The moment when the grapes change colour and gain sugar.

VERTICAL TASTING A tasting of consecutive vintages of one wine.

VIGNERON A grape-grower or vineyard worker.

VINEGAR Acetic acid produced from fruit.

VINIFY The process of turning grapes into wine.

VINTAGE The year of harvest, and the produce of a particular year.

VOLATILE Excessive volatile acids in a wine.

YEAST The micro-organism which converts sugar into alcohol.

Tasting Terms

The following terms refer to the sensory evaluation of wine.

AFTERTASTE The taste (sensation) after the wine has been swallowed. It is usually called the finish.
ASTRINGENT (ASTRINGENCY) Applies to the finish of a wine. Astringency is caused by tannins that produce a mouth-puckering sensation and coat the teeth with dryness.
BALANCE 'The state of . . .'; the harmony between components of a wine.
BILGY An unfortunate taste like the bilge of a ship. Usually caused by mouldy old oak.
BITTERNESS A sensation detected at the back of the tongue. It is not correct in wine but desirable in beer.
BOUQUET The aroma of a finished or mature wine.
BROAD A wine that lacks fruit definition; usually qualified as soft or coarse.
CASSIS A blackcurrant flavour common in cabernet sauvignon. It refers to a liqueur produced in France.
CHALKY A sensation on the finish; extremely dry.
CHEESY A dairy character sometimes found in wine, particularly sherries.
CIGAR BOX A smell of tobacco and wood found in cabernet sauvignon.
CLOUDY A fault in wine which is caused by suspended solids that make it look dull.
CORKED Spoiled wine that has reacted with a tainted cork, and smells like wet cardboard. (The taint is caused by trichloroanisole, a mould.)
CLOYING Excessive sweetness that clogs the palate.
CREAMY The feeling of cream in the mouth, a texture.
CRISP Clean acid on the finish of a white wine.
DEPTH The amount of fruit on the palate.

DULL Pertaining to colour; the wine is not bright or shining.
DUMB Lacking nose or flavour on the palate.
DUSTY Applies to a very dry tannic finish; a sensation.
DRY A wine that does not register sugar in the mouth.
EARTHY Not as bad as it sounds, this is a loamy/mineral character that can add interest to the palate.
FINESSE The state of a wine, refers to balance and style.
FINISH (*see* aftertaste)
FIRM Wine with strong, unyielding tannins.
FLABBY Wine with insufficient acid to balance ripe fruit flavours.
FLESHY Wines of substance with plenty of fruit
FLINTY A character on the finish that is akin to sucking dry creek pebbles.
GARLIC *see* Mercaptan (in Wine Terms)
GRASSY A cut-grass odour, usually found in semillon and sauvignon blancs.
GRIP The effect on the mouth of tannin on the finish; a puckering sensation.
HARD More tannin or acid than fruit flavour.
HERBACEOUS Herbal smells or flavour in wine.
HOLLOW A wine with a lack of flavour in the middle palate.
HOT Wines high in alcohol that give a feeling of warmth and a slippery texture.
IMPLICIT SWEETNESS A just detectable sweetness from the presence of glycerin (rather than residual sugar).
INKY Tannate of iron present in a wine which imparts a metallic taste.
INTEGRATED (WELL) The component parts of a wine fit together without gaps or disorders.
JAMMY Ripe fruit that takes on the character of stewed jam.
LEATHERY A smell like old leather, not necessarily bad if it is in balance.
LENGTH (LONG) The measure of the registration of flavour in the mouth (the longer the better).
LIFTED The wine is given a lift by the presence of either volatile acid or wood tannins; eg. vanillian oak lift.
LIMPID A colour term usually applied to star-bright white wine.
MADEIRISED Wine that has aged to the point where it tastes like a madeira.
MOULDY Smells like bathroom mould; dank.

MOUTHFEEL The sensation the wine causes in the mouth; a textural term.
MUSTY Stale, flat, out-of-condition wine.
PEPPER A component in either the nose or the palate that smells or tastes like cracked pepper.
PUNGENT Wine with a strong nose.
RANCIO A nutty character found in aged fortifieds that is imparted by time on wood.
RESIDUAL SUGAR The presence of unfermented grape sugar on the palate; common in sweet wines.
ROUGH Unpleasant, aggressive wine.
ROUND A full-bodied wine with plenty of mouthfeel (*qv*).
SAPPY A herbaceous character that resembles sap.
SHORT A wine lacking in taste and structure (*see also* Length).
SPICY A wine with a high aromatic content; spicy character can also be imparted by wood.
STALKY Exposure to stalks (eg. during fermentation) leaves a bitter character in the wine.
TART A lively wine with a lot of fresh acid.
TOASTY A smell of cooked bread.
VANILLAN The smell and taste of vanilla beans; usually imparted by oak ageing.
VARIETAL Refers to the distinguishing qualities of the grape variety used in the wine.

Directory of Wineries

AFFLECK VINEYARD
RMB 244
Gundaroo Rd
Bungendore NSW 2651
(06) 236 9276

ALAMBIE WINES
Campbell Ave
Irymple Vic 3498
(050) 24 6800
fax (050) 24 6605

ALKOOMI
Wingeballup Rd
Frankland WA 6396
(098) 55 2229
fax (098) 55 2284

ALL SAINTS
All Saints Rd
Wahgunyah Vic 3687
(060) 33 1922
fax (060) 33 3515

ALLANDALE
Lovedale Rd
Pokolbin NSW 2320
(049) 90 4526
fax (049) 90 1714

ALLANMERE
Lovedale Rd
Pokolbin NSW 2320
(049) 30 7387

AMBERLEY ESTATE
Wildwood & Thornton Rds
Yallingup WA 6282
(097) 55 2288
fax (097) 55 2171

ANDERSON WINERY
Lot 13 Chiltern Road
Rutherglen Vic 3685
(060) 32 8111
fax (060) 32 9028

ANDREAS PARK ESTATE
PO Box 504
Chatswood NSW 2067
(02) 9415 1649

ANDREW GARRETT
Kangarilla Rd
McLaren Vale SA 5171
(08) 323 8853
fax (08) 323 8550

ANGELSEY
Heaslip Rd
Angle Vale SA 5117
(085) 24 3157

ANGOVES
1320 North-East Rd
Tea Tree Gully SA 5091
(085) 85 1311
fax (085) 85 1583

ANTCLIFFE'S CHASE
RMB 4510
Caveat
via Seymour Vic 3660
(057) 90 4333

ARROWFIELD
Denman Rd
Jerry's Plains NSW 2330
(065) 76 4041
fax (065) 76 4144

ASHTON HILLS
Tregarthen Rd
Ashton SA 5137
(08) 390 1243
fax (08) 390 1243

AVALON
RMB 9556
Whitfield Rd
Wangaratta Vic 3677
(057) 29 3629

BABICH WINES
Babich Rd
Henderson, NZ
(09) 833 8909

BAILEYS
Taminick Gap Rd
Glenrowan Vic 3675
(057) 66 2392
fax (057) 66 2596

DIRECTORY OF WINERIES

BALDIVIS ESTATE
Lot 165 River Rd
Baldivis WA 6171
(09) 525 2066
fax (09) 525 2411

BALGOWNIE
Hermitage Rd
Maiden Gully Vic 3551
(054) 49 6222
fax (054) 49 6506

BALNARRING VINEYARD
Bittern-Dromana Rd
Balnarring Vic 3926
(059) 83 5258

BANNOCKBURN
Midland Highway
Bannockburn Vic 3331
(052) 81 1363
fax (052) 81 1349

BAROSSA SETTLERS
Trial Hill Rd
Lyndoch SA 5351
(085) 24 4017

BAROSSA VALLEY ESTATE
Heaslip Rd
Angle Vale SA 5117
(08) 284 7000
fax (08) 284 7219

BARWANG
(see McWilliam's)

BASEDOW
165 Murray Valley Hwy
Tanunda SA 5352
(085) 63 2060
fax (085) 63 2060

BASS PHILLIP
Tosch's Rd
Leongatha South
Vic 3953
(056) 64 3341

BERRI ESTATES
Sturt Highway
Glossop SA 5344
(085) 82 0300
fax (085) 83 2224

BESTS GREAT WESTERN
Western Hwy
Great Western
Vic 3377
(053) 56 2250
fax (053) 56 2430

BETHANY
Bethany Rd
Bethany
via Tanunda
SA 5352
(085) 63 2086
fax (085) 63 2086

BIANCHET
187 Victoria Rd
Lilydale Vic 3140
(03) 9739 1779
fax (03) 9739 1277

BIRDWOOD ESTATE
PO Box 194
Birdwood SA 5234
(08) 263 0986

BLACKJACK VINEYARD
Calder Hwy
Harcourt Vic 3452
(054) 74 2528
fax (054) 75 2102

BLEASDALE
Wellington Rd
Langhorne Creek
SA 5255
(085) 37 3001

BLEWITT SPRINGS
Recreational Rd
McLaren Vale
SA 5171
(08) 323 8689

BLUE PYRENEES ESTATE
Vinoca Rd
Avoca Vic 3467
(054) 65 3202
fax (054) 65 3529

BLOODWOOD ESTATE
4 Griffin Rd
via Orange NSW 2800
(063) 62 5631

BOSTON BAY
Lincoln Hwy
Port Lincoln SA 5605
(086) 84 3600

BOTOBOLAR
Botobolar Lane
PO Box 212
Mudgee NSW 2850
(063) 73 3840
fax (063) 73 3789

BOWEN ESTATE
Penola-Naracoorte Rd
Coonawarra SA 5263
(087) 37 2229
fax (087) 37 2173

BOYNTONS OF BRIGHT
Ovens Valley Hwy
Porepunkah Vic 3740
(057) 56 2356

BRANDS LAIRA
Naracoorte Hwy
Coonawarra SA 5263
(087) 36 3260
fax (087) 36 3208

DIRECTORY OF WINERIES

BREMERTON LODGE
Strathalbyn Rd
Langhorne Creek SA 5255
(085) 37 3093
fax (085) 37 3109

BRIAGOLONG ESTATE
118 Boisdale Street
Maffra Vic 3860
(051) 47 2322
fax (051) 47 2400

BRIAR RIDGE
Mount View
Mt View NSW 2321
(049) 90 3670
fax (049) 98 7802

BRIDGEWATER MILL
Mount Barker Rd
Bridgewater SA 5155
(08) 339 3422
fax (08) 339 5253

BRINDABELLA HILLS
Woodgrove Close
Via Hall ACT 2618
(06) 230 2583

BROKENWOOD
McDonalds Rd
Pokolbin NSW 2321
(049) 98 7559
fax (049) 98 7893

BROOK EDEN
Adams Rd
Lebrina Tas 7254
(003) 95 6144

BROOKLAND VALLEY
Caves Rd
Willyabrup WA 6284
(097) 55 6250
fax (097) 55 6214

BROWN BROTHERS
Meadow Crk Rd (off the Snow Rd)
Milawa Vic 3678
(057) 20 5500
fax (057) 20 5511

BROWNS OF PADTHAWAY
PMB 196
Naracoorte SA 5271
(087) 65 6063
fax (087) 65 6083

BUCHANAN WINES
Glendale Rd
Loira
West Tamar Tas 7275
(003) 94 7488
fax (003) 94 7581

BULLER & SONS, R L
Calliope
Three Chain Rd
Rutherglen Vic 3685
(050) 37 6305

BULLER (RL) & SON
Murray Valley Highway
Beverford Vic 3590
(050) 37 6305
fax (050) 37 6803
fax (060) 32 8005

BURGE FAMILY WINEMAKERS
Barossa Hwy
Lyndoch SA 5351
(085) 24 4644
fax (085) 24 4444

BURNBRAE
Hargraves Rd
Erudgere
Mudgee NSW 2850
(063) 73 3504
fax (063) 73 3601

CALAIS ESTATE
Palmers Lane
Pokolbin NSW 2321
(049) 98 7654
fax (049) 98 7813

CALLATOOTA ESTATE
Wybong Rd
Wybong NSW 2333
(065) 47 8149

CAMPBELLS
Murray Valley Hwy
Rutherglen Vic 3685
(060) 32 9458
fax (060) 32 9870

CANOBOLAS–SMITH
Cargo Rd
Orange NSW 2800
(063) 65 6113

CAPE CLAIRAULT
via Caves Rd
or Bussell Hwy
CMB Carbunup River
WA 6280
(097) 55 6225
fax (097) 55 6229

CAPE MENTELLE
Wallcliffe Rd
Margaret River
WA 6285
(097) 57 3266
fax (097) 57 3233

CAPELVALE
Lot 5
Capel North West Rd
Capel WA 6271
(097) 27 2439
fax (097) 27 2164

DIRECTORY OF WINERIES

CASSEGRAIN
Fern Bank Ck Rd
Port Macquarie
NSW 2444
(065) 83 7777
fax (065) 84 0353

CASTLE ROCK ESTATE
Porongarup Rd
Porongarup WA 6324
(098) 53 1035
fax (098) 53 1010

CHAIN OF PONDS
Gumeracha Cellars
PO Box 365
Main Rd
Gumeracha SA 5233
(08) 389 1415
fax (08) 336 2462

CHAMBERS ROSEWOOD
Corowa-Rutherglen Rd
Rutherglen Vic 3685
(060) 32 8641
fax (060) 32 8101

CHAPEL HILL
Chapel Hill Rd
McLaren Vale SA 5171
(08) 323 8429
fax (08) 323 9245

CHARLES CIMICKY
Gomersal Rd
Lyndoch SA 5351
(085) 24 4025
fax (085) 24 4772

CHARLES MELTON
Krondorf Rd
Tanunda SA 5352
(085) 63 3606
fax (085) 63 3422

CHARLES STURT UNIVERSITY
Boorooma St
North Wagga Wagga
NSW 2650
(069) 22 2435
fax (069) 22 2107

CHATEAU REYNELLA
Reynella Rd
Reynella SA 5161
(08) 392 2222
fax (08) 392 2202

CHATEAU TAHBILK
Tabilk Vic 3607
via Nagambie
(057) 94 2555
fax (057) 94 2360

CHATEAU XANADU
Terry Rd, off Railway Tce
Margaret River
WA 6285
(097) 57 2581
fax (097) 57 3389

CHATEAU YALDARA
Gomersal Rd
Lyndoch SA 5351
(085) 24 4200
fax (085) 24 4678

CHATSFIELD
O'Neill Rd
Mount Barker WA 6324
(098) 51 1704
fax (098) 41 6811

CLARENDON HILLS
(not open to public)
(08) 364 1484

CLEVELAND
(by appointment only)
Shannons Rd
Lancefield Vic 3435
(054) 29 1449
fax (054) 29 2017

COBAW RIDGE
Perc Boyer's Lane
East Pastoria
Via Kyneton Vic 3444
(054) 23 5227

CLONAKILLA
Crisps La
Murrumbateman
NSW 2582
(06) 251 1938 (A.H.)

CLOUDY BAY
(see Cape Mentelle)

CLOVER HILL
(see Taltarni)

COLDSTREAM HILLS
31 Maddens La
Coldstream Vic 3770
(059) 64 9388
fax (059) 64 9389

COOLANGATTA ESTATE
Coolangatta Resort,
via Berry NSW 2535
(044) 48 7131
fax (044) 48 7997

COOMBEND
Swansea Tas 7190
(002) 57 8256
fax (002) 57 8484

COOPERS CREEK WINERY
Highway 16
Haupai Auckland NZ
(09) 412 8560

COPE WILLIAMS WINERY
Glenfern Rd
Romsey Vic 3434
(054) 29 5428
fax (054) 29 2655

DIRECTORY OF WINERIES

CORIOLE
Chaffeys Rd
McLaren Vale SA 5171
(08) 323 8305
fax (08) 323 9136

COWRA ESTATE
Boorowa Rd
Cowra NSW 2794
(063) 42 3650

CRABTREE WATERVALE CELLARS
North Tce
Watervale SA 5452
(08) 8843 0069
fax (08) 8843 0144

CRAIG AVON
Craig Avon La
Merricks North Vic 3926
(059) 89 7465

CRAIGIE KNOWE
Cranbrook Tas 7190
(002) 23 5620

CRAIGLEE
Sunbury Rd
Sunbury Vic 3429
(03) 9744 1160

CRAIGMOOR
Craigmoor Rd
Mudgee NSW 2850
(063) 72 2208

CRAIGOW
Richmond Rd
Cambridge Tas 7170
(002) 48 5482

CRANEFORD
Main St
Springton SA 5235
(085) 68 2220
fax (085) 68 2538

CRAWFORD RIVER
Condah Vic 3303
(055) 78 2267

CULLENS
Caves Rd
Willyabrup via
Cowaramup
WA 6284
(097) 55 5277

CURRENCY CREEK
Winery Rd
Currency Creek SA 5214
(085) 55 4069

DALFARRAS
(*see* Chateau Tahbilk)

DALRYMPLE
Pipers Brook Rd
Pipers Brook Tas 7254
(003) 82 7222

DALWHINNIE
Taltarni Rd
Moonambel Vic 3478
(054) 67 2388

d'ARENBERG
Osborn Rd
McLaren Vale SA 5171
(08) 323 8206

DARLING PARK
Lot 1 Browne Lane
Red Hill 3937
(059) 89 2732
fax (059) 89 2254

DAVID TRAEGER
399 High St
Nagambie Vic 3608
(057) 94 2514

DAVID WYNN
(*see* Mountadam)

DEAKIN ESTATE
(*see* Katnook)

De BORTOLI
De Bortoli Rd
Bibul NSW 2680
(069) 64 9444
fax (069) 64 9400

De BORTOLI
Pinnacle La
Dixons Creek Vic 3775
(059) 65 2271

DELAMERE
Bridport Rd
Pipers Brook Tas 7254
(003) 82 7190

DELATITE
Stoney's Rd
Mansfield Vic 3722
(057) 75 2922
fax (057) 75 2911

DENNIS'S OF McLAREN VALE
Kangarilla Rd
McLaren Vale SA 5171
(08) 323 8665
fax (08) 323 9121

DEVIL'S LAIR
Rocky Rd
Forrest WA 6285
(09) 386 2200
fax (09) 381 5423

DIAMOND VALLEY VINEYARDS
Kinglake Rd
St Andrews Vic 3761
(03) 9710 1484
fax (03) 9739 1110

DIRECTORY OF WINERIES

DOMAINE A STONEY VINEYARD
Teatree Rd
Campania Tas 7026
(002) 62 4174
fax (002) 62 4390

DOMAINE CHANDON
Maroondah Hwy
Coldstream Vic 3770
(03) 9739 1110
fax (03) 9739 1095

DOONKUNA ESTATE
Barton Hwy
Murrumbateman NSW 2582
(06) 227 5885
fax (06) 227 5085

DRAYTON'S BELLEVUE
Oakey Creek Rd
Pokolbin NSW 2320
(049) 98 7513
fax (049) 98 7743

DROMANA ESTATE
Bittern-Dromana Rd
Dromana Vic 3936
(059) 87 3275
fax (059) 81 0714

DUNCAN ESTATE
Spring Gully Rd
Clare SA 5453
(088) 43 4335

EDEN RIDGE
(see Mountadam)

ELAN VINEYARD
17 Turners Rd
Bittern Vic 3918
(059) 83 1858

ELDERTON
3 Tanunda Rd
Nuriootpa SA 5355
(085) 62 1058 or
(008) 88 8500
fax (085) 62 2844

ELGEE PARK
(no cellar door)
Junction Rd
Merricks Nth
PO Box 211
Red Hill South Vic 3926
(059) 89 7338
fax (059) 89 7553

EPPALOCK RIDGE
Metcalfe Pool Rd
Redesdale Vic 3444
(054) 25 3135

EVANS & TATE
Metricup Rd
Willyabrup WA 6284
(09) 296 4666
fax (09) 296 1148

EVANS FAMILY
Palmers La
Pokolbin NSW 2320
(049) 98 7333

EYTON ON YARRA
Cnr Maroondah Hwy
& Hill Rd
Coldstream Vic 3770
(059) 62 2119
fax (059) 62 5319

FERGUSSON'S
Wills Rd
Yarra Glen Vic 3775
(059) 65 2237

FERN HILL ESTATE
Ingoldby Rd
McLaren Flat SA 5171
(08) 383 0167
fax (08) 383 0107

FIDDLER'S CREEK
(see Blue Pyrenees Estate)

FIRE GULLY
(see Pierro)

FRANKLAND ESTATE
RMB 705
Frankland WA 6396
(098) 55 1555
fax (098) 55 1583

FREYCINET VINEYARD
Tasman Hwy
Bicheno Tas 7215
(002) 57 8587

GALAFREY
114 York St
Albany WA 6330
(098) 41 6533

GALAH WINES
Box 231
Ashton SA 5137
(08) 390 1243

GARDEN GULLY
Western Highway
Great Western Vic 3377
(053) 56 2400

GEOFF MERRILL
(see Mount Hurtle)

GIACONDA
(not open to public)
(057) 27 0246

DIRECTORY OF WINERIES

GILBERT'S
Albany Hwy
Kendenup WA 6323
(098) 51 4028
(098) 51 4021

GLENARA
126 Range Rd Nth
Upper Hermitage
SA 5131
(08) 380 5056
fax (08) 380 5056

GOONA WARRA
Sunbury Rd
Sunbury Vic 3429
(03) 9744 7211
fax (03) 9744 7648

GOUNDREY
Muir Hwy
Mount Barker WA 6324
(098) 51 1777
fax (098) 48 1018

GRAMP'S
(see Orlando)

GRAND CRU ESTATE
Ross Dewell's Rd
Springton SA 5235
(085) 68 2378

GRANT BURGE
Jacobs Creek
Barossa Valley Hwy
Tanunda SA 5352
(085) 63 3700
fax (085) 63 2807

GREEN POINT
(see Domaine Chandon)

GREENOCK CREEK
Radford Rd
Seppeltsfield SA 5360
(085) 62 8103
fax (085) 62 8259

GROSSET
King St
Auburn SA 5451
(088) 49 2175

HANGING ROCK
Jim Rd
Newham Vic 3442
(054) 27 0542
fax (054) 27 0310

HANSON WINES
'Oolorong'
49 Cleveland Ave
Lower Plenty Vic 3093
(03) 9439 7425

HAPP'S
Commonage Rd
Dunsborough WA 6281
(097) 55 3300
fax (097) 55 3846

HARCOURT VALLEY
Calder Highway
Harcourt Vic 3453
(054) 74 2223

HARDYS
(see Chateau Reynella)

HASELGROVE WINES
Foggo Rd
McLaren Vale
SA 5171
(08) 323 8706
fax (08) 323 8049

HEATHCOTE WINERY
183 High St
Heathcote Vic 3523
(054) 33 2595
fax (054) 33 3081

HEEMSKERK
Pipers Brook Tas 7254
(003) 82 7133
fax (003) 82 7242

HEGGIES
(see Yalumba)

HELM'S
Yass River Rd
Murrumbateman
NSW 2582
(06) 227 5536 (A.H.)
(06) 227 5953

HENSCHKE
Moculta Rd
Keyneton SA 5353
(085) 64 8223
fax (085) 64 8294

HERITAGE WINES
Seppeltsfield Rd
Marananga
via Tunanda SA 5352
(085) 62 2880

HICKINBOTHAM
(not open to public)
(03) 9397 1872
fax (03) 9397 2629

HIGHBANK
Main Naracoorte/Penola Rd
Coonawarra SA 5263
(087) 37 2020

HILL SMITH ESTATE
(see Yalumba)

HILLSTOWE WINES
104 Main Rd
Hahndorf SA 5245
(08) 388 1400
fax (08) 388 1411

DIRECTORY OF WINERIES 445

HOLLICK
Racecourse Rd
Coonawarra SA 5263
(087) 37 2318
fax (087) 37 2952

HOUGHTON
Dale Rd
Middle Swan
WA 6056
(09) 274 5100

HOWARD PARK
Lot 11
Little River Rd
Denmark WA 6333
(098) 48 1261
fax (098) 48 2064

HUGH HAMILTON WINES
PO Box 615
McLaren Vale SA 5171
(08) 323 8689
fax (08) 323 9488

HUGO
Elliott Rd
McLaren Flat SA 5171
(08) 383 0098
fax (08) 383 0446

HUNGERFORD HILL
(see Tulloch or Lindemans)

HUNTER'S WINES
Rapaura Rd
Blenheim, NZ
(03) 572 8489
fax (03) 572 8457

HUNTINGTON ESTATE
Cassilis Rd
Mudgee NSW 2850
(063) 73 3825
fax (063) 73 3730

IAN LEAMON
Calder Hwy
Bendigo Vic 3550
(054) 47 7995

IDYLL
Ballan Rd
Moorabool Vic 3221
(052) 76 1280
fax (052) 76 1537

INGOLDBY
Ingoldby Rd
McLaren Flat
SA 5171
(08) 383 0005

INNISFAIL
(not open to public)
(052) 76 1258

JAMES IRVINE
Roeslers Rd
Eden Valley SA 5235
PO Box 308
Angaston SA 5353
(085) 64 1046
fax (085) 64 1046

JASPER HILL
Drummonds La
Heathcote Vic 3523
(054) 33 2528

JEIR CREEK WINES
Gooda Creek Rd
Murrumbateman
NSW 2582
(06) 227 5999

JENKE VINEYARDS
Jenke Rd
Rowland Flat SA 5352
(085) 24 4154
fax (085) 24 4154

JIM BARRY
Main North Rd
Clare SA 5453
(088) 842 2261

JOHN GEHRIG
Oxley Vic 3678
(057) 27 3395

JOSEPH
(see Primo Estate)

KAISER STUHL
Tanunda Rd
Nuriootpa SA 5355
(085) 62 0389 &
(085) 62 0408
fax (085) 62 8028

KARINA VINEYARDS
Harrisons Rd
Dromana Vic 3936
(059) 81 0137

KARRIVALE
Woodlands Rd
Porongurup WA 6324
(098) 53 1009
fax (098) 53 1129

KARRIVIEW
RMB 913
Roberts Rd
Denmark WA 6333
(098) 40 9381

KATNOOK ESTATE
Narracoorte Rd
Coonawarra SA 5263
(087) 37 2394
fax (087) 37 2397

KAYS
Kays Rd
McLaren Vale
SA 5171
(08) 323 8211
fax (08) 323 9199

446 DIRECTORY OF WINERIES

KIES ESTATE
Hoffnungsthal Rd
Lyndoch SA 5351
(085) 24 4511

KILLAWARRA
(see Kaiser Stuhl)

KILLERBY
Minnimup Rd
Gelorup WA 6230
(097) 95 7222
fax (097) 95 7835

KINGS CREEK
(not open to public)
(059) 83 2102

KNIGHTS
Burke and Wills Track
Baynton
via Kyneton Vic 3444
(054) 23 7264
mobile 015 843 676
fax (054) 23 7288

KOPPAMURRA
(no cellar door)
PO Box 110
Blackwood SA 5051
(08) 271 4127
fax (08) 271 0726

KRONDORF
Krondorf Rd
Tanunda SA 5352
(085) 63 2145
fax (085) 62 3055

LAANECOORIE
(cellar door by arrangement)
RMB 1330
Dunolly Vic 3472
(054) 68 7260
018 518 887

LAKE'S FOLLY
Broke Rd
Pokolbin NSW 2320
(049) 98 7507
fax (049) 98 7322

LANCEFIELD WINERY
Woodend Rd
Lancefield Vic 3435
(054) 29 1217

LARK HILL
RMB 281 Gundaroo Rd
Bungendore NSW 2621
(062) 38 1393

LEASINGHAM
7 Dominic St
Clare SA 5453
(088) 42 2555
fax (088) 42 3293

LECONFIELD
Penola-Narracoorte Rd
Coonawarra SA 5263
(087) 37 2326
fax (087) 37 2285

LEEUWIN ESTATE
Stevens Rd
Margaret River WA 6285
(097) 57 6253
fax (097) 57 6364

LELAND ESTATE
PO Lenswood SA 5240
(08) 389 6928

LENGS & COOTER
24 Lindsay Tce
Belair SA 5052
(08) 278 3998

LENSWOOD VINEYARDS
3 Cyril John Crt
Athelstone, SA 5076
Tel and fax (08) 365 3766

LEO BURING
Stuart Hwy
Tanunda SA 5352
(085) 63 2184
fax (085) 63 2804

LILLYDALE VINEYARDS
Davross Crt
Seville Vic 3139
(059) 64 2016

LILLYPILLY ESTATE
Farm 16
Lilly Pilly Rd
Leeton NSW 2705
(069) 53 4069
fax (069) 53 4980

LINDEMANS
McDonalds Rd
Pokolbin NSW 2320
(049) 98 7501
fax (049) 98 7682

LONG GULLY
Long Gully Rd
Healesville Vic 3777
(059) 62 3663
fax (059) 807 2213

LONGLEAT
Old Weir Rd
Murchison Vic 3610
(058) 26 2294
fax (058) 26 2510

LOVEGROVE OF COTTLES BRIDGE
Heidelberg Kinglake Road
Cottlesbridge Vic 3099
(03) 9718 1569
fax (03) 9718 1028

McALISTER
(not open to public)
(051) 49 7229

DIRECTORY OF WINERIES 447

McGUIGAN BROTHERS
Cnr Broke and McDonalds Rd
Pokolbin NSW 2320
(049) 98 7400
fax (049) 98 7401

McWILLIAM'S
Hanwood NSW 2680
(069) 63 0001
fax (069) 63 0002

MADEW WINES
Appletree Hill Vineyard
Queanbeyan NSW 2620
(06) 299 2303

MADFISH BAY
(*see* Howard Park)

MAGLIERI
Douglas Gully Rd
McLaren Flat SA 5171
(08) 383 0177

MAIN RIDGE
Lot 48 Williams Rd
Red Hill Vic 3937
(059) 89 2686

MALCOLM CREEK
(not open to public)
(08) 264 2255

MARIENBERG
2 Chalk Hill Rd
McClaren Vale
SA 5171
(08) 323 9666
fax (08) 323 9600

MASSONI
Mornington-Flinders Rd
Red Hill Vic 3937
(059) 89 2060
fax (059) 89 2348

MASTERSON
(*see* Peter Lehmann)

MAXWELL
26 Kangarilla Rd
McLaren Vale SA 5171
(08) 323 8200

MEADOWBANK
Glenora Tas 7140
(002) 86 1234
fax (002) 86 1133

MERRICKS ESTATE
Cnr Thompsons Lane
& Frankston-Flinders Rd
Merricks Vic 3916
(059) 898 416
fax (03) 9629 4035

MIDDLETON ESTATE
Flagstaff Hill Rd
Middleton SA 5213
(085) 55 4136
fax (085) 55 4108

MILBURN PARK
(*see* Salisbury Estate)

MILDARA
(various locations)
(03) 9690 9966
(head office)

MILDURA VINEYARDS
Campbell Ave
Irymple Vic 3498

MINTARO CELLARS
Leasingham Rd
Mintaro SA 5415
(088) 43 9046

MIRAMAR
Henry Lawson Dr
Mudgee NSW 2850
(063) 73 3874

MIRANDA WINES
57 Jordaryan Ave
Griffith NSW 2680
(069) 62 4033
fax (069) 62 6944

MIRROOL CREEK
(*see* Miranda)

MITCHELL
Hughes Park Rd
Skillogalee Valley
via Clare SA 5453
(088) 43 4258

MITCHELTON WINES
Mitcheltstown
Nagambie 3608
(057) 94 2710
fax (057) 94 2615

MONTANA
PO Box 18-293
Glen Innis Auckland NZ
(09) 570 5549

MONTARA
Chalambar Rd
Ararat Vic 3377
(053) 52 3868
fax (053) 52 4968

MONTROSE
Henry Lawson Dr
Mudgee NSW 2850
(063) 73 3853

MOONDAH BROOK
(*see* Houghton)

MOORILLA ESTATE
655 Main Rd
Berridale Tas 7011
(002) 49 2949

DIRECTORY OF WINERIES

MOOROODUC ESTATE
Derril Rd
Moorooduc Vic 3933
(059) 78 858

MORNING CLOUD
(cellar door by appointment)
15 Ocean View Ave
Red Hill South Vic 3937
(059) 89 2762
fax (059) 89 2700

MORNINGTON VINEYARDS
(by appointment only)
Mooroobuc Rd
Mornington Vic 3931
(059) 74 2097
fax (03) 416 1084

MORRIS
off Murray Valley Hwy
Mia Mia Vineyards
Rutherglen Vic 3685
(060) 26 7303
fax (060) 26 7445

MOSS BROTHERS
Caves Rd
Willyabrup WA 6280
(097) 55 6270

MOSS WOOD
Metricup Rd
Willyabrup WA 6280
(097) 55 6266
fax (097) 55 6303

MOUNT AVOCA
Moates La
Avoca Vic 3467
(054) 65 3282

MOUNT HORROCKS
Mintaro Rd
Watervale SA 5452
Tel & fax (08) 884 92243

MOUNT HURTLE
291 Pimpala Rd
Woodcro SA 5162
(08) 381 6877
fax (08) 322 2244

MOUNT LANGI GHIRAN
Vine Rd
Buangor Vic 3375
(053) 54 3207
fax (053) 54 3277

MOUNT MARY
(not open to public)
(03) 9739 1761
fax (03) 9739 0137

MOUNT PRIOR VINEYARD
Cnr River Rd
& Popes La
Rutherglen Vic 3685
(060) 26 5591
fax (060) 26 7456

MOUNTADAM
High Eden Ridge
Eden Valley SA 5235
(085) 64 1101
fax (08) 362 8942

MT PLEASANT
Marrowbone Rd
Pokolbin NSW 2320
(049) 98 7505

MT WILLIAM WINERY
Mount William Rd
Tantaraboo Vic 3764
(054) 29 1998
fax (054) 29 1595

MURRINDINDI
(not open to public)
(057) 97 8217

NATTIER
(*see* Mitchelton)

NAUTILUS
(*see* Yalumba)

NGATARAWA
Ngatarawa Rd
Bridge Pa
Hastings NZ
(070) 79 7603

NICHOLSON RIVER
Liddells Rd
Nicholson Vic 3882
(051) 56 8241

NINTH ISLAND
Pipers Brook
Tas 7254
(003) 82 7197
fax (003) 82 7226

NORMANS
Grants Gully Rd
Clarendon SA 5157
(08) 383 6138

NUTFIELD
(*see* Hickinbotham)

OAKRIDGE ESTATE
Aitken Rd
Seville Vic 3139
(059) 64 3379
fax (059) 64 2061

OAKVALE WINERY
Broke Rd
Pokolbin NSW 2320
(049) 98 7520

OLD KENT RIVER
Turpin Rd
Rocky Gully Wa 6397
(098) 55 1589
fax (098) 55 1589

DIRECTORY OF WINERIES

ORLANDO
Barossa Valley Way
Rowland Flat SA 5352
(085) 21 3111
fax (085) 21 3102

PANKHURST WINES
Woodgrove Rd
Hall ACT 2618
(06) 230 2592

PARINGA ESTATE
44 Paringa Rd
Red Hill South
Vic 3937
(059) 89 2669

PARKER COONAWARRA ESTATE
Penola Rd
Coonawarra SA 5263
(Contact Leconfield)
(087) 37 2946
fax (087) 37 2465

PASSING CLOUDS
Powlett Rd
via Inglewood
Kingower Vic 3517
(054) 38 8257

PAULETT'S
Polish Hill River Rd
Sevenhill SA 5453
(08) 843 4328
fax (08) 843 4202

PEEL ESTATE
Fletcher Rd
Baldivis WA 6171
(095) 24 1221

PENDARVES ESTATE
Lot 12 Old North Road
Belford NSW 2335
(065) 74 7222

PENFOLDS
Stuart Hwy
Nuriootpa SA 5355
(085) 609 389
fax (085) 609 669

PENINSULA ESTATE
Red Hill Rd
Red Hill Vic 3937
(059) 89 2866

PENLEY ESTATE
McLean's Rd
Coonawarra 5263
(087) 36 3211
fax (087) 36 3211

PEPPERS CREEK
Broke Rd
Pokolbin NSW 2321
(049) 98 7532

PETALUMA
(not open to public)
(08) 339 4122
fax (08) 339 5253

PETER LEHMANN
Para Rd
Tanunda SA 5352
(085) 63 2500
fax (085) 63 3402

PETERSONS
Mount View Rd
Mount View
NSW 2325
(049) 90 1704

PFEIFFER
Distillery Rd
Wahgunyah Vic 3687
(060) 33 2805
fax (060) 33 3158

PIBBIN FARM
Greenhill Rd
Balhannah SA 5242
(08) 388 7375
fax (08) 388 7685

PICCADILLY FIELDS
(not open to public)
(08) 390 1997

PIERRO
Caves Rd
Willyabrup WA 6280
(097) 55 6220
fax (097) 55 6308

PIKES POLISH HILL ESTATE
Polish Hill River Rd
Seven Hill SA 5453
(08) 8843 4370

PIPERS BROOK
(by appointment only)
(003) 82 7197
fax (003) 82 7226

PIRRAMIMMA
Johnston Rd
McLaren Vale SA 5171
(08) 323 8205
fax (08) 323 9224

PLANTAGENET
Albany Highway
Mount Barker WA 6324
(098) 51 2150
fax (098) 51 1839

PLUNKETT'S WINEGATE
Hume Highway
Avenel, Vic 3664
(057) 96 2275
fax (057) 96 2147

DIRECTORY OF WINERIES

POOLE'S ROCK
Wollombi Rd
Broke NSW 2330
(065) 69 1251

PORT PHILLIP ESTATE
261 Red Hill Rd
Red Hill Vic 3937
(059) 89 2708
fax (059) 89 2891

PORTREE VINEYARD
RMB 700
Lancefield Vic 3435
(054) 29 1422
fax (054) 29 2205

PREECE
(*see* Mitchelton)

PRIMO ESTATE
Cnr Old Port Wakefield
& Angle Vale Rds
Virginia SA 5120
(08) 380 9442

PRINCE ALBERT
Lemins Rd
Waurn Ponds Vic 3221
(052) 43 5091
fax (052) 41 8091

QUEEN ADELAIDE
(*see* Seppelt)

QUELLTALER ESTATE
Main North Rd
Watervale SA 5452
(088) 843 0003
fax (088) 843 0096

REDBANK
Sunraysia Hwy
Redbank Vic 3467
(054) 67 7255

REDMAN
Penola-Narracoorte Rd
Coonawarra SA 5263
(087) 36 3331
fax (087) 37 3013

RENMANO
Renmark Ave
Renmark SA 5341
(085) 86 6771
fax (085) 83 2224

RIBBON VALE ESTATE
Lot 5 Caves Rd
via Cowaramup
Willyabrup WA 6284
(097) 55 6272

RICHARD HAMILTON
Willunga Vineyards
Main South Rd
Willunga SA 5172
(085) 56 2288
fax (085) 56 2868

RICHMOND GROVE
(*see* Orlando)

RIDDOCH
(*see* Katnook)

ROBERT HAMILTON & SON
Hamiltons Rd
Springton SA 5235
(085) 68 2264

ROBERT THUMM
(*see* Chateau Yaldara)

ROBINVALE WINES
Sealake Rd
Robinvale Vic 3549
(050) 26 3955
fax (050) 26 4399

ROCHFORD
Romsey Park
via Woodend Rd
Rochford Vic 3442
(054) 29 1428

ROCKFORD
Krondorf Rd
Tanunda SA 5352
(085) 63 2720

ROMSEY VINEYARDS
(*see* Cope Williams)

ROSEMOUNT
Rosemount Rd
Denman NSW 2328
(065) 47 2467
fax (065) 47 2742

ROTHBURY ESTATE
Broke Rd
Pokolbin NSW 2321
(049) 98 7555
fax (049) 98 7553

ROUGE HOMME
(*see* Lindemans)

ROWAN
(*see* St Huberts)

RYECROFT
Ingoldby Rd
McLaren Flat SA 5171
(08) 383 0001

RYMILL COONAWARRA WINES
The Riddoch Run Vineyards
off Main Rd
Coonawarra SA 5263
(087) 36 5001
fax (087) 36 5040

DIRECTORY OF WINERIES 451

SADDLERS CREEK WINERY
Marrowbone Rd
Pokolbin NSW 2321
(049) 91 1770
fax (049) 91 1778

SALISBURY ESTATE
see Alambie

SALITAGE
Vasse Hwy
Pemberton WA 6260
(097) 76 1599
fax (097) 76 1504

SALTRAM
Angaston Rd
Angaston SA 5353
(085) 63 8200

SANDALFORD
West Swan Rd
Caversham WA 6055
(09) 274 5922
fax (09) 274 2154

SANDSTONE VINEYARD
(cellar door by appointment)
Caves & Johnson Rds
Willyabrup WA 6280
(097) 55 6271
fax (097) 55 6292

SAXONVALE
Fordwich Estate
Broke Rd
Pokolbin NSW 2330
(065) 79 1009

SCARBOROUGH WINES
Gillards Rd
Pokolbin NSW 2321
(049) 98 7563

SCARPANTONI
Kangarilla Rd
McLaren Flat SA 5171
(08) 383 0186
fax (08) 383 0490

SCHINUS
(see Dromana Estate)

SCOTCHMAN'S HILL
Scotchmans Rd
Drysdale Vic 3222
(052) 51 3176
fax (052) 53 1743

SEAVIEW
Chaffeys Rd
McLaren Vale SA 5171
(08) 323 8250

SEPPELT
Seppeltsfield via Tanunda
SA 5352
(085) 62 8028
fax (085) 62 8333

SEVENHILL
College Rd
Sevenhill via Clare 5453
(088) 43 4222
fax (088) 43 4382

SEVILLE ESTATE
Linwood Rd
Seville Vic 3139
(059) 64 4556
fax (059) 43 4222

SHANTELL
Melba Hwy
Dixons Creek Vic 3775
(059) 65 2264
fax (03) 819 5311

SHAREFARMERS
(see Petaluma)

SHAW & SMITH
(not open to public)
(08) 370 9725

SHOTTESBROOKE
(see Ryecroft)

SIMON HACKET
(not open to public)
(08) 331 7348

SIMON WHITLAM
(see Arrowfield)

SKILLOGALEE
Skillogalee Rd
via Sevenhill 5453
(08) 8843 4311
fax (08) 8843 4343

SMITHBROOK
(not open to public)
(097) 72 3557
fax (097) 72 3579

ST FRANCIS
Bridge St
Old Reynella SA 5161
(08) 381 1925
fax (08) 322 0921

ST HALLETT'S
St Halletts Rd
Tanunda SA 5352
(085) 63 2319
fax (085) 63 2901

ST HUBERTS
Maroondah Hwy
Coldstream Vic 3770
(03) 9739 1118
fax (03) 9739 1015

452 DIRECTORY OF WINERIES

ST LEONARDS
St Leonard Rd
Wahgunyah Vic 3687
(060) 33 1004
fax (060) 33 3636

ST MARY'S VINEYARD
V and A Lane
via Coonawarra SA 5263
(087) 36 6070
fax (087) 36 6045

STAFFORD RIDGE
Geoff Weaver
(not open to public)
(08) 272 2105

STANTON & KILLEEN
Murray Valley Highway
Rutherglen Vic 3685
(060) 32 9457

STEVENS CAMBRAI
Hamiltons Rd
McLaren Flat SA 5171
(08) 323 0251

STONELEIGH
Corbans Wines
Great Northern Rd
Henderson NZ
(09) 836 6189

STONIER'S WINERY
362 Frankston-Flinders Rd
Merricks Vic 3916
(059) 89 8300
fax (059) 89 8709

SUMMERFIELD
Main Rd
Moonambel Vic 3478
(054) 67 2264
fax (054) 67 2380

SUTHERLAND
Deasey's Rd
Pokolbin NSW 2321
(049) 98 7650

TALTARNI VINEYARDS
off Moonambel–Stawell Rd
Moonambel Vic 3478
(054) 67 2218
fax (054) 67 2306

TAMBURLAINE WINES
McDonalds Rd
Pokolbin NSW 2321
(049) 98 7570
fax (049) 98 7763

TANGLEWOOD DOWNS
Bulldog Creek Rd
Merricks North
(059) 74 3325

TAPESTRY
Merrivale Wines
Olivers Rd
McLaren Vale SA 5171
(08) 323 9196
fax (08) 323 9746

TARRAWARRA
Healesville Rd
Yarra Glen Vic 3775
(059) 62 3311
fax (059) 62 3311

TATACHILLA WINERY
151 Main Rd
McLaren Vale SA 5171
(08) 323 8656
fax (08) 323 9096

TAYLORS
Mintaro Rd
Auburn SA 5451
(088) 49 2008

TEMPLE BRUER
Angas River Delta
via Strathalbyn SA 5255
(085) 37 0203
fax (085) 37 0131

T'GALLANT
Lot 2
Mornington-Flinders Rd
Main Ridge Vic 3937
(059) 89 6565
fax (059) 89 6577

THALGARA ESTATE
De Beyers Rd
Pokolbin NSW 2321
(049) 98 7717

THOMAS FERNHILL ESTATE
Ingoldby Rd
McLaren Flat SA 5171
(08) 383 0167
fax (08) 383 0107

TIM ADAMS
Wendouree Rd
Clare SA 5453
(08) 8842 2429
fax (08) 8842 2429

TIM GRAMP
PO Box 810
Unley Sa 5061
(08) 379 3658
fax (08) 338 2160

TIM KNAPPSTEIN
2 Pioneer Ave
Clare SA 5453
(088) 42 2600
fax (088) 42 3831

TISDALL
Cornelia Creek Rd
Echuca Vic 3564
(054) 82 1911
fax (054) 82 2516

DIRECTORY OF WINERIES 453

TOLLANA
(see Penfolds)

TOLLEYS PEDARE
30 Barracks Rd
Hope Valley SA 5090
(08) 264 2255
fax (08) 263 7485

TORRESAN ESTATE
Manning Rd
Flagstaff Hill SA 5159
(08) 270 2500

TRENTHAM ESTATE
Sturt Hwy
Trentham Cliffs
via Gol Gol NSW 2738
(050) 24 8888
fax (050) 24 8800

TULLOCH
De Beyers Rd
Pokolbin NSW 2321
(049) 98 7503
fax (049) 98 7682

TUNNEL HILL
(see Tarrawarra)

TURKEY FLAT
James Rd
Tanunda Sa 5352
(085) 63 2851
fax (085) 63 3610

TYRRELL'S
Broke Rd
Pokolbin NSW 2321
(049) 98 7509
fax (049) 987 723

VASSE FELIX
Cnr Caves & Harmans Rds
Cowaramup WA 6284
(097) 55 5242
fax (097) 55 5425

VERITAS
94 Langmeil Rd
Tanunda SA 5352
(085) 63 2330

VIRGIN HILLS
(not open to public)
(054) 23 9169

VOYAGER ESTATE
Stevens Rd
Margaret River WA 6285
(097) 57 6358
fax (097) 57 6405

WANDIN VALLEY ESTATE
Wilderness Rd
Rothbury NSW 2321
(049) 30 7317
fax (049) 30 7814

WANINGA
Hughes Park Rd
Sevenhill via Clare
SA 5453
(088) 43 4395
fax (08) 232 0653

WANTIRNA ESTATE
(not open to public)
(03) 9801 2367

WARDS GATEWAY CELLARS
Barossa Valley Hwy
Lyndoch SA 5351
(085) 24 4138

WARRAMATE
27 Maddens La
Gruyere Vic 3770
(059) 64 9219

WARRENMANG
Mountain Ck Rd
Moonambel Vic 3478
(054) 67 2233
fax (054) 67 2309

WATERWHEEL VINEYARDS
Lyndhurst St
Bridgewater-on-Loddon
Bridgewater Vic 3516
(054) 37 3060
fax (054) 37 3082

WELLINGTON WINES
34 Cornwall St
Rose Bay Tas 7015
(002) 48 5844

WENDOUREE
Wendouree Rd
Clare SA 5453
(088) 842 2896

WESTFIELD
Memorial Ave
Baskerville WA 6056
(09) 296 4356

WIGNALLS KING RIVER
Chester Pass Rd
Albany WA 6330
(098) 41 2848

WILD DUCK CREEK
Springflat Rd
Heathcote Vic 3523
(054) 33 3133

WILDWOOD
St Johns Lane via
Wildwood Vic 3428
(03) 9307 1118

WILLESPIE
Harmans Mill Rd
Willyabrup WA 6280
(097) 55 6248
fax (097) 55 6210

WILLOWS VINEYARD, THE
Light Pass Rd
Barossa Valley SA 5355
(085) 62 1080

454 DIRECTORY OF WINERIES

WILSON VINEYARD, THE
Polish Hill River
via Clare SA 5453
(088) 43 4310

WILTON ESTATE
Whitton Stock Route
Yenda NSW 2681
(069) 68 1303
fax (069) 68 1328

WINCHELSEA ESTATE
C/o Nicks Wine
Merchants
(03) 9639 0696

WING FIELDS
(see Water Wheel)

WIRILDA CREEK
Lot 32
McMurtrie Rd
McLaren Vale SA 5171
(08) 323 9688

WIRRA WIRRA
McMurtrie Rd
McLaren Vale SA 5171
(08) 323 8414
fax (08) 323 8596

WOLF BLASS
Sturt Hwy
Nuriootpa SA 5355
(085) 62 1955
fax (085) 62 2156

WOODSTOCK
Douglas Gully Rd
McLaren Flat SA 5171
(08) 383 0156
fax (08) 383 0437

WOODY NOOK
Metricup Rd
Metricup WA 6280
(097) 55 7547
fax (097) 55 7547

WYANGA PARK
Baades Road
Lakes Entrance Vic
(051) 55 1508
fax (051) 55 1443

WYANGAN ESTATE
(see Miranda)

WYNDHAM ESTATE
Dalwood Rd
Dalwood NSW 2321
(049) 38 3444
fax (049) 38 3422

WYNNS
Memorial Dr
Coonawarra SA 5263
(087) 36 3266

YALUMBA
Eden Valley Rd
Angaston SA 5353
(085) 61 3200
fax (085) 61 3392

YARRA BURN
Settlement Rd
Yarra Junction Vic 3797
(059) 67 1428
fax (059) 67 1146

YARRA RIDGE
Glenview Rd
Yarra Glen Vic 3775
(03) 9730 1022
fax (03) 9730 1131

YARRA VALLEY HILLS
Old Don Rd
Healesville Vic
(059) 62 4173
fax (057) 62 4059

YARRA YERING
Briarty Rd
Gruyere Vic 3770
(059) 64 9267

YELLOWGLEN
White's Rd
Smythesdale Vic 3351
(053) 42 8617

YERING STATION
Melba Hwy
Yering Vic 3775
(03) 9730 1107
fax (03) 9739 0135

YERINGBERG
(not open to public)
(03) 9739 1453
fax (03) 9739 0048

ZEMA ESTATE
Penola–Narracoorte Rd
Coonawarra SA 5263
(087) 36 3219
fax (087) 36 3280